Thomas De Quincey

Routledge Studies in Romanticism

Keats's Boyish Imagination
Richard Marggraf Turley

Leigh Hunt
Life, Poetics, Politics
Edited by Nicholas Roe

Leigh Hunt and the London Literary Scene
A Reception History of his Major Works, 1805–1828
Michael Eberle-Sinatra

Tracing Women's Romanticism
Gender, History and Transcendence
Kari E. Lokke

Metaphysical Hazlitt
Bicentenary Essays
Uttara Natarajan, Tom Paulin and Duncan Wu

Romantic Genius and the Literary Magazine
Biography, Celebrity, Politics
David Higgins

Romantic Representations of British India
Edited by Michael Franklin

Sympathy and the State in the Romantic Era
Systems, State Finance, and the Shadows of Futurity
Robert Mitchell

Thomas De Quincey
New Theoretical and Critical Directions
Edited by Robert Morrison and Daniel Sanjiv Roberts

Thomas De Quincey
New Theoretical and Critical Directions

**Robert Morrison
Daniel Sanjiv Roberts**

Routledge
Taylor & Francis Group
New York London

Routledge
Taylor & Francis Group
270 Madison Ave,
New York, NY 10016

Routledge
Taylor & Francis Group
2 Park Square,
Milton Park, Abingdon,
Oxon, OX14 4RN

© 2008 by Taylor & Francis Group, LLC
Routledge is an imprint of Taylor & Francis Group, an Informa business

Transferred to Digital Printing 2009

International Standard Book Number-13: 978-0-415-39963-0 (Hardcover)

No part of this book may be reprinted, reproduced, transmitted, or utilized in any form by any electronic, mechanical, or other means, now known or hereafter invented, including photocopying, microfilming, and recording, or in any information storage or retrieval system, without written permission from the publishers.

Trademark Notice: Product or corporate names may be trademarks or registered trademarks, and are used only for identification and explanation without intent to infringe.

Library of Congress Cataloging-in-Publication Data

Thomas de Quincey : new theoretical and critical directions / edited by Robert Morrison and Daniel Sanjiv Roberts.
   p. cm. -- (Routledge studies in romanticism)
   Includes bibliographical references and index.
   ISBN 978-0-415-39963-0 (hardback : alk. paper)
   1. De Quincey, Thomas, 1785-1859--Criticism and interpretation. I. Morrison, Robert, 1961- II. Roberts, Daniel Sanjiv.

PR4537.T5 1995
828'.809--dc22   2007011497

ISBN10: 0-415-39963-7 (hbk)
ISBN10: 0-415-87668-0 (pbk)

ISBN13: 978-0-415-39963-0 (hbk)
ISBN13: 978-0-415-87668-1 (pbk)

Visit the Taylor & Francis Web site at
http://www.taylorandfrancis.com

and the Routledge Web site at
http://www.routledge.com

Contents

List of Illustrations	vii
Acknowledgments	ix
Abbreviations	xi

1. 'I Was Worshipped; I Was Sacrificed':
   A Passage to Thomas De Quincey   1
   ROBERT MORRISON AND DANIEL SANJIV ROBERTS

2. 'Mix(ing) a Little with Alien Natures':
   Biblical Orientalism in De Quincey   19
   DANIEL SANJIV ROBERTS

3. Brunonianism, Radicalism, and 'The Pleasures of Opium'   45
   BARRY MILLIGAN

4. 'Earthquake and Eclipse':
   Radical Energies and De Quincey's 1821 *Confessions*   63
   ROBERT MORRISON

5. De Quincey and Men (of Letters)   81
   JOHN WHALE

6. Wooing the Reader: De Quincey, Wordsworth
   and Women in *Tait's Edinburgh Magazine*   99
   JULIAN NORTH

7. De Quincey and the Secret Life of Books   123
   JOSEPHINE MCDONAGH

8. National Bad Habits: Thomas De Quincey's
   Geography of Addiction   143
   JOEL BLACK

9 On the Language of the Sublime and the Sublime Nation in
De Quincey: Toward a Reading of 'The English Mail-Coach'   165
IAN BALFOUR

10 Chambers of Horror: De Quincey's 'Postscript' to
'On Murder Considered as One of the Fine Arts'   187
GREGORY DART

11 'A Deafening Menace in Tempestuous Uproars':
De Quincey's 1856 *Confessions*, the Indian Mutiny,
and the Response of Collins and Dickens   211
CHARLES RZEPKA

Contributors   235
Index   237

List of Illustrations

Frontispiece	Thomas De Quincey by Sir John Watson-Gordan	xiii
Figure 2.1	*The Protestant's Family Bible*	22
Figure 2.2	'A Scene of Sati'	25
Figure 2.3	'Juggernaut Procession'	26
Figure 2.4	'London from Greenwich Park'	30
Figure 4.1	John Leslie	71
Figure 4.2	David Ricardo	73
Figure 11.1	'Hindoo Thugs and Poisoners'	214
Figure 11.2	'The Massacre at Delhi'	220
Figure 11.3	'The Campbells are Coming'	221

Acknowledgments

All essays in this volume were stringently peer-reviewed by both the editors and detailed responses provided to each contributor. Several of our contributors have commented (we take it appreciatively!) that our procedure has been more rigorous than that of most collections. We would like to thank our contributors for their collective brilliance, good humour, hard work, and, not least, for sharing our sense of urgency—in some cases at very difficult periods in their lives—all in order to meet that devil at the door, the printer's devil. At Routledge, we acknowledge with gratitude Liz Thompson, Terry Clague, and Max Novick for their commitment to this publication. We thank Grevel Lindop and Barry Symonds for their helpful responses to our queries, and Averill Buchanan for her superb work on the index. Carole Morrison provided selfless assistance with proofing and referencing, while her unfailing support helped retain the sanity of at least one of the editors of this volume. Robert Morrison would like to thank the Social Sciences and Humanities Research Council of Canada and the Office of Research Services, Queen's University, Kingston, for their continuing support of his research on Thomas De Quincey. Daniel Sanjiv Roberts thanks Florence Gray of Queen's University Library, Belfast, for help with inter-library loans, the Research and Regional Services of Queen's University Belfast for support with costs of illustrations and indexing, and the School of English, QUB, for supporting applications to the above, and, above all, providing space and time.

Abbreviations

DQW, I Writings, 1799–1820. Ed. Barry Symonds. London: Pickering and Chatto, 2000.

DQW, II Confessions of an English Opium-Eater, 1821–1856. Ed. Grevel Lindop. London: Pickering and Chatto, 2000

DQW, III Articles and Translations from the London Magazine, Blackwood's Magazine and Others, 1821–24. Ed. Frederick Burwick. London: Pickering and Chatto, 2000.

DQW, IV Articles and Translations from the London Magazine; Walladmor, 1824–25. Ed. Frederick Burwick. London: Pickering and Chatto, 2000.

DQW, V Articles from the Edinburgh Saturday Post, 1827–28. Ed. David Groves. London: Pickering and Chatto, 2000.

DQW, VI Articles from the Edinburgh Evening Post, Blackwood's Magazine, and the Edinburgh Literary Gazette, 1826–29. Ed. David Groves and Grevel Lindop. London: Pickering and Chatto, 2000.

DQW, VII Articles from the Edinburgh Literary Gazette and Blackwood's Magazine, 1829–31. Ed. Robert Morrison. London: Pickering and Chatto, 2000.

DQW, VIII Articles from Blackwood's Magazine and the Gallery of Portraits; Klosterheim: or, The Masque, 1831–32. Ed. Robert Morrison. London: Pickering and Chatto, 2001.

DQW, IX Articles from Blackwood's Magazine and Tait's Magazine, 1832–38. Ed. Grevel Lindop, Robert Morrison, and Barry Symonds. London: Pickering and Chatto, 2001.

DQW, X Articles from Tait's Magazine, 1834–38. Ed. Alina Clej. London: Pickering and Chatto, 2003.

DQW, XI   Articles from *Tait's Magazine* and *Blackwood's Magazine*, 1838–41. Ed. Julian North. London: Pickering and Chatto, 2003.

DQW, XII   Articles from *Blackwood's Magazine*, 1840–41. Ed. Grevel Lindop. London: Pickering and Chatto, 2001.

DQW, XIII Articles from *Blackwood's Magazine* and the *Encyclopedia Britannica*, 1841–42. Ed. Grevel Lindop and John Whale. London: Pickering and Chatto, 2001.

DQW, XIV   Articles from *Blackwood's Magazine*, 1842–43. Ed. John Whale. London: Pickering and Chatto, 2001.

DQW, XV   Articles from *Blackwood's Magazine* and *Tait's Magazine*, 1844–46. Ed. Frederick Burwick. London: Pickering and Chatto, 2003.

DQW, XVI   Articles from *Tait's Magazine*, *MacPhail's Edinburgh Ecclesiastical Journal*, the *Glasgow Athenaeum Album*, the *North British Review*, and *Blackwood's Magazine*, 1847–49. Ed. Robert Morrison. London: Pickering and Chatto, 2003.

DQW, XVII Articles from *Hogg's Instructor* and *Tait's Magazine*, 1850–52. Ed. Edmund Baxter. London: Pickering and Chatto, 2001.

DQW, XVIII Articles from *Hogg's Instructor* and *Titan*, 1853–58. Ed. Edmund Baxter. London: Pickering and Chatto, 2001.

DQW, XIX   *Autobiographic Sketches*, Ed. Daniel Sanjiv Roberts. London: Pickering and Chatto, 2003.

DQW, XX   *Prefaces &c. to the Collected Editions; Published Addenda; Marginalia; Manuscript Addenda; Undatable Manuscripts*. Ed. Grevel Lindop, et al. London: Pickering and Chatto, 2003.

DQW, XXI   *Transcripts of Unlocated Manuscripts*. Ed. Grevel Lindop. London: Pickering and Chatto, 2003.

Thomas De Quincey (c. 1845) by Sir John Watson-Gordan. National Portrait Gallery, London.

1 'I Was Worshipped; I Was Sacrificed'
A Passage to Thomas De Quincey

*Robert Morrison and
Daniel Sanjiv Roberts*

'I have [. . .] always intended of course that *poems* should form the cornerstones of my fame', wrote the seventeen-year-old Thomas De Quincey (*DQW*, I: 38). As it turned out, he wrote very little poetry, but he did achieve fame, and in several instances infamy. An essayist with the magazine press for nearly forty years, De Quincey wrote on a broad range of topics, from politics, science, philosophy, economics, and history to aesthetics, drugs, famous contemporaries, murder, and himself. When, near the end of his life, he brought his writings together in a fourteen-volume edition of *Selections Grave and Gay* (1853–60), critical opinion was sharply divided. Naysayers such as the *British Quarterly* declared that De Quincey had written 'not one great work, not a single essay, discussion, or treatise, or tale, on which a lasting literary reputation can be built' (Anon. 1863: 14). More than a century later, he was still being dismissed as a 'Manchester journalist whose enormous output contains, among much flatulent and pretentiously overwritten stuff, just a few essays thanks to which he deserves his small niche in the gallery of the minor English romantics' (Hemmings 1982: 157). But there have always been enthusiasts. The *Eclectic Review* was convinced that De Quincey had produced 'the most valuable and most enduring [. . .] papers, which had originally appeared in a periodical form, to be found in the entire world of literature' (Anon. 1854: 399). This view too has long had staunch support. De Quincey brought to 'the art of prose autobiography something entirely new, and his influence has been felt by every self-conscious English writer, whether of reminiscences or of autobiographical novels, ever since' (Hayter 1971: 24). In the last thirty years, De Quincey's status has risen dramatically as a result of several groundbreaking monographs and a new collected edition of his writings. In the 1980s the battle lines were sharply drawn between those who believed that 'the best contemporary critics of De Quincey' retained the 'more traditional forms of appreciation and analysis' and those who viewed him as an 'aesthete' and a 'pure stylist' who lent himself 'to deconstructive readings' (Thron 1985: 3; Leighton 1992: 164). In the 1990s the upsurge of historicist criticism 'produced yet another [. . .] De Quincey [. . .] this one more sensitive to the social and political context of his life and work' (McDonagh 1994: 10). The present essay collection is a testimony to his vital place in nineteenth-century literature and culture, as well as to his enduring—indeed burgeoning—relevance in our own age.[1]

Critics have approached De Quincey from many different angles. His style has been deplored for 'four evil qualities': 'Pedantry, Digression, Prolixity, and Facetiousness' (Sackville West 1936: 240). The demands of nineteenth-century popular journalism too often forced him to produce 'mere prose' that is characterized by 'discursiveness' and 'triviality' (De Luca 1980: 9–10). Even his signature style—the elaborate, impassioned periods of works such as 'The English Mail-Coach'—has conjured up 'irrepressible memories of, well, Walt Disney and *Fantasia*' (Amis and Rose 1989: 367). Yet De Quincey has also been greatly admired as a stylist. He marks the culmination of a '*digressive tradition*' that runs from Jonathan Swift and Laurence Sterne to Jean Paul Richter (Black 1985: 310). De Quincey proceeds obliquely and convolutedly, and 'yet the effect of his strange beetle-like activity is somehow to fill up a previously hollow void of experience' (Adams 1966: 37). All of his writings are part of one interrelated project. 'We can read his journalistic pieces on the Roman Empire just as we read "The English Mail-Coach", for the Opium-Eater's history and his dreams are only versions of one consistent kind of writing in which the pariah is saving himself' (Maniquis 1976: 88). Yet for all his consistency, De Quincey moved with great fluency between several different prose registers, from the humorous to the sentimental, the reportorial to the satiric, the conversational to the suspenseful, the rambunctious to the refined. 'It is difficult to think of another figure with so varied a stylistic repertoire as De Quincey' (McFarland 1987: 104). His impassioned prose is his most significant stylistic achievement. It evinces a 'painstaking mastery of assonance, alliteration, balance, swelling and falling rhythms, and haunting and evocative diction' (Jordan 1960: xv). With it, he shifted 'the values of familiar things [. . . .] which makes us wonder whether, then, [prose] is quite so limited as the critics say, and ask further whether the prose writer, the novelist, might not capture fuller and finer truths than are now his aim if he ventured into those shadowy regions where De Quincey has been before him' (Woolf 1994: 367).

De Quincey wrote a good deal of literary criticism, much of which was informed by his readings of and conversations with Samuel Taylor Coleridge and William Wordsworth. He 'cannot be ranked among the very great critics because his work is too fragmentary and unreliable' (Jordan 1973: 46). In the most ungenerous light, De Quincey 'is disgracefully slack about verifying things, muddles his favourite authors, and is so often faulty in his quotations that one wonders if anything he quotes is right' (V. R. 1939: 417). He is a 'stupid or very ignorant critic' (V. R. 1940: 435). Viewed much more positively, De Quincey's 'reflections upon the theory of literature are penetrating and suggestive [. . . .] He is the first of English critics to support consistently [. . .] the theory that in literature, as in all the arts, substance and form are inseparable' (Darbishire 1909: 31). He 'combines most of the characteristic traits of the impressionistic temperament with a fine power of purely intellectual analysis' (Proctor 1943: 5). One of De Quincey's most well-known literary formulations is the difference between the 'literature of knowledge' and the 'literature of power'. For some, the 'distinction seems to amount to little more than the distinction between imaginative and applied literature'; and 'the vagueness and multiplicity of meaning which it is possible to assign to the term "power" and the fact that also "knowledge is power" have discredited De Quincey's terminology' (Wellek 1944: 268–69). But for others, the definition provides 'the best single example of what De Quincey expected of literature and of the persistent dualism in his thought' (Jordan 1952: 38). The concept is 'meaningful to him principally because it enables him to surmount a metaphysics of absence' (Snyder 1986: 692). Perhaps De Quincey's most famous critical essay is 'On the Knocking at the Gate in Macbeth', a 'characteristic performance' that 'tells us as much about its author' as about the play. 'De Quincey offers it as "psychological criticism", an attempt to explain the emotional impact of a particular moment in the play' (Lindop 1996: xiii). The essay 'brings the murderer and the writer into the same orbit, for both are interested in pleasure and power, and both seek freedom by outstripping or subverting the social institutions they feel thwart or confine them' (Morrison 2006: xi–xii).

As a scholar, De Quincey has frequently been maligned as a plagiarist, hack, charlatan, and bore who 'read extensively and thought acutely by fits, [ate] an enormous quantity of opium, wrote a few pages which revealed new capacities in the language, and provided a good deal of respectable padding for magazines' (Stephen 1871: 329). Nine decades later and the verdict was much the same. De Quincey's 'many works of a scholarly or intellectual nature are almost all derived in the most direct way from printed sources, and in almost every case from a single volume. In every article of this kind, De Quincey has produced a clever piece of hack work, writing with the source book in one hand and the pen in the other' (Goldman 1965: 9). Several commentators, however, have lauded De Quincey as an intellectual. He is 'a man of very considerable genius [....] a German, a Kantist; a Mystic also, I suppose', declared Thomas Carlyle in 1828 (Morrison 1995: 16). Guided by the philosophical writings of Immanuel Kant, De Quincey explored the workings of the unconscious mind, and the correspondence between the moral law in human nature and the natural law in the heavens. His explorations, like Coleridge's, 'both extend the scope and question the validity of Romantic conceptions as they were being severally set forth in the various European cultures of the time' (Beer 1985: 347). De Quincey took his engagement with Kant even further in his first two essays 'On Murder Considered as One of the Fine Arts' (1827 and 1839), where he pushes Kant's acknowledgement that natural violence was a potential source of the sublime to the logical conclusion that human violence might be regarded in the same light, and possibly to even greater effect. The result is a disorientating and exhilarating world of irony that represents murder as a source of aesthetic satisfaction, and that points the way toward Friedrich Nietzsche's 'full-blown aesthetic critique of morality in general later in the century' (Black 1991: 16).

De Quincey translated several tales of terror, and wrote a number of others. His gothic romance *Klosterheim* (1832) produced a decidedly mixed reaction. On the one hand, it made 'no noise' (Robinson 1938: II. 482). It was 'a complete failure' (Gilfillan 1845: 156). 'The scenery and architecture were over-described; the historic and processional part of the affair completely overlaid the romantic element, and the characters had about as much vitality as the pasteboard "Miller and his Men" of a child's theatre' (Sotheby 1861: 66). In works 'of this kind De Quincey is doing no more than echo a defunct manner' (Praz 1956: 76). But on the other hand, *Klosterheim* reached 'in purity of style and idiom [. . .] an excellence to which Sir W. Scott [. . . .] appears never to have aspired' (Coleridge 1971: 911). It is a text in which De Quincey 'constructs a heroized image of himself, sublimating fears of his own weakness and complicity through the fantasy of one who aggressively controls his fate' (Snyder 1981: 137). The town of Klosterheim 'strangely resembles the mind of the opium-eater, isolated from its surroundings, controlled in its waking consciousness, yet taking on by night an anarchic aspect at once threatening and creative' (Wordsworth 1993: 233). De Quincey's most successful tale of terror, 'The Avenger' (1838), explores a disturbing world of violence, vigilantism, and religious persecution. As events unravel, 'all lesser passions are swallowed up, and the empire of a blank, rayless revenge is triumphant; we are spellbound amid the successive stages of the demoniac tragedy; we start up convulsively, as from the horrors of nightmare, at its ghastly catastrophe' (Spring 1864: 662). 'The Avenger' shows the influence 'of the *Blackwood's*-type tale of terror in its explicit treatment of multiple murder, but at the same time it is one of De Quincey's most obviously Gothic and "German" [. . .] as well as being one of his most certainly personal texts' (Bridgwater 2004: 151). In its aestheticization and commodification of crime, as well as in its rhetoric, suspense, violence, reversals, and ingenuity, 'The Avenger' put in place 'salient features' of detective fiction as they were soon to manifest themselves in the works of Edgar Allan Poe, Wilkie Collins, Arthur Conan Doyle, and a host of others (Morrison 2001: 430). De Quincey capped his career as a terror writer with his 'Postscript' to 'On Murder Considered as One of the Fine Arts' (1854), a text in which he returns again to the bloody scenes of the John Williams murders of 1811. 'I know of no writer but De Quincey who invests mysteries of this tragic order with their appropriate drapery, so that they shall, to our imaginations, unfold the full measure of their capacities for striking awe into our hearts' (Alden 1863: 362). The 'Postscript' lays bare De Quincey's 'oscillation between fascination with and repulsion at violent crime', leaving us 'with a sense of nausea like that induced by the Marquis de Sade's repetitive scenes of torture' (Plumtree 1985: 160). Eve Kosofsky Sedgwick concludes that De Quincey was 'a great Gothic novelist'. The subjects he approached 'with the most characteristic sympathy were certain heightened versions of privation and immobilization: dreams and trances, submergence under a massive space, the unspeakable. If we add to these themes, those of the pariah and of the loss of the past, and mention the sense of helplessness washing over everything else, we have a sketch of the most powerful part of De Quincey's ... prose' (Sedgwick 1986: 37).

De Quincey's biographical essays on Wordsworth, Coleridge, and Robert Southey are magazine articles *par excellence*. Their combination of anecdote, criticism, and insider gossip drew the ire of many. 'All the persons I have met with who have read them, have risen from them with the same disgust' (Hare 1835: 25). The articles were 'an act of treachery scarcely paralleled, we hope, in the history of Literature' (Martineau 1869: 98). Wordsworth called De Quincey 'a pest in society, and one of the most worthless of mankind', while an enraged Southey urged Hartley Coleridge to 'take a strong cudgel, proceed straight to Edinburgh, and give De Quincey, publicly on the streets there, a sound beating—as a calumniator, cowardly spy, traitor, base betrayer of the social hearth, for one thing!' (Jordan 1963: 336, 347). Henry Crabb Robinson, however, spoke for the majority when he described the articles as 'scandalous, but painfully interesting' (Robinson 1938: I. 273). Coleridge's daughter Sara labeled them 'infamous' but gave De Quincey his due: 'of all the censors of Mr Coleridge, Mr De Quincey is the one whose remarks are the most worthy of attention [. . . .] He] had sufficient inward sympathy with the subject of his criticism to be capable in some degree of beholding his mind, as it actually existed, in all the intermingling shades of individual reality' (Wright 1970: 15). The essays are 'easily the most famous biographies of the Romantic era', and have left a deep mark on subsequent criticism (Cafarelli 1990: 151). More than one hundred years after they first appeared, De Quincey's articles on Wordsworth were still referred to as 'much the best biography' of the poet (Bateson 1954: 44). De Quincey's recollections of Coleridge have been seen as even more penetrating. In them he 'first broached the vexed problem of Coleridge's plagiarisms, and commented on the relation between Coleridge's opium habit and loss of poetic creativity. He also depicted Coleridge's unhappy marriage and raised the issue of his political "apostasy". At the same time, he drew attention to Coleridge's varied and original interest in psychology, German literature, metaphysics and classical philosophy, and defended his moral integrity'. He is Coleridge's 'first important critical biographer' (Roberts 2000: 12).

De Quincey as autobiographer has always attracted a great deal of attention. *Confessions of an English Opium-Eater* (1821; revised 1856) made an immense impact when it first appeared. Not all the attention was favourable. 'The work is written throughout in the tone of apology for a secret, selfish, suicidal debauchery', declared the *Eclectic Review*: 'it is the physical suffering consequent upon it, that alone excites in the Writer a moment's regret' (Anon. 1823a: 371). But *The Album* praised the *Confessions* as a 'physical and metaphysical wonder [. . .] We thought it one of the most interesting, and certainly the very most extraordinary, production that we had ever seen' (Anon. 1822: 177). Some avoided opium after reading De Quincey's account. 'Nobody in his senses is likely to be allured to the practice of eating this insane drug [...] by reading the *Confessions of an Opium Eater*' (Montgomery 1821: 3). Others, however, sought the drug as De Quincey had done to heighten their pleasure in music, solitude, books, and conversation. In the *Confessions* De Quincey 'invented the concept of recreational drug use' (Boon 2002: 37). Still others tried opium and were more fatally tempted. 'Many persons had greatly injured themselves by taking Opium experimentally, which trial they had been enticed to make by the fascinating description of the exquisite pleasure attendant on the taking of that drug, given in a recent publication on the subject' (Anon. 1823*b*: iv). Indeed, De Quincey is still being blamed for pushing experimentation and seducing people into addiction. 'In modern society the main cause of drug addiction, apart from the fact that many people have nothing to live for, is a literary tradition of romantic claptrap, started by Coleridge and De Quincey, and continued without serious interruption ever since [....] This claptrap is the main source of popular and medical misconceptions on the subject' (Dalrymple 2006: 61).

The *Confessions* were originally published in the *London Magazine* in September and October 1821. They derived much of their complexity 'from an unresolved combination of extreme experiential concerns and a politeness which is in keeping with their periodical magazine context' (Whale 1985: 35). Wordsworth played an enormous role in shaping De Quincey's account of his teenage sufferings and the growth of his imaginative mind. 'The influence of *The Prelude* is everywhere in the *Confessions*; in the structure, in the areas of experience explored in both works and in the techniques of exploration' (Devlin 1983: 67). Coleridge's *Biographia Literaria* (1817) is equally significant, for the 'structural fabric and thematic development' of De Quincey's text are 'parasitic' upon Coleridge's book (Leask 1992: 187). The evident theme of the *Confessions* is the power of the dreaming mind in interaction with the agencies of opium. 'De Quincey was the first writer, and he is perhaps still the only one, to study deliberately, from within his personal experience, the way in which dreams and visions are formed, how opium helps to form them and intensifies them, and how they are then recomposed and used in conscious art' (Hayter 1968: 103). The 'implicit and more important themes' of the *Confessions* 'include the disembodied nature of textual self-representation, the sublating of material relations between writer and reader in the act of reading, and the mystification of the origin of the work of art as a commodity' (Rzepka 1995: 4). For some, the *Confessions* are a unified narrative in which De Quincey's brings coherence and depth to his experience. 'The fear of unconnectedness and isolation compels De Quincey to make a meaningful order out of his autobiography' (Porter 1980: 593). For others, De Quincey inevitably erases what he seeks to delineate. 'What is named "De Quincey" is effacement, metaphorization, and metamorphosis without beginning, without centre, and without end' (Spector 1979: 520).

Suspiria de Profundis (1845), De Quincey's belated sequel to the original *Confessions*, is a haunting account of the tragically early death of his sister Elizabeth. It has been the subject of intense and provocative critical scrutiny. In his highly influential reading, J. Hillis Miller argues that Elizabeth's death brings the destruction of a previously indissoluble unity that De Quincey bridges only when he realizes at the last that we know God through the absence of God. 'At the moment of death, we shall experience a fathomless solitude, but through it we shall also experience, by anticipation, our reconciliation with God and with all we lost when we were exiled from the Paradise of childhood' (Miller 1963: 79). In John Barrell's view, the complex set of images De Quincey associates with Elizabeth's death expand outward to inform his speculations on a broad range of political and historical issues, including British imperialism, the Indian Mutiny of 1857, and much else. 'It seems best [. . .] to think of the relation between childhood and the oriental in De Quincey's writings as a relation between two forms of guilt, personal and political, in which each can be a displaced version of the other, and in which each aggravates the other in an ascending spiral of fear and of violence' (Barrell 1991: 21). To Alina Clej, the Miltonic and Wordsworthian echoes that pervade De Quincey's account of Elizabeth's death make it 'not primarily a fantasy of incestuous transgression, but the "secret" of modern literary production—the secret that the modern authorial subject, even in its high Romantic mode, is a rhetorical construct fashioned out of echoes, a "self" opened up to and by others and thoroughly penetrated by them'. De Quincey is 'one of the first writers, if not the very first, to experience and work out the symptoms of modernity' (Clej 1995: 249, 8).

'The English Mail-Coach' follows the narrative pattern first established by De Quincey in the *Confessions*, where autobiographical episodes and engaging conversational banter gradually give way to nightmare worlds of personal tragedy and apocalypse played out with horrifying repetitiveness in the tortured mind of the dreamer. Critics have often seen it as De Quincey's most powerful work. It is 'a case study in ekphrastic paralysis', for it reveals 'how De Quincey's experience of heightened perception accompanied by bodily torpor gave rise to images of action and stasis' (Burwick 2001: 127). Though 'firmly set in memory, in the past, in specific lost events', 'The Mail-Coach' voices the aspirations 'of one who has been stranded by political history. The result is curious, because it means that hope and hopelessness occupy the same mental space' (Baxter 1990: 126). In the opening section of the work, the race between the English mail-coach and the Birmingham commercial coach 'is figured as one between England and an enemy [. . . .] The mail-coach rather than the commercial conveyance embodies the version of Englishness that matters most in De Quincey's system' (Milligan 1995: 50). In 'The Vision of Sudden Death', De Quincey assumes 'unapologetically what is intimated in Rousseau and implicit in Wordsworth: that social contract and *convention* [...] always carries a trace of coercion that figures, in extremity, as violence' (Russett 1997: 74). The section demonstrates too the ways in which De Quincey's 'own lost potency, his own imminent death, can be the subject of his best prose' (McDonagh 1994: 152). The 'Dream-Fugue' with which 'The Mail-Coach' concludes emphasizes 'the endless resurrection of De Quincey's own love for his sister even as it celebrates the endless resurrection of divine love' (McFarland 1987: 121). At the same time, it is the most 'mind-boggling fantasy of patriotism [...] written in the nineteenth century. The self, the nation, the world, Christendom are gathered into one historical light cast against the darkness' (Maniquis 1976: 75).

De Quincey's influence on his fellow writers has been profound. His enormous impact on nineteenth-century French literature can be felt in the works of Nerval, Balzac, Gautier, and especially Baudelaire, whose reading of De Quincey 'affected his whole emotional and aesthetic orientation' (Lyon 1969: 181–82). De Quincey's 'vein of fantasy, introspection and unease' tinges the work of 'Poe, Stevenson, Dickens, Baudelaire, Proust, Dostoevsky, Borges and many others' (Lindop 1981: 392). James Joyce 'knew by heart whole pages of [...] De Quincey' (Budgen 1934: 181). D. H. Lawrence liked De Quincey 'because he [...] dislikes such people as Plato and Goethe, whom I dislike' (Lawrence 1984: 407). 'It is to De Quincey that Virginia Woolf may owe much of her perceptual method, especially the sense of the contraction and expansion of time, space, and matter, and the projection of internal emotions, notably certain fears, on the external visual field' (Richter 1970: 91). Jorge Luis Borges declared that his 'debt' to De Quincey was 'so vast that to specify one part seems to repudiate or to silence the others' (Christ 1969: 152). 'I abhor the star-system fashions and all the novelists who play at that', Stevie Smith asserted in a 1963 interview, '... I read De Quincey. I like Evelyn Waugh' (Williams 1991: 45). In W. S. Burroughs's *The Place of Dead Roads*, the lead character Kim Carson 'opens the door to go out of the druggist's shop' just as 'someone comes in with a puff of fog and cold air. Boy about eighteen, angular English face, blue eyes, red scarf. Rather like the younger De Quincey [....] The boy's eyes widened in startled recognition' (Burroughs 1983: 49). 'Few writers had so keen and horrified a sense of place' as De Quincey, Peter Ackroyd observes in *Dan Leno and the Limehouse Golem*. 'He evokes a sinister, crepuscular London, a haven for strange powers, a city of footsteps and flaring lights, of houses packed close together, of lachrymose alleys and false doors' (Ackroyd 1994: 38). Bankim Chandra Chatterjee's *Kamalakanta*—first published in Bengali in 1875—was seen as 'a Bengali version of De Quincey's *Confessions of an Opium Eater*' (Chatterjee 1997: xv), and Rushdie's 'Mail Coach' section (a postcolonial Indian version of 'The English Mail-Coach') of *Haroun and the Sea of Stories* provides yet another case of the empire writing back in a way that ironically fulfills De Quincey's predictions regarding the spread of English through colonialism. De Quincey has haunted, entertained, and influenced some of the most significant names in nineteenth and twentieth-century literature.

The flurry of scholarship in recent years has culminated in the publication of the new, twenty-one volume *Works of Thomas De Quincey* (2000–03), under Grevel Lindop's magisterial general editorship. All scholarship is shaped by its moment and so, no doubt, it is with this collection of essays on De Quincey. Its merits, we believe, will speak out clearly and immediately; its limitations will inevitably become more evident with time. Yet, we believe this is a singularly propitious moment to engage in such an effort. Twentieth-century professional endeavour and technology have achieved what Gabriel and his multipotent adversary—in De Quincey's view—were deemed incapable of. One may quibble with some of the explanatory notes and wish ardently for a more detailed index to the volumes, but certainly the texts are out there, and much new material is available to scholarship. This much was evident to the reviewers who hailed the edition as a major editorial success, and the basis for all future work on De Quincey.[2]

Yet, while the De Quincey editors were digging in archives, in the more rarefied theoretical atmosphere above them, other developments were taking place. (Such a stark separation between archival and theoretical work is of course merely a rhetorical device: many of the De Quincey editors were also specialists in theory, and De Quincey himself was notably theoretical in his critical thinking, rivalled in his lifetime perhaps only by Coleridge). During the years that the De Quincey edition took shape (commencing in 1989), the linguistical and rhetorical excesses of deconstruction had given way to the more grounded theories of New Historicism and Cultural Materialism. De Quincey's identity as an autobiographer was now linked to his political thought on the one hand (ideationally), and to his drug-addicted and penurious circumstances on the other (materially). De Quincey's magazine-context, and his imbrication in Romantic-period cultures of imperialism, gender, sexuality, race, religion, language and medical theory, and aesthetics emerged in significant studies from the nineties. This spate of books was clearly the consequence of a conjunction of theory and praxis, part of their work in progress for many of the editors who were involved in the project, though others not on the team were also influenced by the climate of industry. Many of the above-mentioned scholars, inspired by the winds of change blown in by contemporary theory, and the new material posed by the De Quincey edition, have seen fit to re-enter the critical arena in the following collection. Other voices reflect the interests of newer scholars who have been drawn by the thinking that has emerged and is emerging in this area. Critical work on De Quincey continues to appear with ever-greater frequency, and from a position of peripheral and eccentric significance to Romantic literature, he is now deeply embedded in our notions of Romanticism, and increasingly of Victorianism too. Inevitably it has not been possible to include every active critic of De Quincey here; the field of his scholarship is clearly too large to be held within the bounds of a single volume.

It seemed appropriate to organize the collection in a roughly chronological fashion following De Quincey's career, and to open with a reading of De Quincey's religious thought (an area of scholarship treated memorably by Hillis Miller) in the light of postcolonial theory. Postcolonialist critiques of Romanticism have been among the most vigorous of recent times, and De Quincey's imperialistic attitudes have been the focus of much critical attention (most notably by John Barrell). So much so that De Quincey's presence on the undergraduate literature syllabus is often predicated on his orientalism: the opium nightmares and the encounter with the Malay in the 1821 *Confessions* being the most obvious sites of his colonialist anxieties. Rather than relegating De Quincey's orientalism to the realms of pathology however, Daniel Sanjiv Roberts shows how De Quincey's colonialist fantasies are deeply imbued by his English evangelical upbringing and increasingly conservative Protestantism, during a period when imperial expansion was usually understood in providential terms by Christian thinkers. By linking De Quincey's orientalism to biblical scholarship, Roberts incidentally points to a lacuna in much postcolonial scholarship which has largely ignored the enormous importance of the Bible in the arena of orientalism. Ranging over De Quincey's career, from his early discussions with his East India Company uncle through his anxious opium dreams and Christian apologetical essays of the 1840s to his later nostalgic descriptions of his nursery readings of the Bible in the *Autobiographic Sketches* of the 1850s, Roberts's essay opens a panoramic view of De Quincey's career within a discursive framework of evangelical imperialism. Politics, of course, was never far from De Quincey's mind even in his most religious essays—or perhaps, as we have just seen, *especially* in his most religious essays—and his reputation as a magazine writer was forged in the crucible of political journalism. The bulk of his political journalism was however excluded in the nineteenth-century editions, including his own *Selections Grave and Gay*, that were standard until recently. Consequently much ink has been spilt by historicist critics of De Quincey on the issue of his politics and the ways in which these inform his visionary writings. If nineteenth-century disciples of De Quincey tended to be reverential to the point of protecting his reputation by excising his texts—as Masson and Japp did—to augment his reputation of piety, it was perhaps inevitable that the twentieth century should proceed in the opposite direction and denounce him for his unacceptable political views—his 1821 *Confessions* have often been read in this way as endorsing a deep-seated conservatism.

This view is challenged in two separate and robustly argumentative essays by Barry Milligan and Robert Morrison respectively, concentrating on medical professionalism and extracting a radical subtext in the *Confessions*. As Morrison argues, in the *Confessions*, De Quincey enjoys an elitist education and preens himself on being thought a gentleman and a scholar. He fraternizes with aristocrats and Etonians, quotes Edmund Burke and the older Wordsworth, and comments rather glibly on the pleasures of wandering among London's working classes. He experiences terrifying nightmares in which his identity is threatened by the tyranny of urban masses and the terror of revolutionary battle and strife. His fear of the East is brought vividly to life in the frantic xenophobia of the Malay dream, where he fantasizes about racial superiority and the genocidal exercise of imperial power. Yet as Morrison points out the *Confessions* also contain a radicalized subtext that complicates and destabilizes De Quincey's often truculent Toryism. His narrative celebrates both power and defiance. De Quincey bolts from educational and parental authority and lives outside traditional social structures, an exile who befriends waifs and prostitutes, a thinker who is immersed in recondite German philosophy, and a hedonist who swallows opiates at an unprecedented rate. The text is packed with references to liberal and radical writers, including Thomas Clarkson, Thomas Erskine, William Hazlitt, John Keats, John Leslie, David Ricardo, William Roscoe, Percy Bysshe Shelley, and William Wilberforce, all of whom energize and betray the breadth of De Quincey's political, social, and intellectual sympathies. In the *Confessions*, his aristocratic and colonial preoccupations collide with his delight in disobedience and over-indulgence.

In a parallel argument, Barry Milligan indicates the polemical nature of De Quincey's engagement with medical orthodoxy on the subject of opium, aligning the opium-eater's views with the Brunonian school of medical thought—following the work of the medical authority John Brown (1735–88) and his disciples. However, as Neil Vickers has argued in *Coleridge and the Doctors*, the Brunonian system had become 'inextricably linked with social and political radicalism' by the 1790s. Milligan argues consequently that opium works with respect to De Quincey's sense of class much as it acts upon his sense of national identity, unearthing a quasi-primordial unity with 'the Other' that is both liberating and disturbing. Opium's destabilization of De Quincey's otherwise notoriously conservative political views is reflected not only in his advocacy of Brunonianism, but also in his solidarity with workers and prostitutes in his Saturday night rambles. As both Milligan and Morrison show in different ways, far from promoting hard-line conservatism in any direct fashion, the *Confessions* reveal the paradoxes and strains at the centre of De Quincey's attitude toward race, class, slavery, imperialism, and political violence.

Gender and sexuality—yet other areas in which traditional literary studies have been shaken by recent theory—are next in line for treatment in three distinct and complementary essays by John Whale, Julian North and Josephine McDonagh respectively. In her essay on 'De Quincey, Wordsworth and Women in *Tait's Edinburgh Magazine*', North questions recent accounts of De Quincey's 'anxiety of reception' (in Newlyn's presentation of him) by looking at his writing for *Tait's* in relation to his construction of audience. 'The Lake Reminiscences' show De Quincey 'wooing the reader'—especially the female reader—in a way that offers a critique of what is represented as Wordsworth's unchivalrous disregard for his audience. The influence of

Christian Johnstone, Tait's female editor, is evident in De Quincey's enthusiastic references to women writers which intersect with his writings on the male Lakers. De Quincey's respect for female literary achievement contrasts with what he represents as Wordsworth's contempt for contemporary women's fiction, thus identifying the opium-eater with the poet's female relatives, particularly Dorothy Wordsworth. Together, he and Dorothy become emblematic of Wordsworth's readers, upon whom the poet depends without sufficiently acknowledging his debt.

Another essay interrogating the familiar ground of De Quincey's relationship with Wordsworth in a newly critical way is John Whale's 'De Quincey and Men (of Letters)' which complements recent feminist critiques of De Quincey by the likes of Leighton, Fulford and McFarland, by drawing attention to De Quincey's engagement with different forms of nineteenth-century masculinity in their connection with literary culture. Whale reassesses De Quincey's complex relationship to Wordsworth in this new light, and explores his long-standing and embattled relationship to John Wilson, aka Christopher North of *Blackwood's Edinburgh Magazine*. The connections between privacy, reputation, professional integrity, and the gendered activity of literature for the professional man of letters, form the basis for Whale's enquiry, rather than canonical concerns with poetic genius which have dominated such discussions. The production of a new form of masculinity out of a combination of conduct, sexuality, and writing in the magazine culture of the first three decades of the century are measured against conflicting and more pervasive forms of corporeal masculine culture which also, in turn, formed competing ideas of national identity.

An essay on De Quincey's much-vaunted interest in books is long overdue, and Josephine McDonagh obliges by productively contextualizing this interest in terms of the cultural politics and discourses of 'bibliomania', the strange affliction conceived of in the early decades of the nineteenth century as a medical condition. Bibliomania formed the basis of male homosociality among book connoisseurs and collectors who met at the Roxburghe Club (which included the famous book collector Richard Heber, who in the 1820s allegedly engaged in a homosexual relationship with an aspiring young male bibliographer, Charles Hartshorne). While De Quincey was not a member of the club, he had attended the famous Roxburghe sale of 1812 (which inaugurated the Club's anniversary meetings), and his keen interests would have drawn him into proximity with these homosocial and book-loving circles. Yet another scandal involving homosexual propensities within a bibliophilic context which McDonagh speculatively invokes involved a fellow of All Souls College in Oxford, Charles Shipley, who intriguingly may have met and pressed a guinea on De Quincey's brother, Richard (otherwise known as 'Pink' on account of his exceeding prettiness), while De Quincey was in Oxford. This background regarding the homosocial and homosexual aspects of bibliomania may help to explain the particular anxieties that De Quincey expresses regarding books, especially his grotesque fantasy about a potentially unlimited order for books that is elaborated in the *Suspiria de Profundis*, and also more generally, his discussions of his own library, and those of friends and associates.

Two essays focus on texts of the 1840s, Joel Black's 'Temperance and Temperament: De Quincey's Politics of Global Addiction' which looks at a relatively overlooked essay on 'National Temperance Movements', and Ian Balfour's reading of 'The English Mail-Coach' in relation to 'the Sublime of the Nation'. While De Quincey's journalistic writings dealing with the opium trade have been the subject of some recent studies, Black rewardingly follows a supplementary line by focussing on alcoholism as the subject of 'National Temperance Movements'. Why was De Quincey so enthusiastic about temperance movements in Britain and America while he vigorously opposed the contemporaneous political campaign to eliminate opium addiction in China? Rather than ascribing such contradictions to nationalism, Black sees them as stemming from De Quincey's imagined affinity with the temperate Asiatics whom he perceived as being susceptible to opium while he saw the northern nations as being susceptible to alcohol. While De Quincey sees Europeans as creating an unnatural craving and dependency on alcohol in the temperate regions they colonize, he fails to acknowledge the West's far more flagrant exploitation of the East in the case of Britain's opium trade with China. Instead he portrays himself as a victim of the global opium exchange who has been implanted with insatiable desires originating in the East.

Yet another structure of global politics—this time seen in terms of aesthetics—underpins Balfour's analysis of the discourses of sublimity and nationality in 'The English Mail-Coach', which he links most interestingly with De Quincey's seminal translation of Kant's *Observations on our Feelings of the Beautiful and the Sublime*. Kant's characterization of various nations of the world on the basis of a graduated discrimination between their propensities to the polar aesthetic categories of beauty and sublimity supplies the framework for Balfour's analysis of 'The English Mail-Coach'. In Balfour's analysis, the titular mail-coach becomes a vehicle of national sublimity in more ways than one, so much so that the message is inherent in the medium: the mail-coach is the medium of the sublime news regarding the great Napoleonic victories and traumas, but at the same time its own unstoppable velocity (and the consequent associations with sudden death) render it an object of sublimity in itself.

Both of the preceding essays as well as those by Gregory Dart and Charles Rzepka draw our attention to the *Victorian* De Quincey, an aspect of his literary career which ought to be very apparent from his publishing dates, but is often overlooked in favour of the opium-eater's (also undoubted) imbrication in *Romantic* literary culture and theory. The problem is clearly one of our own construction (of period categories) rather than of De Quincey's making. The essays by Dart and Rzepka address this fallacy of period-categorization head-on by reading De Quincey in symbiotic relation to his

14 *Thomas De Quincey*

Victorian contemporaries. As Dart suggests in his exemplary reading of the 1854 'Postscript' to the celebrated essays on murder, De Quincey's life-long obsession with murder is inflected by the 1830s and 40s phenomenon of the 'Newgate Novel' and responds to criticisms of this low form of literature by elevating murder into high art with distinctively Tory overtones. De Quincey emerges in this analysis as an early theorist and dramatist of the metropole: as issues of individuality and community, virtue and vice, are represented in spatial, almost geometrical terms in his text, mapped onto the ambivalent landscape of early nineteenth-century Wapping. Also turning to mid-Victorian contexts for his readings, Rzepka reconsiders the 1856 *Confessions* which have tended to fall out of favour with critics in recent years, drawing attention to the new meanings generated by the 1856 version which Masson's edition standardized for over a century. Appearing only a year before the Indian 'mutiny' (or first war of independence) of 1857, De Quincey's work fed into mid-Victorian anxieties regarding orientalism and addiction, intertwining them in the popular imagination. Such an influence can be traced through works such as Wilkie Collins's *The Moonstone* (1867–8), Charles Dickens's *The Mystery of Edwin Drood* (1870), and the early Sherlock Holmes stories by Arthur Conan Doyle. Interestingly, both Dart and Rzepka relate De Quincey to popular and sensational forms of literature during the Victorian period, though his reputation remains that of a High Romantic.

If not God's plenty, then certainly this volume has De Quincey's plenty. His works are viewed in relation to politics, religion, medical and orientalist discourses, gender and sexuality, high aesthetics, theory, literary history, philosophy and popular culture among other contexts; the list of his works examined include familiar and unfamiliar material, the 1803 *Diary*, writings for the *London Magazine*, *Blackwood's Magazine*, and *Tait's Magazine*, as well as the 1821 *Confessions*, 'The English Mail-Coach', the *Suspiria de Profundis*, the 'Murder' essays, the *Autobiographic Sketches* and the 1856 *Confessions*, not to mention manuscript correspondence and newly published material from the Pickering and Chatto *Works*; new evidences are unearthed and speculative ventures launched in the following pages; materialist and historicist approaches, global and contemporary politics, orientalism and aesthetics, gender theory, queer theory, and postcolonial theory, have all been pressed into service; his political colours seem to shift from a Tory blue to a colonial pink to a radical red depending on which way one reads him; he is Romantic and Victorian, compassionate and snobbish; a reader and a writer; a patient and a doctor; a literary giant and a wretched journalist; an addict and an agent. We have not attempted any schematization of De Quincey, beyond what the contributors have achieved in their own differing ways. The introduction above orders and groups together articles in ways that we hope will be illuminating and productive, but at the same time we recognize that the essays will speak to each other across the volume in ways we have not fully anticipated or cannot now hear. This collection of essays does not offer itself as definitive in any way, except perhaps, as of a theoretical and critical moment. The very disparities and divergences that it offers seems to us to display the best evidence of a lively and fruitful area of study.

NOTES

1. The most important surveys of De Quincey's critical reputation are Green 1908, Jordan 1966, Dendurent 1978, North 1997, and Morrison 1998.
2. For a selection of reviews of the De Quincey edition see the Pickering and Chatto website: http://www.pickeringchatto.com/dequincey.htm.

WORKS CITED

Ackroyd, Peter. (1994) *Dan Leno and the Limehouse Golem*. London: Sinclair-Stevenson.
Adams, Robert Martin. (1966) *Nil: Episodes in the Literary Conquest of the Void during the Nineteenth Century*. New York: Oxford University Press.
Alden, H. M. (1863) 'Thomas De Quincey'. *The Atlantic Monthly*, 12, 345–68.
Amis, John and Rose, Michael. (1989) *Words About Music*. London: Faber.
Anon. (1822) 'Confessions of an English Opium Eater'. *The Album*, 2, 177–207.
———. (1823a) 'Confessions of an English Opium Eater'. *Eclectic Review*, 19, 366–71.
———. (1823b) *Advice to Opium Eaters, with a Detail of the Effects of that Drug upon the Human Frame*. London: Goodluck.
———. (1854) 'Selections Grave and Gay'. *Eclectic Review*. New Series, 8, 385–99.
———. (1863) 'The Works of Thomas De Quincey'. *British Quarterly Review*, 38, 1–29.
Barrell, John. (1991) *The Infection of Thomas De Quincey: A Psychopathology of Imperialism*. New Haven, CT: Yale University Press.
Bateson, F. W. (1954) *Wordsworth: A Reinterpretation*. London: Longman.
Baxter, Edmund. (1990) *De Quincey's Art of Autobiography*. Edinburgh: Edinburgh University Press.
Beer, John. (1985) 'The Englishness of De Quincey's Ideas'. *English and German Romanticism: Cross-Currents and Controversies*. Ed. James Pipkin. Heidelberg: Carl Winter, 323–47.
Black, Joel. (1991) *The Aesthetics of Murder: A Study in Romantic Literature and Contemporary Culture*. Baltimore: Johns Hopkins University Press.
———. (1985) 'Confession, Digression, Gravitation: Thomas De Quincey's German Connection' in *Thomas De Quincey: Bicentenary Studies*. Ed. Robert Lance Snyder. Norman: University of Oklahoma Press, 308–37.
Boon, Marcus. (2002) *The Road of Excess: A History of Writers on Drugs*. Cambridge, MA: Harvard University Press.
Bridgwater, Patrick. (2004) *De Quincey's Gothic Masquerade*. Amsterdam: Rodopi.
Budgen, Frank. (1934) *James Joyce and the Making of Ulysses*. London: Grayson and Grayson.
Burroughs, W. S. (1983) *The Place of Dead Roads*. New York: Holt, Rinehart and Winston.
Burwick. Frederick. (2001) *Thomas De Quincey: Knowledge and Power*. Houndmills: Palgrave.

Cafarelli, Annette Wheeler. (1990) *Prose in the Age of Poets: Romanticism and Biographical Narrative from Johnson to De Quincey.* Philadelphia: University of Pennsylvania Press.
Chatterjee, Bankim Chandra. (1997) *Kamalakanta*, trans. Monish Chandra Chatterjee. New Delhi: HarperCollins India.
Christ, Ronald. (1969) *The Narrow Act: Borges's Art of Allusion.* New York: New York University Press.
Clej, Alina. (1995) *A Genealogy of the Modern Self: Thomas De Quincey and the Intoxication of Writing.* Stanford, CA: Stanford University Press.
Coleridge, Samuel Taylor. (1971) 'To William Blackwood ... May 26, 1832'. *Collected Letters.* Vol. 6. Ed. E. L. Griggs. Oxford: Clarendon Press, 911–13.
Dalrymple, Theodore. (2006) *Romancing Opiates: Pharmacological Lies and the Addiction Bureaucracy.* New York: Encounter Books.
Darbishire, Helen. (1909) 'Introduction'. *De Quincey's Literary Criticism.* London: Henry Frowde, 7–36.
De Luca, V. A. (1980) *Thomas De Quincey: The Prose of Vision.* Toronto: University of Toronto Press.
Dendurent, H. O. (1978) *Thomas De Quincey: A Reference Guide.* Boston: G. K. Hall.
Devlin, D. D. (1983). *De Quincey, Wordsworth and the Art of Prose.* London: Macmillan.
Goldman, Albert. (1965) *The Mine and the Mint: Sources for the Writings of Thomas De Quincey.* Carbondale: Southern Illinois University Press.
Gilfillan, George. (1845) *A Gallery of Literary Portraits.* Edinburgh: William Tait.
Green, J. A. (1908) *Thomas De Quincey: A Bibliography Based upon the De Quincey Collection in the Moss Side Library.* Manchester: Manchester Public Free Libraries.
Hare, Julius. (1835) 'Samuel Taylor Coleridge and the English Opium-Eater'. *British Magazine*, 7, 15–27.
Hayter, Alethea. (1971) 'Introduction'. *Confessions of an English Opium-Eater.* Ed. Alethea Hayter. Harmondsworth: Penguin, 7–24.
——. (1968) *Opium and the Romantic Imagination.* London: Faber.
Hemmings, F. W. J. (1982) *Baudelaire the Damned.* London: Hamish Hamilton.
Japp, A. H. (ed.) (1891) *The Posthumous Works of Thomas De Quincey*, 2 vols., London: Heinemann.
Jordan, John E. (1973) 'Introduction'. *De Quincey as Critic.* Ed. John E. Jordan. London: Routledge and Kegan Paul, 1–48 .
——. (1966) 'Thomas De Quincey'. *The English Romantic Poets and Essayists.* Ed. Carolyn Washburn Houtchens and Lawrence Huston Houtchens. New York: New York University Press, 289–331.
——. (1963) *De Quincey to Wordsworth.* Berkeley: University of California Press.
——. (1960) 'Introduction'. *The Confessions of an English Opium-Eater.* London: Dent, v–xv.
——. (1952) *Thomas De Quincey, Literary Critic.* Berkeley: University of California Press.
Lawrence, D. H. (1984) 'To Catherine Carswell [30 October 1919]'. *The Letters of D. H. Lawrence.* Vol. III. Ed. James T. Boulton and Andrew Robertson. Cambridge: Cambridge University Press, 407.
Leask, Nigel. (1992) *British Romantic Writers and the East.* Cambridge: Cambridge University Press.
Leighton, Angela (1992). 'De Quincey and Women'. *Beyond Romanticism: New Approaches to Texts and Contexts, 1780–1832.* Ed. Stephen Copley and John Whale. London: Routledge, 160–77.

Lindop, Grevel. (1996) 'Introduction'. *Confessions of an English Opium-Eater*. Ed. Grevel Lindop. Oxford: Oxford University Press, vii–xxi.
———. (1981) *The Opium-Eater: A Life of Thomas De Quincey*. London: Dent.
Lyon, Judson S. (1969) *Thomas De Quincey*. New York: Twayne.
Maniquis, Robert. (1976) 'Lonely Empires: Personal and Public Visions of Thomas De Quincey'. *Literary Monographs*, 8. Ed. Eric Rothstein and J.A. Wittreich. Madison: The University of Wisconsin Press, 47–127.
Martineau, Harriet. (1869) *Biographical Sketches*. New York: Leypoldt and Holt.
Masson, David. (ed.) (1889–90) *The Collected Writing of Thomas De Quincey*, 14 vols., Edinburgh: Adam and Charles Black.
McDonagh, Josephine. (1994) *De Quincey's Disciplines*. Oxford: Clarendon Press.
McFarland, Thomas. (1987) *Romantic Cruxes: The English Essayists and the Spirit of the Age*. Oxford: Clarendon Press.
Miller, J Hillis. (1963) *The Disappearance of God: Five Nineteenth-Century Writers*. Cambridge, MA: Belknap Press of Harvard University Press.
Milligan, Barry. (1995) *Pleasures and Pains: Opium and the Orient in Nineteenth-Century British Culture*. Charlottesville: University of Virginia Press.
Montgomery, James. (1821) 'Sheffield, Tuesday, Oct. 23, 1821'. *The Iris; or, Sheffield Advertiser*, 33, 3.
Morrison, Robert. (2006) 'Introduction'. *Thomas De Quincey: On Murder*. Ed. Robert Morrison. Oxford: Oxford University Press, vii–xxvii.
———. (2001) 'Poe's De Quincey, Poe's Dupin'. *Essays in Criticism*, 51.4, 424–41.
———. (1998) 'Essayists of the Romantic Period: De Quincey, Hazlitt, Hunt, and Lamb'. *Literature of the Romantic Period: A Bibliographical Guide*. Ed. Michael O'Neill. Oxford: Clarendon Press, 341–63.
———. (1995) '"The Bog School": Carlyle and De Quincey'. *Carlyle Studies Annual*. Special Issue, 13–20.
North, Julian. (1997) *De Quincey Reviewed: Thomas De Quincey's Critical Reception, 1821–1994*. Columbia, SC: Camden House.
Plumtree, A. S. (1985) 'The Artist as Murderer: De Quincey's "On Murder Considered as One of the Fine Arts"'. *Thomas De Quincey: Bicentenary Studies*. Ed. Robert Lance Snyder. Norman: University of Oklahoma Press.
Porter, Roger J. (1980) 'The Demon Past: De Quincey and the Autobiographer's Dilemma'. *Studies in English Literature*, 20, 591–609.
Praz, Mario. (1956) *The Hero in Eclipse in Victorian Fiction*. London: Oxford University Press.
Proctor, Sigmund. (1943) *Thomas De Quincey's Theory of Literature*. Ann Arbor: University of Michigan Press.
Richter, Harvena. (1970) *Virginia Woolf: The Inward Voyage*. Princeton, NJ: Princeton University Press.
Roberts, Daniel. (2000) *Revisionary Gleam: De Quincey, Coleridge, and the High Romantic Argument*. Liverpool: University of Liverpool Press.
Robinson, Henry Crabb. (1938) *On Books and their Writers*. 3 vols. Ed. Edith Morley. London, Dent.
Rushdie, Salman. (1990) *Haroun and the Sea of Stories*, London: Granta.
Russett, Margaret. (1997) *De Quincey's Romanticism: Canonical Minority and the Forms of Transmission*. Cambridge: Cambridge University Press.
Rzepka, Charles. (1995) *Sacramental Commodities: Gift, Text, and the Sublime in De Quincey*. Amherst: University of Massachusetts Press.
Sackville West, Edward (1936). *A Flame in Sunlight: The Life and Work of Thomas De Quincey*. London: Cassell.
Sedgwick, Eve Kosofsky. (1986) *The Coherence of Gothic Conventions*. New York: Methuen.

Snyder, Robert Lance. (1986) 'De Quincey's Literature of Power: A Mythic Paradigm'. *Studies in English Literature*, 26, 691–711.
———. (1981) '*Klosterheim*: De Quincey's Gothic Masque'. *Research Studies*, 49, 129–42.
Sotheby, H. W. (1861) 'Life and Writings of Thomas De Quincey'. *Fraser's Magazine*, 63, 51–69.
Spector, Stephen J. (1979) 'Thomas De Quincey: Self-effacing Autobiographer'. *Studies in Romanticism*, 18, 501–20.
Spring, L. W. (1864) 'Thomas De Quincey and his Writings'. *The Continental Monthly*, 5, 650–62.
Stephen, Leslie. (1871) 'Thomas De Quincey'. *Fortnightly Review*, 15, 310–29.
Thron, E. Michael. (1985) 'Thomas De Quincey and the Fall of Literature'. *Thomas De Quincey: Bicentenary Studies*. Ed. Robert Lance Synder. Norman: University of Oklahoma Press, 3–19.
V. R. (1940) 'De Quincey: Some Objections and Corrections'. *Notes and Queries*, 179, 434–36.
———. (1939) 'De Quincey: Some Objections and Corrections'. *Notes and Queries*, 176, 417–18.
Wellek, René. (1944) 'De Quincey's Status in the History of Ideas'. *Philological Quarterly*, 23, 248–72.
Whale, John. (1985) '"In a Stranger's Ear": De Quincey's Polite Magazine Context'. *Thomas De Quincey: Bicentenary Studies*. Ed. Robert Lance Synder. Norman: University of Oklahoma Press, 35–53.
Williams, Jonathan. (1991) 'Much Further Out Than You Thought'. *In Search of Stevie Smith*. Ed. Sanford Sternlicht. Syracuse, NY: Syracuse University Press. 38–49.
Woolf, Virginia. (1994) 'Impassioned Prose'. *The Essays of Virginia Woolf, Volume IV*. Ed. Andrew McNeillie. London: The Hogarth Press, 361–69.
Wordsworth, Jonathan. (1993) *Visionary Gleam*. London: Woodstock Books.
Wright, David. (1970) 'Introduction'. *Recollections of the Lakes and the Lake Poets*. Harmondsworth: Penguin, 7–27.

2 'Mix(ing) a Little with Alien Natures'
Biblical Orientalism in De Quincey

Daniel Sanjiv Roberts

Thomas De Quincey's opium nightmares, reported to sensational acclaim in his *Confessions of an English Opium-Eater* (1821), have become a touchstone of Romantic orientalism in the wake of Edward Said's seminal work, *Orientalism* (1978). In a passage which finds quotation in all the standard anthologies of Romantic literature[1] one may recognize the formative expression of a stereotypical English view of a teeming, undifferentiated and deeply repulsive orient: the attitudinal basis, as Said has argued, for orientalism's imperialist progression through the nineteenth century:

> Under the connecting feeling of tropical heat and vertical sunlights, I brought together all creatures, birds, beasts, reptiles, all trees and plants, usages and appearances, that are found in all tropical regions, and assembled them together in China or Indostan. From kindred feelings, I soon brought Egypt and all her gods under the same law. [...] I was kissed, with cancerous kisses, by crocodiles; and laid, confounded with all unutterable slimy things, amongst reeds and Nilotic mud. (*DQW*, II: 71)

Under the stimulus of opium it would appear that the entire panoply of Eastern 'usages and appearances' were lumped together by De Quincey in a way that corresponds to Said's influential thesis. Despite the controversial reception of Said's work and his subsequent qualification of it in some respects, this fundamental binary separation between East and West is an aspect of his critique that he has stood by in later publications, and it remains influential as a basic parameter of postcolonial criticism. As Said explains in *Culture and Imperialism*:

> Throughout the exchange between Europeans and their 'others' that began systematically half a millennium ago, the one idea that has scarcely varied is that there is an 'us' and a 'them', each quite settled, clear, unassailably self-evident. [...] the division goes back to Greek thought about barbarians, but, whoever originated this kind of 'identity' thought, by

the nineteenth century it had become the hallmark of imperialist cultures as well as those cultures trying to resist the encroachments of Europe. (Said 1993: xxviii)

Said's insistence on the cleavage between East and West is of course crucial to his critique and without admission of it, his thesis fails (somewhat paradoxically) to cohere. Yet he himself is imprecise about the origins of 'this kind of "identity" thought' as he styles it—though he is clear that it is fully in place on both sides of the imperial divide by the nineteenth century.

While De Quincey's opium nightmares are often cited as evidence of the operation of Said's binary thesis regarding orientalism, and while De Quincey himself has been increasingly criticized for the rampant imperialism of his later political journalism[2]—an aspect of his thinking that is foreshadowed undoubtedly in earlier canonical works such as the 1821 *Confessions*—yet his development of these ideas has, I believe, not been properly examined so far. While opium as De Quincey represents it is evidently a stimulus for the process, it is even by his own admission not the cause of it; those who talk of oxen, as he said, being prone to dream of oxen (*DQW*, II: 12). This chapter proposes to address the issue of De Quincey's development of an orientalist mentality, and to see if his example sheds any light on the hardening of imperialist attitudes by the nineteenth century which Said indicates, though in elusive and unspecific terms. At the outset I will adduce three factors of importance to this examination: (1) De Quincey's late-eighteenth-century evangelical upbringing and the attitudes implied thereby; (2) the orientalist, biblical and classical studies of the late eighteenth century which were deeply interlinked with each other; and (3) the commercial and utilitarian aims of imperialism which were often opposed to missionary interests in the colonies. Thus I would like to extend the criticism of De Quincey's orientalist imagination to include reference to his evangelical upbringing, and in particular his childhood reading of the Bible which was crucially presented to him as an oriental work owing to developments in Biblical criticism of the eighteenth century.[3] This aspect of the Bible, its eastern origin, may be seen at once to pose some problems for Said's binary thesis in that moral justifications for nineteenth-century imperialism were typically premised on a western superiority subsumptive of a civilizing Christian element—which in De Quincey's case, of course, was of a rosy English Protestant hue. However, as we shall also see, during the course of the nineteenth century, evangelical attitudes to the orient were profoundly influenced and altered by developments in orientalist scholarship and debate as well as imperial governance. I will try and suggest that these social and intellectual changes may help us to understand the development of De Quincey's imperialist attitudes and may even provide a rationale for interpreting the bizarre imagery of his famous orientalist nightmares and dreams.

II

In the first chapter of his *Autobiographic Sketches*, De Quincey identifies the favourite item of his nursery days as an illustrated Bible which he explains was the source of his first visual imagining of the orient:

> It had happened, that amongst our vast nursery collection of books was the Bible illustrated with many pictures. And in the long dark evenings, as my three sisters with myself sat by the firelight round the guard of our nursery, no book was so much in request with us. [. . .] Our younger nurse, whom we all loved, would sometimes, according to her simple powers, endeavour to explain what we found obscure. [. . .] The nurse knew and explained to us the chief differences in oriental climates; and all these differences (as it happens) express themselves, more or less, in varying relations to the great accidents and powers of summer. (*DQW*, XIX: 10–11).

De Quincey's fond description of his nursery points to the use of the Bible as a tutelary aid for the education of children during the late eighteenth and nineteenth centuries, a period in which the Bible itself became a chief object and often a target of Enlightenment critique. In particular the higher biblical criticism, as it was called, of scholars such as Robert Lowth, Johann Gottfried Eichhorn and J.D. Michaelis, sought to historicize the Bible, typically reading the scriptures as an oriental literary product, and hence subject to oriental 'usages and appearances'. Evangelical codes of education, such as those evoked by De Quincey, sought to accommodate these modes of thinking within a Christian framework, rendering biblical criticism compatible with evangelical orthodoxy. The simple younger nurse in De Quincey's description is an ideal teacher of the Bible in that her knowledge, though informed by oriental geography, is uncontaminated by the subversive aspects of biblical criticism. This kind of conservative and rationalizing impulse behind evangelical adaptation of biblical criticism from the late eighteenth century resulted in the production of 'family' bibles which presented themselves as educational books, with maps, pictures and notes. As David Daniell notes in *The Bible in English,* 'Romantic interest in the exotic East was a strand in the growing fashion, towards the middle of the [nineteenth] century, for books recording with new accuracy both the places mentioned in Scripture and the traditions found there' (Daniell 2003: 675). In the *Autobiographic Sketches*, then, De Quincey was recording with nostalgia the beginnings of this trend. An early example of the kind of Bible that the child De Quincey may have read in his nursery was *The Protestant's Family Bible*, 1780–81, with engravings by William Blake (see Figure 2.1). This Bible contained several maps and illustrations accompanying key scriptural passages, and thus brought a certain realism to the reading of the Bible. Its footnotes identified oriental customs and sought to explain perplexities of the Biblical text to lay readers. The resultant depiction of the orient was in fact of a strongly

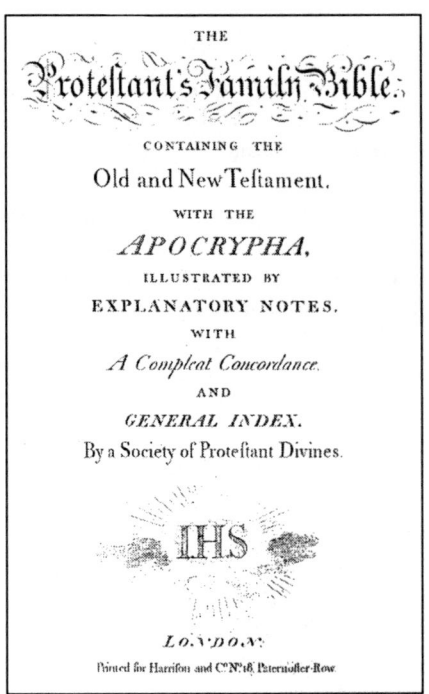

Figure 2.1 Title page of *The Protestant's Family Bible* (1780–81).

favourable nature, portraying the oriental nations as being in general simple, honourable, hospitable, and wise.[4] De Quincey's family Bible would typically have been one such production, a treasured possession which he recalled in later years as his first introduction to the orient.

In his fine study of the scholarly inflections of British orientalism in India entitled *Aryans and British India* (1997), Thomas Trautmann has shown how British 'Indophobia' of the mid to late nineteenth century had in fact been preceded in the late eighteenth century by what he calls 'Indomania'.[5] Indomania (as described as Trautmann) may be understood as the early European enthusiasm for classical Indian civilization following recognition of the great antiquity of Indian civilization (comparable to the Egyptian) by early scholars such as Sir William Jones and Charles Wilkins—East India Company officials who were encouraged in their scholarly activities by Warren Hastings, governor-general of India until 1784. Their scholarship, especially the Mosaic ethnology and linguistic researches of the pre-eminent Sir William Jones, displayed a powerful synthetic impulse to link Hindu, and generally oriental thought and practices with Christianity in a way that initially appealed to conservative and evangelical interpretations of Indian/Hindu civilization as being in a radical sense compatible with Christianity. According to this Mosaic ethnology of Jones, Indian civilization could be traced back to the diasporic rehabitation of the earth following Noah's flood. The ancient nature of Indian civilization, and its pristine preservation by the Brahmins, suggested therefore that this ancient civilization was a well-preserved version of Biblical patriarchy.[6] Hence Christianity, as a development of Judaism, could find affirmation in India. A tattered but, in this context, crucial manuscript of De Quincey's illuminates the impact of Jonesian scholarship on De Quincey's evangelical mother:

> (My mother's fancy—y^t Sir W. J had found in the East proofs of X$^{ty.}$—having gone out an Infidel.—To do her justice, <she> never once after she had adopted a theory of X$^{ty.}$—did she inquire further or feel anxious about it's proof. But to review the folly {torn} this idea—.
>
> 1. That X$^{ty.}$ There where it reigned and was meant to reign should be insufficient in it's proofs, but in a far distant land <hid in> lurking in some hole or corner, should be proof of it's <exis> truth. Just precisely where these proofs were not wanted. And again reserved for one scholar rambling <out> into a solitary path, where in a moral sense nobo<by>dy could follow him (for it is nobody—this or that oriental scholar). And we are sure y^t <H> his proof was not of that order to shine by it's own light: else it w$^{d.}$ have resounded thro' Engl$^{d.}$
>
> 2. That for thousands of years X$^{ty.}$ should have been received—gener$^{n.}$ after gener$^{n.}$ should have lived under its vital action—upon no suff$^{t.}$ arg^t: and suddenly such an arg$^{t.}$ sh$^{d.}$ turn up as a reward to a man {↑in a country not Xtian} for <his> being more incredulous y^n his neighbours—how impossible! (*DQW*, XXI: 417)

It is not difficult to piece together De Quincey's argument here. He is responding to the supposition that Sir William Jones had gone to India as an atheist,[7] and 'discovered' proofs of Christianity there through the linkage between Indian civilization and the Mosaic dispensation (whereby Indians were seen as descendants of Noah's son, Ham).[8] Such a notion had presumably made a great impression on his mother, a fervent Christian and a follower of the evangelical Hannah More, who found it all the more convincing that a reputed sceptic such as William Jones, could have been convinced by such proofs and converted to Christianity thereby. De Quincey suggests however that it was very unlikely for someone like Jones, supposedly ignoring the Christian presumptions of his original English society with culpable negligence, to simply discover Christian truth in a land which was not Christian at all. Why should such important divine truths be buried in a non-Christian land? Why would God's light be hidden under a bushel?

In fact then, De Quincey implies, the Jones phenomenon was something of a hoax. Jones's arcane scholarship was an area where few people could follow, nor was it likely to lead anywhere significant. His mother's fault however was merely that of gullibility; she herself once committed to Christian belief required no additional proofs. The whole business of oriental scholarship was a fraud, and oriental scholars were charlatans who sought attention by discovering self-evident truths regarding Christianity by means of obscure and unnecessary scholarship. In short, scholarly orientalism of the Asiatic Society kind was merely a flash in the pan which did not shed any new light on old and well-established beliefs and doctrines.[9] It must be remembered however that these views of De Quincey are certainly post-1841[10] responses to scholarship of the 1790s and as such represents a revisionary view of orientalist researches by De Quincey. In order to understand why De Quincey returns so suspiciously in later years to scholarly arguments that he had read decades earlier, I would suggest we need to return to the context of changing attitudes to the orient in the period. Returning then to Trautmann's account of Indomania yielding to Indophobia in the course of the nineteenth century, it is notable that the chief instigators of this movement according to Trautmann were the new evangelical faction of the East India Company and the utilitarians, notably lead by Charles Grant and James Mill respectively. Their effects were felt in British attitudes from the first decade of the nineteenth century, commencing in the decade after Sir William Jones's death in 1794. Like De Quincey, these later interventionists in India, for different reasons characteristic of their position, poured scorn on orientalist scholarship and mocked its pretensions. For the evangelicals concerned with conversion, the idea that the religious customs of Hinduism were in any way allied to a Christian tradition was strenuously to be rebuffed, and for utilitarians such as Thomas Babington Macaulay and James Mill concerned with governance, the privileging of European learning was to be asserted at all costs in favour of commercial and imperial interests in India. The Indian practice of sati, the immolation of Hindu widows on their husbands' funeral pyres, was of course the *cause célèbre* of evangelical attacks on India and Hinduism. Far from being the representatives of an unalloyed patriarchal tradition of natural religion, the Brahmin priests were now seen as the corrupt agents of 'priestcraft' and institutional oppression of the common people. The watercolour in Figure 2.2 of a sati scene from the early 1800s shows the woman raising her hands in supplication—this would become a standard gesture in sati representations—while the Indian men are shown stoking her pyre, or brandishing swords or making music in unholy adoration of the sati mata, as she was known. Similarly, De Quincey's reference to the 'mighty Juggernaut of social life' (*DQW*, IX: 211) makes reference to the Jaggarnath chariot procession of Orissa (see Figure 2.3), which several evangelical reports described as a licentious and gory Hindu carnival, marked by numerous deaths of devotees beneath the wheels of the relentless chariot even while the Brahmin priests engaged in sexual misconduct (Oddie 2006: 75–83).[11] Such writings and visual representations, as they emerged in the aftermath of the so-called Vellore massacre of 1806 and in the context of the puritanical backlash against the corruption of East India Company officials, has been described as a

'Mix(ing) a Little with Alien Natures' 25

Figure 2.2 Watercolour: Anon., 'A Scene of Sati'. The sati mata raises her hand piteously while around her Indian men are shown celebrating and participating in the ritual. Copyright British Library Board. All rights reserved WD248.

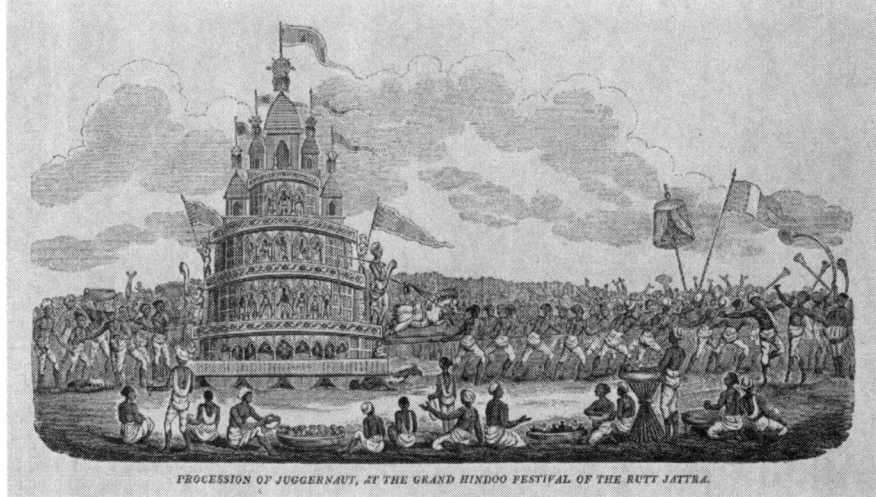

Figure 2.3 Etching: 'Procession of Juggernaut', Missionary Register, 1817. The crowd passes over the corpses of devotees crushed beneath the chariot wheels, while yet another devotee prostrates himself before the chariot. The carnivalesque atmosphere of the scene contrasts with the grim reminder of the deaths caused by the chariot.

pamphlet war between the older commercialist policies of non-interference and the new evangelical spirit that was promoting a more interventionist approach to empire on moral grounds (Kopf, 136–44). De Quincey's narcotized repugnance in the *Confessions* to the 'ancient, monumental, cruel, and elaborate religions of Indostan' (*DQW*, II: 70), as may be evident, owes a great deal to such evangelical representations of the East. Clearly these religions were to be dissociated at any cost from Christianity.

Yet, as we have seen, such an attitude though it gained acceptance with the rise of imperialist evangelicalism in the nineteenth century, was not characteristic of the earlier synthetic and scholarly orientalist approach which sought to harmonize Christianity with the orient and its religious practices. As we have already noted, the orient was not always portrayed unfavourably in the cultural landscape of De Quincey's early years. Through the Bible and through reports of orientalist scholarship, De Quincey had also received versions of orientalism which were far from merely critical of the Eastern nations and their ways. While recent critical scholarship has been largely oblivious to these favourable strains of orientalism in relation to the young De Quincey, my contention is that they deeply inform the development of his later imperialism, disturbing and complicating his ideology in revealing and anxious ways. Among the more puzzling and outrageous effects of opium as De Quincey describes it in the *Confessions*, is a fusion of mythological systems, as Egyptian gods are 'inosculated' with the Hindu pantheon through 'kindred feelings' of revulsion:

I fled from the wrath of Brama through all the forests of Asia: Vishnu hated me: Seeva laid wait for me. I came suddenly upon Isis and Osiris ... (*DQW*, II: 71)

Such fusions are often ascribed to the action of the drug, as if opium itself may be credited with casting a certain confusion over nineteenth-century orientalism, suffusing its users with a geographical and mythological haziness whereby the East was homogenized into a Saidian form of orientalism. On the other hand, opium, it must be pointed out, is not actually an hallucinogenic drug, nor by any means was De Quincey's geography hazy, however prejudiced his later pronouncements on the Eastern nations were. My more mundane thesis is that these imagistic and mythological fusions can be traced back to some of the earlier orientalist scholarship of the Indomania variety, prior to Indophobia, when the commercial interests of the East India Company gave way to a muscular evangelical form of missionary intervention in the colonies on one hand and to utilitarian forms of imperialism in governance and education on the other.

To return to De Quincey's oriental nightmares with this context in mind, it is not surprising to note that the dream linkages he finds between India, China and Egypt had been anticipated by a good deal of orientalist scholarship. In his famous anniversary discourses as President of the Asiatic Society, William Jones had influentially suggested an oriental ethnology linking the Greeks, Egyptians and Indians as being of similar racial stock and sharing the same popular religion. He also suggested, drawing on Hindu traditions, that the Chinese were an outcaste from Hindu society, being lapsed *Kshatriyas* who had established themselves north-east of Bengal and gradually taken over the vast area of China. Another eighteenth-century scholarly authority whom De Quincey had certainly studied in some detail as a schoolboy was James Burnett, Lord Monboddo, the author of two dauntingly ambitious scholarly works, *Of the Origin and Progress of Language* (6 vols., 1773–92), and *Ancient Metaphysics, or the Science of Universals* (6 vols., 1779–99). In these works Monboddo argued that Egypt could be considered a parent-country of language and the arts to both Europe and western Asia, '[the] Egyptian and Greek languages being originally the same' (Monboddo 1779–99, I: 466), and that furthermore Sanskrit and Greek were 'dialects of the same language: And that language could be no other than the language of Egypt, brought into India by Osiris' (Monboddo 1779–99, IV: 323). Both Monboddo and Jones, then, agreed on the nature of Sanskrit's antiquity; its great perfection, superior to Greek, was ascribed to the conservatism of the Brahminical tradition. De Quincey's nightmares bringing together Hindu and Egyptian deities seem less mystifying perhaps in the light of such knowledge: 'I fled from the wrath of Brama through all the forests of Asia: Vishnu hated me: Seeva laid wait for me. I came suddenly upon Isis and Osiris' (*DQW*, II: 71).

If De Quincey's oriental dreams were partially a by-product of this late eighteenth-century orientalist scholarship, as I have been suggesting, it remains to be explained why this form of learning took on a particularly anxious and nightmarish aspect in his life. As we have seen, orientalist scholarship in its early days was in fact deeply aligned with the Biblical orient, and a corollary of this alignment was that oriental studies might have a great deal to offer in understanding some of the pristine revelations of Christianity which may even have been obscured or lost through their Western mediation in translated forms of the Bible. In his *Lectures on the Sacred Poetry of the Hebrews*, Robert Lowth sought to lay bare one of the greatest difficulties besetting a translator of the Bible, that the imagery borrowed from nature which the Hebrew poets frequently used, could appear on the one hand exaggerated, or on the other, merely trite, owing to the unfamiliarity of the modern English reader with oriental scenes and customs. This work, first published in Latin in 1753 and translated into English in 1787, was to prove immensely influential as a new scholarly way of understanding the Old Testament in relation to its Hebraic poetic and cultural traditions. Lowth had introduced his critical method as a means of restoring such imbalances in perception, orienting the English reader to a better understanding of the Bible through an engagement with the historical and geographical specificity of its source material:

> It is the first duty of the critic, therefore, to remark, as far as is possible, the situation and habits of the author, the natural history of his country, and the scene of the poem. Unless we continually attend to these points, we shall scarcely be able to judge with any degree of certainty concerning the elegance or propriety of the sentiments: the plainest will sometimes escape our observation; the peculiar and interior excellencies will remain totally concealed. (Lowth 1787: 139–40)

The only remedy for such distancing in the view of Lowth and the Biblical critics who translated and annotated his text influentially for English readers was in fact an immersion in oriental works which might allow the reader not only to understand but even to experience the Bible accordingly.

German critics such as Michaelis and Eichhorn carried the implications of his work even further, downplaying the miraculous aspects of the Bible and explaining these in merely human and historical terms. In a lengthy footnote to the passage quoted above which Lowth's English translator Gregory records, the German critic Michaelis suggested that:

> We must not omit noticing in this place, those images which are derived from rivers and fountains, and the earth recreated with rain; which are indeed used by our poets, but more frequently by the Orientals. For the scarcity of water, and the extreme heat of summer, together with the wonderful fertility of the soil, when watered, render this a more elegant and jocund comparison in the East than with us. [. . .] Mahomet makes use of this idea frequently, as figurative of the resurrection; and in this

he shews himself no less of a philosopher than a poet. Dr. Russel described this regeneration of nature in most lively colours in his *Natural History of Aleppo*, a book which every man ought to read, who wishes not only to understand the Oriental writers, but to feel them. (Lowth 1787: 140n)

Hence the Bible was to be accompanied by readings in the Koran and middle-eastern natural history for its full effects to be felt. Christian revelation thus required orientalist (including Islamic) scholarship to be fully understood by English readers. This was challenging indeed. Certainly a backlash set in with the higher biblical criticism being seen as subversive of Christian doctrine.[12] Though Lowth himself was well respected by the establishment in his own lifetime (he died in 1787, two years before the onset of the French Revolution), for post-revolutionary dissenting and radical Christians, including the early Lake poets whom De Quincey worshipped as a boy, such ideas would have carried heady overtones of revolutionary import.[13] Yet Michaelis's comments on the regenerative symbolism of the oriental summer, a prefiguration of Christ's resurrection, are precisely the terms in which De Quincey records his celebrated visionary experience following his sister's death in the *Autobiographic Sketches*: 'Summer, therefore, had connected itself with death, not merely as a mode of antagonism, but also as a phenomenon brought into intricate relations with death by scriptural scenery and events' (*DQW*, XIX: 11). If De Quincey recalls the footnote in Lowth's well-known text making this connection, he does not acknowledge it however, returning his thanks solely to the simple nurse who had explained it to him: her version offering clearly a more pious version of Michaelis's radical scholarship.

It is interesting to note in this context how far De Quincey's oriental dreams are suffused by oriental imagery of the Biblical kind, apart from the more virulent Sino- and Indophobic images cited earlier. The dream of 'tropical heat and vertical sunlights' quoted at the beginning of this chapter—one that has attracted a great deal of recent criticism—was followed by another oriental dream, but this of a very different character.

> The scene was an oriental one; and there also it was Easter Sunday, and very early in the morning. And at a vast distance were visible, as a stain upon the horizon, the domes and cupolas of a great city—an image or faint abstraction, caught perhaps in childhood from some picture of Jerusalem. (*DQW*, II: 73)

The distancing perspective employed is suggestive of Wordsworth's famous sonnet 'Composed upon Westminster Bridge, September 3, 1802' or similarly of Turner's 'London' painted from Greenwich, 1809, wherein the city is envisaged at a vast remove, its detail and bustle etherialized as a consequence (see Figure 2.4). De Quincey's explicit obligation however is to

30 Thomas De Quincey

Figure 2.4 Oil on canvas: J.M.W. Turner, 'London from Greenwich Park', 1809. Turner's verses accompanying the painting were critical of the city's materialism; his perspective however, foregrounding a natural scene, imparts a quality of picturesque abstraction to the city. © Tate, London 2007.

the oriental illustrations of his childhood, obtained no doubt from the 'vast nursery collection of books' he was so proud of. In the dream that follows De Quincey meets Ann, a young prostitute he had befriended in London, as a runaway from the Manchester Grammar School:

> And not a bow-shot from me, upon a stone, and shaded by Judean palms, there sat a woman; and I looked; and it was—Ann! (*DQW*, II: 73)

The meeting with Ann, though joyous, carries undertones of sexuality which threaten to disturb the innocence of the memory:

> Seventeen years ago, when the lamp-light fell upon her face, as for the last time I kissed her lips (lips, Ann, that to me were not polluted), her eyes were streaming with tears: the tears were now wiped away; she seemed more beautiful than she was at that time, but in all other points the same, and not older. (*DQW*, II: 73)

De Quincey's childhood experiences are here absorbed into an oriental setting: Jerusalem's sanctity and the Easter occasion render Ann an evidently

Magdalene figure redeemed by her Biblical associations of repentance and weeping, her figure is framed by Judean palms, and her beauty is even enhanced by the location.

Placing the two oriental dreams from the *Confessions* together, as indeed their placement in the text demands, it is worth noticing that the evident bigotry of the earlier oriental dream, wherein De Quincey responds with fear and loathing to all things Chinese and Indian, is followed by a dream of a different character wherein the Hebraic or Biblical orient promises a salvific and regenerative potential. At one level these dreams may be read as reflective of the well-documented transition from 'Indomania' to 'Indophobia' experienced in Britain from the late eighteenth to early nineteenth century. Insofar as these dreams, however, are dreamed and recorded by the same person, they expose an unresolved tension at the heart of late Enlightenment Christian thinking such as De Quincey was deeply aware of through his readings of the German and English Biblical critics,[14] an area of scholarship in which he felt he was only matched by Coleridge. However much such philosophies were to be shunned in their more subversive forms, one could achieve theological sophistication only through acquaintance with their major spokesmen. Comparing Coleridge for instance with the Bishop of Llandaff as theological controversialists, De Quincey establishes Coleridge's far more sophisticated understanding of this field precisely on the basis of his reading of such philosophies:

> Coleridge was armed, at all points, with the scholastic erudition which bore upon all questions that could arise in polemic divinity. [. . .] Having been personally acquainted with Eickhorn and Michaelis, he knew the whole cycle of schisms and audacious speculations, through which Biblical criticism, or Christian philosophy, has revolved in modern Germany. All this was ground upon which the Bishop of Llandaff trode with the infirm footing of a child. (*DQW*, X: 329)

As the greater antiquity of the Eastern religions of India, China, and Egypt became increasingly recognized over the course of the century, in order to keep its origins unsullied by paganism, Christianity itself required to be purged of its oriental (and even Judaic[15]) associations rather than to embrace them. Yet at the heart of Christian belief a doubt had been sown of its essential purity. The vast reaches of geological time emerging from fossil records (far greater than Mosaic orthodoxy allowed), the anthropological view of religion that this ushered in (building on the Higher Biblical scholarship), and the idea that Christianity was linked with other major world religions in mythological import were all deeply challenging to simpler evangelical notions of scriptural belief.

Recent criticism of De Quincey has revealed him uncompromisingly as a diehard imperialist in his later journalism on China and India, an aspect of his politics that has been read retrospectively into his earlier works such as the *Confessions* as well as in relation to the famous oriental nightmares and opium dreams therein. He appears in this light an English Tory patriot who wears his hard imperialist heart on his sleeve. Yet it is perhaps worth pointing out that De Quincey's upbringing by his own admission was characterized by intense arguments about imperial matters. The *Autobiographic Sketches* record the 'altogether serious [. . .] disputes upon INDIA [at his family home of the Priory]—a topic on separate grounds equally interesting to us all, as the mightiest of English colonies, and the superbest monument of demoniac English energy, revealing itself in such men as Clive, Hastings, and the two Wellesleys'. In De Quincey's description these disputes assumed the character of a standoff between the imperialist viewpoint and the evangelical one, his energetic and ambitious colonial uncle against his fervent and pious mother:

> To my mother as the grave of one brother, as the home of another, and as a new centre from which Christianity (she hoped) would mount like an eagle; for just about that time the Bible Society was preparing its initial movements: whilst to my uncle India appeared as the *arena* upon which his activities were yet to find their adequate career. (*DQW*, XX: 277)

De Quincey reminiscing on these matters adopts a strongly imperialist tone, aligning himself with his uncle's Indian viewpoint, 'dutifully' dismissing his mother's arguments against the colonial custom of receiving 'nuzzers'[16] (whereby East India Company officials could expect to gain huge personal fortunes),[17] as being based upon her 'mere ignorance of India' (*DQW*, XX: 277). The high moral ground taken by the evangelicals with regard to the Christianization of India implied of course that East India Company officials reformed their practices of compliance (or at least non-interference) with local customs. De Quincey's reminiscence of the debate provides a revisionary spin to its logic, as he insists that 'With respect to the Christianization of India, my uncle assumed a hope which he did not really feel' (*DQW*, XIX: 277). While his mother's moral rectitude is hardly to be questioned, the situation is complicated by the degree of laxness which could be allowed to local custom. While upholding the former, De Quincey seems to be suggesting that colonial officials were to be allowed some latitude in their dealings abroad. If the Christianization of India so ardently desired by his mother were only a chimera, then it followed that his uncle's compliance with her Christian standards of rectitude was unnecessarily limiting. He may as well have pocketed the bribes. Yet, the playful nature of the anecdote, and De Quincey's care in recalling his uncle's implicit acknowledgement through his own actions—or the non-action of not accepting such bribes—of the superiority of his sister's stern English Christian principles over those of native custom suggests his own implicit acceptance of the former in spite of the thwarting of personal and familial interests that it implied.

The erratic play of personal loyalties versus Christian imperatives in the above reminiscence may be seen to find a correlative in De Quincey's unconventional evaluation of the respective merits of the Hebrew and Greek languages, a comparative theory which I will show brings us back to his eccentric theory of biblical orientalism. Through the course of the nineteenth-century, linguistic and antiquarian researches, as we have seen, continued to mount a challenge to traditional Christian beliefs, particularly of the more literal sort of Biblical interpretation characteristic of evangelicalism. Orientalism may have commenced its course with Lowth's biblical criticism and Jones's Mosaic ethnology suggesting a potential affirmation of Christianity, but increasingly such views were problematized by further researches which had the effect of disturbing the orthodoxy. If De Quincey's first lessons in orientalism were gained through his nurse's Biblical explanations in the somewhat naïve and cosy way he records in the *Autobiographic Sketches*, his later reading of other orientalists (in whose works he shows interest throughout his life[18]) would not have reinforced those early intimations that orientalist researches might deliver Christian orthodoxy in the end. With the decipherment of the Egyptian hieroglyphics by Champollion in the 1820s, it became evident that the ancient Egyptian language was not a close relation of Greek and Sanskrit as earlier thought, though the two latter languages were admittedly related. A further blow to the credibility of the earlier orientalist scholarship though came in the form of an elaborate hoax perpetuated on one of the later orientalists, the hapless Captain Francis Wilford, a later disciple of William Jones. In an article entitled 'On the sacred isles of the west' (1805), Wilford put forward the thesis that references to the *śveta-dwīpa* (White Island) in the ancient Hindu scriptures, the *Puranas*, were to England, and that the (supposedly) fabled 'sacred isles' of Puranic geography were the British isles. Wilford developed this thesis, conveniently attractive to English patriotic sentiments, through the researches of a pandit, but later discovered himself to be the victim of a hoax whereby the pandit had composed in great abundance the evidence that Wilford so ardently desired. His work was further compromised by the discovery that the original impulse for his research had emanated from an imposture on the late Sir William Jones who too had been deceived in his reading of the *Padma Purāna*. This celebrated case of scholarly hoaxing did not silence Wilford who continued to publish his work in the *Asiatic Researches*, but it did bring orientalist research into disrepute and contributed to the demise of Indomania. De Quincey's suspicious references to Sir William Jones in later life may be seen to betray these disappointments in orientalist scholarship whereby orthodox hopes of discovering Christian truths in India were dashed by further investigations. While the later De Quincey seems to suggest that he had always already been sceptical of such claims, one may suggest more plausibly that his scepticism is a revisionary interpretation more likely to be based on hindsight than any extraordinary premonition of the course of orientalist researches in the nineteenth century.

If orientalism did not provide the support to Christian orthodoxy that evangelicals such as De Quincey's mother might earlier have hoped for, perhaps it was up to a more astute linguistic scholar—such as De Quincey preened himself on being—to remedy the situation. I would like to examine in this regard De Quincey's above-mentioned comparative theory of Greek and Hebrew. A crucial distinction between the oriental and the occidental for De Quincey may be found in his comparison between Hebrew and Greek literatures. In opposition to the standard eighteenth and nineteenth-century judgements of Grecian pre-eminence over other classical literatures, De Quincey adopts a somewhat unusual position—deriving clearly from Lowth's influence[19]—that it is the Hebrew which must be seen as more enduring:

> Speaking in the deep sincerities of the solitary and musing heart, which refuses to be duped by the whistling of names, we must say of the Greek that—*laudatur et alget*—he has brilliancies of earth, but on the deeper and more abiding nature of man he has no hold. [. . .] Whereas the Hebrew, by introducing himself to the secret places of the human heart, and sitting there as incubator over the awful germs of the spiritualities that connect man with the unseen worlds, has perpetuated himself as a power in the human system (*DQW*, XVIII: 59)

In De Quincey's judgement Greek literature is characterized by brilliance and intellectual energy—characteristics which (as his uncle's example reminds us) are particularly associated with imperialism for him—whereas Hebrew, 'dull and inert intellectually', is yet deeply spiritual in a way that renders it superior in the final analysis. The judgement invokes his own famous critical distinction between power and knowledge, Hebrew literature being that of power, whereas by implication Greek with its greater intellectual resources is yet in itself largely a literature of knowledge.

The full implications of this judgement for De Quincey's Protestant imperialism may be gleaned from his late essay on Christianity, 'On the Supposed Scriptural Expression for Eternity' (1853), though the ideas it expresses are fitfully glimpsed in essays of Christian apologetics such as 'The Essenes' (1840), 'The Pagan Oracles' (1842), 'Greece under the Romans' (1844), 'On Christianity as an Organ of Political Movement' (1846), and 'Protestantism' (1847–48) among others. This corpus of writings clearly merits a more extensive treatment than I can afford in the space of this chapter; my focus is on De Quincey's discussion of the Septuagint in the first of the above essays. As De Quincey helpfully explains to his 'illiterate reader'—a growing category of readership he discerned in nineteenth-century reading audiences—the Septuagint was 'the earliest translation of the Hebrew Scriptures ever made into Greek'. This work was often cited in scriptural scholarship; yet, as De Quincey properly insists, on all controversial matters pertaining

'Mix(ing) a Little with Alien Natures' 35

to the Old Testament, it is inappropriate to refer to the Greek version. It is the Hebrew version that is authoritative. Yet, paradoxically, it was the Greek version, and not the Hebrew, that was far more effective in spreading Christianity, on account of Grecian influence in the Roman empire.[20] The influence of pre-Christian Jewish thought and language on Grecian Alexandria—a 'preternatural shock [...] upon the jaded and exhausted intellect of the Grecian race'—for over three centuries prior to this translation; the location of the Alexandrian metropolis as 'a centre of communication between the East and the West'; and the imperial destiny of its king Ptolemy Philadelphus—'a king both learned in his tastes and liberal in his principles of religious toleration'—who had encouraged the translation, all conspire towards regarding the Septuagint as a providential event:

> Such a king—a king whose father had been a personal friend of Alexander, the mighty civilizing conqueror, and had shared in the liberalisation connected with his vast revolutionary projects for extending a higher civilization over the globe, such a king, conversing with such a language, having advantages so absolutely unrivalled, and again this king and this language concurring with a treasure so supernatural of spiritual wisdom as the subject of their ministrations, and all three concurring with political events so auspicious—the founding of a new and mighty metropolis in Egypt, and the silent advance to supreme power amongst men of a new empire, martial beyond all precedent as regarded *means*, but not as regarded *ends*—working in all things towards the unity of civilization and the unity of law, so that any new impulses, as, for instance, impulse of a new religion, was destined to find new facilities for its own propagation, resembling electric conductors, under the unity of government and law—concurrences like these, so many and so strange, justly impress upon this translation, the most memorable, because the most influential of all that have ever been accomplished, a character of grandeur that place it on the same level of interest as the building of the first or second temple at Jerusalem. (*DQW*, XVIII: 7)

It is not difficult to see the connection between Christian providentiality in Alexandria in relation to the western world, and that faced by Britain in the nineteenth century with regard to the east. Imperialism, like the 'electric conductors' of the telegraph, 'under the unity of government and law', provides the means for propagating Christianity. What is perhaps more interesting is the emphasis placed on martial supremacy as a means but not an end of empire. In this respect De Quincey adopts the evangelical perspective of his mother against the martial imperialism of the East India Company (such as his energetic uncle may have represented) prior to its evangelization.

III

Despite the high moral ground he adopts in his writings with regard to other religions and cultures, it should be evident by now that De Quincey's sense of Christianity, and of the Biblical text in particular, as in an original sense 'oriental' in nature, opens up some radical suspicions with regard to western appropriations of its sublime truths. Was Britain truly qualified to reclaim the east in a spiritual sense (as his mother had hoped with regard to India)—or were its territorial and commercial interests too strong for that? Had the west truly shed its own pagan past, or did these live on in the bloody and barbarous progress of European imperialism? Such doubts exposed a 'dreadful ulcer' such as he feared in 'The English Mail-Coach' 'lurking far down in the depths of human nature'. It is in one's dreams that such fears regarding human nature, 'its deep-seated Pariah falsehood to itself', are revealed (*DQW*, XVI: 432). The very partiality and fervour of his apologetics in relation to topics such as the Essenes, Greece under the Roman empire, and other such controversial subjects, mark his arguments as being robustly committed in outcome and tone before pen was ever put to paper. Yet the anxieties of his dreams betray a more tenuous position than he overtly allows. Recent attempts to pathologize De Quincey as an incest-ridden or paedophilic writer[21] in my view tend only to distance his work from those of his contemporaries; his imperialism becoming apparently a function of his childhood traumas and repressions. Yet most of his contemporaries who knew him personally judged him differently, and in the context of the high imperialism of the Victorian period, his views are perhaps no more extraordinary than many another imperialist spokesman. In the light of present day fears over Islamic terrorism and a clash of civilizations between the west and its alleged enemies, however, De Quincey is alarmingly contemporaneous, and not defunct; his writings articulate in shifting and evolving ways the kinds of separation between 'us' and 'them' that emerged (as Said maintains) by the nineteenth century, and that have become endemic to political discourse today. The ease with which the Christian providentiality he represents could move from hopes of Christianizing the East to dominating and destroying its peoples through explicit retribution and warfare (as De Quincey's Indian Mutiny and Chinese war essays display), allowing ends to cynically override means, prefigures for us the rhetoric of democratic, civilizational and cultural values which slips easily into the commercially-fuelled and nakedly aggressive foreign policies of the Bush-Blair alliance. Yet, the extent to which these discursive strains are in evident conflict in De Quincey helps us to understand the process by which Said's binary separation was wrought. His works help us to understand the insecurities and anxieties attending imperialistic hubris even as it was articulated and hardened in the course of the century.

Despite the way in which De Quincey's texts seem to reiterate themselves endlessly by repeated themes and images, I wish to argue in conclusion that they are not consistent or synchronic as several of his critics seem not only to accept but even replicate in their own work.[22] In doing so however, I would suggest that their criticism only reads De Quincey on his own terms of unity and coherence: a critical seduction that we should resist. Instead I would suggest that a better recognition of developmental and sometimes contradictory strains in his writings would be more helpful in achieving a correct understanding of his work. As I have attempted to show in a previous book, *Revisionary Gleam*, De Quincey is in fact an assiduous and clever manipulator of his own texts, revising and recasting his views in the context of changing political and writerly imperatives. Our current reading of De Quincey in terms of a providential imperialism, a persistent discourse in his writings as I have indicated, should recognize therefore the existence of conflicting readings within his *oeuvre* which are justified by other contexts in which he wrote. Though brought up by an evangelical mother, De Quincey clearly rebelled against orthodoxy quite early in his intellectual life, and later returned to a qualified form of Anglican commitment. The relatively benign providential strain though well-marked in De Quincey may be challenged by reference to some of the more savage of his imperialistic writings, in particular his late Chinese and Indian journalism which seems to abandon the civilizing mission of Christianity in favour of a retributory and racially purgative direction for imperialism, more in keeping with a Hitler than a Wilberforce. In the Preface to his 1857 pamphlet on China he explicitly abandons the missionary hope of conversion by suggesting instead that 'few of us who read this chapter of Chinese spoliation altogether go along with these Missionaries in their proselytising views upon a people so unspiritual as our brutal friends the Chinese' (*DQW*, XVIII: 136). Here he affirms English commercial and martial imperatives for imperialism and so far denies the Chinese any spiritual nature as to depict them as unworthy of conversion. Yet, despite his frenzied war-mongering and prejudice against the Chinese in his journalism and pamphleteering, an earlier critical text of his, 'On the Present Stage of the English Language' indicates apparent goodwill to the Chinese as late as 1840—suggesting that 'mis-translations must be many between ourselves and the Chinese'—and going on to propose that Chinese references to the English as barbarians were to be explained by 'the probability [. . .] that this reputedly arrogant expression means only "the aliens, or external people, who speak in tongues foreign to China"' (*DQW*, XVII: 61). This earlier view can hardly excuse the participatory nature of De Quincey's later war-mongering journalism; however it does alert us to the contradictory and provisional nature of his writings in different contexts and at different times. Perhaps it is this disjunction between his points of view that exposes De Quincey's fear of a loss of identity among the myriad articles for the journals that he wrote. The new De Quincey edition commences with a memorable quotation regarding his own view in 1850 of ever achieving a collective edition of his works: 'Sir, the thing is absolutely, insuperably, and forever impossible'. His interlocutor, Gilfillan, responds with a disciple's fervour, speaking wistfully of the 'unsounded abysses' and 'treasures' that might be recovered. As Grevel Lindop has declared in his Introduction to the new *Works,* we now have an edition approximating as far as knowledge allows to completeness (*DQW*, I: xi). But perhaps De Quincey's abysses have proved ironically more compelling than his treasures. De Quincey's own collective edition of 1853–60 was explicitly a selective one, and represented his last attempt at achieving unity in his writings. Needless to say, it left out several of his texts. Despite De Quincey's pessimism regarding the practicality of achieving a complete edition, his response has usually been seen as favourable to the notion in an ideal sense. Yet equally he may have regarded it as a dread consummation of his writing career, recovering the fragmentary and inconsistent corpus of his texts in one accessible form, open to scholarly scrutiny and investigation. As with the Bible, that work of purely divine inspiration to the bibliolatrous Protestant, our scholarship reveals the frailties of the human text, the political and historical exigencies that shape its texts and meaning.

I will end with a dream description from the section entitled 'The Apparition of the Brocken' in De Quincey's *Suspiria de Profundis* which I wish to offer as emblematic of the late Enlightenment Christian anxieties that I consider to be at the centre of his imperialism. De Quincey's description is of an ascent of the Brocken in the Hartz mountains of Germany, a location famous for its Spectre, a natural phenomenon caused by certain effects of light and shade which project a giant figure of the observer into clouds. This striking phenomenon had generated pagan ritualistic practices for centuries. In his dream ascent of the Brocken, De Quincey invites his Christian reader to test the Brocken apparition for its faithfulness to the new order of Christianity. This is done by making the sign of the cross, a movement which the Spectre, on account of 'driving showers [which] perplex the images', follows with 'the air of one who acts reluctantly or evasively'. The Spectre becomes an image of De Quincey's 'Dark Interpreter', a shadowy figure whom De Quincey explains as 'originally a mere reflex of my inner nature', and a metaphorical representation of opium's material agency in De Quincey's texts. Yet, as De Quincey continues, the Dark Interpreter's presence becomes oddly disturbing to the sanctuary of the opium-eater's selfhood:

> But as the apparition of the Brocken sometimes is disturbed by storms or by driving showers, so as to dissemble his real origin, in like manner the Interpreter sometimes swerves out of my orbit, and mixes a little with alien natures. [. . .] No man can account for all things that occur in dreams. Generally, I believe this—that he is a faithful representative of myself; but he also is at times subject to the action of the god *Phantasus*, who rules in dreams.

As he explains the significances attached to the anemones and the crude pagan altar, named respectively the Sorcerer's flower and the Sorcerer's altar, that remain as evidences of pagan practice in the Hartz, the orthodox gestures of De Quincey's text are undercut by a footnote which explains these phenomena as vestiges of 'the gloomy realities of Paganism, when the whole Hartz and the Brocken formed for a very long time the last asylum to a ferocious but perishing idolatry'. De Quincey's oriental dreams, it may be suggested, owe their peculiar anxieties to the problematics of late Enlightenment Biblical orientalism as it was absorbed uneasily into the dominant discourses of Victorian imperialism and evangelicalism in the course of the following century.

NOTES

1. Represented for instance in standard anthologies of Romantic literature for undergraduate students (Mellor 1996: 863; Wu 1998: 635–6; and Wolfson 1999: 1015–6).
2. Notable studies of De Quincey's imperialism include those by Robert Maniquis (1976), John Barrell (1991) and Nigel Leask (1992). Several journal articles and chapters on De Quincey's imperialism have also emerged in recent years including those by Charles Rzepka (1991), Josephine McDonagh (1992), Rajani Sudan (1994), Judith Plotz (2001), Diane Simmons (2002) and Anna Frey (2005). Maniquis's monograph was the first to broach the intimate connection between De Quincey's imperialistic journalism and his 'impassioned' and autobiographical writings. His lead was taken up more than a decade later as Said's influence on literary studies became clearer.
3. In his essay 'On the Essenes' De Quincey points out that for the Romans in the history of the early church, 'the word 'Oriens' had a technical and limited meaning; it was restricted to Syria, of which Palestine formed a section [. . .] But some years after the Epi-christian generation, the word began to extend' (*DQW*, XI: 457). Here De Quincey recognizes the orient as specifically Christian in opposition to the western paganism of Rome.
4. So marked is this tendency, that deviations from such behaviour seem to require explanation of their own. For example a footnote to Genesis 19:5 (wherein the men of Sodom challenge Lot's hospitality) explains that the men of Sodom were 'so wicked that even the laws of hospitality, held sacred among all the oriental nations, were no security in that city'.
5. The separation is certainly a broad one and not meant to be taken as hard and fast. Favourable attitudes to India in orientalist scholarship persisted throughout the nineteenth century as evidenced in the work of scholars such as Henry Thomas Colebrook, Horace Hayman Wilson and Max Müller. Undoubtedly, however, the power balance had shifted away from scholarly orientalism towards a utilitarian form of governance in India. Horace Wilson's 1840s edition of Mill's influential *History of British India* is a good example of damage limitation by the orientalists, as Wilson strives to correct and ameliorate Mill's harsh criticisms on many points, arguing that Mill's tendency was 'evil' even while providing a new edition of his *History* (Mill 1997, I: vii–xiv).
6. For example, Thomas Maurice, author of the well-known *Indian Antiquities*, asserted that the Vedas were 'derived to them [the Brahmins] from NOAH, the MENU of the Sanscreet theologians, or else from his more immediate descendants of the righteous line of Shem, who first settled in India' (II: 14).
7. De Quincey's characterization of Jones's atheistical reputation may have had a popular basis, possibly based on Gibbon's effusive praise for Jones in footnotes

to his *The History of the Decline and Fall of the Roman Empire*, though it would be more accurate to say that Jones moved from a position of Christian acceptance on the basis of probability to one of more explicit commitment and piety in later years (Garland 1990: 60, 268–9). De Quincey's suspicion of Jones's Christian credentials may also have been exacerbated by the Clapham evangelical John Shore's biography of Jones in 1807 which attempted to cover up Jones's rationalism by casting him as a pious Christian especially in his later years.

8. In his 'Passing Notices of Indian Affairs' (1857) De Quincey deploys a version of the orientalists' Mosaic ethnology when he suggests that if British troops were to be designated as Europeans (a practice that rouses his patriotic ire) then in proper antithesis, native troops in India were to be referred to as Asiatics: 'Scripturally, we are the children of Japhet; and, as all Asiatics are the sons of Shem, then we shall be able to mortify their conceit, by calling to their knowledge our biblical prophecy, that the sons of Japhet shall sit down in the tents of Shem' (*DQW*, XVIII: 172). De Quincey clearly uses Bryant's version of the Mosaic ethnology which was largely compatible in its conclusions with Jones's, though Jones had famously attacked Bryant's methodology. Suggestively connecting ethnology with Providence, Bryant wrote: 'It seems, as if the design of Providence was that the three branches of *Noah's* family should divide the earth between them: that Asia was to be allotted to the sons of *Shem, Europe* to *Japhet,* and *Africa* to *Ham*' (Bryant 1767: 213).

9. That De Quincey was a close (though strongly combative) reader of Asiatic orientalism is evident from the following comment from his essay of 1841 on 'The Dourraunee Empire', treating with scepticism William Jones's theory regarding the supposed Mosaic origins of the Sikhs and Afghans: 'Sir William Jones was amongst those who countenanced the belief of a descent from the ten tribes in the Sikhs and the Affghans; and in the *Asiatic Researches* he has given four arguments, not very strong in support of it' (*DQW*, XII: 181). De Quincey rejects the evidence of Jewish names among Afghans (which Jones cites in evidence), as he ascribes such correspondences to 'the sterility of invention in Mahomet'. The Muslims did not have the wit to invent their own names, and hence they 'pillaged' them from the Jews.

10. Such being the evidence of the watermark; see *DQW*, XXI: 417.

11. Both sati and 'temple prostitution' are depicted in Robert Southey's 1810 epic poem, *The Curse of Kehama*, which De Quincey had certainly read. My introduction to the poem for the Pickering and Chatto edition (2004) shows the extent to which Southey was influenced by changing attitudes to India while drafting the poem.

12. In his essay on 'Protestantism' for *Tait's Edinburgh Magazine* in 1847, De Quincey registers the disquiet shown by pious English Protestant readers (who were often accused of bibliolatry) to this kind of scholarship: 'once aware that much of their Bibliolatry depends upon ignorance of Hebrew and Greek, and often upon peculiarity of idiom or structures in their mother dialect, cautious people begin to suspect the whole. Here arises a very interesting, startling, and perplexing situation for all who venerate the Bible; one which must always have existed for prying, inquisitive people, but which has been incalculably sharpened for the apprehension of these days by the extraordinary advances made and making in Oriental and Greek philology. It is a situation of public scandal even to the deep reverencers of the Bible; but a situation of much more than scandal, of real grief, to the profound and sincere among religious people' (*DQW*, XVI: 237).

13. Coleridge in particular was deeply influenced by the higher biblical criticism as Elinor Shaffer has shown in her excellent study *'Kubla Khan' and 'The Fall of Jerusalem'* (1975).
14. In his 'Notes on Gilfillan's "Gallery of Literary Portraits"', De Quincey described his library as being 'rich in the wickedest of German speculations', and hence potentially of greater interest to a self-declared free-thinker and atheist such as Shelley than Southey's tamer though larger collection which Shelley visited (*DQW*, XV: 293–4).
15. De Quincey's essay 'On the Essenes' for example is a detailed and convoluted attempt to incorporate the Jewish sect of the Essenes into the Christian fold on account of the Christian values they evidently practice and at the same time to discredit Josephus (the original historian of the Essenes) for his blindness in failing to recognize the Essenes as Christians (*DQW*, XI: 442–88).
16. Translated by his mother uncompromisingly as 'bribes'. 'A very ugly word was that', De Quincey ruefully exclaims, reflecting that his uncle could easily have remitted £200,000 to England, had he not been overcome by his sister's scruples which he had found 'imperfectly convincing' in any case. Had he been less scrupulous, this might have proved a tidy inheritance for the impoverished opium-eater.
17. The figure of the 'nabob' (the wealthy East India Company official) in late eighteenth-century England had become a byword for corruption and despotism as Samuel Foote's popular play, *The Nabob* (1772) depicts. In 1773 Lord North's Regulating Act prohibited Company officials from engaging in private trade and accepting presents. Yet criticisms of the nabobs' corrupt practices continued, most famously with Burke's impeachment of Warren Hastings in 1787.
18. In particular, De Quincey is influenced by Alexander Murray, the Scottish orientalist whom he refers to with admiration in his 'Letters to a Young Man whose Education has been Neglected' (*DQW*, III: 61). Murray is less famed than the Asiatic Society orientalists of Calcutta such as Jones and Colebrook, but he exercised an important influence on the Scottish Enlightenment which evolved an alternative historiography and methodology to evangelical and utilitarian approaches; see Jane Rendell: 1982.
19. Lowth writes: 'For the Greek, beyond every other language [. . .] is copious, flowing, and harmonious, possessed of a great variety of measures [. . .]. But in the Hebrew language the whole economy is different. Its form is simple above every other; the radical words are uniform, and resemble each other almost exactly; nor are the inflexions numerous, or materially different: whence we may readily understand, that its metres are neither complex, nor capable of much variety; but rather simple, grave, temperate; less adapted to fluency than dignity and force' (Lowth 1787, I: 70–71). De Quincey's preference for Hebrew over Greek absorbs Lowth's linguistic framework into his own Wordsworthian and evangelical critical sensibility.
20. In relation to the Biblical resonances of De Quincey's dream description of the prostitute Ann discussed earlier in this chapter, it is worth noting that in the *Autobiographic Sketches*, the scriptural image of a weeping woman under the Judean palms is related to an image De Quincey had encountered on Roman coins (*DQW*, XIX: 20). The association clarifies the fierce and bloody route by which Biblical imagery was given currency by means of the Roman empire. As John Barrell has pointed out, the image of the woman on the coin represents the subjugation of Judea by Vespasian in the context of the first Jewish-Roman war (66–73 C.E.) which ended with Roman victory and the fall of Jerusalem (Barrell 1991: 33–4, 41, 69–70, 145–6, 158). The coin was

issued in celebration of Jewish humiliation and massacre. Barrell fails to note however that the image of Judea weeping is the opening image of Jeremiah's *Lamentations* in the Bible, hence turning the Roman desolation of Judea into a prophetic event of providential imperialism.

21. I refer to the influential and in many ways rewarding books by John Barrell (1991) and Margaret Russett (1997). Their willingness to explain De Quincey's imperialism and canonical status in terms of childhood events or traumas however seems to me reductive and ultimately disabling, tending to read broader cultural phenomena as psychological aberrations. Revealingly, one of the texts cited by Barrell in evidence of the incest theme in De Quincey, *The Stranger's Grave*, has been proved to be a misattribution; see Symonds (1993). The continued influence of this psychoanalytical approach may be seen in the following explanation of De Quincey's Sinophobia in a recent article: 'In his fabrication of an Asian persona, in his irrational rage at a people about whom he knows virtually nothing, we see the author obsessively, if unconsciously, reliving the fury of a child at the cold omnipotence of the parent' (Simmons 2002: 187).

22. An insightful article which critiques De Quincey scholarship on the grounds of synchronicity is Daniel O'Quinn's 'Murder, Hospitality, Philosophy: De Quincey and the Complicitous Grounds of National Identity'. O'Quinn argues that De Quincey's texts often draw the reader into complicity with the author's narrative compulsions, favouring a synchronic and unifying approach to his varied texts.

WORKS CITED

Barrell, John. (1991) *The Infection of Thomas De Quincey: A Psychopathology of Imperialism*, New Haven, CT: Yale University Press.

Bryant, Jacob. (1767) *Observations and Inquiries relating to various parts of Ancient History*, Cambridge: J. Archdeacon.

Burnett, James (Lord Monboddo). (1779–99) *Ancient Metaphysics, or the Science of Universals*, 6 volumes, London: T. Cadell.

———. (1773–92) *Of the Origin and Progress of Language*, 6 volumes, London: T. Cadell.

Daniell, David. (2003) *The Bible in English: Its History and Influence*, New Haven, CT: Yale University Press, 2003.

Frey, Anna. (2005) 'De Quincey's Imperial Systems', *Studies in Romanticism*, 44: 41–61.

Garland, Cannon. (1990) *The Life and Mind of Oriental Jones: Sir William Jones, the Father of Modern Linguistics*, Cambridge: Cambridge University Press.

Kopf, David. (1969) *British Orientalism and the Bengal Renaissance: The Dynamics of Indian Modernization, 1773–1835*. Berkeley: University of California Press.

Leask, Nigel. (1992) *British Romantic Writers and the East: Anxieties of Empire*, Cambridge: Cambridge University Press.

Lowth, Robert. (1787) *Lectures on the Sacred Poetry of the Hebrews*, 2 volumes, London: J. Johnson.

McDonagh, Josephine. (1992) 'Opium and the Imperial Imagination', in Philip W. Martin and Robin Jarvis (eds.) *Reviewing Romanticism*, London: Macmillan, 116–33.

Maniquis, Robert. (1976) 'Lonely Empires: Personal and Public Visions of Thomas De Quincey'. *Literary Monographs*, 8. Ed. Eric Rothstein and J. A. Wittreich. Wisconsin: The University of Wisconsin Press, 47–127.

Mellor, Anne K. and Matlak, Richard E. (1996) *British Literature: 1780–1830*, New York: Harcourt Brace and Co.
Mill, James. (1997) *The History of British India*, 10 volumes, London: Routledge/Thoemmes.
Oddie, Geoffrey. (2006) *Imagined Hinduism: British Protestant Missionary Constructions of Hinduism, 1793–1900*. London: Sage Publications.
O'Quinn, Daniel. (1999) 'Murder, Hospitality, Philosophy: De Quincey and the Complicitous Grounds of National Identity', *Studies in Romanticism*, 38: 135–70.
Plotz, Judith. (1996) 'Imaginary Kingdoms with Real Boys in them: or, How the Quincey Brothers Built the Empire', *The Wordsworth Circle*, 27: 131–36.
The Protestant's Family Bible: Containing the New and Old Testament, with the Apocrypha, illustrated by explanatory notes. With a Compleat Concordance, and general index. (1780) London: Harrison and Co.
Rendell, Jane. (1982) 'Scottish Orientalism: From Robertson to James Mill', *The Historical Journal*, 25: 43–69.
Roberts, Daniel Sanjiv. (1999) *Revisionary Gleam: De Quincey, Coleridge and the High Romantic Argument*, Liverpool: Liverpool University Press.
———. (2004) *Robert Southey: Poetical Works 1793–1810*, Volume 4: *The Curse of Kehama*, London: Pickering and Chatto.
Russett, Margaret. (1997) *De Quincey's Romanticism: Canonical Minority and the Forms of Transmission*. Cambridge: Cambridge University Press.
Rzepka, Charles. (1991) 'The Literature of Power and Imperial Will: De Quincey's Opium War Essays', *South Central Review*, 8: 37–45.
Shaffer, Elinor. (1975) *'Kubla Khan' and 'The Fall of Jerusalem': The Mythological School in Biblical Criticism and Secular Literature, 1770–1880*. Cambridge: Cambridge University Press.
Simmons, Diane. (2002) 'Narcissism and Sinophobia: The Case of Thomas De Quincey', *Journal for the Psychoanalysis of Culture and Society*, 7: 179–89.
Sudan, Rajani. (1994) 'Englishness A'muck: De Quincey's *Confessions*', *Genre*, 27: 377–94.
Symonds, Barry. (1993) '*The Stranger's Grave*: Laying a De Quinceyan Ghost', *The Charles Lamb Bulletin*, n.s. 83: 105–7.
Trautmann, Thomas R. (1997) *Aryans and British India*, Berkeley: University of California Press.
Wilford, Francis. (1805) 'An Essay on the Sacred Isles in the West, with other Essays', *Asiatic Researches*, 8: 245–375.
Wolfson, Susan and Manning, Peter. (1999) *The Longman Anthology of British Literature: The Romantics and their Contemporaries*. New York: Longman.
Wu, Duncan. (1998) *Romanticism: An Anthology with CD-Rom*, 2nd edn., Oxford: Blackwell.

3 Brunonianism, Radicalism, and 'The Pleasures of Opium'[1]

Barry Milligan

Critics have often regarded Thomas De Quincey as adhering to an almost caricaturish High Tory line, but several critics more recently have begun to hear a dissonant counterpoint of radical sentiment woven into his otherwise supposedly conservative ideology. Josephine McDonagh, for instance, notes a 'language of balance', particularly in De Quincey's writings of the early 1830s, and regards it as a rhetorical ploy by a committed Tory, 'perpetrated in panic and heavy-handed', rather than as an indication of deeper conflict and questioning (McDonagh 1994: 36). Daniel Sanjiv Roberts, however, sees the origins of De Quincey's radical subtext as more fundamental and sincere, tracing 'lines of influence and development in De Quincey's thought that come from . . . a radical politics and poetics that he absorbs from his early influences' (Roberts 2000: 26). Robert Morrison suggests that the dominance of De Quincey's conservative voice is delusive, evidence not necessarily of ideological commitment but rather of shrewd rhetorical positioning: much of his writing was for notoriously conservative periodicals such as *Blackwood's* and De Quincey knew how to provide a saleable commodity (Morrison 1998). Morrison's chapter in the current volume extends this argument, attributing the tension between conservative and radical leanings in *Confessions of an English Opium-Eater* (1821, D*QW*, II) to twistings and turnings in the work's evolution: it was begun as an essay for *Blackwood's* but assumed its final shape as a contribution to the more progressive *London Magazine*.[2]

Of course, any attempt to delineate coherent conservative and liberal camps is probably a losing enterprise in any age and place, but nineteenth-century Britain is perhaps even more than usually elusive in this respect. The nation and century that could produce, for instance, a Disraeli, who began his political life as a putative independent radical but ultimately led an idealistically aristocratic Tory party, defies easy divisions. In this respect De Quincey might be the paradigmatic nineteenth-century British intellectual, with his characteristically paradoxical tendency both to delineate dichotomies and to dissolve them. Such corrosiveness is enhanced by opium, which has the power not simply to blur divisions between ostensible binary opposites, but indeed to lay bare the identity that has always existed between them. This simultaneously threatening and thrilling unity is evident, for instance, with the supposed division between England and the East, as De Quincey elaborates especially in the *Confessions* and 'The English Mail-Coach' (1849, *DQW*, XVI). But he shows at the same time, if perhaps more subtly, a similar unity between supposedly separate social classes within Britain. The eponymous mail-coach, for instance, spatially maps a 'revolution' afoot in English society during the last years of the Napoleonic Wars: the outside-riding 'pariahs' scorned by the more affluent inside passengers were in fact sons of the up-and-coming middle classes, and, by the time the essay appeared at mid-century, these former Oxonians were administering the ever-expanding British Empire. This instability is revealed by the corrosive agency of opium, which dissolves the obscuring writing on the palimpsests of both collective history and individual consciousness to reveal that the current top of the hierarchy is not just an upstart challenger to the originary authority but is in fact a degraded descendant of it.[3]

But whereas De Quincey's exposure of England's troubling Oriental origins is suffused with a fearful resistance, his revelation of class unity is more playful, vacillating between reverent imitation and corrosive parody, polemic and pastiche. The specific physiological properties he attributes to opium place him within a controversial confluence of medical, professional, and social radicalism closely implicated with the so-called Brunonian system of medicine arising from John Brown's *Elementa Medicinae* (1780, translated as *Elements of Medicine*, 1788), later famously edited and introduced by Thomas Beddoes (1795), himself a more radical figure than was generally acknowledged during his life and immediately after his death.[4] These tendencies and affinities are most focused in one section of the *Confessions*, the 'Pleasures of Opium', where De Quincey both throws down the gauntlet before supposedly 'benighted' medical professionals (*DQW*, II: 58, note) and recounts his sympathetic sojourns among the London poor on Saturday nights. Thus 'The Pleasures of Opium' challenges the familiar conception of a High Tory Opium-Eater, but not simply by replacing him with a flaming radical one. With this in mind, this essay will close-read 'The Pleasures of Opium', placing it within the intersecting contexts of Brunonian medicine, medical professional reform, and radical politics in late eighteenth- and early nineteenth-century Britain, thus illuminating otherwise unexamined facets of De Quincey's elusively ironic, proto-deconstructive sensibility.

'AN UPHEAVING, FROM ITS LOWEST DEPTHS, OF THE INNER SPIRIT!'

Throughout 'The Pleasures of Opium', De Quincey does in a more focused, even exaggerated way what he does throughout the *Confessions* in particular and his whole oeuvre in general: he wryly notes, critiques, and celebrates the tendency of supposed dichotomies to collapse upon themselves. But even more specifically, he dwells upon opium's idiosyncratic ability to expose such instability. The drug is paradoxically the 'dread agent of unimaginable pleasure and pain' (*DQW*, II: 42) that throws its user into an oxymoronic 'abyss of divine enjoyment' (*DQW*, II: 43); the man who first sold it to De Quincey is simultaneously as 'dull and stupid . . . as any mortal druggist' and the 'beatific vision of an immortal druggist' (*DQW*, II: 42); the Opium-Eater scruples that it would be 'impolite to pursue an argument which must [presume] a man mistaken in a point belonging to his own profession' (*DQW*, II: 46) while insisting that 'professors of medicine' write nothing but 'Lies! lies! lies!' about the drug (*DQW*, II: 43). Prominent among such collapsed breaches are communication gaps: musical phrases, otherwise 'like a collection of Arabic characters', release through the agency of opium 'the whole of my past life . . . as if present and incarnated in the music' (*DQW*, II: 48). Similarly revealed is 'the music of the Italian language', even though the opium-eater is 'a poor Italian scholar, reading it but little and speaking it not at all' (*DQW*, II: 49).

Chief among De Quincey's illustrations of opium's unifying capacity is its supposed breaching of socio-economic boundaries: it acts upon 'the hearts of poor and rich alike' (*DQW*, II: 51) and incites the middle-class intellectual opium-eater to mingle with the poor. In a centerpiece to 'The Pleasures of Opium' recounting his Saturday night 'debauch[es] of opium' (*DQW*, II: 47), he notes his sympathy with the poor and recounts how it was enhanced by his Saturday night doses:

> I feel always, on a Saturday night, as though I also were released from some yoke of labour, had some wages to receive, and some luxury of repose to enjoy. For the sake, therefore, of witnessing, upon as large a scale as possible, a spectacle with which my sympathy was so entire, I used often, on Saturday nights, after I had taken opium, to wander forth, without much regarding the direction or the distance, to all the markets, and other parts of London, to which the poor resort on a Saturday night, for laying out their wages. [. . .] I joined their parties, and gave my opinion upon the matter in discussion, which, if not always judicious, was always received indulgently. If wages were a little higher, or expected to be so, or the quartern loaf a little lower, or it was reported that onions and butter were expected to fall, I was glad: yet, if the contrary were true, I drew from opium some means of consoling myself. For opium (like the bee that extracts its materials indiscriminately from roses and from the soot of chimneys) can overrule all feelings into a compliance with the master key. (*DQW*, II: 49–50)

Thus, even though the opium-eater 'had no labours that I rested from; no wages to receive', he felt during his Saturday night opium debauches as if he had, and his sympathy became 'so entire . . . after I had taken opium' that he 'joined their parties' (*DQW*, II: 49–50).

As is the case with every other set of binary terms De Quincey encounters, however, this supposed levelling is by no means so simple. First, he breaches the divide between bourgeois intellectual and poor worker only to impose within the supposedly resulting unity the same bifurcation that characterizes his experience of opium, that between pleasures and pains: 'I ... was disposed to express my interest by sympathizing with their pleasures. The pains of poverty I had lately seen too much of' (*DQW*, II: 49). It does not require a priggish sensibility to question the merits of such a fair-weather sympathy, as several critics have done. Alina Clej scorns it as 'the counterpart of his class prejudices and racial intolerance .... a reflection of De Quincey's (and his readers') own bad conscience and vague fears of the masses' (Clej 1995: 83), while Josephine McDonagh finds the Opium-Eater's account of his Saturday night sojourns 'glibly' representing urban workers as 'frivolous' (McDonagh 1994: 42). John Barrell discriminates more finely: 'The pleasure is not at all to pretend to be *one of* an inferior class, but to pretend to be *like* them, fundamentally the same, but different in all that really concerns one's sense of identity and self-esteem', thus making the apparent unification of classes 'a means of reassurance, of making safe what seems to be threatening in the poor, in the "masses"' (Barrell 1991: 2).

However questionable the alleged class unification might appear under close critical scrutiny, De Quincey offers it as an example of opium's beneficent ability to 'overrule all feelings into a compliance with the master key.' More specifically, the drug's facilitation of class sympathy parallels its action upon the palimpsest of the human brain as described in *Suspiria de Profundis* (1845, *DQW*, XV: 171–77): it etches away obscuring layers of imposed distractions to reveal the original essence that lies beneath. In this case it enables the 'removal' of obstacles to 'the impulses of a heart originally just and good' (*DQW*, II: 45). The oceanic benignity manifested in the opium-eater's supposed unity with poor London labourers, then, is for him the essence of his true self, for like wine, opium is the antidote to the state in which 'most men are disguised by sobriety', and both substances cause their users to 'display themselves in their true complexion of character' (*DQW*, II: 45). Whereas alcohol seems merely to dredge up the sediment beneath the surface, however, opium on the contrary 'always seems to compose what had been agitated, and to concentrate what had been distracted' (*DQW*, II: 45). The effects of such a revealing and organizing force are felt most profoundly at a moral level, where the true self is allegedly laid bare by opium's cleansing effect:

> the expansion of the beniger feelings, incident to opium is no febrile access, but a healthy restoration of that state which the mind would naturally recover upon the removal of any deep-seated irritation of pain that had disturbed and quarreled with the impulses of a heart originally just and good..... In short, to sum up all in one word, a man

who is inebriated, or tending to inebriation, is, and feels that he is, in a condition which calls up into supremacy the merely human, too often the brutal, part of his nature: but the opium-eater (I speak of him who is not suffering from any disease, or other remote effects of opium) feels that the diviner part of his nature is paramount; that is, the moral affections are in a state of cloudless serenity; and over all is the great light of the majestic intellect. (*DQW*, II: 45)

The calm-after-a-storm motif here (composing what had been agitated, cloudless serenity, great and majestic light), is consistent with a significant strain of imagery throughout the 'Pleasures of Opium' hearkening to the biblical flood. A few pages later De Quincey compares the zenith of opium's effects to 'overlook[ing] the sea at a mile below me', seeing it 'in everlasting but gentle agitation, and brooded over by a dove-like calm . . . as if the tumult, the fever, and the strife, were suspended' (*DQW*, II: 51). With or without an olive branch, the dove hovering above the recently tumultuous sea here further associates opium's ordering effects with the flood's washing away of sin, the restoration of 'the diviner part of his nature' (*DQW*, II: 45). Likewise, opium's sublimely just quality—it is 'just, subtle, and mighty . . . and dost reverse the sentences of unrighteous judges' (*DQW*, II: 51)— recalls the divine justice of the New Covenant following the biblical flood, even unto King James Version diction.

The flood metaphor appears earlier in the 'Pleasures' as well. De Quincey characterizes the ordered, benign state of the opium-eater's faculties as consistent with 'a bodily constitution of primeval or antediluvian health' (*DQW*, II: 44), suggesting that opium washes away layers of sediment obscuring the essential human state beneath, much as it erases the obscuring writing on the 'palimpsest of the human brain' to reveal the originary text of buried memory in *Suspiria de Profundis*.[5] But there is also a dissonant counterpoint here: the 'antediluvian' quality of this true self suggests the silt obscuring it was deposited by a flood, that by extension, the true nature beneath predates the First Covenant. Thus what opium washes away is not necessarily the sin eradicated by Noah's flood, but the obfuscation of the postdiluvian dispensation that followed.

This quasi-Blakean subversive view is also subtly implied by the characterization of opium's cleansing qualities as 'revers[ing] the sentences of unrighteous judges' (*DQW*, II: 51), suggesting that God's imposition of the flood was an unjust, even 'unrighteous' sentence.[6] Furthermore, opium implicitly usurps the Judeo-Christian God's status not only as ultimate lawgiver, but even as creator: much as 'the Spirit of God moved upon the face of the waters' when 'the earth was without form, and void; and darkness was upon the face of the deep' (Genesis 1:1–2, KJV), opium 'buildest upon the bosom of darkness, . . . and 'from the anarchy of dreaming sleep', callest into sunny light the faces of long-buried beauties' (*DQW*, II: 51). Furthermore, opium is not just God's rival here but is instead the 'only' giver of such gifts: 'Thou only givest these gifts to man; and thou hast the keys of Paradise, oh, just, subtle, and mighty opium!' (*DQW*, II: 51).

Among God's unjust sentences reversible by opium is that most consequential one, exile from Paradise, the locked gates of which can be opened by just and mighty opium. This apocalyptic reversal smears yet another dividing line, shifting fluidly from the Old Testament rhetoric of the flood to the New Testament imagery of Revelation, whose language is most explicitly echoed in the Opium-Eater's pronouncement of 'the doctrine of the true church on the subject of opium: of which church I acknowledge myself to be the only member—the alpha and the omega' (*DQW*, II: 45). 'Alpha and Omega' is of course Revelation's recurrent epithet for the redeemer (Revelation 1:8, 1:11, 21:6, 22:13), who promises to 'give unto him that is athirst of the fountain of the water of life freely' (21:6). The opium-eater stops just short of calling laudanum 'the water of life', characterizing it as 'the secret of happiness, about which philosophers had disputed for so many ages' and exulting that 'happiness might now be bought for a penny, corked up in a pint bottle: and peace of mind could be sent down in gallons by the mail coach' (*DQW*, II: 43).

Thus opium is not just a health restorative but a cosmic force of redemption, reinstating with its 'exquisite order, legislation, and harmony' (*DQW*, II: 44) the prelapsarian order obscured by subsequent pollutions. Likewise, the opium-eater is the prophet of 'an upheaving, from its lowest depths, of the inner spirit! . . . an apocalypse of the world within me' (*DQW*, II: 43). His casting himself as alpha-and-omega redeemer would smack to some of blasphemy, a problem implicitly addressed, albeit to raise other problems, by his recasting himself in the 1856 revision as 'the Pope' (*DQW*, II: 220). Even more extreme, however, is his characterization of the opium-induced restoration of lost order, legislation, and harmony as 'revers[ing] the sentences of unrighteous judges' (*DQW*, II: 51), casting himself as a sort of Miltonic Satan or Shelleyan Prometheus, toppling a cosmically tyrannical hierarchy to liberate those it oppresses.

In a characteristically De Quinceyan paradox, order is restored to the self only to eradicate that self on another level: the world thus reconfigured is much wider than 'the world within me' (*DQW*, II: 43), as the specific originary state at the heart of 'The Pleasures of Opium' is a fundamental unity among otherwise artificially separated socio-economic classes. Thus, in a metaphorical move so characteristic of eighteenth-century political discourse as to be a sort of cliché, the individual's body figures in miniature the body politic,[7] and in this instance opium is a means of restoring health and balance not only to the former but also to the latter, which has been thrown out of equilibrium by its own forms of 'deep-seated irritation of pain that had disturbed and quarreled with the impulses of a heart originally just and good' (*DQW*, II: 45).

'THE ART OF MEDICINE . . . NOW REDUCED TO AN EXACT SCIENCE'

The suggestion that class unity is a fundamentally natural state and needs to be restored is, of course, Revolutionary with a capital 'R', obscured though it might be in 'The Pleasures of Opium' beneath layers of metaphor and biblical allusion. Similarly, it is also revolutionary in a less obvious sense to argue that opium is a means of restoring fundamental balance to even an individual bodily economy, especially by means of the kind of stimulation De Quincey details. When the *Confessions* appeared in 1821, the medical community was not merely divided upon the question of whether opium was a stimulant or narcotic (terms that have themselves become so familiar by the early twenty-first century as to obscure their idiosyncratic origins in the debates in question here); indeed the dispute lay at the heart of a long-standing but still heated controversy regarding whether the 'Brunonian' system originated by John Brown's *Elementa Medicinae* was an accurate and practically applicable medical theory or merely a quackish instance of the supposedly Godless materialism rampant in Jacobin circles during the decades surrounding the French Revolution.

As the hard-drinking, earthy-talking son of a rural Scots weaver, John Brown (1735–88) was perhaps destined never to be a true insider to the Edinburgh medical establishment. Nevertheless, his prodigious reading and skill at Latin landed him a position as tutor to the children of William Cullen (1710–90), the eminent physician and professor of medicine (originally of chemistry) at Edinburgh University, most lastingly remembered for his innovative explorations of the relationships between the operations of the nervous system and the development of illnesses. This close personal association with a scientific luminary emboldened Brown to put his name forward for election to the Edinburgh Philosophical Society. When he was blackballed, he conceived a lifelong resentment for his former mentor and began teaching his own system of medicine in pointed opposition to Cullen's. Brown's system was notable for its simplicity, reducing aspects of Cullen's complex considerations of nervous factors and physical symptoms to a straightforward question of balance between two fundamental forces Brown called 'stimulus' and 'excitability.' Illness ensued when a lack of stimulation resulted in an excess of unused excitability ('asthenic' disorders) or, conversely, when too much stimulation depleted the body's finite resources of excitability ('sthenic' disorders). Medical treatment, then, was a matter of restoring equilibrium by increasing or decreasing stimulation, but the majority of diseases, according to Brown, were asthenic and thus called for the administration of stimulants.

Of such stimuli, he says, 'the highest of all, as far as experiments have yet thrown light upon the subject, is opium' (Brown 1803: 144), an assertion that flew in the face of received medical wisdom.[8] The professional iconoclasm of the assertion was hardly lost upon Brown, who places it at the centre of one of the most polemical passages in the book, calling the whole profession onto the carpet for its ignorance. His professional brethren have erred seriously,

> as they senselessly enough supposed excessive motions to be occasioned by an excess of the principle of life, at least in the labouring parts, so they either thought, or taught, that opium possessed the virtue of checking or allaying, as a sedative, these motions; an hypothesis contrary to the whole analogy of nature, and to the certain proof afforded by all the exciting powers, every one of which has proved to be stimulant, not one sedative. . . . In truth, opium is not a sedative; on the contrary, . . . it is the most powerful of all the agents that support life, and that restore health. (Brown 1803: 218–19)

But such senseless suppositions regarding opium's powers in particular are merely a symptom of an entirely wrongheaded medical orthodoxy in general, to which Brown's new system provides a revolutionary alternative:

> This stimulant plan of cure, in all its parts, is new, whether the reasoning part, or the merely practical be regarded; and whether the cause and the exciting powers, or the indication of cure and the remedies, be considered. May it not, therefore, be put as a question, whether the whole doctrine, which has been delivered, has not, at last, brought forward clear proof, that the art of medicine, hitherto conjectural, inconsistent with itself, and altogether incoherent, is now reduced to an exact science, proved not by mathematical principles, which is only one kind of evidence, but by physical ones, and established by the certain testimony of our senses, nay, and by the very axioms of the mathematical elements? (Brown 1803: 278–79)

Brown thus takes the radically empirical position that a systematic scientific method can conquer age-old ignorance. But his position is even more revolutionary in that he proposes to unseat the wrongly enthroned medical professional powers and replace them with a more democratic system based upon Painean common sense. As he says in his preface to the English translation,

> Both this, and the original work, are intended not for the exclusive use of medical readers, but also for that of the public at large . . . The public are presented with a work, that claims the merit of having reduced the doctrine and practice of medicine to scientific certainty and exactness. With respect to the form, in which it is delivered, it is stripped of that jargon of numerous unmeaning or misleading terms, and all that mystery either in style or matter, that has hitherto rendered the pretended

healing art impenetrable to the most intelligent and discerning, and locked it fast up in the schools. (Brown 1803: xiv)

Although it is difficult to know for certain whether De Quincey read Brown, a number of factors indicate that he was familiar with the *Elementa Medicinae*. As Thomas Beddoes asserted in the biographical sketch that prefaced his edition, 'the opinions of Brown [have] been so widely diffused by oral communication, as to affect the whole practice of medicine in Great Britain' (Beddoes 1803: lxxxi), and that influence only broadened and deepened throughout the early nineteenth century, as Christopher Lawrence recounts (Lawrence 1988). As Beddoes also noted, 'In pamphlets recommending repeated doses of opium to support excitement, and in other publications, it would be easy to detect attempts to purloin [Brown's] language and ideas' (Beddoes 1803: lxxxi). De Quincey read enough medical literature regarding opium to have encountered such dissemination of Brown's ideas, and he was only one degree of separation from Beddoes himself through their mutual friend Coleridge. Furthermore, De Quincey refers directly at least once in his writings to 'the theory of the Scotch physician Brown', which he characterizes (ostensibly echoing Kant's assessment) as 'not only . . . a great step taken for medicine, but even for the general interests of man . . . . something analogous to the course which human nature has held in still more important inquiries, viz. first of all, a continual ascent towards the more and more elaborately complex, and then a treading back, on its own steps, towards the simple and elementary' (*DQW*, VI: 83–84). Whether or not De Quincey consciously intended to 'purloin' Brown's ideas, he would at least have found Brown's reforming and unifying system appealing in the mode of Ricardo's 'laws which first gave a ray of light into the unwieldy chaos of materials, and had constructed what had been but a collection of tentative discussions into a science of regular proportions' (*DQW*, II: 64).

De Quincey's specific contentions and rhetorical stance are conspicuously akin to Brown's, especially in the 'Pleasures of Opium':

> upon all that has been hitherto written on the subject of opium . . . . by professors of medicine, writing *ex cathedrâ*,—I have but one emphatic criticism to pronounce—Lies! lies! lies! . . . . therefore, worthy doctors, as there seems to be room for further discoveries, stand aside, and allow me to come forward and lecture on this matter.
>
> First, then, it is not so much affirmed as taken for granted, by all who ever mention opium, formally or incidentally, that it does, or can, produce intoxication. Now, reader, assure yourself, *meo periculo*, that no quantity did, or ever could, intoxicate . . . . whereas wine disorders the mental faculties, opium, on the contrary (if taken in a proper manner), introduces amongst them the most exquisite order, legislation, and harmony. . . . I speak from the ground of a large and profound personal experience: whereas most of the unscientific authors who have at all

treated of opium, and even those who have written expressly on the materia medica, make it evident, from the horror they express of it, that their experimental knowledge of its action is none at all. (*DQW*, II: 44–46)

De Quincey recapitulates all of Brown's otherwise idiosyncratic main points. By opposing his 'large and profound personal experience' of opium to that of the medical professionals', whose 'experimental knowledge of its action is none at all' (*DQW*, II: 46), De Quincey stands beside Brown as an empirical scientific revolutionary who would have medicine 'reduced to an exact science, proved ... by physical [principles], and established by the certain testimony of our senses' (Brown 1803: 278–79). Even more specifically, De Quincey's extended comparison and contrast of alcohol and opium, establishing that opium increases and focuses the powers while alcohol decreases and disorders them, directly reiterates Brown's controversial assessments. Just as Brown's medical colleagues 'senselessly enough supposed ... that opium possessed the virtue of checking or allaying, as a sedative' (Brown 1803: 218), so have De Quincey's 'professors of medicine .... taken for granted ... that it does, or can, produce intoxication' (*DQW*, II: 44).

One might say that echoing Brown's call for medical professional reform does not in itself paint De Quincey as a more comprehensive radical, but it is important to note that, in the late eighteenth and early nineteenth centuries, the cause of medical reform was becoming ever more closely associated with growing efforts toward social reform in general. Given the hegemony of the medical community at the University of Edinburgh, Brown's challenge immediately assumed the outlines not just of an intellectual dispute but of a socially revolutionary act. As Christopher Lawrence notes, 'opposed to the orthodoxies of Cullen in particular and of Edinburgh medicine in general, Brown's system of medicine appears to have been popular in Edinburgh among outsiders in the medical profession and was supported by those seeking wider political reform in the city. Indeed it seems to have had its greatest popularity elsewhere in Britain, among political radicals, such as Beddoes, or among more humble practitioners and military and naval surgeons' (Lawrence 2004). As Lawrence also notes elsewhere, 'Cullen was being associated with the past, the establishment, orthodoxy and tradition, and Brown was being identified, not with reform, ... but with revolution' (Lawrence 1988: 10). De Quincey's own relationship with the Edinburgh university faculty was somewhat checkered, as he both derided and admired especially its philosophy professors, another of the many self-contradictory patterns even in the *Confessions*.[9] However, De Quincey does not seem to have been well acquainted with any of Edinburgh's medical faculty, and he seems in general to group orthodox medical professionals together as 'professors of medicine, writing *ex cathedrâ*', who spout 'Lies! lies! lies!' (*DQW*, II: 44). Given De Quincey's own self-emphasized status as an excellent classical scholar squaring off again and again with less educated people in positions of higher status, he presumably would also have sympathized with Brown's similar status as an excellent classicist who was nonetheless excluded from the elite intellectual ranks to which he aspired.

In the *Elementa Medicinae*, Brown's most pointed challenges are to the state of medical knowledge, but it was well known that he was at least equally opposed to professional medicine's institutional dimensions. Having failed to secure a faculty position at the University of Edinburgh, Brown was a vocally challenging outsider to the Edinburgh medical establishment, which tended to regard him as a drunken Scots rube, despite his acknowledged distinction as a classicist and the respect accorded his system by a number of reputable practitioners beyond the closed circle of the Edinburgh elite. But orthodox medical professionals' perception of Brown as a comprehensively dangerous threat also extended well beyond Edinburgh. Systematically surveying contemporary responses to Brown throughout Britain, Europe, and the United States, Christopher Lawrence notes that detractors scorned his system as

> materialist, irreligious, and thus potentially productive of the very worst social consequences. . . . Here was something familiar and very nasty: French materialism, irreligion and Jacobinism dressed up in 'crude notions', arrived at by either a simple misunderstanding of the nature of life or devised with some more sinister intent. . . . Brunonianism posed the threat of democracy and equality among medical practitioners. (Lawrence 1988: 13–14)

There were pronounced social overtones to Brown's system beyond the professional community as well: as Neil Vickers has argued, *Elementa Medicinae*'s emphasis on balancing intellectual activity and luxury with physical exertion notably anticipates Wordsworth's radical idealization of the lives of rustic labourers (Vickers 2004: 40). Less subtly, as Beddoes notes in his biographical preface, 'Brown was the first person I ever saw absurd enough to profess himself a Jacobite' (Beddoes 1803: xxxviii), and it was difficult to separate his strongly stated political ideas from his equally disputatious scientific ones. As if all this were not enough to establish Brown's credentials as a radical, he also placed his English translation of the *Elementa* with the London publisher Joseph Johnson, whose catalog included works by Joseph Priestley, William Blake, Mary Wollstonecraft, and John Horne Tooke (Overmeier 1982: 311).[10]

One of the most radical features of Brown's medical system was its attribution of life to a single, identifiable physical principle—in Brown's case 'excitability'—and this materialism, as it came to be branded, kept Brown among the frontrunners of medical radicalism for nearly two generations. By the end of the eighteenth century, longstanding speculation about the principle by which life originates and is maintained was taking on more and more explicitly political dimensions. Humphry Davy's shift from the materialist inquiries of his youth to the staunchly vitalist orthodoxies of his old age, for instance, is emblematic of the general shift from radical to conservative politics that characterized his intellectual circle, including De Quincey's erstwhile idols Wordsworth, Coleridge, and Southey. By the second decade of the nineteenth century, battle lines were starkly drawn. Those who believed the processes of life were governed by an invisible, immaterial force opposed the more empirically inclined, who looked for a demonstrable principle of life in a physical form. Thus the so-called Vitality Debate evolved from a philosophical conversation into a standoff between religious conservatives and putatively atheistic Jacobins. The debate became especially focused and celebrated between the eminent London surgeons John Abernethy and William Lawrence shortly before the *Confessions* appeared. In his 1815 lectures to the Royal College of Surgeons (published in 1816 as *Introduction to Comparative Anatomy and Physiology*), Lawrence concentrated on the functions of the bodily organs as the principle of life, criticizing others' emphasis upon an immaterial and externally imposed vitalist force.[11] Rightly recognizing himself as Lawrence's chief implicit target, John Abernethy counter-attacked in his *Physiological Lectures* (1817), accusing Lawrence of materialism, atheism, and the overall 'pernicious tendency' of French anatomists such as Bichat (qtd. Ruston 2005: 54). Abernethy identified in Lawrence's rejection of an externally imposed principle of life the kind of resistance to organizational forces that underlay the French Revolution. Lawrence rebutted the accusation in his subsequent lectures, finding in Abernethy's charges an anti-democratic principle evident also in his insistence on an externally imposed regulation of life.

Lawrence was one of a new generation of reformers including the *Lancet*'s founder Thomas Wakley, who wanted the influence-bound profession of medicine shifted to a more meritocratic basis and the science underlying it grounded in more recognizably empirical principles. Allying themselves with prominent social reformists such as William Cobbett, this new generation of medical men challenged professional luminaries besides Abernethy, such as Astley Cooper and Charles Bell. Several of these eminent medics were friends and advisors to the Lake Circle, prompting Coleridge to comment disapprovingly in his correspondence on 'the Lawrenciens' and their reformist efforts (qtd. Ruston 2005: 51). Lawrence, who often peppered his lectures with praise of the revolutionary advances in France and the United States, came to be revered as both a revolutionary and something of a visionary among the second generation of Romantic poets, most especially Shelley, with whom he was personally acquainted and whose work De Quincey much admired.[12] Although Lawrence officially withdrew his offending lectures from publication shortly after they first appeared, pirated editions began to circulate just as the *Confessions* was published and were to become a mainstay of the radical press for several decades to come (Desmond 1989: 120), a situation that was possible in part because Lawrence's assertion of copyright was denied by then Chancellor Lord Eldon on the grounds that the lectures were blasphemous and consequently not worthy of protection (Jacyna 2004).

Although De Quincey never refers directly to the vitalism/materialism dispute anywhere in his writings, he does skirt it in several ways. Two of the most notable editors of the *Confessions*, for instance, suggest that De Quincey comments directly and derogatorily upon Abernethy and his politics: Grevel Lindop, in both of his editions of the *Confessions* (Oxford World's Classics and Pickering and Chatto), seconds Alethea Hayter's suggestion (in her 1971 Penguin Classics edition) that the surgeon who, De Quincey says, 'bore evidence to [opium's] intoxicating power, such as staggered my own credulity' (*DQW*, II: 46) is in fact John Abernethy. Both editors describe Abernethy as a fellow opium addict, though Lindop stops short of Hayter's additional assertion that Abernethy treated De Quincey. Although De Quincey did provide additional information about the nameless surgeon in his 1856 revision of the *Confessions*, there is no clear substantiation for these hypotheses there. Nonetheless it is intriguing to think that De Quincey might himself have coyly weighed in on Abernethy as a man given to 'talking nonsense on politics' (*DQW*, II: 46), especially given that Abernethy's most public and lastingly remembered political pronouncements were his salvos in the vitalist skirmishes with Lawrence.

De Quincey's passing jokes on medicine and materialism also implicitly hearken to the Vitality Debates. He evinces a facetious temptation to see opium as an immaterial, motivating principle, paradoxically countered by an equally jocular insistence upon its materiality. When he first took it, as he recounts in 'The Pleasures of Opium', he equated it with the biblical water of life (as discussed above). Everything about opium tempts him to view it as a metaphysical principle: Oxford Street on a rainy Sunday appears as 'the Paradise of Opium-Eaters' while a 'dull and stupid . . . mortal druggist' becomes a 'minister of celestial pleasures . . . the beatific vision of an immortal druggist' by association (*DQW*, II: 42). Nonetheless, De Quincey insists, all these things are in fact material after all: opium can be corked up in bottles and sent down by coach, and the druggist 'out of my shilling, returned to me what seemed to be real copper halfpence, taken out of a real wooden drawer' (*DQW*, II: 42). This mock debate over whether opium is a metaphysical force acting upon the soul or a material force acting upon the body suggests that De Quincey is deliberately trivializing the contemporary tendency to tie medical questions to broader debates regarding materialism, a more mediated version of the kind of orthodoxy-challenging gesture he makes by echoing Brown.[13]

In the end, however, it would be a mistake to regard these revolutionary impulses as the cleverly hidden *real* political gist of the *Confessions*. If the present discussion has erred on the side of emphasizing the revolutionary or at least subversive subtext, it is because that dimension is the less discussed rather than because it is somehow the more authoritative. Anyway, most readers of De Quincey would not recognize in him a univocal polemicist; they already know him too well as an elusive, digressive, even sometimes frustratingly evasive ironist. Although John Brown's self-proclaimed 'merit of having reduced the doctrine and practice of medicine to scientific certainty and exactness' (Brown 1803: xiv) and Ricardo's 'laws which ... constructed what had been but a collection of tentative discussions into a science of regular proportions' (*DQW*, II: 64) would have equally appealed to De Quincey's unifying tendencies, so would they presumably have spurred his drive toward erecting a 'barrier of utter abhorrence' between elements whose proximity aggravated his anxieties (*DQW*, II: 70). Similarly, just as De Quincey's acknowledgement of a deep-seated unity between Britain and the East raises troubling questions about the imperial enterprise, so does his recognition of a fundamental identity among socio-economic classes undercut the assumptions at the heart of a class system that would render a term such as 'conservative' meaningful in the first place. To be revolutionary is finally to be reactionary in so far as it pushes back toward a state that existed long before the current one, and just as opium was the catalyst for a corrosive revelation of the unity between East and West, so does it wash away the layers of sediment otherwise obscuring the identity between what Disraeli famously coined 'Two Nations' just four years before 'The English Mail-Coach' appeared. But to say that De Quincey finally breaks down the boundaries between the rich and the poor would belie the degree to which he fails to challenge the distinction at its most basic levels, allowing that he 'had no labours that [he] rested from; no wages to receive' and limiting his boundary-crossing to the sanitized 'sympathizing with their pleasures' (*DQW*, II: 49). It is likewise notable that he fails to come down on either side of the Vitality Debate, or indeed even to acknowledge its terms directly—somewhat ironic at least, given both the closeness with which he skirts those terms and the debate's centrality as a watershed issue in the increasingly intertwined worlds of science and politics. Even his assumption of both Old and New Testament prophetic modes or his seemingly direct echoes of John Brown walk that fine line between reverent imitation and scathing parody, sometimes seemingly with a foot in both camps at once.

Still, though, in his emphasis upon opium's ability to blur such boundaries and increase their permeability, and in his subtle call to restore a lost order to the medical professions, English society, or no less than the cosmos at large, De Quincey shows himself in 'The Pleasures of Opium' as a far more slippery political commentator than the High Tory mouthpiece who has often emerged from De Quincey criticism and biography.

NOTES

1. This chapter is much indebted to the sensitive reading and shrewd advice of several people the author would like to thank here: Carol Engelhardt, Rick Incorvati, Joan Milligan, Robert Morrison, Christopher Oldstone-Moore, Tammy Proctor, and Daniel Sanjiv Roberts. Any remaining faults are the author's own.
2. On a related but slightly different note, Grevel Lindop noted in the standard biography published a quarter of a century ago that De Quincey regarded

Brunonianism, Radicalism, and 'The Pleasures of Opium' 59

conservative and radical agendas as equally desirable and leading to necessary compromise, a strangely uncommitted political philosophy which led to his often 'taking the side assigned to him in the political shadow-boxing, opposing for the sake of opposing.' Lindop, Grevel, *The Opium Eater: A Life of Thomas De Quincey*, London: J. M. Dent, 1981, p. 286.

3. This argument is elaborated in the present author's *Pleasures and Pains*, Charlottesville: University Press of Virginia, 1995.
4. As Roy Porter has said, 'Beddoes was to recognize that illness . . . spoke about absolute and relative distributions of plenty and poverty, of power and oppression, of education and ignorance, succour and neglect. . . . To such a doughty political radical as Beddoes, the techniques of medicine could thereby underpin the causes of popular rights and citizenship, of liberty, equality and fraternity.' Porter, Roy, *Doctor of Society: Thomas Beddoes and the Sick Trade in Late Enlightenment England*, London: Routledge, 1992, p. 2.
5. De Quincey elsewhere uses the same biblically loaded adjective to evoke a similar sense of a sort of gold standard of essential humanity when he notes in 'The Pains of Opium' that 'a young Chinese seems to me an antediluvian man renewed' (*DQW, II*, p. 70). Elsewhere in the present volume, Daniel Sanjiv Roberts expands upon these implications, noting that an unpublished manuscript of De Quincey's acknowledges the theory current in both the German Higher Criticism of the Bible and British Orientalist scholarship that the major world religions all traced their origins to the descendants of Noah, who settled in different parts of the globe following the great flood.
6. This otherwise seemingly iconoclastic reading is arguably consistent with God's own assessment after the cleansing is concluded: 'the LORD said in his heart, I will not again curse the ground any more for man's sake; for the imagination of man's heart is evil from his youth; neither will I again smite any more every thing living, as I have done' (Genesis 8: 21). Rather than a lesson to humanity and an initiation of a new state, then, the flood could be seen as the mistake from which God must learn, the exercise that makes him finally accept the state of humanity that pertained equally both before and after the flood. In other words, it is an 'unrighteous' judgment whose very unrighteousness is obscured by the false rhetoric of cleansing and redemption, a point De Quincey might be seen as subtly underscoring.
7. The trope was perhaps most evident in eighteenth-century cartoons such as those of Gillray and Rowlandson, which often depicted England as John Bull subjected to the dubious practices of politicians depicted as quack doctors. The tradition persisted well into the nineteenth century. See, for instance, Haslam, Fiona, *From Hogarth to Rowlandson: Medicine in Art in Eighteenth-Century Britain*. Liverpool: Liverpool University Press, 1996, and Helfand, William H., 'Medicine and Pharmacy in British Political Prints: The Example of Lord Sidmouth', *Medical History*, 1985, vol. 29, 375–85.
8. Although some of the earliest medical commentators acknowledge what might be called a stimulating effect, even they emphasize the converse. John Jones's introduction (*The Mysteries of Opium Reveal'd*, London: Richard Smith, 1700), for instance, acknowledges an effect 'like a most delicious and extraordinary *Refreshment* of the Spirits upon very *good News*, or any other great cause of *Joy*' or even 'a permanent gentle *Degree* of that Pleasure which Modesty forbids the naming of' (p. 20), but his chapter headings tell a different story, emphasizing 'Inhability, or Listlessness to do any thing', 'A dull, moapish, and heavy Disposition', 'Decay of Parts', 'Weakness of Memory', etc.
9. See, for instance, Grevel Lindop's overview of De Quincey's close but conflicted relationship with the Edinburgh university faculty in his 'De Quincey

and the Edinburgh and Glasgow University Circles', in Jeremy Treglown and Bridget Bennett (eds.) *Grub Street and the Ivory Tower: Literary Journalism and Scholarship from Fielding to the Internet*, Oxford: Clarendon Press, 1998.
10. Although Helen Braithwaite has interestingly argued that Johnson's list was dominated by more moderate titles and his radicalism was more qualified than has previously been acknowledged (*Romanticism, Publishing and Dissent: Joseph Johnson and the Cause of Liberty*, London: Palgrave-Macmillian, 2003), he nonetheless did publish works by the aforementioned authors and did the initial printing if not the final publication of Paine's *Rights of Man*. This milieu at least ensured that Johnson's imprint on Brown's title page would have given the book more than a whiff of radicalism.
11. For this discussion of the Vitalism Debates in general and Abernethy and Lawrence in particular, I am significantly indebted to three sources: Ruston, Sharon, *Shelley and Vitality*, London: Palgrave-Macmillan, 2005, ch. 2; Desmond, Adrian, *The Politics of Evolution: Morphology, Medicine, and Reform in Radical London*, Chicago: University of Chicago Press, 1989, ch. 3; and Butler, Marilyn, in Mary Shelley, *Frankenstein, or The Modern Prometheus: The 1818 Text*, Oxford: Oxford University Press, 1994, introduction.
12. For an overview of De Quincey's references to Shelley in the *Confessions* and his implicit sympathy with at least some elements of Shelley's radicalism, see Robert Morrison's essay in this volume.
13. Paul Youngquist has similarly noted the *Confessions*' emphasis upon materialism, but in more abstractly philosophical terms, describing it as De Quincey's 'first and darkest riposte to Kant's philosophy.... Not philosophy but physiology might best administer the test of living.... Habitual opium eating forces De Quincey to see life physiologically, unencumbered by the ruse of representation and the larger claims of critical philosophy' (Youngquist, Paul 'De Quincey's Crazy Body', *PMLA*, 1999, vol. 114, p. 350).

WORKS CITED

Barrell, John (1991) *The Infection of Thomas De Quincey: A Psychopathology of Imperialism*, New Haven, CT: Yale University Press.
Beddoes, Thomas (1803) 'Observations on the Character and Writings of John Brown, M.D.' in John Brown, *The Elements of Medicine of John Brown, M.D.*, Portsmouth, NH: Daniel Treadwell.
Braithwaite, Helen (2003) *Romanticism, Publishing and Dissent: Joseph Johnson and the Cause of Liberty*, London: Palgrave-Macmillian.
Brown, John (1803) *The Elements of Medicine of John Brown, M.D. Translated from the Latin, with Comments and Illustrations, by the Author. A New Edition, Revised and Corrected with a Biographical Preface by Thomas Beddoes, M.D.*, Portsmouth, NH: Daniel Treadwell.
Butler, Marilyn (1994) 'Introduction', in Mary Shelley, *Frankenstein, or The Modern Prometheus: The 1818 Text*, Oxford: Oxford University Press, ix–li.
Clej, Alina (1995) *A Genealogy of the Modern Self: Thomas De Quincey and the Intoxication of Writing*, Stanford, CA: Stanford University Press.
Desmond, Adrian (1989) *The Politics of Evolution: Morphology, Medicine, and Reform in Radical London*, Chicago: University of Chicago Press.
Haslam, Fiona (1996) *From Hogarth to Rowlandson: Medicine in Art in Eighteenth-Century Britain*. Liverpool: Liverpool University Press.
Helfand, William H. (1985) 'Medicine and Pharmacy in British Political Prints: The Example of Lord Sidmouth', *Medical History*, 29: 375–85.

Jacyna, L. S. (2004) 'Lawrence, Sir William, first baronet (1783–1867)', in Lawrence Goldman (ed.) *Oxford Dictionary of National Biography* (online edition), Oxford: Oxford University Press.
Jones, John (1700) *The Mysteries of Opium Reveal'd*, London: Richard Smith.
Lawrence, Christopher (1988) 'Cullen, Brown and the Poverty of Essentialism', in W. F. Bynum and Roy Porter (eds.) *Brunonianism in Britain and Europe*, London: Wellcome Institute for the History of Medicine.
―――. (2004) 'Brown, John (*bap.* 1735, *d.* 1788)', in Lawrence Goldman (ed.) *Oxford Dictionary of National Biography* (online edition), Oxford: Oxford University Press.
Leask, Nigel (1992) *British Romantic Writers and the East: Anxieties of Empire*, Cambridge: Cambridge University Press.
Lindop, Grevel (1981) *The Opium Eater: A Life of Thomas De Quincey*, London: J. M. Dent.
―――― (1998) 'De Quincey and the Edinburgh and Glasgow University Circles', in Jeremy Treglown and Bridget Bennett (eds.) *Grub Street and the Ivory Tower: Literary Journalism and Scholarship from Fielding to the Internet*, Oxford: Clarendon Press.
McDonagh, Josephine (1994) *De Quincey's Disciplines*, Oxford: Clarendon.
Milligan, Barry (1995) *Pleasures and Pains: Opium and the Orient in Nineteenth-Century British Culture*, Charlottesville: University Press of Virginia.
Morrison, Robert (1998) 'Red De Quincey', *The Wordsworth Circle* 29: 131–36.
Overmeier, Judith A. (1982) 'John Brown's *Elementa Medicinae*: an Introductory Bibliographical Essay', *Bull Medical Library Association* 70: 310–17.
Porter, Roy (1992) *Doctor of Society: Thomas Beddoes and the Sick Trade in Late Enlightenment England*, London: Routledge.
Roberts, Daniel Sanjiv (2000) *Revisionary Gleam: De Quincey, Coleridge, and the High Romantic Argument*, Liverpool: Liverpool University Press.
Ruston, Sharon (2005) *Shelley and Vitality*, London: Palgrave-Macmillan.
Vickers, Neil (2004) *Coleridge and the Doctors, 1795–1806*, Oxford: Clarendon and New York: Oxford University Press.
Youngquist, Paul (1999) 'De Quincey's Crazy Body', *PMLA* 114: 346–58.

4 'Earthquake and Eclipse'
Radical Energies and De Quincey's 1821 *Confessions*
Robert Morrison

Drugs in De Quincey's *Confessions of an English Opium-Eater* are simultaneously poison and cure, public and private, paradise and prison, natural and artificial. Critics for the most part have read the *Confessions* as endorsing De Quincey's deep-seated conservatism. But his political outlook in the text is almost as unstable as his opium intake. De Quincey is a staunch believer in social order who revels in subversion and excess, while his Tory dogma is confounded by his embrace of Cockneys, Whigs, abolitionists, economists, and rebels. Far from promoting John Bullism, the *Confessions* reveal the paradoxes at the centre of his attitude toward class, race, imperialism, and political violence.

In the *Confessions*, De Quincey's conservatism—basically 'imperialist, xenophobic, and defensive'—is well to the fore (Evans 1995: 232). The 'specifically "English" gloss' of the title 'signifies a wish to distinguish himself from other nationalities and cultures' (Baxter 1990: 127). As a 'political conservative', he is careful to disassociate 'his *Confessions* from those of Rousseau, the archetypal apologist for himself, who moreover made self-realization and fulfilment a potentially liberal cause' (Butler 1981: 174–75). Unlike the 'stupefying, vulgar habit of alcohol drinking, opium eating is presented as a refined means of educating the senses in a bid obviously meant to appeal to the aristocratic aspirations of the bourgeois public' (Clej 1995: 63). In his nightly wanderings through London's East End, De Quincey identifies with the working class, but he has anaestheticized himself with opium so that their plight is a spectacle for observation rather than a sting to his social conscience. 'The poor, he glibly maintains, are "more philosophic than the rich"' (McDonagh 1994: 42). The visit of the Malay to De Quincey's Dove Cottage door introduces 'a racial, sexual and social paranoia' into his narrative. 'In a stark contrast to his *repression* of class hatred in London [. . .] De Quincey in this passage mobilizes the full armoury of racial discrimination [. . . .] Skin equals culture' (Leask 1992: 210). When the meeting with the Malay and the frantic Asian nightmares that follow are 'examined on moral grounds', the 'aesthetic pleasure generated by the narrative' is revealed as 'inextricably connected to the Opium-eater's racist designs' (O'Quinn 1999: 161). Indeed, the Malay dream itself is the most lurid index of De Quincey's 'psychopathology of imperialism' (Barrell 1991). In the *Confessions*, a persistent Toryism rises in the finale to jingoism.

Yet De Quincey's delighted confidence in his own Englishness is frequently undermined by sympathies that disrupt the political and social ideologies he is ostensibly bent on affirming. His conflicting loyalties may be explained in part by the magazine context in which the *Confessions* emerged. De Quincey originally intended to publish the work in the truculently Tory *Blackwood's Edinburgh Magazine*. He may have written for the magazine as early as 1817, and a *Blackwood's* ledger-book lists him as a contributor beginning in June 1818 (Leask 1992: 181; Groves 1999: 473–74). De Quincey dated the Malay dream 'May 1818', and its bigoted nationalism is well suited to *Blackwood's*. In December 1820 De Quincey promised William Blackwood an 'Opium article', which was 'very far advanced', and which he was writing 'with pleasure to myself' (Symonds 1994: 63). Within weeks, however, De Quincey quarrelled with Blackwood, and six months later he offered his opium article to *Blackwood's* arch rival, the *London Magazine*, which was patterned on *Blackwood's*, but much more polished, dispassionate, and liberal in tone. Hostilities between the two rival magazines had erupted as recently as February 1821, when *Blackwood's* ally Jonathan Christie and the *London*'s editor John Scott fought a duel in which Scott was fatally wounded (Woodhouse 1998: xv–xx). As De Quincey set to work on completing his opium article, he undoubtedly retained those portions originally intended for *Blackwood's*, and then composed new sections aimed directly at the *London* audience. The result is a *London* text which is simultaneously invested in and critical of the *Blackwood's* context.

Had De Quincey stayed in Edinburgh and continued to write for *Blackwood's*, for example, it seems highly improbable that he would have given London such prominence in his *Confessions*. *Blackwood's* had a broad reach, but it rooted itself in Edinburgh's rich literary, political, and cultural traditions. It had made a name for itself mocking London, especially its Cockney poets. But on the *London* the situation was of course very different. The magazine had been founded to celebrate 'the very "image, form, and pressure"' of London as the great English metropolis, and had consciously set itself in opposition to those 'popular Journals' that were based in the 'secondary towns of the Kingdom', like Edinburgh (Scott 1820a: iv). When De Quincey transferred himself from the Scottish to the English capital, he responded astutely to the change in location, playing up the London and English aspects of his opium experience, and exercising those radical sentiments which were anathema to *Blackwood's*. Long sections of his text are set in London, including his harrowing months on the streets as a teenage runaway, his friendship with the young prostitute Ann, his first purchase of opium from a celestial druggist, his weekend debauches as an Oxford student, his nightly wanderings as he composed his *Confessions*, and his vivid dreamscapes in which Ann reappeared and the two walked together again 'by lamp-light in Oxford-Street [. . .] just as we walked seventeen years

'*Earthquake and Eclipse*' 65

before, when we were both children' (*DQW*, II: 73). *Blackwood's* and the *London* both shaped the *Confessions*, and some of the key paradoxes of the work are informed by their rivalry.

De Quincey in the *Confessions* is both hero and anti-hero. His choice of genre—the confessional discourse—has always been linked with the criminal, the subversive, the forbidden. It 'cannot come from above', as Michel Foucault observes, '[. . .] through the sovereign will of a master, but rather from below, as an obligatory act of speech which, under some imperious compulsion, breaks the bonds of discretion or forgetfulness' (Foucault 1978: 62). De Quincey in the *Confessions* is 'little better than an outcast'. He rejects parental and educational authority to escape from Manchester Grammar School. He lives outside traditional social structures, as a wanderer in Wales and then down and out on the streets of London. He flagrantly subverts the religious associations of the confession in proclaiming 'the doctrine of the true church on the subject of opium: of which church I acknowledge myself to be the only member—the alpha and the omega'. A 'Eudaemonist' and poor sinner, he compounds his guilt by refusing 'self-denial and mortification'. De Quincey 'cannot face misery [. . .] with an eye of sufficient firmness', and will not be frightened 'by a few hard words into embarking [. . .] upon desperate adventures of morality'. His body 'should be had into court'. Is he 'the hero of the piece' or 'the criminal at the bar'? (*DQW*, II: 32, 45, 54–5, 60–1).

De Quincey's racial and aristocratic prejudices co-exist with his intense sympathy for the exiled and the abused. When he flees from Manchester, he has a copy of Wordsworth's *Lyrical Ballads* in his pocket, for its account of convicts, outcasts, idiot boys, mad mothers, and female vagrants made an immense impression on him, and convinced him that Wordsworth was the greatest poet of the modern age. In the *Confessions*, De Quincey presents himself as a philosopher who sees beyond the 'narrow and self-regarding prejudices of birth and education', and who views himself 'in an equal relation to high and low—to educated and uneducated, to the guilty and the innocent'. At no time 'of my life have I been a person to hold myself polluted by the touch or approach of any creature that wore a human shape' (*DQW*, II: 25). Wordsworth's description of the rural poor in *Lyrical Ballads* is transposed into vivid accounts of urban despair. During his teenage months in London, De Quincey's 'partner in wretchedness' is a 'hunger-bitten' girl who lives in a cold, rat-infested house full of ghosts conjured by her imagination (*DQW*, II: 24, 22). At night she creeps close to De Quincey

> for warmth, and for security against her ghostly enemies [. . . .] Whether this child were an illegitimate daughter of Mr ———, or only a servant, I could not ascertain; she did not herself know; but certainly she was treated altogether as a menial servant. No sooner did Mr ——— make his appearance, than she went below stairs, brushed his shoes, coat,

&c.; and, except when she was summoned to run an errand, she never emerged from the dismal Tartarus of the kitchens, &c. to the upper air, until my welcome knock at night called up her little trembling footsteps to the front door. (*DQW*, II: 22–23)

De Quincey fraternizes with Etonians, Oxonians, and aristocrats, and takes a sometimes intoxicated pleasure in roaming amongst the working class. But he also speaks out on behalf of 'plain human nature, in its humblest and most homely apparel' with an immediacy and compassion that clearly anticipates Charles Dickens (*DQW*, II: 24). In the *Confessions*, De Quincey is both hidebound by prejudice and a 'Catholic creature' who deems 'nothing human alien to him' (*DQW*, II: 25, 12, 330).

Prostitution reveals his habitual ambivalence. The circumstantial evidence suggests that De Quincey 'sexually exploited' Ann of Oxford Street, and that his inability to trace her may not have been an accident, for 'where he was going, whether it was to the relatively more upscale and independent life of a gentleman-scholar in London or matriculation at Worcester College in Oxford, Ann simply could not follow' (Rzepka 1995: 141, 147). Yet at the same time De Quincey invests Ann with a nobility that transcends class. Hers is 'a case of ordinary occurrence' in a society that is 'harsh, cruel, and repulsive'. She is cut off from the 'stream of London charity', which though 'deep and mighty, is yet noiseless and underground'. A 'brutal ruffian' has stolen from her, and she is 'timid and dejected to a degree which showed how deeply sorrow had taken hold of her young heart' (*DQW*, II: 25–6). De Quincey plans to plead her case in front of a magistrate, as he does in front of the reader. When he collapses in Soho Square, her generosity and presence of mind save him. Though his future holds severe trials, losing her is the 'heaviest affliction' of his life (*DQW*, II: 36). Charles Lamb—who apostrophized London as 'O City abounding in whores'—teased De Quincey about his experiences on Oxford Street (Lamb 1975: 248). De Quincey did not find it funny.

> "There are," said he, "certain places & events & circumstances, which have been mixed up or connected with parts of my life which have been very unfortunate, and these, from constant meditation & reflection upon them, have obtained with me a sort of sacredness, & become associated with solemn feelings so that I cannot bear without the greatest mental agony to advert to the subject, or to hear it adverted to by others in any tone of levity or witticism. It seems to me a sort of desecration & unhallowing analogous to the profanation of a temple, when these subjects are approached in conversation by any one unless in a feeling of sympathy and seriousness—and I would rather suffer the most excruciating bodily pains, than the shock my whole nature feels at hearing these topics discussed in a ludicrous matter [sic], or made the ground of raillery." (Woodhouse 1998: 22)

De Quincey has been criticised for portraying the 'sufferings of urban experience without acknowledgment of repressive attitudes as the cause of these sufferings or of rebellion as the appropriate response' (De Luca 1981: 16). Yet his sympathetic depiction of prostitutes aligns him most closely with William Blake and his *Songs of Experience*. In the dream sequence that closes the *Confessions*, Ann reappears in the midst of an 'oriental' scene, 'upon a stone, and shaded by Judean palms [. . . .] and I said to her at length: "So then I have found you at last"' (*DQW*, II: 73). The most famous depiction of the East in the climax is of course the Malay dream, which portrays the orient as monstrous. But De Quincey follows it immediately with an eastern setting which 'promises a salvific and regenerative potential', as is argued elsewhere in this collection (see above, Roberts: 31). De Quincey may have exploited Ann. He certainly idealized her. But his account is rooted in the harsh realities of her experience, and his memory of her imbued with deep and genuine personal sadness. She is at once commodity and saviour.

Opium places De Quincey both at the centre and on the margins of his society. His designation of himself as the 'English opium-eater' announces his proud nationalism, yet in the minds of his readers his drug of choice is firmly associated with the East as a result of travel-books, oriental novels, and exotic verse tales. Similarly, while a Turkish opium-eater descends into torpor, and a Malay runs a-muck, and a wine drinker becomes maudlin, a specifically English opium-eater 'feels that the diviner part of his nature is paramount; that [. . .] the moral affections are in a state of cloudless serenity' (*DQW*, II: 45). Yet like many before him, De Quincey relished the bodily delights of opium as well. In the *Mysteries of Opium Reveal'd* (1700), Dr John Jones observes that if after taking opium 'the person keeps himself in action, discourse of business, it seems [. . .] like a most delicious and extraordinary refreshment of the spirits upon very good news, or any other great cause of joy . . . It has been compared (not without good cause) to a permanent gentle degree of that pleasure which modesty forbids the name of' (Booth 1998: 31). Samuel Johnson took the drug for 'rheumatism of the loins [. . .] as a means of positive pleasure whenever any depression of spirits made it necessary' (Boon 2002: 20). The Marquis de Sade was even more to the point about opium and sexuality. 'Regarding my temperament, it had acquired strength over the years, and was now something truly terrifying and always under the control of my mind', he writes in *Juliette* (1797):

> when got properly started, it was absolutely indefatigable. But for the purpose of setting it surely into motion I was coming to rely upon wine and spirits; my brain once spinning, I was capable of anything; I also employed opium and other love-stimulants. . .which were on open and profuse sale in Italy. You ought never to fear irritating your lascivious appetites by such means. (Sade 1968: 658–59)

If opium-eating 'be a sensual pleasure', De Quincey declares in his confession, '[. . .] I am bound to confess that I have indulged in it to an excess' (*DQW*, II: 10). In conjoining 'English' and 'Opium', he shows himself at once domestic and foreign, familiar and exotic, majestic and debauched, clean and contaminated.

In 'The Rhetoric of Drugs', Derrida explores the political implications of addiction. What do we hold against drug addicts? It is not transcendence. We all want that. Rather, it is that they have a taste for simulacra and hallucinations, that they undermine the social bond, that they choose solitude and oblivion over the very world which is the world of all of us. Addiction 'leads to suffering and to the disintegration of the self, in short, it desocializes', Derrida argues. Addicts are exiles, and prohibition is necessary. '*Our* society, *our* culture, *our* conventions' require it. 'Let us rigorously enforce it [. . . .] By prohibiting drugs we assure the integrity and responsibility of the legal subject, of the citizens' (Derrida 2003: 25, 37, 21). As De Quincey's hedonism collapses into dependency, opium comes both to define and obliterate his sense of self. He 'loses none of his moral sensibilities, or aspirations: he wishes and longs, as earnestly as ever, to realize what he believes possible, and feels to be exacted by duty; but his intellectual apprehension of what is possible infinitely outruns his power, not of execution only, but even of power to attempt' (*DQW*, II: 65). Drugs gradually hollow out De Quincey's political will. As they exalt his moral sense, they work simultaneously to divest him of citizenship.

Edmund Burke is quoted twice in the *Confessions*, once from *Reflections on the Revolution in France* (1790) and once from *Letters on a Regicide Peace* (1795–7; *DQW*, II: 9, 61). De Quincey lays siege to the arch-conservatism of these two texts, however, with a broad range of reference to activists and intellectuals who aligned themselves well to the political left of Burke. The Edinburgh physician John Brown developed the Brunonian system of medicine, in which all diseases were classified as 'sthenic' or 'asthenic', depending on whether 'they increased or decreased the state of excitement of the nervous tissue' (Leask 1992: 176). Treatment for most diseases was by stimulation, usually in the form of alcohol and opium. Brown championed his system in opposition to most of the medical and political orthodoxies of the day. His decisive impact on the *Confessions* is explored elsewhere in this collection (see above, Milligan: 45–61). Thomas Erskine was one of six men De Quincey knew, 'directly or indirectly', as an opium-eater (*DQW*, II: 11). An intimate of Whig leaders such as Charles James Fox and Richard Brinsley Sheridan, Erskine was a jurist and longtime MP who stood up for the protection of personal and civil liberties during the Pittite crackdowns of the 1790s. He is best known for his impassioned but unsuccessful defence of Thomas Paine. Just one year before the appearance of the *Confessions*, Erskine rose to prominence again for his role in defending Queen Caroline against government attempts to deprive her of the title of queen. De Quincey praised 'many of Mr Erskine's addresses to juries, where political rights were at stake', and described him as 'the greatest of modern advocates' (*DQW*, XI: 32; XII: 72). Erskine was a thorn in the side of the Tories, but De Quincey held him in high esteem.

Thomas Hope was a man of great wealth, refined taste, and wide experience in art and travel. His only novel, *Anastasius* (1819), caused a sensation, and was widely attributed to 'that prince of wickedness and poetry, Lord Byron', as Mary Russell Mitford put it. 'It's altogether Grecian; is not that like Lord Byron?', she argued.

> It's exceedingly sceptical; is not that like Lord Byron? It complains of a jealous wife; is not that like Lord Byron? It is full of fine and gloomy poetry (in prose), which is of the very same style with Lord Byron's. It is still fuller of the light, derisive mockery—the tossing about of all good feeling, so gibing and so Voltaireish, which no one could or would do but Lord Byron. It is a most uncomfortable book—is not that like Lord Byron? And, lastly, it is all full of the sneering, misanthropic, wretched author; is not that Lord Byron? (Mitford 1870: I. 325–26).

Henry Crabb Robinson complained of the novel's 'uniform wickedness and brutal violence', and described its author as—after Charles Maturin and Percy Shelley—'a third imitator of Lord Byron's horrors' (Robinson 1938: I. 274). The eponymous hero is 'a compilation' of various Byronic heroes, declared *Blackwood's*. He is similarly 'liberal, licentious, learned, brave, impassioned, and misanthropic' (Wilson 1821: 201). In the *Confessions*, De Quincey complains that in the novel there is a 'grievous misrepresentation' of the effects of opium, but he lauds its author as 'brilliant' (*DQW*, II: 45). The reference exploits the contemporaneity and notoriety of *Anastasius*, as well as its close association with the most famously subversive poet of the day.

John Keats was flailed by *Blackwood's* as an uneducated Cockney School mediocrity with ideas well above his social station. The *London* deplored the political motivation of these attacks: 'We consider it one of the worst signs of these, the worst times which England, we are afraid, has ever seen, that the miserable selfishness of political party has erected itself into a literary authority' (Scott 1820*b*: 315). De Quincey agreed. 'To speak conscientiously', he wrote to *Blackwood's* linchpin and close friend John Wilson in November 1820, 'I cannot wholly approve of every thing you have done: what I should most condemn, if I had any right to be your judge, is the harsh (and latterly to my feeling more painful than anything simply harsh— *good naturedly contemptuous*) treatment of Keats' (Symonds 1994: 33–4). *Endymion*, Keats's poetic romance, was described by De Quincey as 'the very midsummer madness of affectation, of false vapoury sentiment, and of fantastic effeminacy'. But he had a high opinion of Keats's epic fragment,

Hyperion, which 'presents the majesty, the austere beauty, and the simplicity of Grecian temples enriched with Grecian sculpture' (*DQW*, XV: 307). As he worked on his *Confessions*, De Quincey requested a copy of Keats's *Lamia, Isabella, the Eve of St Agnes, and other Poems* (1820), and there seem to be at least two echoes of the volume in the *Confessions* (Symonds 1994: 98–9; Lindop 1995: 58–65). One, De Quincey's celestial drugstore which mysteriously evanesces is reminiscent of the magically elusive residence of Lamia and Lycius, for 'none knew where / They could inhabit; the most curious / Were foil'd, who watch'd to trace them to their house'. Two, in the Liverpool reverie, De Quincey's consumption of opium makes him feel 'as if the tumult, the fever, and the strife' were suspended. The phrase clearly recalls 'the weariness, the fever, and the fret' of Keats's 'Ode to a Nightingale', a poem in which he 'similarly contemplates a nocturnal landscape, having characterised his state as "a drowsy numbness" resembling one caused by hemlock or "some dull opiate"' (Lindop 1995: 63). While Keats's work was hooted down by the Tory press, De Quincey appears on two occasions to have given the Cockney upstart a place in the *Confessions*.

John Leslie, mathematician and natural philosopher, was an extreme Whig in his youth, and went on to become an important writer for the *Edinburgh Review*, where he was associated with leading liberals such as Francis Jeffrey and Henry Brougham. In 1805 Leslie's candidacy for the Chair in Mathematics at the University of Edinburgh was opposed by the clergy, who accused him of atheism because of his acceptance of David Hume's notion of causality. Leslie succeeded in obtaining the Chair, 'to the great joy of all liberal minds' (Napier 1842: 246). His opinions eventually brought him into conflict with *Blackwood's*, where he was lampooned in the infamous 'Chaldee Manuscript' (1817), and denounced as impious for his attack on Hebrew as '*the rudest and poorest of all written languages*' (Maginn 1820: 501). De Quincey saw beyond such abuse. He believed that the 1805 charges of atheism against Leslie were 'brought forward with a *practical purpose of partisanship*' (*DQW*, IX: 354). He praised Leslie's conduct in his controversy with the French mathematician Adrien Marie Legendre (*DQW*, X: 176). Leslie appears in the *Confessions* as the 'Scotchman of eminent name' who has 'lately told us, that he is obliged to quit even mathematics, for want of encouragement', a reference to Leslie's best-known work, *Elements of Geometry, Geometrical Analysis, and Plane Trigonometry* (1809), where Leslie regrets that there is 'unfortunately very little incitement to the publication of abstract works in this country' (Morrison 1999: 45–6). Charges of scepticism and whiggery dogged Leslie, but De Quincey was a keen admirer.

William Hazlitt was belligerently committed to the cause of political reform. De Quincey felt an often deep antipathy toward him. '*Whatever is*—so much I conceived to have been a fundamental lemma for Hazlitt—*is wrong*', he asserted. In the margins of his copy of Hazlitt's first major work, *An Essay on the Principles of Human Action* (1805), De Quincey observed

Figure 4.1 Sir John Leslie, by John Kay. National Portrait Gallery, London. Leslie's favourable view of David Hume's doctrine of Cause and Effect led the Edinburgh clergy to insinuate that he was an atheist. In the *Confessions*, Leslie appears as the 'Scotchman of eminent name'.

that the 'very intensity of Thought may perhaps serve to account for the Confusion of Ideas that pervades the whole of Mr H's writings' (*DQW*, XX: 235). Yet De Quincey also acknowledged the 'splendid originality' of Hazlitt, who possessed the 'unresting irritability of Rousseau, but in a nobler shape' (*DQW*, X, 269; XV: 274). Hazlitt's *Reply to the Essay on Population by the Rev. T. R. Malthus* (1807) contained two arguments which De Quincey appropriated without acknowledgement in his essay on 'Malthus', prompting Hazlitt to accuse him of something like plagiarism (*DQW*, III: 168–74). *Liber Amoris* (1823), Hazlitt's obsessional tale of his disastrous love for the teenage Sarah Walker, was a gift to his Tory assassins, who read it as confirmation of the degradation and moral confusion bound to result from a commitment to leftwing politics. 'We call down upon [Hazlitt's] head', *Blackwood's* cried in a savage review, 'and upon the heads of those accomplished reformers in ethics, religion, and politics, who are now enjoying his *chef-d'oeuvre*, the scorn and loathing of every thing that bears the name of MAN' (Lockhart 1823: 646). De Quincey had a very different opinion. 'I must reverence a man', he states, 'be he what he may otherwise, who shews himself capable of profound love'. In the *Confessions*, De Quincey criticizes Hazlitt for not reading 'Plato in his youth' and 'Kant in his manhood'. Yet Hazlitt's philosophical abilities are praised, and despite the strong contemporary tendency to read his highly diverse output through the lens of radical politics, De Quincey accords him the remarkably high position of third in England as a 'subtle' or 'acute thinker' (*DQW*, II: 13).

David Ricardo was one of the leading economists of the day, and a searching analyst of Adam Smith's laissez-faire doctrines. His closest supporters included the philosopher and economist James Mill and the utilitarian philosopher Jeremy Bentham. In 1819 Ricardo became a Member of Parliament, where he espoused Whig principles and voted almost exclusively with the Opposition. Political economy at this time was synonymous with Whiggery, or worse. 'I wish that we may be able to take up our ground as good and sound political economists', Henry Malden wrote to the liberal publisher Charles Knight in 1823,

> and yet show that political economy is by no means necessarily connected with the formal and technical French literary taste, the false and selfish morality, and the contempt of all religion, with which, unhappily, it has been accidentally associated. I wish to show that men may be good political economists, and liberal thinkers in politics, without being raving democrats, without reviling *every*thing old, without renouncing the imagination and all its works, without being selfish and hard-hearted, and without being despisers of God and of all religion. (Clowes 1892: 155–56)

Blackwood's attitude was typical of the conservative press. 'The empire prospered until it became cursed with a swarm of political economists, cold, calculating theorists, and speculative rulers', it complained. More specifically, it ascribed Ricardo's 'peculiar errors in his works on Political Economy [...] as well as his excessive refinement and obscurity, to a morbid desire to be profound and original, unaccompanied by a thorough and clear apprehension of the doctrine he endeavours and wishes to inculcate' (McQueen 1828: 891; Stevenson 1824: 651).

De Quincey was fascinated by political economy, a position—it need hardly be said—highly anomalous in a Tory. He began to study the subject in 1811, but it was not until he read Ricardo's most famous work, *Principles of Political Economy and Taxation* (1817), that he cried eureka. 'All other writers had been crushed and overlaid by the enormous weight of facts and documents', he declared in the *Confessions*; 'Mr. Ricardo had deduced, à *priori*, from the understanding itself, laws which first gave a ray of light into the unwieldy chaos of materials, and had constructed what had been but a collection of tentative discussions into a science of regular proportions, now first standing on an eternal basis' (*DQW*, II: 64). De Quincey's own work as a political economist led the *Standard* newspaper to identify him as 'that most incomprehensible, and preposterous of all things—a Tory political economist' (Tave 1966: 119–20). De Quincey had little interest in the 'potential links between political economy and social reform', and he did his best to soften 'the radical implications of distribution theory as presented by Ricardo' (Henderson 1995: 103). But he had a deep understanding of Ricardian theory, and was committed to popularizing and refining it. His celebration of Ricardo—in the *Confessions* and well beyond—allies him closely with philosophical radicals and forward-looking Whigs.

Figure 4.2 David Ricardo by William Holl. National Portrait Gallery, London. 'Thou art the man!', De Quincey cried in enthusiasm after reading Ricardo's *Principles of Political Economy and Taxation*. Ricardo's economic doctrines were anathema to most Tories.

Thomas Clarkson was a leading abolitionist whose *Essay on the Slavery and Commerce of the Human Species* (1786) galvanized interest in the movement. He played a prominent role in the passage of the 1807 bill to abolish the slave trade, and then devoted himself to the campaign to abolish slavery itself in the British colonies. De Quincey alludes to Clarkson in the *Confessions*, and elsewhere describes him as 'that son of thunder, that Titan, who was in fact the one great Atlas that bore up the Slave-Trade Abolition cause' (*DQW*, II, 58; XI: 214). William Wilberforce was an eloquent and indefatigable parliamentarian, and Clarkson's most important co-agitator in the abolition campaign. De Quincey cites Wilberforce in the *Confessions* as a 'benevolent' man 'of eminent station' known to him as an opium eater (*DQW*, II: 11). Like Hazlitt, De Quincey rated Clarkson far higher than Wilberforce, but paired them as 'the two heroes of this period'. Clarkson 'was the Luther of that reformation; and of Mr Wilberforce it is almost too much to say that he was the Melancthon' (*DQW*, VI: 204–05, 370).

William Roscoe, historian, miscellaneous writer, and Whig politician, was a leading member of Liverpool literary society and another important abolitionist. De Quincey met him during a three-month stay in Liverpool in the summer of 1801. Roscoe, De Quincey snidely recalled years later, possessed 'the feebleness of a mere *belle-lettrist*, a mere man of *virtù*, in the style of his sentiments on most subjects'. His poetry evinced 'the most timid and blind servility to the narrowest of conventional usages, conventional ways of viewing things, conventional forms of expression'. And in his 'political writings, especially those which had connected his name with Burke', Roscoe appeared 'not so much as [...] a feeble man, but absolutely as [...] a man emasculated'. Yet Roscoe also impressed De Quincey. He 'was a politician, took an ardent interest in politics, and wrote upon politics—all of which are facts usually presuming some vigour of mind. And he wrote, moreover, on the popular side, and with a boldness which, in that day, when such politics were absolutely disreputable, seemed undeniably to argue great moral courage'.

As Keats's 'Nightingale' inflects De Quincey's Liverpool reverie, so Roscoe's poem 'Mount Pleasant' (1777) seems clearly to stand behind it (Morrison 2005: 54–6). Like the reverie, the poem is set in Liverpool, where 'lightly fled' Roscoe's 'youthful day', and where De Quincey himself spent a good deal of time as a teenager and young adult. Both speakers situate themselves high above the city, Roscoe on 'an agreeable Eminence', and De Quincey at 'an open window'. Both descriptions are panoramas which encompass the urban landscape and the ocean: Roscoe observes 'the thronging buildings' and 'the beating tide' while De Quincey sees 'the great town' and 'the ocean, in everlasting but gentle agitation'. Both visions move through time, in Roscoe's case from sunrise to sunset and in De Quincey's 'from sun-set to sun-rise'. Both writers have known 'strife', and both regard their position above Liverpool as a kind of haven. Roscoe flies 'to these retreats' while De Quincey feels for the first time 'at a distance, and aloof from the uproar of life'. Their shared perspective above Liverpool has the desired effect:

Roscoe's 'sorrow' is 'sooth'd to rest' while De Quincey enjoys a 'sabbath of repose' (Roscoe 1777: 7, 8, 10, 32; *DQW*, II: 51).

There is, however, a crucial difference between the two descriptions: Roscoe is sober while De Quincey's 'repose' is partially indebted to opium. He numbs himself, and then looks down upon Liverpool, 'with its sorrows and its graves'. And 'if we should ask for a specification of the sorrows and graves [. . .] the answer would have to lie in the material history of Liverpool', which 'more than any other British city waxed fat on the slave trade, employing 132 ships solely for that purpose in 1792' (Leask 1992: 208). De Quincey submerged these references in the reverie, but as he later made clear, he knew all about 'the slave trade, by which so many fortunes were made at that era in Liverpool', and he condemned it categorically: 'of the kidnapping, murdering *slave-trade*, there cannot be two opinions' (*DQW*, X: 4). More pointedly, Roscoe too knew all about the slave trade, and in 'Mount Pleasant' he bitterly denounced it:

> Shame to Mankind! But shame to BRITONS most,
> Who all the sweets of Liberty can boast;
> Yet, deaf to every human claim, deny
> That bliss to others, which themselves enjoy:
>
> [. . .] Yet whence these horrors? this inhuman rage,
> That brands with blackest infamy the age?
>
> (Roscoe 1777: 14).

De Quincey's reverie has been characterized as 'the most eloquent expression in [his] writings of that Wordsworthian faith in a secular and internalized centre of transcendence' (De Luca 1980: 24). But Roscoe's poem is a provocative and politicized antecedent that destabilizes De Quincey's sublime experience. In his confession, De Quincey cannot wholly erase Liverpool's material history, or his own abhorrence of the sorrows and graves of the slave trade.

Percy Shelley was one of the most infamously radical poets of the day. The *London* and other leading magazines like the *New Monthly* steered largely clear of him. The *Edinburgh* ignored him altogether during his lifetime. The *Quarterly* reviews were notoriously malicious. De Quincey, on the other hand, praised him highly. Shelley, 'a brother Oxonian', first came to De Quincey's attention 'by the report of his Oxford labours as a missionary in the service of infidelity'. De Quincey heard that Shelley 'looked like an elegant and slender flower, whose head drooped from being surcharged with rain', a description that 'tallied pretty well' with a 'little Indian sketch of him in the academic costume of Oxford' that De Quincey later saw in London. In 1811 Shelley moved to Keswick and became De Quincey's Lake District neighbour. The two did not meet, a source of regret to De Quincey, who believed that Shelley would have enjoyed browsing through his Dove Cottage library, which was 'rich in the wickedest of German speculations' (*DQW*, XV, 293–94, 291). In 1818 De Quincey read *The Revolt of Islam*, in which Shelley reimagines the events of the French Revolution, and found it displayed 'more ability of a particular sort than he expected, or indeed than he had conceived Shelley [. . .] to possess' (Woodhouse 1998: 24). His enthusiasm for the poem was immediately evident. As editor of *The Westmorland Gazette*, he published a long section from Canto X in August 1818 under the heading 'Famine and Pestilence'. He also wrote a long letter to John Wilson 'stating his judgment' of Shelley's poem, and in January 1819 *Blackwood's* followed De Quincey's lead by publishing 'a flaming article' in praise of the *Revolt* (Morrison 1992: 36–41). 'As a philosopher, our author is weak and worthless', it asserted; '—our business is with him as a poet, and, as such, he is strong, nervous, original; well entitled to take his place near to the great creative masters, whose works have shed its truest glory around the age wherein we live' (*DQW*, XX; 198). The review condemns Shelley's politics, but lengthy quotations from the poem make its revolutionary agenda explicit.

De Quincey quotes the *Revolt* three times in the *Confessions*, and the radicalism of the poem bristles just below the surface of his text. First, as he recollects the morning he prepared to bolt from Manchester Grammar School, Shelley comes to mind. 'At half after three I rose', he writes, 'and gazed with deep emotion at the ancient towers [. . .] "drest in earliest light" and beginning to crimson with the radiant lustre of a cloudless July morning' (*DQW*, II: 16). De Quincey's quotation is drawn from Canto V. As Laon gazes at the veiled Cythna and listens to those nations 'gathered there / From the sleep of bondage', the summit of the 'great Pyramid' shines 'Like Athos seen from Samothracia, dressed / In earliest light by vintagers' (Shelley 2000: 150). Second, De Quincey observes that 'certainly, Mr. Shelley is right in his notions about old age: unless powerfully counteracted by all sorts of opposite agencies, it is a miserable corrupter and blighter to the genial charities of the human heart' (*DQW*, II: 21). De Quincey's source is a politically explicit passage from Canto II:

> Old age with its gray hair,
> And wrinkled legends of unworthy things,
> And icy sneers, is nought: it cannot dare
> To burst the chains which life forever flings
> On the entangled soul's aspiring wings,
> So is it cold and cruel, and is made
> The careless slave of that dark power which brings
> Evil, like blight on man, who still betrayed,
> Laughs o'er the grave in which his living hopes are laid.
>
> (Shelley 2000: 105)

Finally, in the epigraph for 'The Pains of Opium', De Quincey draws again from the revolutionary events of Canto V (*DQW*, II: 61). Laon has entered the 'Imperial House, now desolate'. He sees a 'little child [. . .] very pale and wan', and then 'the fallen Tyrant', who

> with gathered brow, and lips
> Wreathed by long scorn, did inly sneer and frown
> With hue like that when some great painter dips
> His pencil in the gloom of earthquake and eclipse.
>
> (Shelley 2000: 142–43)

De Quincey's Tory prejudices ran deep enough that he always regarded Shelley as an object of both suspicion and regret. But this did not prevent him from extolling Shelley's genius, and embedding within his *Confessions* passages in which Shelley champions a radical vision deeply at odds with De Quincey's professed conservatism.

In his 1847 essay on the iconoclast Walter Savage Landor, De Quincey proudly proclaimed his devotion to John Bull. 'For myself, as perhaps the reader may have heard, I was and am a Tory; and in some remote geological aera, my bones may be dug up [. . .] as a specimen of the fossil Tory'. Yet, he continues, 'for all that, I loved audacity; and I gazed with some indefinite shade of approbation upon a poet whom the attorney-general might have occasion to speak with' (*DQW*, XVI: 11). De Quincey's fossilized conservatism has overshadowed his fascination with criminality, insurrection, and illicitness. His works are riven by these tensions, but nowhere more so than in the 1821 *Confessions*, where his conservative and bohemian impulses collide, and where his dedication to intolerance is complicated by his concern for exiles, slaves, and prostitutes, and his portrayal of the redemptive potentials of the East. De Quincey believed in Toryism, but at the heart of his politics is ambivalence, brought most clearly into view in contexts like the *London*, where his attraction to power is subverted by a wide-ranging series of liberal commitments and radical sympathies.

WORKS CITED

Barrell, John. (1991) *The Infection of Thomas De Quincey: A Psychopathology of Imperialism*, New Haven, CT: Yale University Press.
Baxter, Edmund. (1990) *De Quincey's Art of Autobiography*, Edinburgh: Edinburgh University Press.
Boon, Marcus. (2002) *The Road of Excess: A History of Writers on Drugs*, Cambridge, MA: Harvard University Press.
Booth, Martin. (1998) *Opium: A History*, New York: St. Martin's Press.
Butler, Marilyn. (1981) *Romantic, Rebels and Reactionaries*, Oxford: Oxford University Press.
Clej, Alina. (1995) *The Genealogy of the Modern Self: Thomas De Quincey and the Intoxication of Writing*, Stanford, CA: Stanford University Press.

Clowes, Alice. (1892) *Charles Knight: A Sketch*, London: Richard Bentley and Son.
De Luca, V. A. (1980) *Thomas De Quincey: The Prose of Vision*, Toronto: University of Toronto Press.
Derrida, Jacques. (2003) 'The Rhetoric of Drugs', in Anna Alexander and Mark S. Roberts (eds.) *High Culture: Reflections on Addiction and Modernity*, Albany: State University of New York Press, 19–43.
Evans, Eric. (1995) 'Englishness and Britishness: National Identities, *c.* 1790–*c.* 1870', in Alexander Grant and Keith J. Stringer (eds.) *Uniting the Kingdom?: The Making of British History*, London: Routledge, 223–43.
Foucault, Michel. (1978) *The History of Sexuality, Volume One: An Introduction*, Robert Hurley (trans.), New York: Vintage Books.
Groves, David. (1999) 'De Quincey and the Early Issues of *Blackwood's Magazine*', *Notes and Queries*, 244: 473–74.
Henderson, Willie. (1995) *Economics as Literature*, London: Routledge.
Lamb, Charles, (1975) *The Letters of Charles and Mary Anne Lamb, Volume One*, Edwin Marrs, Jr. (ed.) Ithaca, NY: Cornell University Press.
Leask, Nigel. (1992) *British Romantic Writers and the East*, Cambridge: Cambridge University Press.
Lindop, Grevel. (1995) 'De Quincey's Wordsworthian Quotations', *The Wordsworth Circle*, 36: 58–65.
Lockhart, J. G. (1823) '*Liber Amoris; or, the New Pygmalion*', *Blackwood's Magazine*, 13: 640–46.
Maginn, William. (1820) 'Leslie *versus* Hebrew', *Blackwood's Magazine*, 6: 501–03.
McDonagh, Josephine. (1994) *De Quincey's Disciplines*, Oxford: Oxford University Press.
McQueen, James. (1828) 'The British Colonies; Letter to His Grace the Duke of Wellington', *Blackwood's Magazine*, 23: 891–913.
Mitford, Mary Russell. (1870) *The Life of Mary Russell Mitford, Told by Herself in Letters to her Friends*, A. G. K. L'Estrange (ed.), 2 vols, New York: Harper & Brothers.
Morrison, Robert. (2005) 'De Quincey on "Mount Pleasant": William Roscoe and *Confessions of an English Opium-Eater*', *Notes and Queries*, 52: 54–56.
———. (1999) 'The "Scotchman of eminent name" in De Quincey's *Confessions of an English Opium-Eater*', *Notes and Queries*, 46: 45–47.
———. (1992) 'De Quincey, Champion of Shelley', *Keats-Shelley Journal*, 41: 36–41.
Napier, MacVey. (1842) 'Leslie, Sir John', *Encyclopedia Britannica*, 7th edition, 13: 242–52.
O'Quinn, Daniel. (1999) 'Murder, Hospitality, Philosophy: De Quincey and the Complicitous Grounds of National Identity', *Studies in Romanticism*, 38: 135–170.
Robinson, Henry Crabb. (1938) *On Books and Their Writers*, Edith J. Morley (ed.), London: Dent.
Roscoe, William. (1777) *Mount Pleasant: A Descriptive Poem*, London: J. Johnson.
Rzepka, Charles. (1995) *Sacramental Commodities: Gift, Text, and the Sublime in De Quincey*, Amherst: University of Massachusetts Press.
Sade, Marquis de. (1968) *Juliette*, Austryn Wainhouse (trans), New York: Grove Press.
Scott, John. (1820*a*) 'Prospectus of the *London Magazine*', *London Magazine*, 1: iv–viii.
———. (1820*b*) '*Lamia, Isabella, the Eve of St Agnes, and other Poems*', *London Magazine*, 2: 315–21.
Shelley, Percy (2000). *The Poems of Shelley*, Kelvin Everest, Geoffrey Matthews, Jack Donovan, Ralph Pite, Michael Rossington (eds.), London: Longman.

Stevenson, William. (1824) 'The Political Economist. Essay II—Part I', *Blackwood's Magazine*, 15: 643–55.
Symonds, Barry. (1994) *De Quincey and his Publishers: The Letters of Thomas De Quincey to his Publishers, and other Letters, 1819–1832*, Unpublished Doctoral Thesis, University of Edinburgh.
Tave, Stuart (ed.). (1966) *New Essays by De Quincey: His Contributions to the Edinburgh Saturday Post and the Edinburgh Evening Post, 1827–1828*, Princeton: Princeton University Press.
Wilson, John. (1821) 'Familiar Epistles to Christopher North, *From an Old Friend with a New Face*. Letter II', *Blackwood's Magazine*, 10: 200–06.
Woodhouse, Richard. (1998) 'Richard Woodhouse's *Cause Book*: the Opium-Eater, the Magazine Wars, and the London Literary Scene in 1821', in Robert Morrison (ed.) *Harvard Library Bulletin*, n.s. 9.3: i–xxiv, 1–43.

5 De Quincey and Men (of Letters)
John Whale

I

De Quincey's preoccupation with women has been successfully explored by some of his best critics. In particular, the disturbing proliferation of dead women in his writing and their relationship to his idea of the aesthetic has been examined alongside his speculations on language and the nature of 'style'. Much less has been written on De Quincey's masculinity and how this defines and is embedded in his ideas on literature. In this chapter I want to suggest that De Quincey's relationships with literary men might provide an equally revealing subject of inquiry and one just as important for our understanding of his idea of the aesthetic. To this purpose, I explore his well documented and much debated relationship with William Wordsworth and his 'intimate' friendship with the critic, poet, and fellow *Blackwood's* contributor John Wilson. In both of these problematic relationships De Quincey's idea of masculinity is simultaneously defined by notions of friendship and his concept of literature. In the case of Wordsworth it could be said that De Quincey idealistically fuses friendship and literature together; in the case of Wilson he finds a figure who epitomises and straddles the divide between them.

Attention to De Quincey's disturbing representation of women has produced a sharper understanding of the gendered nature of his conception of writing. Along with other male writers of his period, he has long been seen as an exponent of the feminised imagination searching out its feminine other. In this respect, Thomas McFarland's reference to the 'heroic quest' of De Quincey's 'life and art' stands squarely within a central tradition of Romantic criticism. According to McFarland, 'in no other Romantic figure does the "eternal feminine" draw us further'. Following Baudelaire, he focuses on De Quincey's 'feminine' style, what the French poet refers to more paradoxically as 'la manière pénétrante et *feminine* de l'auteur'(McFarland 1987: 97).[1] For McFarland, the status of 'hero' is conferred on De Quincey in spite of his diminutive stature; he remains an enigma, a feminised man for ever separated from the women he seeks in life and literature: most particularly his sister Elizabeth in *Autobiographic Sketches* and Ann of Oxford Street in *Confessions of an English Opium-Eater*. In identifying De Quincey's preoccupation with women as a condition of loss, McFarland touches on a rich vein of De Quincey scholarship which has also engaged productively on how this loss is fundamentally related to his ideas on language and the proliferation of literature in the early nineteenth century.

In her powerfully perceptive account of De Quincey and women, Angela Leighton confidently concludes that he is no exponent or advocate of 'Romantic androgyny' (Leighton 1992: 160–77). In his disturbing preoccupation with aestheticised images of dead women, she finds rather 'a Romantic aesthete who feels perennially guilty about it'. Across the range of De Quincey's writing, she identifies the violence done to the figure of woman as 'the visionariness of the imagination and the ideology of masculinity' come together in 'destructive collusion'. This disturbing, creative dynamic is particularly apparent once again in De Quincey's idea of 'style' where he poses the 'manliness of the British character' against the preservation of 'the mother tongue' whose character, according to this interestingly specific sociological argument, survives in its idiomatic, racy and delicate form amongst letter-writing unmarried women (Leighton 1992: 164, 177, 166). De Quincey's representation of women is thus, for Leighton, always peculiarly attentive to the social realities of women's lives—for all the elaborate phantasmagoria of his dream-visions. What she very helpfully exposes is the fraught nature of his allegiance to literature, particularly as it is constituted by gender and national identity.

Similarly, by examining De Quincey's ambivalent response to 'the language of books', Mary Jacobus has also defined the gendered nature of his response to 'style'. In particular, she draws attention to his sense of a 'prevalent cultural malaise', a '"contagion of bookishness"' which has 'infected the urban populace through the rise of journalism' and which carries with it a deadly threat residing within language which is capable of collapsing De Quincey's distinction between an 'organology' and a 'mechanology' of style and, as a result, of causing 'a fatal accident in which the feminine (the language of feeling) is the casualty'(Jacobus 1989: 130). In similar vein, Josephine McDonagh identifies in De Quincey's anxiety over the 'excessive production of writing' (and a consequent faulty consumption of content) a metonym for the market: an addictive economy of over-production (McDonagh 1994: 70–71).

De Quincey's preoccupation with and proximity to women, then, can make his 'style', his characteristic signature as a Romantic prose-writer, look either feminine or masculine, depending on the perspective. The fluidity of his acts of imaginative identification not just with women, but with a complex host of feminised orientalist others have also led John Barrell to identify 'a confusion in De Quincey about his own sexual orientation; that his identification with the masculine may be more like a desire for it; that his contempt for the effeminate may be functioning as a disavowal of identification with the feminine' (Barrell 1991: 163). This dynamic and relational aspect of gender identity—masculinity's self-conscious assertion of itself against its correlative—is taken up by Edmund Baxter when he recognises that De Quincey's sense of 'manhood' depends upon and is constituted by its 'recognition of the latent ideal of woman', particularly by the excess of what De Quincey refers to as 'the over reverential feeling, sometimes suddenly developed, towards women, and the idea of women' (Baxter 1990: 61).

Tim Fulford's account of De Quincey within the wider context of masculinity and Romanticism takes Burke's distinction between the sublime and the beautiful and the consequent gendering of 'power' as its basis (Fulford 1999:209). Within this politico-literary genealogy, De Quincey's Burkean inheritance—including what Fulford describes as the 'sublime object of Coleridge'—makes him look like an anxious suppressor of his precursors who 'adopt[s] a masculine, sublime literary style in an effort to win power over himself and his public'; and the extremity of his effort, we are told, even makes him resemble 'Burke and Coleridge gone mad' (Fulford 1999: 213, 209, 219).

In this chapter, my concern is not with De Quincey's masculinity as manifest in his will to power through the sublime, but as he defines himself against and alongside other men in a relational process of self-conscious definition. In short, I want to open up a discussion of how De Quincey sees himself as a man who is also a writer and how his role as a man of letters might be thought to construct or compromise his idea of being a man. As I hope my title suggests, being a man and a man of letters might provoke an anxious and, at the same time, creative sense of authorship within early nineteenth-century print culture.

II

De Quincey's bid for friendship with Wordsworth offers an interesting opportunity to explore the relationship between men in early nineteenth-century literary culture and, more particularly, De Quincey's exploration, in his relationships with literary men, of the boundaries between 'real life' and 'literature'. The friendship was initiated as a result of reading *Lyrical Ballads* and discovering in the poems what he took to be a new understanding of the power of genial feelings. Literature provided the young De Quincey with the spur to form an attachment with the author on the basis that it was capable of pre-empting and determining new modes of feeling and conduct. Wordsworth, he presumes, is a man who has broken free from the usual constraints and conventions of social life. The youthful De Quincey's premise seems to be that the genius evident in these poems radically alters the possibilities not only for the importance of certain feelings, but also for relationships between men. De Quincey's letter makes a number of dangerous assumptions, but perhaps the most significant of these for our purposes is the primacy of literature in determining relationships. As he agonised over the text of his letter, his opening sentence shifted from

> To most men what I am going to say would seem strange; and to most men therefore I would *not* say it; but to you I will, because your feelings do not follow the current of the world

to

> I suppose that most men would think what I am going to say—strange or at least rude: but I am bold enough to imagine that, as you are not yourself 'in the roll of common men', you may be willing to excuse anything uncommon in the liberty I am now taking. (Jordan 1962: 28–30)

In the second version, the quotation from Shakespeare explains the leap in faith and bolsters the poetic provenance of his behaviour. 'Friendship' is the keyword of De Quincey's letter of introduction to Wordsworth. He refers to himself 'soliciting ... friendship', 'humbly sue[ing] for ... friendship', and 'hop[ing] for friendship'; and he is profoundly aware that 'the motives to any intimacy must be mutual' and that his request for 'fellowship with a society' such as Wordsworth's is stretching the bounds of conventional behaviour. He perseveres, however, on the basis that he is 'zealously attached' to the poet's 'moral character'.[2] He ends, significantly, with another twist to the idea of friendship. His implied reference to Coleridge simultaneously moderates and situates his zealous attachment in the context of male friendship:

> And I will add that, to no man on earth except yourself and *one* other (a friend of your's), would I thus lowly and suppliantly prostrate myself.
> Dear Sir!
> Your's for ever,
>   Thomas de Quincey (Jordan 1962: 31)

Often seen as a key text in his hero-worship of the poet in a relationship that included high expectations, profound disappointment, acrimony, and cordial toleration, the letter De Quincey wrote to Wordsworth from Liverpool in 1803 is, perhaps, as notable for its assumption of equality as for its affirmation of the difference between the young worshipper and his idol.[3] In this letter, as we have seen, De Quincey firmly establishes 'friendship' as his object and he is profoundly self-conscious about the nature of his request, realising that he is breaking through the bounds of usual politeness and conventional behaviour between men. Late eighteenth-century friendship's appropriation of religious or spiritual functions, its sacredness, and its inclusion of a 'manly love' transcending heterosexual bonds has been well documented.[4] In this instance, a letter of self-introduction, what in today's terms would be called fan-mail, might be thought to obtrude rather rudely on the idea of friendship and, as we shall see, a conflict between fraternity and hero-worship, between 'martyrdom' or self-sacrifice and a bond of mutual respect haunts the relationship between the two writers. In De Quincey's case, however, this by no means rules out the possibility of a spiritual, quasi-religious aspect to the friendship, one based, to quote Keats, on the 'holiness of the Heart's affections' (Keats 1958: I: 184).

Wordsworth's response is kind, supportive, and welcoming, and he ends with a warm invitation to visit Grasmere. But he does baulk at his young correspondent's request for immediate friendship:

> You will then perceive that the main end which you proposed to yourself in writing to me is answered, viz. that I am already kindly disposed towards you. My friendship it is not in my power to give: this is a gift which no man can make, it is not in our own power: a sound and healthy friendship is the growth of time and circumstance, it will spring up and thrive like a wildflower when these favour, and when they do not, it is in vain to look for it (Wordsworth 1935: 400)

While his metaphor establishes the organic nature of friendship, Wordsworth offers a word of caution about the connection between self and writing. He challenges the alacrity with which De Quincey moves from the poems to the 'moral character' of their author: 'How many things are there in a mans character of which his writings however miscellaneous or voluminous will give no idea. How many thousand things which go to making up the value of a frank and moral man concerning not one of which any conclusion can be drawn from what he says of himself or of others in the Worlds Ear' (Wordsworth 1935: 401). If the analogy between friendship and a 'wildflower' confirms a belief in the natural, unforced nature of friendship, it also suggests a degree of fragility, even precariousness. De Quincey's mistake, it seems, lies in the moral enthusiasm with which he seizes on the example of *Lyrical Ballads* as a means of collapsing the boundaries between literature and life; of using the stylized manifestation of 'real feelings' as a way of forcing himself upon Wordsworth's actual feelings and the private, organic workings of male friendship.

When relations between De Quincey and Wordsworth became strained in the 1820s and 1830s, the challenge to fraternity exposed the fault-lines in a relationship fostered by hero-worship or idolisation, but seeking reciprocal intimacy. Faced with what he clearly saw as De Quincey's breach of trust in publishing reminiscences of their friendship, Wordsworth's 'smoldering resentment' is evident in a comment he made in the margin of Barron Field's biography of him. Here Wordsworth focuses on the artificial instigation of their friendship. Claiming that De Quincey had 'written under the influence of wounded feelings' and had committed a 'breach of the laws of hospitality', he angrily concluded that 'a man who [could] set such an example . . . I hold to be a pest in society, and one of the most worthless of mankind'. Tellingly, he reveals that: 'My acquaintance with him was the result of a letter of his own volunteered to me';[5] a revelation which confirms his view that it was a forced and therefore inauspicious mode of initiating a friendship.

In his own disappointed retrospect on their relationship, De Quincey came to see Wordsworth as someone whose egocentric nature made it impossible for him to enter into fraternal intimacy. He described him now as 'a *mixed* creature, made up of special infirmity and special strength'. His presiding flaw was his 'one-sidedness', his '*einseitig*' (*DQW*, XI: 258, 257). His description of the poet's ego chimes with the more famous contemporary accounts of Wordsworth's psychology in relation to the poetic, including Keats's phrase 'egotistical sublime', but it appears under the more specialised question of male friendship. For De Quincey, Wordsworth appears to have been

> a man so diffused amongst innumerable objects of equal attraction, that he had no cells left in his heart for strong individual attachments. I was not singular in this feeling. Professor Wilson had become estranged from him: Coleridge, one of his earliest friends, had become estranged: no one person would be deemed fervently his friend. (*DQW*, XI: 255)[6]

Just as De Quincey's daring request for friendship with Wordsworth was bolstered with a reference to Coleridge so, too, his retrospect of their relationship needs the corroboration of another friend. But, as we shall see, John Wilson provides a point of orientation not only for De Quincey's disappointment with the older poet, but for his sense of masculinity's role within his idea of literature. As he explores the exact nature of his negative feelings towards Wordsworth and reviews the correlation between his motives and what he sees as his strange incapacity for intimate friendship as opposed to a socially cordial relationship, De Quincey answers the charge of having been unfair in his literary treatment of his more famous friend. He admits that his reader may harbour 'the suspicion' of his

> having, at times, yielded to a private prejudice, so far as to colour my account of Wordsworth with a spirit of pique or illiberality. I shall acknowledge then, on my own part—and I feel that I might even make the same acknowledgement on the part of Professor Wilson (though I have no authority for doing so)—that to neither of us, though, at all periods of our lives, treating him with the deep respect which is his due, and, in our earlier years, with a more than filial devotion,—nay, with a blind loyalty of homage, which had in it, at that time, something of the spirit of martyrdom, which, for his sake, courted even reproach and contumely; yet to neither of us has Wordsworth made those returns of friendship and kindness which most firmly I maintain that we were entitled to have challenged. [. . .] I acknowledge myself to have been long alienated from Wordsworth; sometimes even I feel a rising emotion of hostility—nay, something, I fear, too nearly akin to vindictive hatred. Strange revolution of the human heart! (*DQW*, XI: 62)[7]

The structure of this revolution in feeling—from worship to sacrifice and from celebration to guilt—is, in all its frightening abruptness, a familiar one in De Quincey's most famous writings. Many of his explorations of murder are premised on just such proximity: the flimsy domestic boundaries which stand between the individual and his or her violent destruction, between innocence and guilt. One of the most resonant sentences in *Confessions of an English Opium-Eater* ends its Orientalist nightmare with a hauntingly fragmented set of parallel clauses: 'I was the priest; I was worshipped; I was sacrificed.' Here, the 'revolution' takes the form of an inversion of subject/object relations in its terrifying narrative of the self. Reflecting on the ruin of his intimate friendship with former idol Wordsworth, De Quincey offers the following cautionary advice to his reader:

> 'Put not your trust in the intellectual princes of your age'; form no connexions too close with any who live only in the atmosphere of admiration and praise. The love or the friendship of such people rarely contracts itself into the narrow circle of individuals [. . .] Gaze, therefore, on the splendour of such idols as a passing stranger. Look for a moment as one sharing in the idolatry; but pass on before the splendour has been sullied by human frailty . . . (*DQW*, XV: 224)

The pain and disappointment of negotiating between literature, literary fame, and personal experience is clearly evident in such a passage, but De Quincey's advice to his reader exposes a more general intellectual problem in maintaining a healthy distance between literary power and human contact. For a writer whose most compelling texts, including 'The English Mail-Coach' and *Autobiographic Sketches*, spell out the awful implications of a moment's looking, the collusiveness of being a mere spectator, this is horribly ironic. In his instruction to 'gaze' as a 'passing stranger' and 'look for a moment as one sharing in the idolatry' he also advocates a difficult act of dissembling which hovers uneasily between belief and pretence; a combination which is in grave danger of offending against his deeply held conviction of literature's profound connection with sincerity and the almost religious connection between deep feelings and truth.

In retrospect, De Quincey realises, as it were, that the initial 'revolution' in feelings he thought he had discovered in the example of *Lyrical Ballads*—a whole-hearted, moral revelation effected by the genial power of poetry—has given way to a more reserved, sceptical separation: a split between the worshipper and the idol, between literature and life.

III

De Quincey declared in print that 'Professor Wilson [was] the only very intimate male friend I have had' (*DQW*, II: 73).[8] As Grevel Lindop has astutely pointed out, there was 'something symbiotic in the relationship and it flourished' (Lindop 1978: 165). Symbiosis was intensified, as Robert Morrison has noted, by a strange parallelism:[9] as students at Oxford at the same time, they had prided themselves on their personal 'discovery' of Wordsworth and both had earlier sought and succeeded in initiating a friendship with the poet as a result of sending him a letter. In many obvious ways, however, the two men were poles apart in terms of their relationship to conventional notions of masculinity; Wilson was tall, extrovert, and athletic, De Quincey, diminutive, scholarly, and reclusive. In the light of such an intense set of conflicting patterns determining the relationship between the two men it is not surprising that De Quincey's published responses to John Wilson are characterised by anxiety and evasiveness. Writing about a close friend might in itself be thought sufficient to engender such a response, but, as I hope to demonstrate, they betray a more widespread anxiety on De Quincey's part about the nature of masculinity and, more particularly, about the identity of masculinity within his contemporary literary culture.

For De Quincey, Wilson is problematically and symptomatically an 'ambidextrous' creature, a man who inhabits the intersection between the physical and the intellectual. (In this, as we have seen, he offers a sharp contrast to Wordsworth's 'one-sidedness'.) Considering the enormous contribution he made to *Blackwood's*, De Quincey deploys a metaphor that encapsulates his anxious response to his friend's physical prowess and presence. 'Wilson', he writes, 'was its intellectual Atlas'. The phrase immediately highlights a combination of body and mind which haunts, as we shall see, De Quincey's published responses to his friend. And when he goes on to celebrate Wilson as the 'creator' of the magazine's identity embodied in its 'great innovating principle' of 'oscillat[ing] pretty equally between human life on the one hand and literature on the other' he also highlights his anxiety about a division between 'literature' and 'life' which recurs in his estimate of his close friend (*DQW*, XVII: 36). For De Quincey, then, Wilson comes to represent a troubling masculine presence which inhabits the boundary of the literary and which focuses many of his own anxieties as a man and as an author. Precisely because of his 'versatility' and his 'ambidextrous' nature, John Wilson occupies, for De Quincey, a liminal position in the realm of letters. His authority to write on the subject of natural history, for example, as De Quincey makes clear at the beginning of the first article he published on him, derives from first-hand experience, not from books; and elsewhere he writes that his friend 'had won all his knowledge . . . by direct experience, troubling himself little about books' (*DQW*, XIII: 419). Wilson's is, for De Quincey, a decidedly organic, experiential knowledge, pointedly and positively defined against book-learned scholarship. It derives from 'personal observation', 'affections' and 'instincts' as opposed to the 'second-hand acts of memory' which characterise the 'bookish naturalist'. In many ways, Wilson operates as a point of comparison or contrast, but there is always the possibility, because of the coincidence of the year of their birth, of Wilson being considered a double or alter ego, as, for example, when De Quincey claims to be 'so old a friend of Mr. Wilson that I take pride in supposing myself the oldest [. . .] we are almost *ad apicem* of the same age' (*DQW*, VII: 5). Once again, De Quincey draws attention to his 'intimacy' with Wilson: an intimacy which seems peculiarly mobile even as it is conjured as an authority.

This ambivalence about the status of literature and its relationship to masculinity is apparent in the three articles which constitute the 'Sketch of Professor Wilson' De Quincey published in the *Edinburgh Literary Gazette* in 1829. In typical indirect fashion, the 'Sketch' employs an epistolary fiction and is addressed to an anonymous American friend. The use of such a correspondence to reflect on and project the nature of British masculinity is, I would argue, a key component in De Quincey's discourse of gender. As we have seen, the letter is deeply embedded in his thinking about the gendered nature of writing. In addition, this genre provides him with a necessary critical distance as well as the possibility of refracted self-projection. The first of the three articles begins with an extended digression on the physical presence of men and a diatribe as to whether this is a worthy object of attention for men of learning. Here, De Quincey catalogues his disappointment at the way in which literary worthies, including his illustrious contemporaries and heroes, Wordsworth and Coleridge, have failed to transcend a meanness of spirit which allows them to persist in an infantilising curiosity about the physical stature of their fellow men. From his 'earliest years', De Quincey informs us, he has 'considered the interest which men, grown men, take in the personal appearance of each other as one of the meanest aspects under which human curiosity commonly presents itself' (*DQW*, VII: 6). '[N]o man commands me, no man prepossesses me, by any thing in, on, or about his carcass' he states vehemently before concluding that he 'disclaim[s] and disdain[s] any participation in such green-girl feelings'. He then proceeds to detail how even the most eminent intellectuals have failed to rise above such a demeaning curiosity, his account culminating in a revealing comic anecdote about Wordsworth who, he claims, had stated that 'he would not go ten yards out of his road to see the finest specimen of man (intellectually speaking) that Europe had to show', but that 'he would still exert himself to a small extent (suppose a mile or so) for the sake of seeing Belzoni', a celebrated strong-man and explorer (*DQW*, VII: 7).

In *Confessions of an English Opium-Eater* De Quincey plays with his reader's curiosity on precisely this point. Having melodramatically invoked the biographical tendency of his readership with a visual description of his cottage and his library, including the details of the decanter holding his laudanum, he suddenly stops at the prospect of revealing himself:

> . . . but as to myself,—there I demur. I admit that, naturally, I ought to occupy the foreground of the picture; that being the hero of the piece,

> or (if you choose) the criminal at the bar, my body should be had into court. This seems reasonable: but why should I confess, on this point, to a painter? or why confess at all? If the public (into whose private ear I am confidentially whispering my confessions, and not into any painter's) should chance to have framed some agreeable picture for itself, of the Opium-eater's exterior,—should have ascribed to him, romantically, an elegant person, or a handsome face, why should I barbarously tear from it so pleasing a delusion. . . . (*DQW*, II: 60–61)

Such mockery of what he perceives to be the reading public's tendency to focus on the corporeality of the author provides further evidence of De Quincey's sense of the degree to which a prurient and demeaning curiosity about the body has infiltrated his contemporary literary culture.

What De Quincey focuses on in the case of Wordsworth and Coleridge is not just the disappointment of finding his literary idols subject to frailty of judgement. He identifies a structural problem with the nature of early nineteenth-century masculinity. As he informs us, the motive for such a digression is not only his anxiety to 'put on record his own opinions', but to register his 'contempt for men generally in this particular' (*DQW*, VII: 8). In a characteristically interesting manoeuvre, De Quincey positions himself within the feminine realm of letter-writing so that he is able to rail against the shortcomings of his own sex. The problem with men, as he sees it, is that they have not properly grown up. As he pithily puts it:

> The sum of the matter is this: all men, even those who are most manly in their style of thinking and feeling, in many things retain the childishness of their childish years: no man thoroughly weeds himself of all. And this particular mode of childishness is one of the commonest, into which they fall the more readily from the force of sympathy, and because they apprehend no reason for directing any vigilance against it. (*DQW*, VII: 7)

De Quincey's advocacy of maturation here, his sense of the incapacity of men who are unable to grow up, stands in stark opposition to his more celebrated identification with children and his own self-fashioning in this respect. Grevel Lindop and Judith Plotz, for example, have explored his seemingly conscious decision to be seen as a kind of 'child-man'.[10]

When De Quincey returns to the subject of his 'intimate' friend later in his career he continues to view him as a something of a test-case for the interface between literary culture and a more robust form of physical manliness. Once again, Wilson provides De Quincey with a fascinating example of a man not simply caught between two cultures, two modes of life, but someone who illustrates the dangers of being arrested in the process of maturation, what De Quincey refers to as 'the transitional state from boyhood to manhood':

he divided his time and the utmost sincerity of his love between literature and the stormiest pleasures of real life. Cock-fighting, wrestling, pugilistic contests, boat-racing, horse-racing, all enjoyed Mr Wilson's patronage; all were occasionally honoured by his personal participation. I mention this in no unfriendly spirit toward Mr Wilson; on the contrary, these propensities grew out of his ardent temperament and his constitutional endowments—his strength, speed, and agility: and being confined to the period of youth—... can do him no dishonour amongst the candid and the judicious. '*Non lusisse pudet, sed non incidere ludum.*' [11] (*DQW*, XI: 229)

Although he goes on to celebrate Wilson's 'generosity of mind' in this youthful phase by reference to the 'old English chivalric feeling' exemplified in Robin Hood and the courage with which he 'throws himself fearlessly upon his own native powers, as man opposed to man', there remains a lurking suspicion that the transition from 'real life' to 'literature' and from 'youth' to 'manhood' is more troubled and difficult, that the claim for its being 'relieved and emphatically contrasted by his passion for literature' might not be so simple a story. The fact that the 'Sketch' contains two promises to provide an account of 'the particular position [Wilson] occupies in modern literature', but that De Quincey took another twenty years to fulfil the obligation, itself points to a problem (*DQW*, XI: 229–30, VII: 26–7).

De Quincey clearly identified Wilson as someone defined and limited by his attachment to manly sports and as a man inveterately connected with the prowess and the knowledge of his body. 'No man', he wrote, 'was a better judge upon questions of bodily prowess; and no man, at least no gentleman, was better acquainted with the records of the Fancy, as delivered by Mr Pierce Egan' (*DQW*, XIII: 420). Despite his powerful insinuations that Wilson's attachment to the body represents the danger of not growing up and that this is a recognisable and common characteristic of 'manly men', De Quincey was sometimes willing to defend this robust masculine culture against the false refinements of literature: 'In everything Mr Wilson shewed himself an Athenian. Athenians were all lovers of the cockpit; and, howsoever shocking to the sensibilities of modern refinement, we have no doubt that Plato was a frequent better at cockfights' (*DQW*, XI: 230). On occasion, De Quincey even used the slang language of 'the Fancy': an indication, perhaps, not only of the influence of his friendship with Wilson, but of his need to attach himself occasionally to a more corporeal and robust form of national masculine identity.[12]

If De Quincey's published accounts of Wilson point to a deep-seated ambivalence of response to his 'most intimate' friend, a much more obviously fraught aspect to their relationship, especially in 1821, is evident from the records provided by Richard Woodhouse.[13] Here, it transpires, De Quincey conducted what Robert Morrison has defined as a 'policy of treacherous duplicity' and a 'concerted and malicious attack on Wilson' which reveals some degree of paranoia and real fear on De Quincey's part. In order to curry favour with the editors of the *London Magazine* at a key moment in his career De Quincey, it seems, is willing to sacrifice his friend, but the inference is strong that it was, at this point at least, a friendship beset with rivalry and with the real threat of Wilson exposing the embarrassing details of De Quincey's private life, if not publicly, then at least to the Wordsworths.[14] Here again, De Quincey positions Wilson on the boundary between masculine, organic, animal sensibility and literary culture, but this time, apparently, the transition between the two is not envisaged as an act of maturation, but as a fall from innocence. Instead of growing up, Wilson's passage into the literary is seen as corrupting and as involving a loss of emotional integrity:

> The opium-eater described Wilson as an acquaintance of his of long standing, and said that he would have been the best & kindest creature breathing, but for his being a literary man & a Poet. He was originally possessed of much feeling & enthusiasm. (Morrison 1998: 7)

In this reported private context, to be a 'literary man' is to forfeit the openness and geniality that belongs to the 'manly man'.

IV

In the first of his 'Letters to a Young Man whose Education has been Neglected', published in the *London Magazine* in 1823, De Quincey responds to Coleridge's advice in chapter eleven of *Biographia Literaria* 'never to pursue literature as a trade'. While at odds with what he sees as Coleridge's championing of a literary amateurism, he takes the opportunity to present his own version of the 'clerisy'. If literature is not to 'decay', he argues, there must be 'a class *wholly* dedicated to that service, not pursuing it as an amusement only with wearied and pre-occupied minds'. Men from 'our overstocked trades and professions', he urges, should 'compose a garrison on permanent duty for the service of the highest purposes which grace and dignify our nature' (*DQW*, III: 48). While seeing the production of this specialist literary elite as a matter of urgent national importance, however, he has some serious concerns about the limits of literary knowledge. His own intellectually secure foundation in the realm of knowledge, he confidently informs us, has produced a life of 'happiness' in what he claims to have been in an unprecedented state of 'solitude'. Such security rests on a training which ranges across a variety of knowledges, however, and De Quincey reveals his worry about those who might dedicate themselves exclusively to literary or aesthetic concerns. The 'dilemma', as he sees it, for the 'student of pure literature' is that he will be reduced to a 'mere man of taste' and, consequently, that 'his understanding must find a daily want of some masculine exercise to call it out and give it play'. Without recourse to severer studies such as mathematics and philosophy, disciplines 'which present such difficulties as will bend to a resolute effort of the mind' and are capable of 'stimulat[ing] and irritat[ing] the mind to make that effort', there is always the danger of suffering 'cravings of an unsatisfied intellect' and of being 'thrown upon some vulgar excitement of business or pleasure'. '[C]o*ntinuous* thinking and study' are, he claims, capable of 'support[ing] the spirits by perpetual influxes of pleasure, from the constant sense of success and difficulty overcome'(*DQW*, III: 44, 45–6). For De Quincey, masculinity is characterised by competition, conflict, and self-consciousness and defined by metaphors which introduce a sense of the physical and the corporeal in what are otherwise purely intellectual activities. What he also establishes quite clearly is masculinity's dynamic nature: its constant process of testing and being tested. This, in turn, is productive of a healthy psychology and is likely to lead to happiness.

This profoundly gendered sense of what he perceives as the need to bolster the otherwise dangerously effete and feminine domain of the literary by recourse to philosophy or political economy is also reflected in his distinction between the 'literature of knowledge' and 'the literature of power' and in his deep-seated sense of literary power as the product of resistance overcome.[15] It is also evident in his description of the interaction between the subjective and objective in the act of writing where he claims that:

> The exuberance of *objective* knowledge—that knowledge which carries the mind to materials existing *out* of itself, such as natural philosophy, chemistry, physiology, astronomy, geology, where the mind of the student goes for little and the external object for much—has had the effect of weaning men from subjective speculation, where the mind is all in all, and the alien object next to nothing; and in that degree has weaned them from the culture of style. (*DQW*, XII: 66–67)

Once again, De Quincey's metaphor of 'weaning' is indicative of his attachment to the notion of masculine identity and, particularly, its need to be disciplined into maturity. For such an inveterate autobiographer, he maintains a developed critique of the dangers of introspection, seeing it as tending towards both the infantile and the feminine. As we have already seen, 'style' for De Quincey inhabits a particularly fraught and precarious position within his idea of literature and its relationship to gendered identity.

When he came to refine his ideas on the nature of literature and the distinction he had drawn in 1823 between the literature of power and the literature of knowledge in a review of the works of Pope, De Quincey confirms his subscription to an affective view of art which celebrates sincerity over artificiality and sees the truth of feeling as a quasi-religious justification of the aesthetic. And he does so in terms which recall the correlation between life and literature he had made in his analysis of John Wilson's robust and physical masculine presence:

> Were it not that human sensibilities are ventilated and continually called out into exercise by the great phenomena of infancy, or of real life as it moves through chance and change, or of literature as it recombines these elements in the mimicries of poetry, romance, &c., it is certain that, like any animal power of muscular energy falling into disuse, all such sensibilities would gradually droop and dwindle. It is in relation to these great *moral* capacities of man that the literature of power, as contradistinguished from that of knowledge, lives and has its field of action. (*DQW*, XVI: 337)

De Quincey's division between 'literature' and 'real life'—best illustrated in his ambivalent response to his friend John Wilson—provides, on the one hand, an interestingly gendered account of the need for the realm of letters to be compensated for its inherent femininity; and, on the other, it presents the man of letters, in the manner of De Quincey himself, as a mature, autonomous and self-sufficient being who can celebrate the achievement of his solitude: a state of maturity and purity in which the primitive and debasing particularity of the body—what he refers to disparagingly as a man's 'carcass'—can be left behind.

This division is mirrored in the case of De Quincey's associate and fellow journalist William Hazlitt, but in Hazlitt's case, instead of an implicitly gendered account of the difference between the realm of letters and the realm of 'life', there is a highly explicit, sexualised account.[16] For Hazlitt, at his most disappointed at the time of the events recorded in *Liber Amoris*, to have been a man of letters is to have forfeited one's masculine sexual power and to have been duped into the fiction of romance. At this particular point in his life, 'Literature' is seen by Hazlitt to have effected an almost conspiratorial deception about the real nature of sex and sexual appetite; and, consequently, to have hidden the 'true' nature of women. He details his position in a letter of advice to his son—in itself a fascinating document of the way in which such anxiety about masculinity is relayed not just 'between men', but between fathers and sons. Rather than a letter to a young man whose education has been neglected, Hazlitt's text is a letter which suggests that 'education', particularly a literary education, is capable of traducing one's masculine identity, of translating the sexualised body of a man into no more than a tissue of quotations:

> Authors . . . feel nothing spontaneously . . . nothing stirs their blood or accelerates their juices or tickles their veins. Instead of yielding to the first natural and lively impulse of things, in which they would find sympathy, they screw themselves up to some far-fetched view of the subject in order to be unintelligible. Realities are not good enough for them,

till they undergo the process of imagination and reflection ... They are intellectual dram-drinkers; and without their necessary stimulus, are torpid, dead, insensible to every thing. They have great life of mind, but none of body. They do not drift with the stream of company or of passing occurrences, but are straining at some hyperbole or striking out a bye-path of their own. Follow them who list. Their minds are a sort of Herculaneum, full of old, petrified images;—are set in stereotype, and little fitted to the ordinary occasions of life (Hazlitt 1978: 217–18).

While De Quincey's writings don't contain anything quite like this level of self-hatred vented on the figure of the author, they do display a similarly deep-seated anxiety about the degree to which the profession of literature might constitute a threat to one's manliness. And although De Quincey might conjure by way of compensation an image of achieved self-sufficing solitude to match Hazlitt's idea of 'living to one's self', his reflections on friendship with male authors also recognise the dangers of depending solely on letters and, consequently, of becoming removed from 'the ordinary occasions of life'.

NOTES

1. Baudelaire 1993: 169.
2. Daniel Sanjiv Roberts has seen the emotional tenor of De Quincey's letter—particularly the emphasis on spiritual values and 'moral character'—as an indication of his Evangelical leanings at this period of his youth and his eagerness for Wordsworth's friendship as typical of the manner of an 'Evangelical epistolary fraternizer' (Roberts 2002: 5). De Quincey himself later described his attitude to Wordsworth as 'in no respect short of a religious feeling: it had indeed all the sanctity of religion, all the tenderness of a human veneration' and his 'devotion' as being like 'a primitive Christian amongst a nation of pagans' (*DQW*, X: 239, 246).
3. See: Jordan 1962: 14–16, 28–32; Lindop 1981: 103–05.
4. See: Sharp 1986: 113–14; Taussig 2002: 29, 89, 91, 93.
5. See Jordan 1962: 347.
6. Henry Crabb Robinson also records that: 'De Quincey said Wordsworth is very 'secular, 'he loves no one but his own family.' 'he is incapable of friendship towards any' (Robinson 1938: I. 96).
7. See also Lindop 1981: 333. Coleridge's contrasting sense of the sacredness of friendship even in the midst of fraternal break-down is evident from the following quotation: '... It is not in my nature to love those, who after my whole manhood's service of faithful self-sacrificing Friendship have wantonly stripped me of all my comfort and all my hopes—and to hate them is not in *my* nature' (British Museum Add. MS 47,520 fol 84).
8. De Quincey also stated in 1826 that: 'I had known him most intimately for 17 years' (*DQW*, XIII: 419). In a letter to Alexander Blair in 1809 Wilson describes De Quincey as '[a]n intimate friend of Wordsworth's' (Swann: 39). (See Brotherton MSS, University of Leeds, John Wilson Autograph Letters, vol 1, 1809–1842.)
9. For a more detailed account of the context of the relationship between the two writers which engendered in De Quincey a mixture of 'great hostility and

enduring affection', see Morrison 2000 where he considers their shared backgrounds, the possibility of their shared opium habit, and Wilson's role in shaping his friend's writings for *Blackwood's*.
10. See Lindop 1981: 365; Plotz 2001: 129–190.
11. The quotation is from Horace, *Epistles* 1.14.36: 'no shame in having played childish games, shame would be in not having put a stop to them'.
12. See Lindop 1981: 187.
13. See Morrison 1998: 9, 3.
14. See Morrison 1998: xx–xxi. The rivalry seems to have centred on poetry and Wilson seems to have taken a dominating stance by insisting that De Quincey 'stick to metaphysics'. See Morrison 1998: 18. De Quincey's fear of Wilson's exposing him is registered in his statement that 'there are quarters through which he can wound me'. See Morrison 1998: 18.
15. See Whale 1984: 40–58; McDonagh 1994: 71–90; Bate 1993: 137–50; Roberts 2002.
16. See Whale 2005: 56–67.

WORKS CITED

Barrell, John. (1991) *The Infection of Thomas De Quincey: A Psychopathology of Imperialism*, New Haven, CT: Yale University Press.
Bate, Jonathan. (1993) 'The Literature of Power: Coleridge and De Quincey', in Tim Fulford and Morton Paley (eds.) *Coleridge's Visionary Languages: Essays in Honour of J. B. Beer*, Cambridge: Brewer.
Baudelaire, Charles. (1993) *Les Paradis Artificiels*, ed. Claude Pichois, Paris: Folio.
Baxter, Edmund. (1990) *De Quincey's Art of Autobiography*, Edinburgh: Edinburgh University Press.
Fulford, Tim. (1999) *Romanticism and Masculinity: Gender, Politics, and Poetics in the Writings of Burke, Coleridge, Cobbett, Wordsworth, De Quincey and Hazlitt*, London and New York: Macmillan.
Hazlitt, William. (1978) Herschel Moreland Sykes, Willard Hallam Bonner and Gerald Lahey (eds.), *The Letters of William Hazlitt*, London: Macmillan.
Jacobus, Mary. (1989) *Romanticism, Writing, and Cultural Difference*, Oxford: Clarendon Press.
Jordan, John E. (1962) *De Quincey to Wordsworth: A Biography of a Relationship*, Berkeley and Los Angeles: University of California Press.
Keats, John (1958) *The Letters of John Keats 1814–1821*, 2 vols. ed. Hyder Edward Rollins, Cambridge, MA: Harvard University Press.
Leighton, Angela. (1992) 'De Quincey and Women', in Stephen Copley and John Whale (eds.), *Beyond Romanticism: New Texts and Contexts 1789–1832*, London: Routledge, 160–77.
Lindop, Grevel. (1981) *The Opium-Eater: A Life of Thomas De Quincey*, London: J.M. Dent.
McFarland, Thomas. (1987) *Romantic Cruxes: The English Essayists and the Spirit of the Age*, Oxford: Clarendon Press.
McDonagh, Josephine. (1994) *De Quincey's Disciplines*, Oxford: Clarendon Press.
Morrison, Robert. (1998) 'Richard Woodhouse's *Cause Book*: the Opium-Eater, the Magazine Wars, and the London Literary Scene in 1821', *Harvard Library Bulletin* ns, 9:3.
———. (2000) '*Blackwood's* Berserker: John Wilson and the Language of Extremity', *Romanticism on the Net* 20, http://users.ox.ac.uk/~scat0385/20morrison.html
Plotz, Judith (2001) *Romanticism and the Vocation of Childhood*, New York: Palgrave.

Roberts, Daniel Sanjiv. (2002) 'Not "Forsworn with Pink Ribbons": Hannah More, Thomas De Quincey, and the Literature of Power', *Romanticism on the Net* 25, http://users.ox.ac.uk/~scat0385/25roberts.html
Robinson, Henry Crabb. (1938) *On Books and their Writers*. 3 vols. Edith J. Morley (ed.), London: J. M. Dent.
Sharp, Ronald A. (1986) *Friendship and Literature: Spirit and Form*, Durham NC: Duke University Press.
Swann, Elsie. (1934) *Christopher North John Wilson*, Edinburgh: Oliver and Boyd.
Taussig, Gurion. (2002) *Coleridge and the Idea of Friendship, 1789–1804*, Cranberry, NJ, London, Mississauga: University of Delaware Press and Associated University Presses.
Whale, John. (1984) *Thomas De Quincey's Reluctant Autobiography*, Beckenham and Totowa NJ: Croom Helm and Barnes and Noble.
———. (2005) 'Hazlitt and the Selfishness of Passion', in Uttara Natarajan, Tom Paulin, and Duncan Wu (eds.) *Metaphysical Hazlitt: Bicentenary Essays*, London: Routledge, 56–67.
Wordsworth, William. (1935; revised 1967) in Ernest De Selincourt and Chester L. Shaver (eds.), *Letters of William Wordsworth and Dorothy Wordsworth I: The Early Years 1787–1805*, Oxford: Clarendon Press.

6 Wooing the Reader
De Quincey, Wordsworth and Women in *Tait's Edinburgh Magazine*
Julian North

The new edition of De Quincey's collected *Works*, displaying for the first time the full range of his writing for the periodical press, his textual revisions and some of the many fraught negotiations with his editors, suggests that the conditions under which his writing was produced and published will become an important context for reappraising his work. Views of De Quincey have already begun to be shaped by the growth of critical interest in relations between Romanticism, the reading public and the literary marketplace. There has recently been an emphasis on his admissions of anxiety and loss of control in the face of the new readerships and the commercialization of publishing. Lucy Newlyn has presented him as wary of the reading public and the publishing industry, placing him at the centre of a high Romantic 'anxiety of reception' attendant on a proliferation of literary production that threatened to overwhelm the power of the author (Newlyn 2000: 45–8). Cian Duffy has argued that his criticism is influenced by his fear of the rise of the novel, allied to the expanding, middle-class readership, whom he regarded as a 'revolutionary social insurgency', threatening the literature of 'Power' (Duffy 2005: 8). For De Quincey, if the author submitted to this audience, it was in an act of 'treachery', akin to that in his childhood dream of 'lying down before the lion', a betrayal of 'the aristocracy of "Power" to the reading "mob"' (Duffy 2005: 20–21).[1] Others have acknowledged another De Quincey, a canny journalist, adeptly rather than anxiously responding to his medium and to his audience. John Whale, for example, discussed his creation of a magazine persona, working with and against the author-reader relationship as constructed in the *London Magazine* and *Blackwood's* (Whale 1985); and Robert Morrison and David Higgins have shown how he adapted his political and critical views to the radical, reforming ethos of *Tait's Edinburgh Magazine* (Morrison 1998; Higgins 2005: 85–9).

It is important to recognise De Quincey's statements in relation to the reading public, in his magazine journalism, as themselves constructions of and communications with the audience for whom he is writing at that moment. In this chapter I re-examine his attitude to his readers by paying close attention to the publishing context of his work, focusing on the ways in which his extensive series of auto/biographical essays, the 'Sketches of Life and Manners; from the Autobiography of an English Opium Eater', appearing in *Tait's Magazine* between 1834–41, and especially the 'Lake Reminiscences' (1839), were tailored to their audience.[2] William Tait founded his magazine, a month before the Reform Bill of 1832, as a radical, Benthamite journal, 'directly countering the Toryism of its chief Scottish rival *Blackwood's*' (*DQW*, IX: 303) and promising to bring to a popular audience a 'more matured discussion of public affairs than can be expected in the daily and weekly journals'.[3] In February 1834 *Tait's* reduced its price from the already low 2/6 to one shilling, thereby extending its readership from the middle-classes to literate artisans (Houghton 1987: 478).[4] De Quincey's adaptation of his writing to the radical reformist agenda of the magazine may be seen not only in explicit political commentary, but in his efforts to woo the new readerships it targeted. This is especially evident in his writing about Wordsworth, who was a central presence in the *Tait's* essays and crucial to De Quincey's thinking on the contemporary author-reader relationship.

Focusing on the essay 'On Wordsworth's Poetry' (*Tait's* 1845), Newlyn and Duffy argue that De Quincey, like Wordsworth, sought to defend his ideal of the literature of 'Power' from a public he viewed as 'hostile and undiscerning' (Newlyn 2000: 176). For De Quincey, writing in 1823, 'All, that is literature, seeks to communicate power; all, that is not literature, to communicate knowledge' (*DQW*, III: 71).[5] The literature of power was opposed to 'books of knowledge' (*DQW*, III: 70) as, in Jonathan Bate's words, 'writing which must be judged according to the criterion of significant form, that is to say, on the basis of aesthetic more than cognitive effect' (Bate 1993: 142). De Quincey's conception of power was influenced by Wordsworth's 'Essay Supplementary to the Preface' (1815), but we need to recognise the ways in which he diverged from Wordsworth in the relationship between author and audience he implied.[6] For Wordsworth, power was opposed to popularity and the 'PUBLIC' taste (Owen and Smyser 1974: 3, 84).[7] It was a quality beyond the capacities of most readers to recognise immediately, and for this precise reason it was where the value of a work of literature inhered. But in both De Quincey's major statements on the literature of 'Power' in 1823, for the *London Magazine* and for the *North British Review*, in 1848, this argument was absent. Indeed, it is notable that in these essays, in a way quite different to Wordsworth's stance, De Quincey adopted the position of the reader, rather than the writer, when describing the effects of power:

> Now, if it be asked what is meant by communicating power, I in my turn would ask by what name a man would designate the case in which I should be made to feel vividly, and with a vital consciousness, emotions which ordinary life rarely or never supplies occasions for exciting, and which had previously lain unawakened, and hardly within the dawn of

consciousness—as myriads of modes of feeling are at this moment in every human mind for want of a poet to organize them?—I say, when these inert and sleeping forms *are* organized—when these possibilities *are* actualized,—is this conscious and living possession of mine *power*, or what is it? (*DQW*, III: 71)[8]

Contrary to Duffy's argument, De Quincey defended the novel as a popular form in 1823 and, in 1848, included it in the category of the literature of 'Power'.[9] By looking at the complete cycle of 'Sketches' and 'Reminiscences' within the *Tait's* context, we can see him interrogating the relationship between Wordsworth and his readers, and the balance of power in the author-reader relationship more generally.

An examination of the ways in which De Quincey's 'anxiety of reception' issues strategically in his practice as a magazine journalist will also lead us to re-evaluate his representations of women. The female figures in his writing have often been discussed as autobiographical projections, especially of guilt and violence, but the *Tait's* 'Sketches' and 'Reminiscences' reveal an interest in women as the representative writers and readers of the contemporary literary marketplace.[10] Duffy draws attention to passages in 'Style'(*Blackwood's*, 1840–41) in which De Quincey satirised the new readerships, imagined as ill-educated females (Duffy 2005: 14–16).[11] But in his substantial body of work for *Tait's* he took a quite different attitude to his female readers, showing his awareness of the magazine's particular interest in this audience constituency. Uniquely, for a national monthly journal, *Tait's* was co-edited by a woman. The novelist, critic and journalist, Christian Johnstone (1781–1857), had worked on the magazine from its beginnings, but took over as active editor and as a major contributor from June 1834–46.[12] Johnstone continued William Tait's efforts to make this a journal of the people, but shifted the balance of articles from the political to the literary and introduced a distinctive focus on women's issues.[13] Throughout her articles and those of fellow contributors, there was a strong interest in the female perspective and a feminist advocacy of reform in the social, political and legal position of women.[14] As Alexis Easley has shown, for Johnstone, 'the question of how to promote social justice for the working classes was inextricably linked to the problem of how to empower women within literary and political realms' (Easley 2004: 71). She published work by Harriet Martineau, Catherine Gore, Eliza Lynn Linton, Mary Russell Mitford, Amelia Opie and Mary Howitt, amongst others.[15] In her editorials, her short reviews contained in the monthly 'Literary Register', and in longer articles and reviews she was able to showcase women's writing and to discuss female genius and the condition of women more generally.[16] Whilst she sometimes assumed a female audience in her writing—as did other writers for the magazine—she worked within a community of writers and readers that she and fellow contributors typically constructed as male.[17] Nevertheless, as Easley demonstrates, Johnstone's anonymity as editor of and writer for the magazine allowed the question of the gender-perspective of the journal to remain open:

> During the 1830s, *Tait's* became a multi-layered text, capable of being read by multiple audiences from diverse class- and gender-based perspectives, while at the same time maintaining its identity as a reformist periodical aimed primarily at middle-class men. Reading with and against the grain, readers could uncover explicit and implicit dialogues over class and gender that both confirmed and challenged the dominance of men as writers and editors in the discourse on social reform (Easley 2004: 72).

This is an important if little-recognised, context for reading De Quincey's essays.[18] He continued to publish in the Tory *Blackwood's,* but his new connection with *Tait's* from 1833 meant that he was also producing material for a radical journal whose reformist agenda was based on actively, if ambiguously, courting a broad-based audience in terms of class and gender. Robert Morrison has suggested that working for *Tait's* gave him the opportunity to moderate his Tory politics and to vent 'the compassionate and rebellious side of his political ideology' (Morrison 1998: 134), but the *Tait's* context also had significant effects on his projection and discussion of the reader-author relationship and on his portraits of the literary men and women of the age.

The 'Sketches' and 'Reminiscences' were characterised by an awareness of the reader-constituency addressed by the magazine.[19] De Quincey wrote with the aim of attracting a broad audience with a wide spectrum of educational backgrounds. When the 'Sketches' were originally projected as a series for the *London Magazine,* in the early 1820s, he already imagined them as answering the needs of a readership seeking not just entertainment, but education—he would give 'special attention', he said, 'to communicate in every No. some knowledge that the reader is likely to value' (*DQW*, X: xiii).[20] As composed for *Tait's,* the early 'Sketches', particularly, with their disquisitions on Oxford University and the philosophy of Kant, were clearly still directed at this kind of readership.[21] His own persona, as projected in the essays, contributed to his stance as educator of the populace. In the *Confessions* he had stressed his social mobility, as a bourgeois gentleman who, chameleon-like, adapted to all walks of life, and was as capable of conversing and sympathising with the aristocracy, as with the street-child or common prostitute. The 'Sketches' showed him moving between bourgeois, aristocratic and intellectual circles. There was an element of appeal here to an aspirational middle-class audience, with tales of his schoolboy friendship with 'Lord W—' [Westport] and his encounter with the King—but he also tells his readers how, on coming to manhood, he renounced this hierarchical world as one in which he would always be an outsider, for a life of 'Peace, liberty to think, solitude' (*DQW*, X: 211). He enters the republic of letters, significantly, not as a writer, but as a reader. The 'Sketches' and 'Reminiscences' describe De Quincey's formative years, not as the preparation for creative genius, but as the Odyssey of a reader, journeying from his childhood browsing in his father's library, to his life-changing encounters with the works of Kant, Coleridge and Wordsworth, and especially, of course, '"the ray of a new morning"' that dawned after opening *Lyrical Ballads* (*DQW*, X: 287). In these episodes De Quincey was vaunting his exceptional powers as a reader, suggesting that, having mastered Greek, German philosophy, and, above all, recognised the genius of Wordsworth so precociously, his unique range of knowledge and critical acumen fitted him to instruct the aspirational readership of *Tait's*.[22] But the exceptional reader is a less distant figure than the exceptional writer and scattered comments suggest a conscious effort by De Quincey to signal support for a democratization of reading. Early on in the series he argues strongly for public right of access to national copyright libraries and suggests that even he had benefited from being introduced to great literature in more accessible forms (*DQW*, X: 34–6). The first of his many allusions to his unique insight into Wordsworth's genius follows a recollection of having come to a knowledge of eighteenth-century poetry, as a young man,

> . . . through those pleasant miscellanies, half gossip, half criticism—such as Warton's *Essay on Pope,* Boswell's *Johnson,* Mathias's *Pursuits of Literature,* and many scores beside of the same indeterminate class—a class, however, which do a real service to literature, by diffusing an indirect knowledge of fine writers in their most effective passages, where else, in a direct shape, it would often never extend. (*DQW*, X: 145)

As we shall see, his self-projection as friend of the popular readership is central to his essays on Wordsworth.

De Quincey's working relationship with Johnstone, and his awareness of the prominence she was giving to women's writing and gender issues in the magazine also appears to have had a distinct influence on the content of his articles for *Tait's*.[23] His memoirs of the male Lake poets, especially Coleridge and Wordsworth are the best-known of these essays, but the 'Sketches' and 'Reminiscences' also include accounts of his meetings with Hannah More, Mary Lamb, the first biographical portrait of Dorothy Wordsworth and an extended account of the life of Elizabeth Smith.[24] De Quincey scattered his articles with numerous, enthusiastic allusions to female authors including Mary Wollstonecraft, Susan Ferrier, Frances Trollope, Mary Mitford, Joanna Baillie, Elizabeth Hamilton, Mrs Inchbald, Sophia and Harriet Lee, Ann Radcliffe and Christian Johnstone herself.[25] He also mentioned his encounters with a number of other literary ladies—Mrs Green ('the Saracen's Head'), with whom he and the Wordsworths dined (*DQW*, XI: 168–71), the novelist Margaret Cullen, and her sister Mrs Millar (*DQW*, XI: 184–91), Sarah Ponsonby and Lady Eleanor Butler (the 'ladies of Llangollen') (*DQW*, XI:

213). The inclusion of this material, in itself, suggests his efforts to appeal to the female readership courted by Johnstone. By following her editorial policy with regard to women's writing, his decision to place his sketches of the male Lake poets besides portraits of the literary women of the Lakes also countered an exclusively masculine conception of genius and implied that male and female genius were deserving of comparable attention. His recollections of Wordsworth were, in practice, a joint memoir of the poet and his sister. He wrote of Dorothy Wordsworth, very much in the Johnstone style, that she 'would have merited a separate notice in any biographical dictionary of our times, had there even been no William Wordsworth in existence' (*DQW*, XI: 108). The ways in which De Quincey represented these literary women in relation to himself and to their male counterparts, raised issues relating to reading, writing and gender that intersected with the themes that typified the writing for *Tait's*.

The model of the author-reader relationship with which De Quincey most closely associated his own practice was that of a courtship—an initial submission of masculine power, on the part of the writer, rewarded by the reader's feminine indulgence. Early on in the 'Sketches', he described the attainment of manhood as defined by the onset of 'the reverential feeling, sometimes suddenly developed, towards woman, and the idea of woman . . . . when the ideal of womanhood, in its total pomp of loveliness and purity, dawns like some vast aurora upon the mind' (*DQW*, X: 90). His illustrative anecdote suggests a connection between this dawning and a fantasised relationship between himself and his magazine readers. Aged fourteen and onboard a boat, in the company of his aristocratic school friend, he is publicly humiliated by a middle-aged blue-stocking who recognises the social inequality between the two boys. The experience leaves him tongue-tied until he is rescued by a beautiful young woman, herself aristocratic, who then repays his gratitude with her own blushes. His rescuer, compared to Spenser's warrior maiden, Britomart, allows him to complete the ritual courtly love exchange of submissive for dominant roles, by becoming an indulgent audience for De Quincey's public performance:

> . . . my replies were no longer stifled in noise and laughter. . . . literature was extensively discussed; and that is a subject which, offering little room to argument, offers the widest to eloquent display. I had immense reading; vast command of words, which somewhat diminished as ideas and doubts multiplied; and speaking no longer to a deaf audience, but to a generous and indulgent protectress, I threw out, as from a cornucopia, my illustrative details and recollections. . . . I remained the lion of that company which had previously been most insultingly facetious at my expense . . . (*DQW*, X: 92).

The episode implies a conservative vision of social harmony, promoted by an alliance of the bourgeoisie and the aristocracy, and, in its final resolution, a conservative sexual politics. But the courtly exchange between reader and writer becomes associated in the course of his essays, with a critique of the author-reader relationship, in which the aristocratic, masculine 'Power' of the poet stands aloof from the reader and the marketplace. The rival models are most fully present in his representation of the relationship between De Quincey and Wordsworth.

De Quincey's own first (and last) relationship with Wordsworth, as represented in the 'Reminiscences', is as his reader[26], but the courtly exchange is thwarted from the outset. De Quincey courts Wordsworth, with a self-immolating intensity that is never fully reciprocated. In the first of the 'Reminiscences' he looks back to 1803 and his youthful reverence for Wordsworth as a 'nympholepsy', figuring the poet as the feminine and unattainable object of the reader's desire (*DQW*, XI: 43). In another passage the genders are reversed, but the poet still remains in a position of splendid—and destructive—dominance—'the very image of Wordsworth, as I prefigured it to my own planet-struck eye, crushed my faculties as before Elijah or St Paul' (*DQW*, XI: 45). At their first meeting in Westmoreland, De Quincey figures himself as Semele, incinerated by Zeus's lightening (*DQW*, XI: 49). It is an ominous opening to the reader-writer relationship and one that prefigures De Quincey's sense in the 'Reminiscences' that both he and Professor Wilson—Wordsworth's earliest and for many years, as De Quincey tells it, his only readers—were ultimately treated with indifference.[27] He had hoped, at first, to talk with Wordsworth 'on something like equal terms, as respected the laws and principles of poetry' (*DQW*, XI: 46), but Wordsworth eventually failed to make 'those returns of friendship and kindness' he believed he, and Wilson deserved (*DQW*, XI: 62). The relationship is represented, from the vantage point of 1839, as irretrievably damaged:

> ... by error, more or less, on one side or the other, either on Wordsworth's in doing too little, or on mine in expecting too much.... *now*, I find myself standing aloof, gloomily granting (because I cannot refuse) my intellectual homage, but no longer rendering my tribute as a willing service of the heart, or rejoicing in the prosperity of my idol! (*DQW*, XI: 62–3)

This is a comment on a personal rift between the two men, but the withdrawal of De Quincey's heartfelt tribute cannot be fully dissociated from his earlier forecast that Wordsworth's poetry will have an enduring power to touch 'the human heart' (*DQW*, XI: 61). Whilst De Quincey, writing in the late 1830s, works from the premise of Wordsworth's fame, he returns again to one of his favourite themes: the poet's early failure to attract an audience.[28] The frequency with which he mentions this in the *Tait's* articles may be read in several ways. It is, in part a means for De Quincey to assert his unique critical acuity, by contrast with the obtuse or vindictive responses of the periodical press of the time. It may also be read in the context of

Wordsworth's 'Essay Supplementary to the Preface', as a defence of Wordsworth's own position, that an initial failure in popularity is, itself, a sign of the original genius of a literary work. Yet, in conjunction with the representation of the poet's relationship with De Quincey and other readers, it raises the question of Wordsworth's degree of responsibility to his audience.

With wry humour, De Quincey narrates Wordsworth's life as a fairy tale of liberation from the constraints of the marketplace. Supported by a series of providential windfalls, he inhabits a fantasy world of pre-industrial patronage (*DQW*, XI: 96–102). That it is an illusion is clear, for his early problems with publishing have never entirely disappeared. De Quincey informs his readers on several occasions that his great philosophical poem is, for reasons never stated, still in manuscript.[29] In paraphrasing and quoting from this poem, as the basis for a substantial portion of his biographical narrative, he displays his own power to publicise Wordsworth's work in the periodical press. It is significant, in this light, that De Quincey reminds his *Tait's* readers that it is not Southey's poetry which '*made the pot boil*', but his prose in the *Quarterly Review* (*DQW*, XI: 122), and states that 'with all his immeasurable genius, Wordsworth has not, even yet, and from long experience, acquired any popular talent of writing for the current press' (*DQW*, XI: 98). As one who, manifestly, *has* acquired such a talent, De Quincey sets out to prove it to his audience even as he represents Wordsworth's refusal to concede to their needs. He does so, crucially, by demonstrating what has been a running theme of the essays: the congruence of a writer's relationships with his public and with women.

Both Coleridge and Wordsworth are represented as deficient, compared to De Quincey, in submitting to the female communities who support them, and this becomes a sign of their inability to woo the reader. In 1823 De Quincey had disputed Coleridge's argument, in the *Biographia Literaria*, that literature should never be pursued as a trade and his account of the part-time writer who could devote three hours in the evening to the pursuit of literature, whilst in the 'social silence' of female relatives. Querying the sociability of such a silence and the absence of noisy children, De Quincey presented himself, by contrast, as happy to listen to his female relatives, thereby signalling his disapproval of a model of authorship that isolates itself from the very readers upon whom it is dependent (*DQW*, III: 47–8). He developed this theme in his *Tait's* essays on Coleridge, as I have shown elsewhere (North 2003), but also made Wordsworth's lack of chivalry a keynote of his character and his relationship with his readers. Wordsworth's masculinity is presented as unyielding—his 'character, in all its features, wore a masculine and Roman harshness' (*DQW*, XI: 197). De Quincey recalls his own and Professor Wilson's astonishment that he could ever have submitted himself to the 'self-surrender' of courtship:

> That self-surrender—that prostration of mind, by which a man is too happy and proud to express the profundity of his service to the woman

of his heart—it seemed a mere impossibility that ever Wordsworth should be brought to feel for a single instant. . . . There never lived the woman whom he would not have lectured and admonished under circumstances that should have seemed to require it; nor would he have conversed with her in any mood whatever without wearing an air of mild condescension to her understanding (*DQW*, XI: 93).

Unlike De Quincey, who rhapsodises on his own awakening love for Margaret, his future wife, Wordsworth 'had not the feelings within him which make this total devotion to a woman possible' (*DQW*, XI: 93).[30] He could never forget himself sufficiently to indulge in this worship of the opposite sex, to 'burthen himself with a lady's reticule, parasol, shawl, "or anything that was hers." He needed '[f]reedom—unlimited, careless, insolent freedom—unoccupied possession of his own arms—absolute control over his own legs and motions' (*DQW*, XI: 73). It is an image of the sublime self-containment of the poet. In a passage directly following this he made the connection between Wordsworth, his public and his lack of chivalry, in a way that he retrospectively judged to be too pointed to go into print.[31] The passage contains two anecdotes. The first illustrates Wordsworth's lack of public esteem in 1810, as evidenced by a dinner party conversation in which a stuttering lawyer says he has made 'a d-d-d-amnation fool of himself' in his poems (*DQW*, XI: 579). The second is of a quarrel between William and Dorothy. De Quincey, walking in the darkness along a Lakeland road, unwillingly overhears an irritable exchange between the poet and his sister. The only phrase he relays to us is from Dorothy: 'O <brother> William, I will walk by myself' (*DQW*, XI: 581). In embarrassment, De Quincey avoids joining them. It is another example of Wordsworth's deficiencies in his relationships with women, this time in the form of an ironic commentary on the sibling relationship as represented by himself in 'Tintern Abbey', from which De Quincey quotes in the passage (*DQW*, XI: 579). It suggests, in juxtaposition with the preceding dinner-party gossip, that he has the capacity to alienate not only the general public but also his truest readers.

A running theme in the later 'Sketches' is the failure of either Coleridge or Wordsworth to impress their female neighbours with their writing. De Quincey's own, amicable relations with the female social networks in the Lakes give him an insight into how unpopular the work of both Coleridge and Wordsworth is with this potential audience of women. Although fully aware of the existence of their work, they refuse to read it. The refusal is politically motivated—the Misses Cullen and Mrs Millar, Scottish sisters, influenced by the *Edinburgh Review*, will not mention either author or have anything to do with them (*DQW*, XI: 184–5).[32] We might expect some censure of this devotion to the *Edinburgh Review*, which is, earlier in the series, taken to task for its vindictive sabotage of Wordsworth's early career and which was one of *Tait's* main rivals. But De Quincey comments that the prejudices of the Misses Cullen and Mrs Millar would only have been confirmed if they had read Coleridge's *The Friend*, nominated the Delphic Oracle, on account of its obscurity, by the daughter of the Bishop of Llandaff, a judgment De Quincey thinks justified on the grounds of Coleridge's 'shocking want of adaptation to his audience' (*DQW*, XI: 186).

Wordsworth's lack of feeling for his public is most overtly criticised by De Quincey in terms of the poet's deficiencies as a reader and, more specifically as a reader of contemporary fiction by women. His contempt for books generally is a theme of the essays and clearly one of the means by which De Quincey competitively ingratiates himself with his audience.[33] The 'extreme limitation of his literary sensibilities', helped on by his natural '*one-sidedness, (einseitigkeit,)*' (*DQW*, XI: 96) means that

> Thousands of books, that have given the most genuine and even rapturous delight to millions of ingenuous minds, for Wordsworth were absolutely a dead letter—closed and sealed up from his sensibilities and his powers of appreciation, not less than colours from a blind man's eye (*DQW*, XI: 96–7)

He is especially dismissive of female novelists. De Quincey, who believes that two of Harriet Lee's *Canterbury Tales* are 'absolutely unrivalled as specimens of fine narration' (*DQW*, XI: 257), lends 'The German's Tale' to Wordsworth, who 'for once, having, I suppose, nothing else to read ... condescended to run through it'. The poet's verdict is merely that it leaves 'an uncomfortable impression of a woman as being too clever' (*DQW*, XI: 257). Wordsworth reads Ann Radcliffe's *The Italian*, 'by some strange accident ... only to laugh at it' (*DQW*, XI: 258). De Quincey's outrage at these reactions chimes with the championship of women's writing encouraged by Johnstone in *Tait's*. The poet's lack of appreciation for women's fiction, combined with his unaccountable preference for the morally 'disgusting' novels of Smollett, Fielding and Le Sage, convince De Quincey of his 'defective sympathy ... with the universal feelings of his age' (*DQW*, XI: 258).[34] The passage shows how De Quincey expresses an enthusiasm for contemporary popular fiction by women that is, precisely, directed *against* the Wordsworthian aristocracy of 'power', and towards engaging the sympathies of a broadly-based readership.[35]

By contrast to his portrait of Wordsworth and as a mark of his solicitude towards the readers of *Tait's*, De Quincey sets out to demonstrate throughout the 'Reminiscences', his own chivalrous devotion to women and especially his affinities with Wordsworth's female associates. He arrives in Westmorland, as the travelling companion of Mrs Coleridge, in the role of protector of women. Temporarily diverted by his first sight of Wordsworth, he confesses that he forgot to hand her down from the carriage, but, having passed into Wordsworth's cottage, his sympathies with the feminine perspective re-establish themselves:

> A little semi-vestibule between two doors prefaced the entrance into what might be considered the principal room of the cottage. It was an oblong square, not above eight and a half feet high, sixteen feet long, and twelve broad; very prettily wainscotted from the floor to the ceiling with dark polished oak, slightly embellished with carving. (*DQW*, XI: 50)

The 'stunned' poet-worshipper descends to a prosy catalogue of interior décor. De Quincey here, as everywhere in his *Tait's* essays, intercuts the sublime and the prosaic—the mathematical mode (a parody of the famously tedious narrator of 'The Thorn') continues at intervals during these essays—he even counts the stairs ('fourteen in all') as he is led up to the dining room ('It was not fully seven feet six inches high') (*DQW*, XI: 54). The home is where the poet becomes flesh—a transition which interests De Quincey throughout his biographical writing. In the prolonged account of Wordsworth's body that follows, the weaknesses of the flesh at once suggest that genius is and is not transcendent. This double perception is what mediates genius to a popular readership and publicly reminds Wordsworth of what De Quincey at one point calls 'the *human* tenure' of his 'mighty blessings'—something, he argues, that the poet needs to recall (*DQW*, XI: 101). Such passages make a specific appeal to the female reader. Johnstone included lengthy descriptions of interiors, fabrics and female fashions in her reviews and valued literature which opened up a feminine, domestic perspective. In her review of *Scenes and Characteristics of Hindoustan*, by Emma Roberts, for instance, she dwelt on the details given of Anglo-Indian domestic life and pointed out that:

> From the writings of Forbes, Tod, Malcolm, Monro, Heber, and others, we had obtained very considerable information regarding India; but the lively and minute pen of a woman was still required to give us those indoor details which none save a woman could note, and none describe so well (Johnstone, October 1835: 684).

De Quincey's own attention to 'in-door details' throughout his *Tait's* essays, challenges this last assumption, but shows a similar, canny eye to the readership.[36]

Having described Wordsworth's home, De Quincey turns his attention to its female inmates—Mary and Dorothy Wordsworth, whose appearance and characters are given, again in some detail, as a preface to Wordsworth's. The order of precedence is significant, for it establishes De Quincey's affiliations with the feminine domestic world by which Wordsworth is sustained but from which he stands apart. In his description of Mary, he draws on Wordsworth's lyric, 'She was a Phantom of Delight' in which the poet describes his future wife as a harmony of angelic femininity and real woman, in such a way as to return her real presence almost completely to a sublimated ideal.

De Quincey defers to Wordsworth's description and even imitates his strategy, but also points out that Mary's passive intellect was what made her the perfect wife for Wordsworth. 'She was a Phantom of Delight' is quoted as an illustration of 'how much better this [intellect] was adapted to her husband's taste, how much more adapted to uphold the comfort of his daily life, than a blue-stocking loquacity, or even a legitimate talent for discussion' (*DQW*, XI: 51). This re-instates Mary as a socially-situated subject, stresses Wordsworth's dependency on her and suggests an identification between her present situation and De Quincey's own, as it will unfold, since neither is granted an equality of intellectual relationship. His description of Dorothy develops these critical hints much more fully.

He introduces Dorothy with another quotation from one of Wordsworth's lyrics—'The Beggars'.[37] The poem describes a wild but beautiful female beggar, whom the poet encounters whilst walking. The poet judges both her and her sons to be liars, but allows them their difference, admiring them for their beauty and joy. He chooses not to enter sympathetically into the situation of the beggar woman, who is voiceless in the poem. He is content to acknowledge her strangeness as an object of aesthetic contemplation and move on. As in the description of Mary, De Quincey develops and problematizes the Wordsworth lyric, implying here only a limited satisfaction with his sublimated visions of the feminine. He emphasises Dorothy's uncomfortable Otherness—her foreign appearance, her wild eyes, indicative of future mental instability, her lack of conventional femininity. The key-note to her character is 'self-conflict' (*DQW*, XI: 52). She is the opposite of Mary's contented femininity: 'some subtle fire of impassioned intellect apparently burned within her', sometimes visible, but at other times 'checked, in obedience to the decorum of her sex and age, and her maidenly condition, (for she had rejected all offers of marriage, out of pure sisterly regard to her brother and his children,)' (*DQW*, XI: 52). De Quincey is full of admiration for her self-sacrifice, but he recognises it as such. Here, as elsewhere in these essays, we find what Angela Leighton has described as his 'quiet undercurrent of criticism of the social and sexual structures, whether "conjugal" or "parental", in which most women are caught' (Leighton 1992:167–8). It was an undercurrent that the *Tait's* context encouraged in his writing. Later, discussing the predicament of Dorothy as an unmarried woman and citing Mrs Trollope in support of his argument, he mounts a passionate defence of the right of women to choose to remain single and not be mocked for it:

> ... how important it is that the dignity of noble-minded (and, in the lowest case, of firm-minded) women, should be upheld by society in the honourable election they make of a self-dependent state of virgin seclusion, by preference to a heartless marriage!' (*DQW*, XI: 102).

He still, traditionally enough, sees the life of the single woman primarily in terms of service to others, but there are doubts here too.

De Quincey dwells at length on Dorothy's role as her brother's sympathetic nurturer. Her name, 'gift of God', perfectly described

> ... the mission with which she was charged—to wait upon him as the tenderest and most faithful of domestics; to love him as a sister; to sympathize with him as a confidante; to counsel him as one gifted with a power of judging that stretched as far as his own for producing; to cheer him and sustain him ... (*DQW*, XI: 104)

The catalogue, as always, suggesting De Quincey's identification with Dorothy, slips in her equal 'power' as a critic, in the midst of the more conventionally feminine attributes of loving solicitude. He names her greatest 'service' to her brother as her ability to listen sympathetically. She is the ideal, indulgent reader:

> The pulses of light are not more quick or more inevitable in their flow and undulation, than were the answering and echoing movements of her sympathizing attention. Her knowledge of literature was irregular, and not systematically built up. She was content to be ignorant of many things; but what she knew and had really mastered, lay where it could not be disturbed—in the temple of her own most fervid heart. (*DQW*, XI: 53)

Despite her irregular knowledge, De Quincey suggests his identification with Dorothy, for both are represented as Wordsworth's best audience. But, again, he does not accept Dorothy's role as passive nurturer unquestioningly. He stresses the active contribution of her sympathising attention to her brother's poetry. Readers will owe her a debt in futurity, he says, for having

> ... first *couched* his eye to the sense of beauty—humanized him by the gentler charities, and engrafted, with her delicate female touch, those graces upon the ruder growths of his nature, which have since clothed the forest of his genius with a foliage corresponding in loveliness and beauty to the strength of its boughs and the massiness of its trunks (*DQW*, XI: 53).

Where Dorothy has 'engrafted' her sense of beauty onto the masculine austerity of her brother's work, De Quincey has, in his *Tait's* articles, revealed the poet as a man. Both have 'humanized him' (*DQW*, XI: 53) for the benefit of the reader. He writes that Wordsworth has acknowledged his debts to his sister for this, but he also casts doubt on the reciprocity of the relationship. He compares the happiness of Dorothy's early life to that promised to Ruth in Wordsworth's poem of the same title. This is a troubling allusion, since Ruth is, of course, a jilted bride. De Quincey's modified quotation reminds the reader of this at the same time as it alludes to Dorothy's single status:

> . . . she, like Ruth, was for years allowed
>
> 'To run, though *not* a bride
> A sylvan huntress, by the side'
>
> of him to whom, like Ruth, she had dedicated her days; and to whose children, afterwards, she dedicated a love like that of mothers. (*DQW*, XI: 103)

Wordsworth appears here in the position of the feckless husband, a man who, in the poem, is devoted to nature and his own will. As a result of her desertion, Ruth falls victim to melancholy, is put in an asylum and then becomes a vagrant. The link to the earlier allusion to 'The Beggars' is clear, as is the parallel with Dorothy's own life, which, as De Quincey tells us, has been marked by mental illness (*DQW*, XI: 107–8).[38] The allusions to 'Ruth' question the idyll of Dorothy's self-sacrificing devotion to her brother. Beneath the surface there is inequality and even a betrayal of trust. As always, De Quincey's representation of Dorothy's relationship with her brother suggests his own relationship with the poet, but also that between the poet and his reading public.

Wooing the readership nurtured by Johnstone, De Quincey identifies himself with Dorothy not only as a member of Wordsworth's early, coterie audience, but also as a fellow author. In keeping with the *Tait's* identity, he gives high praise for Dorothy's prose, comparing it favourably with that of male writers. Her 'Journal of a Tour in Scotland, 1802' is 'a monument to her power of catching and expressing all the hidden beauties of natural scenery with a felicity of diction, a truth, and strength, that far transcend Gilpin, or professional writers on those subjects' (*DQW*, XI: 106). He also acknowledges his own debts to her 'simple but fervid memoir' of the tragedy of George and Sarah Green in his later narrative of these events in the 'Sketches' series.[39] He feels less convinced by her performance as a poet. Her verse is at best 'wild and pretty', at worst, 'feeble and trivial' (*DQW*, XI: 106). The adjectives betray an assumption of the incompatibility of poetic greatness and female genius, but this is accompanied by a conviction of the value of the alternative path chosen by women who have sought a career as professional prose journalists. Alluding to Dorothy's later mental illness, he suggests that she might have been happier if she had been 'in good earnest, a writer for the press' (*DQW*, XI: 107). This career would have produced an emotional and financial stability in her life and at no sacrifice to her femininity—Joanna Baillie, Mary Mitford and Christian Johnstone are all cited here as examples of women who have followed this path (*DQW*, XI: 107). Johnstone, particularly is held up as the model of the writer who

> . . . has pursued the profession of literature—the noblest of professions, and the only one open to both sexes alike . . . as a *daily* occupation; and,

I have every reason to believe, with as much benefit to her own happiness, as to the instruction and amusement of her readers: for the petty cares of authorship are agreeable, and its serious cares are ennobling. More especially is such an occupation useful to a woman without children ... (*DQW*, XI: 107–8).

In imagining this career for Dorothy De Quincey suggests an alternative vision of authorship to that represented by Coleridge or Wordsworth, and an alternative vision of the author-reader relationship. Prose journalism is characterised not only as a profession within which a woman can flourish, but as a kind of writing attentive to the needs of the readers, imagined as a surrogate family.

As is already clear from the examples cited, De Quincey's defence of women writers was hampered by his contempt for the 'bluestocking' who claims intellectual equality with men. To some extent, his chivalrous stance also replicated a characteristic manoeuvre of reviewers at the period, who allowed female genius, but at an implicitly lowered estimate.[40] Similarly, it would be wrong to ignore the fact that De Quincey's debts to Wordsworth were clearly profound, and his questioning of the Wordsworthian sublime in his writing for the *Tait's* audience, of course, entailed a homage to the poet. Whilst recognising these tensions in his writing, we need also to acknowledge the extent to which he cultivated a popular, and particularly a female readership in his work for *Tait's* and the ways in which his response to Wordsworth's critical views and poetic practice in this important series of essays was shaped by that aim. I want to conclude by reappraising De Quincey's essay 'On Wordsworth's Poetry', published in *Tait's* in 1845, since it offers a notably more critical account of the poet's readers than had been present in the earlier essays for the magazine. Whilst acknowledging this fact, I would argue that, especially when read in the light of an unpublished, epistolary article on the same subject, the 'Letter to Mr Tait Concerning the Poetry of Wordsworth' (1838), we can see the ways in which this essay, too, derives from De Quincey's active interest in cultivating the new readerships.[41]

In 'On Wordsworth's Poetry' De Quincey echoed the poet's own defensive stance in arguing that, unlike Young or Cowper, he was initially unpopular because '[w]hatever is too original will be hated at the first' (*DQW*, XV: 242). If *Lyrical Ballads* had appeared without prefatory material explaining the experiment in diction 'the mass of readers would have been too blind or too careless to notice it' (*DQW*, XV: 225). The first battle-line of readers always includes 'a majority of the young, the common-place, and the unimpassioned', unable, therefore, to identify with the situations described by a great poet (*DQW*, XV: 230):

> The meditative are interested by all that has an interest for human nature. But what cares a young lady, dreaming of lovers kneeling at her feet, for the agitations of a mother forced into resigning her child, or of

> a shepherd at eighty parting for ever amongst mountain solitudes with an only son of seventeen, innocent and hopeful, whom soon afterwards the guilty world seduces into ruin irreparable. Romances and novels in verse constitute the poetry which is *immediately* successful; and that is a poetry, it may be added, which, after one generation, is unsuccessful for ever. (*DQW*, XV: 230)

The passage recurs to the earlier theme of Wordsworth's lack of chivalry as a figure for his relationship with the reader, but here the 'young lady, dreaming of lovers kneeling at her feet' is the inadequate party, rather than the poet. She is the consumer of the ephemeral productions of the press, the 'Romances and novels in verse' that flood the market and evaporate without a trace. The literature of power, dealing with tragedies of the human heart, will be appreciated only by a 'meditative' minority.

These comments run counter to the populist agenda of *Tait's* and to the tenor of the attitude to audience in the 'Sketches' and the 'Reminiscences' and are more akin to the picture of the contemporary mass readership De Quincey produced three years later in 'Life and Adventures of Oliver Goldsmith'. But, as whole, 'On Wordsworth's Poetry' is more critical of the poet than of his readers. The essay begins with another prolonged outpouring of personal disillusionment with Wordsworth as the autocratic betrayer of his disciple's trust, suggesting the same critique of the author's attitude to his audience that has run throughout the biographical essays (*DQW*, XV: 224–5). The essay is a calculated display of De Quincey's superior sensitivity to the popular audience, and to the necessity of making sensible marketing decisions when seeking an audience.[42] He argues that Wordsworth's decision to include his theory of diction in *Lyrical Ballads* and the partial falsity of that theory were the prime causes of the collection's lack of success. *The Excursion* was a failure because of the tedium of its conversational style (*DQW*, XV: 236–7).[43] Indeed, Wordsworth has been less successful in 'big books', such as this than in his shorter lyrics and in individual lines and phrases (*DQW*, XI: 237). *Lyrical Ballads*, without its prefatory material, would have sold, he argues. A volume of extracts would have worked better than *The Excursion* (*DQW*, XV: 237, 241).

The suggestion for this volume of extracts, appealing to a popular audience, alludes to a project explained in De Quincey's unpublished 'Letter to Mr Tait Concerning the Poetry of Wordsworth', written for *Tait's* in May 1838. In this article De Quincey expressed his sympathy with Tait's radical politics (*DQW*, XI: 583) and, in this context, proposed a popular edition of Wordsworth's poetry. A 'literary man', known to him, he writes, had had the original idea

> ... that an edition of Mr. Wordsworth's poems upon coarse paper, and in every other way adapted to purchasers of the lowest rank, would form a most acceptable present to the great number (now annually growing

rapidly) of grave meditative men in the class of mechanics and artizans both here and in the . . . American United States, and throughout our vast colonial empire (*DQW*, XI: 586–7)

Here, by contrast to the later essay 'On Wordsworth's Poetry', the new readerships are characterised as 'meditative'. In order to appeal to these readers, De Quincey suggests, instead of a complete edition, a selected one, containing about half the poems, thus avoiding questions of copyright and 'much more acceptable to those for whom it was designed, because better and more portably and here and there more intelligibly prepared for their {↑separate}<especial> use' (*DQW*, XI: 587). Unlike Wordsworth he will anticipate the tastes of readers, excluding 'poems not adapted to the . . . taste which is likely to grow up in such classes of society', an editorial decision which will have 'corresponding advantages to the purse of the buyers' (*DQW*, XI: 588). He will also

> . . . add a very few and brief notes . . . which {↑indeed} are absolutely necessary {↑ at times to those}<to any> readers of Wordsworth {↑who are} not classically educated, and {↑ secondly to those who are} not familiar by long habit with his style of thinking. It is also <necessary> {↑ proper} to confess, and there is no shame in confessing, that <not merely to> other classes of readers beside the two here indicated will <b> sometimes find a Delphic obscurity in <poems> some of Wordsworth's poems, and in separate passages of many: but this is no more than that inevitable gloom or murkiness which besieges all very profound descents into our human nature. (*DQW*, XI: 588)

'Delphic obscurity' is a phrase he had used in 1823, to describe Coleridge's explanations of Kant—himself, an 'oracle' of obscurity (*DQW*, III: 95). It also picks up on the impression left by *The Friend*. In applying the phrase to Wordsworth, De Quincey impugns the poet's ability to communicate in a particularly pointed manner. He excuses the obscurity as a sublime effect, but also asserts his own critical power to meet the need of all readers, but especially the less well-educated and the newcomer, for clarification of the sublime.[44] He asks Tait, in the 'Letter', to allow him to write, 'preparatory to such a publication', 'a {↑general} review of Wordsworth's poetry and of it's special adaptation to the purposes . . . and occasions of human life' (*DQW*, XI: 589).

I would suggest that this proposed 'review' was the origin of the later essay 'On Wordsworth's Poetry'. Certainly, De Quincey's concern with the popular readership in that essay falls into place in the context of the 'Letter' and the projected edition. In 1838, in the 'Reminiscences' and in the 'Letter to Mr Tait', De Quincey imagined the readership of the future expanding outwards into the British colonies, sustained by the great voices of English literature in popular editions. In the 'Reminiscences' he envisaged these readers as young women, seduced by Shakespeare:

> ... even in the farthest depths of Canada, many a young innocent girl, perhaps, at this very moment—looking now with fear to the dark recesses of the infinite forest, and now with love to the pages of the infinite poet, until the fear is absorbed and forgotten in the love ... (DQW, XI: 61)

He predicted here, in his 'Letter' to Tait and in the concluding sentence of 'On Wordsworth's Poetry', that the poet would find a place beside Shakespeare in the hearts of readers. In 1838 he spoke of this audience as one of self-educating colonialists, for whom Wordsworth's work would become a secular,

> ... bead-roll of sentiments suited to his human {↑ condition} ... teaching him benignity towards man and resignation towards heaven; instructing him finally (in the very words of the Poet) 'To prize the breath we share with human kind. / And look upon the dust of man with awe.' (DQW, XI: 594–5)[45]

The people's *Wordsworth*, edited by De Quincey, did not materialise, but it was a project encapsulating his desire to create a role for himself as a magazine journalist, mediating the sublime to a popular audience on the largest possible scale and wooing that readership on behalf of a poet who was, as he saw it, ill-fitted to do so for himself.

NOTES

1. Duffy's most convincing evidence is from De Quincey's 'The Life and Adventures of Oliver Goldsmith', *North British Review* (1848), DQW, XVI: 309–31.
2. 'Sketches of Life and Manners; From the Autobiography of an English Opium-Eater', ran in *Tait's* from February 1834 to February 1841. The 'Lake Reminiscences', which centred on De Quincey's recollections of Wordsworth, ran in *Tait's* from January to August 1839. The 'Reminiscences' were, in some ways a self-contained series, but they were also closely related to the 'Sketches'. For details of the publication and textual history of these essays, see *DQW*, XI: 40–42.
3. William Tait's pre-launch 'Prospectus', quoted in Houghton 1987: 475.
4. See also Hyde 1981: 137–9.
5. 'Letters to a Young Man Whose Education has been Neglected'. His second important statement on the literature of power came in 'The Works of Alexander Pope', *North British Review* (1848), see *DQW*, XVI: 335–8.
6. Wordsworth wrote that the poet's role was 'to call forth and to communicate *power*' (Owen and Smyser: 3: 82). See Bate 1993: 143–4, for a discussion of the relationship between De Quincey's conception of power in 1823, Wordsworth's 'Essay Supplementary' and Coleridge's *Biographia Literaria*.
7. Wordsworth was eager not to seem dismissive of the reader. He distinguished between the 'PUBLIC', by which he appears to mean the literary world, and the 'PEOPLE', a more abstract conception of the reader, towards whom he

expressed respect (Owen and Smyser 1974: 3, 83). Nevertheless he was contemptuous of 'the word, *popular*, applied to new works in poetry' and argued that the poet of power 'must reconcile himself for a season to few and scattered hearers' (Owen and Smyser 1974: 3, 84).
8. See also in 1848: power is 'exercise and expansion to your own latent capacity of sympathy with the infinite' (*DQW*, XVI: 337). In 1823 he expressed an anxiety at the proliferation of print in the modern world, but again, it was from the reader's point of view, rather than that of the embattled writer, who, for Wordsworth, was the primary victim (*DQW*, III: 63–5).
9. In 1823 he wrote that it was better to have produced a popular novel 'which has given pleasure to myriads' than showy, but empty criticism, like that of Bouterwek or Schlegel (*DQW*, III: 68). For his inclusion of the novel in the category of the literature of 'Power', see *DQW*, XVI: 338. See also C. I. Patterson who reviewed the evidence and concluded, rightly I think, that 'De Quincey considered prose fiction within the literature of power but at the bottom of the scale, that is, "among the meanest that moves" the spirit, still pre-eminent above all that "merely teaches"' (Patterson 1955: 380).
10. See e.g. Barrell 1991. Angela Leighton moved away from the autobiographical readings, recognising a tension between the aestheticised, and 'figuratively dead' females in De Quincey's work, and 'a politics of woman as the actual victim of some external destructive force' (Leighton 1992: 163).
11. See *DQW*, XII: 15–16 and a passage in 'Schlosser's Literary History', *Tait's* (1847), where he personifies the 'public' as a fickle woman (*DQW*, XVI: 184–213).
12. Johnstone made substantial contributions to each issue, producing nearly 20% of the material between 1832–46 (Houghton 1987: 479). The magazine was edited collaboratively by William Tait and Johnstone who 'made the editorial decisions and chose the contents of each issue' (Houghton 1987: 478). See also Easley 2004: 61–79.
13. Her editorship coincided with a change in format to what she described as the 'cheap *People's size*' (Houghton 1987: 478). Easely argues that she was committed to encouraging working-class readers and that her 'definition of reformist journalism was premised on the idea that positive social change would result if the literary tastes of the general public were improved' (Easley 2004: 65).
14. See e.g. 'When Mrs Postans laments the hard fate of the Cutchee matrons, and their daily drudgery, is she aware, that not much better is that of the women, in a similar condition, in England and Ireland, if, as we fully believe, their menial toils do not greatly exceed those of their simple-minded sisters of the East?' (Johnstone, January 1839: 32). See also the polemical feminism of her reviews of Anna Jameson's *Winter Studies and Summer Rambles in Canada* (Johnstone, February 1839) and Lady Morgan, *Woman and her Master* (Johnstone, June 1840). For feminist arguments in contributions by other women writers, see e.g. 'M. L. G.' [Mary Leman Grimstone] March, 1834, arguing, within a reformist political context, for female education and for the opening of civil offices to women.
15. Women contributors increased from c. 19%–37% under her editorship (Easley 2004: 69).
16. See e. g, 'In the present month we owe all our entertainment, and the greater part of our instruction, to female pens—to Miss Edgeworth, Miss Martineau, Miss Stickney, Mary Howitt, and, lastly, to the rarely gifted authoress of THE HAMILTONS—Mrs. Gore' (Johnstone, April 1834: 208).
17. For the assumption of a female reader, see Easley 2004: 69. See also 'Gentle reader! (and if that thou art *fair* as well as gentle, so much the better, the more

glad shall we be of thy company,) is it asking too much of thy good nature to request the loan of thine arm for a brief space, whilst we take a pleasant ramble together . . . ?' (Onwhyn, June 1840: 341).

18. Lindop 1981: 305 notes that, in writing for *Tait's*, De Quincey was working for 'a Radical competitor' to *Blackwood's*, but he does not mention Johnstone and the gender politics of the magazine.
19. There are one or two signs, in these essays, of distrust of the poorly educated reader. See *DQW*, X: 189 on the 'poor stall women' of Paris, reading Voltaire and Rousseau, with no improvement to their minds, anticipating comments on the 'contagion of bookishness' in 'Style', *Blackwood's* (1840) (*DQW*, XII: 15–16). Yet this comes after a complaint against literary men who exclude '[o]rdinary people' by their superior airs (*DQW*, X: 187).
20. Letter to Hessey (1822).
21. See e.g. the chapter on Kant, *Tait's* (June, 1836) (*DQW*, X: 165), where De Quincey presents an exposition of his philosophy for 'the curiosity of *some* readers', acknowledging that he might have strayed beyond the realms of popular education with this subject.
22. De Quincey's *Diary* of 1803 (*DQW*, I: 12-69) testifies to the importance of reading in his life at this period as well as to his catholic tastes.
23. For evidence that he admired her work, see *DQW*, XI: 107-8. See also letter from De Quincey to John Johnstone [her husband], 22 September, 1827 (Pierpont Morgan, MA3007), referring to 'the great pleasure with which I have lately read *Elizabeth De Bruce* [by Christian Johnstone, 1827], an admirable work, and in my judgement by many degrees superior to the novels of Miss Ferrier—of which so many fine things are said'. I am grateful to Barry Symonds for drawing my attention to this letter. De Quincey evidently read her contributions to *Tait's* carefully, see e. g. 'The Opium and The China Question', *Blackwood's* (June 1840) (*DQW*, XI: 672, n. 29), where he alludes, apparently working from memory, to an anecdote cited by Johnstone in a review of Elizabeth Broughton's *Six Years' Residence in Algiers* (Johnstone, June 1839). She, in turn, was a supportive editor, defending him in a dispute with William Tait, over revisions to an article—see *DQW*, XI: 142 and letter from Johnstone to Tait, 22 August 1840, NLS, MS 1670. She also defended him against a reader's complaint, see below n. 36.
24. For Hannah More, see *Tait's* (August 1840) (*DQW*, XI: 238–43). His second contribution to *Tait's* (December, 1833) was an essay on Hannah More, originally submitted to *Blackwood's* but rejected by William Blackwood. For Mary Lamb, see *Tait's*, (April 1838) (*DQW*, X: 239–41). For the portrait of Dorothy Wordsworth, intertwined with that of William Wordsworth, see 'Lake Reminiscences', *Tait's* (January, February and April, 1839) (*DQW*, XI: 52–108). For the biographical sketch of Elizabeth Smith (1776–1806), oriental scholar and linguist, author of *Vocabulary, Hebrew, Arabic, and Persian*, (1814), see 'Sketches', *Tait's* (June 1840) (*DQW*, XI: 209–19). The account of Elizabeth Smith is largely derived from a biographical edition of her work by Henrietta Maria Bowdler (Bowdler 1809).
25. See *DQW*, X: 205; XI: 56, 102–3, 105–7; X: 205; XI: 217; X: 100, 257–8; XI: 107.
26. He also collaborated, uneasily, with Wordsworth in editing his pamphlet on the *Convention of Cintra* and some subsequent essays. For details of this aspect of the writers' relationship see Morrison, 1998, review of Margaret Russett.
27. Wordsworth was, in fact, welcoming and considerate in responding to De Quincey's first fan letters (Jordan 1962; Lindop 1981: 118). De Quincey's later resentments did not prevent him from acknowledging his own responsibility

for delaying their first meeting and for burdening their relationship with excessive emotional demands (*DQW*, XI: 43–7). He also acknowledged the kindness and hospitality with which Wordsworth treated him on that first visit (*DQW*, XI: 50).
28. See, *DQW*, X: 145–6, 239–40, 287 and XI: 83–4.
29. See e.g. *DQW*, XI: 80.
30. Part of De Quincey's motivation for these comments derived from his resentment of the coldness of Wordsworth and his circle towards Margaret (*DQW*, XI: 64, *n* 53; Lindop, 1981: 220). Wordsworth's letters to Mary Wordsworth show that, in his private correspondence, at least, he did submit to the self-abnegating role of the courtly lover (e.g. Darlington, 1982: 39).
31. '[Cancelled Passage from "William Wordsworth"]', *DQW*, XI: 578–81.
32. See also the reaction of Miss Wilkes, future wife of Francis Jeffrey, *DQW*, XI: 188–9.
33. See *DQW*, XI: 117–18 and 132.
34. The records we have of Wordsworth's reading from 1770 to 1815 confirm De Quincey's claims. While Wordsworth was an appreciative reader of women's poetry, he seems to have read very little women's fiction (Wu 1993 and 1995).
35. 'Novels' (1830), a piece apparently written for a young lady's album, *DQW*, VII: 289, is De Quincey's most substantial defence of the novel as a form fulfilling the need of readers—and particularly young female readers—for an ideal of sexual love. It also shows him adapting his views carefully to his audience. De Quincey's *Diary* (*DQW*, I: 12–69) shows that he was an enthusiastic reader of women's fiction, memoirs and poetry. In 1803 he read work by Clara Reeves, Mary Robinson, Mary Hopkins Pilkington, Charlotte Smith and Sophia Lee, amongst others.
36. Johnstone liked detailed biographical revelations of private life. Whilst she agreed with the widespread disapproval of Lady Blessington's gossip (Jonstone, April 1834), in her review of a *Life of Mrs Siddons*, immediately preceding De Quincey's 'Sketches' for that month, she wished that the author had not 'fancied himself bound, in biographic decorum, or social propriety, to suppress' material (Johnstone, August 1834). She actively encouraged De Quincey's biographical revelations, with an eye to increasing her readership and went into print to defend him from the objections of one of his subjects, the Revd. William Shepherd (Johnstone, May 1837).
37. 'Her face was of Egyptian brown' (*DQW*, XI: 52).
38. De Quincey concluded the third instalment of the 'Reminiscences' with a valediction to Dorothy ('Farewell, Miss Wordsworth! farewell, impassioned Dorothy! . . .'), that echoed the final stanza of 'Ruth' (*DQW*, XI: 108).
39. 'Sketches', *Tait's* (September 1839), *DQW*, XI: 143–60, see 144.
40. See Newlyn 2000: 38–9.
41. The 'Letter to Mr. Tait' was published for the first time in *DQW*, XI. For my transcription see *DQW*, XI: 582–95.
42. He broaches the subject of sublimity but draws back: 'This subject might be pursued into profounder recesses; but in a popular discussion it is necessary to forbear' (*DQW*, XV: 241).
43. In some respects De Quincey echoes the criticisms of Wordsworth made by Francis Jeffrey in the *Edinburgh Review*—especially his notorious review of *The Excursion* in 1814. Jeffrey's strategy is also, like De Quincey's, to appeal to the needs of the reader, but there are important differences too, most fundamentally that Jeffrey sanctions the readers' supposed objection to the low diction and subject-matter of Wordsworth's poetry.

44. As part of this De Quincey proposed to restore Wordsworth's poems to their original versions in his edition (*DQW*, XI: 588).
45. Compare 'Reminiscences', *DQW*, XI: 61–2.

WORKS CITED

Barrell, J. (1991) *The Infection of Thomas De Quincey. A Psychopathology of Imperialism*, New Haven, CT: Yale University Press.

Bate, J. (1993) 'The Literature of Power: Coleridge and De Quincey', in T. Fulford and M. D. Paley (eds.), *Coleridge's Visionary Languages. Essays in Honour of J. B. Beer*, Cambridge: D. S. Brewer, 137–50.

Bowdler, H. M. (1809) *Fragments in Prose and Verse: By Miss Elizabeth Smith, Lately Deceased. With Some Account of her Life and Character*, 2 vols, Bath: Richard Cruttwell; London: Cadell and Davies; Edinburgh: S. Cheyne.

Darlington, B. (ed.) (1982) *The Love Letters of William and Mary Wordsworth*, London: Chatto and Windus.

De Quincey, Thomas, Letter to John Johnstone [her husband], 22 September, 1827 (Pierpont Morgan, MS MA3007).

Duffy, C. (2005) '"His *Canaille* of an Audience": Thomas De Quincey and the Revolution in Reading', *Studies in Romanticism*, vol. 44, no. 1: 7–22.

Easley, A. (2004) *First Person Anonymous. Women Writers and Victorian Print Media, 1830–70*, Aldershot: Ashgate.

'G., M. L.' [Grimstone, Mary Leman]. (March 1834) 'Men and Women', *Tait's Edinburgh Magazine*, 5 o.s., 1 n.s.: 101-3.

Higgins, D. (2005) *Romantic Genius and the Literary Magazine. Biography, Celebrity, Politics*, Abingdon: Routledge.

Houghton, W. E. et al. (eds.) (1987) *The Wellesley Index to Victorian Periodicals 1824–1900*, vol. 4, Toronto: University of Toronto Press.

Hyde, M. (1981) 'The Role of "Our Scottish Readers" in the History of *Tait's Edinburgh Magazine*', *Victorian Periodicals Review*, 14. 4: 135–40.

[Jeffrey, F.] (1814) Review of *The Excursion*, *Edinburgh Review*, 24: 1–30.

Johnstone, C. (April 1834) Review of Catherine Gore, *The Hamiltons, or the New Era*, 'Literary Register', *Tait's Edinburgh Magazine* 5 o.s., 1 n.s.: 208.

———. (April 1834) 'The Duchess D'Abrantès and the Countess of Blessington', *Tait's Edinburgh Magazine* 5 o.s., 1 n.s.: 204–6.

———. (August 1834) Review of the 'Life of Mrs. Siddons by Thomas Campbell Esq.', *Tait's Edinburgh Magazine* 5 o.s., 1 n.s.: 467–9.

———. (October 1835) 'Anglo-Indian Society' [Review of Emma Roberts, *Scenes and Characteristics of Hindoustan*], *Tait's Edinburgh Magazine* 6 o.s., 2 n.s.: 683–93.

———. (May 1837) 'Mr De Quincey, and the Literary Society of Liverpool in 1801', *Tait's Edinburgh Magazine*, 8 o.s., 4 n.s.: 337–40.

———. (January 1839) Review of Mrs Postans, *Cutch; or Random Sketches, taken during a Residence in one of the Northern Provinces of Western India*, *Tait's Edinburgh Magazine* 10 o.s., 6 n.s.: 28–35.

———. (February 1839) Review of Anna Jameson's *Winter Studies and Summer Rambles in Canada*, *Tait's Edinburgh Magazine* 10 o.s., 6 n.s.: 69–81.

———. (June 1839) Review of Elizabeth Broughton, *Six Years' Residence in Algiers* (London: Saunders and Otley, 1839), *Tait's Edinburgh Magazine* 10 o.s., 6 n.s.: 399–406.

———. (June 1840) Review of Lady Morgan [formerly Sydney Owenson], *Woman and her Master*, 2 vols (London: Colburn, 1840), *Tait's Edinburgh Magazine* 11 n.s., 7 n.s.: 390–97.

———. Letter to William Tait, 22 August 1840, NLS, MS 1670.
Jordan, J.E. (1962), *De Quincey to Wordsworth: A Biography of a Relationship*, Berkeley: University of California Press.
Leighton, A. (1992) 'De Quincey and Women', in S. Copley and J. Whale (eds.), *Beyond Romanticism. New Approaches to Texts and Contexts 1780–1832*, London: Routledge, 160–77.
Lindop, G. (1981) *The Opium-Eater. A Life of Thomas De Quincey*, London: J. M. Dent & Sons Ltd.
Morrison, R. (1998) 'Red De Quincey', *The Wordsworth Circle*, 29, no. 2: 131–6.
———. (1998) Review of Margaret Russett, *De Quincey's Romanticism: Canonical Minority and the Forms of Transmission*, *Romanticism On the Net* 10 (May 1998) at http://www.erudit.org/revue/ron/1998/v/n10/005803ar.html
Newlyn, L. (2000) *Reading, Writing, and Romanticism. The Anxiety of Reception*, Oxford: Oxford University Press.
North, J. (2003) 'Self-Possession and Gender in Romantic Literary Biography', in A. Bradley and A. Rawes (eds.), *Romantic Biography*, Aldershot: Ashgate, 109–38.
Onwhyn, Thomas ['Palette, Peter Paul'] (June 1840) 'The Green Lane—No. 1', *Tait's Edinburgh Magazine* 11 o.s., 7 n.s.: 341–6.
Owen, W. J. B. and J. W. Smyser (eds.) (1974) *The Prose Works of William Wordsworth*, 3 vols, Oxford: Clarendon Press.
Patterson, C. I., (1955) 'De Quincey's Conception of the Novel as Literature of Power', *PMLA*, vol. 70, no.1: 375–89.
Whale, J. C. (1985) '"In a Stranger's Ear": De Quincey's Polite Magazine Context', in R.L. Snyder (ed.), *Thomas De Quincey. Bicentenary Studies*, Norman: University of Oklahoma Press, 35–53.
Wu, D. (1993) *Wordsworth's Reading 1770–1799*, Cambridge: Cambridge University Press.
———. (1995) *Wordsworth's Reading 1800–1815*, Cambridge: Cambridge University Press.

7 De Quincey and the Secret Life of Books

Josephine McDonagh

In his late autobiographical work, *Suspiria de Profundis* (1845), De Quincey tells a story about an incident in a bookshop when he was about seven which, he says, had a profound effect on the subsequent development of his adult psyche.[1] The facts of the case are these. Encouraged by his guardian and sometime Latin tutor, Samuel Hall, to purchase books, he had already acquired a precocious taste in book collecting. He had also accrued growing debts as a result.[2] On this particular occasion he went to the bookshop to order a multivolume work, which would be a 'general history of navigation' and would include narratives of all the famous sea voyages from history (*DQW*, XV: 165).[3] His usual bookseller, an avuncular man, was otherwise occupied, and in his stead young Thomas is served by a 'smiling young man': 'Never did human creature, with his heart palpitating at Delphi for the solution of some killing mystery', he writes, 'stand before the priestess of the oracle, with lips that moved more sadly than mine' (*DQW*, XV: 165–6). Recalling the scene in *Suspiria* more than fifty years later, De Quincey writes of his childish self with the understanding and indulgence of an older man, but slips in and out of his former child's consciousness. The young bookseller was 'handsome, good-natured, but full of fun and frolic', and he looked at the forward child with 'drollery' that the boy De Quincey misinterpreted as contempt. On asking how many volumes to which the work would extend, the young man replies, mimicking the boy's seriousness, 'Oh! Really I can't say, maybe a matter of 15,000, be the same more or less. . . . there might be some trifle over, as suppose 400 or 500 volumes, be the same more or less' (*DQW*, XV: 166). Oblivious to the joke, the boy De Quincey is horrified: 'What, then, here there might be supplements to supplements—the work might positively never end'. Stunned by the fear of having unwittingly made an order so outrageously large, and contracted a debt so egregiously deep, he presents a series of elaborate images to express his feelings of shame and guilt: he is the object of an ancient spider's anger for having damaged his web; he is accused (in print) by the Stationer's Company of an unknown crime; and finally, the most baroque expression of them all, he is the recipient in a 'great opera-house 'scena' of the [book] delivery'. He imagines the following scene:

> There would be a ring at the front door. A waggoner in the front, with a bland voice, would ask for 'a young gentleman who had given an order to their house'. Looking out, I should perceive a procession of carts and waggons, all advancing in measured movements; each in turn would present its rear, deliver its cargo of volumes, by shooting them, like a load of coals, on the lawn, and wheel off to the rear, by way of clearing the road for its successors. Then the impossibility of even asking the servants to cover with sheets, or counterpanes, or tablecloths, such a mountainous, such a 'star-y-pointing' record of my past offences lying in so conspicuous a situation! (*DQW*, XV: 167)

The passage underlines the particular moral failings that play on his conscience: first that he is overly acquisitive; second, that he's an impostor, posing as the gentleman of the house, when in reality he is no more than a child. There is a very obviously scatological dimension to the fantasy too: the ever increasing pile of books ignominiously excreted onto his family lawn is irrefutable and unconcealable evidence of his anal transgressions.

The situation calls to De Quincey's mind a story from the *Arabian Nights*, the retelling of which completes this sequence.[4] In this a young porter finds a beautiful young woman imprisoned in the harem of an aged magician, 'and', De Quincey writes, 'recommends himself as her suitor more in harmony with her own years than a withered magician' (*DQW*, XV: 168). The magician returns, and the porter escapes, but gives himself away by leaving behind his porter's ropes. In both this story and that of De Quincey, the protagonists implicate themselves by leaving behind traces of themselves and their unruly desires. In fact, De Quincey claims that in his bookshop drama he is doubly caught out, once by his own desires, and twice by the fact that his own dilemma has been told already in the *Arabian Nights*: 'I had been contemplated in types a thousand years before on the banks of the Tigris' (*DQW*, XV: 168). Cast adrift in a sea of guilt, De Quincey cannot even claim that his predicament is his own.

Young De Quincey's craving for books is gargantuan.[5] 'Had the Vatican, the Bodleian, and the *Bibliothèque du Roi* been all emptied into one collection for my private gratification, little progress would have been made towards content in this particular craving' (*DQW*, XV: 163). But it is not merely the size of his longing that matters; it is also the way it makes him feel. Books open for him a new kind of desire: not, he writes, 'a state of languishing desire tending to torpor'; rather one that generates extraordinary psychic energy, 'feverish irritation and gnawing care that kept alive the activity to my understanding'. Within his autobiographical narrative, the scene in the bookshop holds a crucial importance recalling a moment when a kind of guilty, insatiable desire is born. His longing for books acts as a primary compulsion, and one that will later be repeated or paralleled in his unhealthy longings for opium in a better known way (Rzepka 1995: 175). His book mania thus seems to provide the origins of addiction, the perverse style of unstoppable consumption that gives shape to his life and bestows his identity as the English Opium Eater.

Elsewhere in his writings De Quincey expresses a similarly profound concern for the proliferation of books. Since the invention of the steam press, De Quincey thinks, there are simply too many books. In the context of an expanded print culture, he frequently returns to the need for sound principles for their selection: in his 'Letters to a Young Man whose Education has been Neglected' (1823), for instance, and in the careful distinctions that he makes within his own works, between the transcendent Literature of Power, and the useful Literature of Knowledge. These are categories that have a significant legacy in disseminating Romantic or Wordsworthian ideas of literature to a mid nineteenth-century reading public (Russett 1997). But what is curious in the scene in *Suspiria*, however, is that expressed here is not a desire to limit or manage books, but in fact, the fantasy of having them all, being buried by them, being, as it were, consumed by the books he has consumed. This seems to be part of the erotic charge that the scene conveys: he is swamped by books sent by the handsome and flirtatious young bookseller; they have been dumped from the twice repeated erotogenic 'rear' of the carts; and, to seal it all, the framing narrative of the *Arabian Nights*, transposes what hitherto had been a homoerotically charged scene into a heterosexual romance.

The two responses to books and book acquisition outlined in De Quincey's works conform to two strands in the wider culture of books and book collecting at the time. As is well documented, factors including the end of perpetual copyright, technological changes in the printing industry which dramatically accelerated book production while reducing costs, and the increased demand with the spread of literacy, had combined to transform the literary market place in the late eighteenth and early nineteenth centuries (Keen 1999: 99–131; St Clair 2004). On the one hand, the expansion of books provoked a concern regarding notions of literary value, an emerging discourse of literary criticism that discriminated between works of art on the basis of stylistic features; and on the other hand, an antiquarian preoccupation with the book as a material object. One emanation of the latter was the creation of national libraries, such as the British Library, that preserved books and manuscripts as part of a national heritage. But this antiquarian impulse also found a more extreme expression in the obsessions of private collectors, or self-confessed 'bibliomaniacs', who were an eccentric feature of literary culture in the first decades of the nineteenth century. As Philip Connell has pointed out, these private collectors also considered themselves to be custodians of national treasures, and through donation or sale of their libraries to public collections, regarded themselves to be contributing to the nation's wealth and prestige (Connell 2000: 27). Indeed De Quincey notes how George IV gave his immense library of more than 120,000 volumes to the British Museum to 'swell' the Museum's collection, and in doing so, translated his eccentric, private obsession with the 'health of books' into a public good (*DQW*, X: 22–24; see also XIX: 101–3). In this account, De Quincey evokes the medical vocabulary that, as we shall see, pervades discussions of bibliomaniacs, but here he projects the ill health onto the book rather than the collector—perhaps in deference to the King.

In two recent essays, Ina Ferris and Deirdre Lynch have examined the peculiar relationship between the public and private cultures of collecting, and provide a suggestive context for considering De Quincey's intense emotional and financial investments in books (Ferris 2004, Lynch 2004). In this chapter I build on this work, especially Lynch's suggestion that we should take seriously the affective aspects of book collecting. I ask, what do De Quincey's strange fantasies about books tell us about the early nineteenth-century culture of books? And what does this culture tell us about De Quincey? The chapter is divided into three unequal sections. In the first section, I discuss bibliomania as an especially symptomatic form of book collecting, to which I suggest De Quincey responded. In the second section, I look at some examples of libraries and bookshops in De Quincey's work, and consider the meanings that they carry. And finally I will discuss a particularly perverse instance of book purchasing that took place in Oxford in 1808. Throughout I explore the idea that bookshops and libraries (which in this period usually overlapped [Brewer 1997: 178]) are sexually charged social arenas, and that De Quincey's experience of them, and fantasies of them, have consequences for his self-representation, his conception of masculinity, and his late-Romantic subjectivity.

BIBLIOMANIA

In his longings for books expressed in this episode in *Suspiria*, De Quincey was not alone. The condition of 'bibliomania' had been the subject of a spate of works published in the early decades of the nineteenth century, when De Quincey was a young man, but it continued to denote a pathological relationship to books that afflicted certain kinds of genteel men throughout the century. In the early decades, it was chiefly associated with a group of bibliophiles, including private collectors and librarians, who were organised loosely around the great book collections and libraries of London, Oxford and Cambridge. These particular bibliophiles were part of a wider culture of antiquarianism that emerged in this period, counting among its numbers such prominent literary figures as Sir Walter Scott and Isaac D'Israeli. Philip Connell has written convincingly of 'bibliomania' as representing a genteel and conservative, neo-Burkean response to the 'demographic expansion of print culture' in the early nineteenth century. He argues that the work of self-confessed bibliomaniacs in establishing book collections as a repository of a national past reconciled aristocratic wealth with the conspicuous consumption of the connoisseur, under the umbrella of 'patriotic, patrician *virtù*'. Here was excessive consumption for the public good: it promoted a 'notional permeability between private, aristocratic wealth and an evolving sense of public, literary *heritage*—while still effectively excluding the impolite, unlearned, or simply undesirable' (Connell 2000: 27). But in emphasising a purposive strategy in bibliomania, Connell may underplay the irrational aspects of this strikingly eccentric project. For even those who supported the idea of book collecting to excess also regarded it as a mania. And its effects are most clearly apparent in the styles of desire and the intimate forms of masculine sociability that the culture of book collecting engendered.

The *Oxford English Dictionary* cites usages of the term bibliomania through the eighteenth century, but it becomes newly fashionable around the 1810s. In 1809, two works entitled *Bibliomania* were published, both of which were addressed to the book collector, Richard Heber. The first of these works was a long poem by a Manchester-based doctor with an antiquarian interest in books, John Ferriar; the second, and more influential, was the bibliographer Thomas Frognall Dibdin's response to Ferriar, first published in one volume in 1809, and in an expanded two volume version in 1811 under the title, *Bibliomania; or Book Madness: A Bibliographical Romance in Six Parts*.[6] As these works attest, excessive passion for books resulted in a disordered sense of reality and a dissipation of the will; in many of its characteristics it resembled the more familiar condition of erotomania that is discussed in many medical treatises of the time.[7] According to a frequently cited French writer, Peignot, it is 'a passion for possessing books; not so much to be instructed by them as to gratify the eye by looking on them. He who is affected by this mania knows books only by their titles and dates, and is rather seduced by the exterior than interior' (cited in Dibdin 1809: 57–58; see also D'Israeli 1807: I: 10). Both Ferriar, the doctor, and Dibdin pursued a medical idiom in their works, but neither with any particular rigour: the symptoms of bibliomania, a disease that 'has almost uniformly confined its attacks to the male sex, and among these, to people in the higher and middling classes of society', (Dibdin 1809: 14–15) are not somatic symptoms so much as disorders of property, located not on the body, but in the bookshelves of the suffering individual: an excessive collection of 'Large paper copies', 'uncut copies', 'illustrated copies', and so on, finishing with the most serious symptom of all, a 'general desire for the Black Letter', (Dibdin 1809: 58) the most *recherché* of early printed books. According to Dibdin, the 'cure' for this condition is to turn private indulgences into a public good, and he lists measures such as the systemization of the principles of bibliography and the creation of libraries as public institutions among antidotes to book madness. But despite this ostensible commitment to more wholesome forms of library loving, both works record the intense pleasures of collection in highly erotic terms: bibliomaniacs, it seems, love their symptoms and have little real interest in 'cure'. Both Dibdin and Ferriar document the delights of book collecting by focusing on the one hand on the beauty and allure of books as physical objects ('How pure the joy, when first my hands unfold ,' writes Ferriar, 'The small, rare volume, black with tarnish'd gold' [Ferriar 1809: 11, l.138]); and on the other hand the thrill of possessing them, or attempting to possess them: 'the wild desires' and 'restless torments' that 'seize/ the hapless man, who feels the book disease' (Ferriar 1809: 3 ll.1–2). Ferriar often positions books coyly in places where they can flicker in and out of view, as the unobtainable object of desire: 'The Princeps-copy, clad in blue and gold, / Where the tall Book-case with partition thin, / Displays, yet guards the tempting charms within' (Ferriar 1809: 4 ll. 5–7). Here is a vocabulary of temptation and seduction, in which the book is a tantalising, erotic object.

Dibdin was the author of a panoply of bibliographic works (Ferris 2004: 9). He also played a key role in the establishment of the Roxburghe Club in 1812, a gentlemen's society formed to commemorate the sale of the family library of the fifth duke of Roxburghe (Barker 1964; Bigham 1928). As Connell notes, an opportunity to purchase such a distinguished array of antiquarian books rarely occurred, and 'book dealers, wealthy private collectors, and curious but impecunious men of letters' (among whom was De Quincey),[8] 'congregated for the sale in a London auction room' (Connell 2000: 24). The event was celebrated in particular for the sale of a 1471 edition of Boccaccio's *Decamerone* for the unprecedented sum of £2260, an event that took on mythic status in the history of book selling. The Roxburghe Club met annually on the date of the sale, and celebrated its anniversary with the publication of an edition of an early English text, funded by an individual member, and a lavish dinner. It thus combined a commitment to a form of public cultural benefit (the publication) with the private pleasures of friendly masculine society and fine dining.[9] The Roxburghe Club was one of a number of societies of gentlemen connoisseurs which were founded in this period, that revised older forms of aristocratic male societies, such as, most notoriously, the Hell-Fire Club, with a more socially diverse group of men, and in a more polite and genteel fashion. Another such society of connoisseurs, the Athenaeum Club, whose members overlapped with those of the Roxburghe, was founded in 1824. Elite, socially exclusive, and exclusively male, these societies of connoisseurs secured networks of sociability that extended far beyond the dining room, and carried significant forms of political influence and patronage. Richard Heber, the addressee of Ferriar and Dibdin's works, was a founder member of both the Roxburghe and the Athenaeum. The eldest son of a wealthy land owner and Church of England clergyman, from whom he inherited large estates in Shropshire and Yorkshire, he became Member of Parliament for Oxford University in 1821. Heber allegedly spent over £100,000 on books in his life time. When he died his eight houses in Britain (including one in Oxford High Street) and on the Continent housed untold riches of books, and lacking an heir (Heber was a confirmed bachelor), his library was dispersed, and much of it bought by the British Library and the Bodleian (*Oxford Dictionary of National Biography* 2004).

De Quincey's compulsion for books suggests that he had something in common with Heber and the bibliophiles of the Roxburghe group, but although he was an habitué of bookshops from early boyhood, and even attended the auction of the Roxburghe collection, his social milieu does not appear to have overlapped directly with that of these other self-avowed slaves to books. Indeed, De Quincey distances himself from, while also showing that he was drawn to, the societies of gentlemen dilettantes in his essays 'On Murder Considered as One of the Fine Arts'. The first and second of these essays which were published in *Blackwood's* in 1827 and 1839, were both styled as dinner addresses to an invented Society of Connoisseurs in Murder, interested in the aesthetic appreciation of killing: '[d]esign, gentlemen, grouping, light and shade, poetry, sentiment, ... are now deemed indispensable to attempts [at murder]' (*DQW*, VI: 113). A fictive editorial note to the first essay locates the satire securely in the diverse culture of gentlemen's societies, evoking the Hell-Fire Club on the one hand, but also parodic versions of the evangelical societies for the moral reformation of society, such as the Society for the Suppression of Vice established in 1802 (*DQW*, VI: 111–12, 346, n.1). An earlier (and less successful) satirical essay by De Quincey was published in the *London Magazine* in January 1825 under the pseudonym of the Rev. Tom Foggy Dribble, entitled 'The Street Companion; or the Young Man's Guide and the Old Man's Comfort in the choice of shoes' (*DQW*, IV: 449–54). It directly parodied Dibdin and the Roxburghe Club, playing especially on the title of Dibdin's work *The Library Companion: or, The Young Man's Guide and the Old Man's Comfort in the Choice of a Library*, published the previous year in 1824 (Axon 1907; Lynch 2004: sections 11–13).[10] But it also evoked the Roxburghe Club's lavish dinners, their peculiar preoccupations, and coy *double entendres*. It pastiches the characteristics of Dibdin's and his associates' style—the black print, the obsession with arcane detail, and especially the extensive footnotes that overwhelm the main body of the text. In De Quincey's skit, the love of shoes stands for the love of books, an extended joke presumably on the obsession with the footnote. De Quincey's suggestion of foot fetishism in his footnote on the feet of London actresses hints at a more perverse and erotically charged world concealed under the sheen of respectability that chimes with an aspect of Dibdin's book fetishism. For when Dibdin writes in *Bibliomania* of the innocuous nature of the bibliomaniac's obsessions, (it has 'the least moral turpitude attached to it' [Dibdin 1809: 80]; and, he insists, it is unlikely to destroy a marriage or break up a family) he likely protested a little too much, and covered over the heterodox sexuality of his fellow bibliomaniacs. But just a few months after De Quincey's satire was published, in the summer of 1825, a much publicised scandal involving Heber and a younger man brought to the surface an aspect of the Roxburghe Club that was less in tune with domestic mores than Dibdin would have it.

At the centre of the Heber scandal was a very young man called Charles Hartshorne.[11] Hartshorne was from Shropshire, the county in which Heber owned a large estate and wielded extensive influence. Before going up to Cambridge, Hartshorne had cultivated a friendship with Heber, through whom he met Dibdin and his circle of bibliophiles, and developed his own antiquarian interest in books. Hartshorne's friends, while warning him of the dangers of debt related to excessive book collecting, seemed oblivious to other kinds of risks he took by consorting with this group of older men, and encouraged him to cultivate Heber for the kinds of social and professional benefits he might bestow on the young man (Hunt 1993: 24–29). Heber and Hartshorne apparently had a strong rapport, and a deep friendship appears to have developed, despite (or probably because of) their difference in age (twenty-nine years). Through Heber and Dibdin, Hartshorne also met and developed friendships based on their shared interests in medieval books with other members of the Roxburghe Club. At New Year of 1825, Hartshorne authored and printed on a printing press in his rooms in St John's College, Cambridge, a whimsical little book written in late middle English, entitled *A Geyffte ffor the Neue Yere: or, A playne, plesaunte, and profytable Pathe=waie to the BLACK LETTRE Paradyse. Dedycated on a Red Lettre Daie to all braue Boke=buying Byblyomanes, by a Black Lettre Byblyophyle* which he gave to various members of this circle, including Heber and Dibdin. The book tells a tale of a bashful bibliophile, who is too shy and too distracted by books to meet with a 'fayre ladye', and ends up claiming that 'a boke off gorlyerrs loked ffayre as a ladie' (Hartshorne 1825: n.p.; Hunt 1993: 38, 191). The close relationship that had developed between Heber and Hartshorne in particular raised eyebrows: even members of the Roxburghe group recorded some disquiet when Heber invited the young man to the Roxburghe dinner the previous summer (Hunt 1993: 38–39; Haslewood 1837: 38–39). But the friendship ended abruptly when the Tory newspaper and scandal-sheet, *John Bull*, printed lines insinuating impropriety—and worse—between them: that 'Mr. Heber, the late Member for Oxford University, will not return to this country for some time—the backwardness of the season renders the Continent more congenial to some constitutions'; and a week later, that 'the complaint from which Mr Heber has been recommended to travel is said to have been an over addiction to Hartshorne' (cited in Cobbett 1827: 265; Hunt 1993: 187). Aware of the imminent exposure (he had been tipped off by a friend), Heber had left for the continent to avoid scandal, and had little intention of returning. Soon after this he resigned his seat in parliament. He refused to defend himself when asked by Hartshorne's friends. Hartshorne, however, who at the time of the publication of the slur, was also out of the country (in Corfu with another aristocratic, bachelor connoisseur, Frederick Norton, on a mission to establish the Ionian University, furthering the cause of Greek nationalism, by creating a library of books and manuscripts, to 'reintroduce Greeks to their culture' [Hunt 1993: 39]), was at pains to clear his name, and took out proceedings for criminal libel against the editor of *John Bull*. He won the case, and the editor, Edward Shackell, was fined £500, although, as Hunt notes, Shackell was not deterred by this in continuing his innuendos against Heber in the pages of *John Bull* (Hunt 1993: 193–6).¹²

In an editorial on the trial in Cobbett's *Weekly Political Register*, Cobbett defended *John Bull* on the grounds of the freedom of the press and its right to express an opinion. *John Bull* was not a paper with which Cobbett would otherwise hold sympathies—throughout he refers to it as the 'vendor of smut', and a muck-raker (Cobbett 1827: 271). But in this instance, Cobbett supports *John Bull*'s publication of the innuendo. He argues that the defence that the paper's lawyers mounted was wrong headed: rather than claiming that the line contained no innuendo, Cobbett argues, the paper should have had the courage of its convictions, and presented the evidence that proved that its allegations were correct. According to Cobbett the 'utility of the press' was 'in correcting the immorality of the people.' There were 'vile dark insinuations, which, though not secret, were private' (Cobbett 1827: 291). It is this notion of privacy that Cobbett challenges. How could a fact be 'not secret', yet 'private'? Cobbett's view is in line with the ambient ideology of domesticity: he holds that private life and personal behaviour should be open to public scrutiny, and moreover provide a model of public standards. Heber and his fellow bibliomaniacs, with their jokey innuendos and risqué intimacies, their appearance of domestic respectability and their references to 'ffare ladyes' that were merely a front, reeked of aristocratic corruption. In his editorial, Cobbett is vocal about his disgust of homosexuality; but he is also critical of the bibliomaniacs' failure to observe the appropriate relationship between private and public life.

As Philip Connell has noted, the bibliomaniacs broached the long standing conflict between excessive and luxurious private consumption and public benefit that had preoccupied social thinkers throughout the eighteenth and early nineteenth centuries, by lauding the role of the private book collector in contributing to national heritage. But the Heber scandal graphically demonstrated that in other ways this soldering of interests had not effectively taken place; that the bibliomaniac's private desires were *against* the public good. This was most apparent in the way in which bibliomania enabled the expression of perverse forms of desire that offended standards of public decency and private morality. And it is the bibliomaniac's library that is the iconographic location of this transgressive desire: a liminal space that is neither fully public nor fully private, a stage for the performance of unseemly masculine desire.

DE QUINCEY'S LIBRARY

De Quincey makes at least one reference to Heber in his work, but it is to Heber's 'liberality in lending the rarest of [his] books' (*DQW*, X: 34) that he refers, not to his sexuality, or the scandal that wrecked his career. But this is not the point that I wish to pursue. Rather Heber and the bibliomaniacs provide a context in which to consider De Quincey and the ways in which books mediate his relationships with others, and his self-representation. In his discussion of William Wordsworth and Robert Southey in *Autobiographic Sketches* (1853–4), for instance, De Quincey contrasts the two poets through their respective libraries: Wordsworth's 'two or three hundred volumes . . . [which] occupied a little, homely painted bookcase' were 'ill bound, or not bound at all—in boards, sometimes in tatters; many were imperfect as to the number of pages' and were 'for use, and not for show'; Southey's huge collection of seven to ten thousand volumes, on the other hand, 'occupied a separate room, the largest, and every way the most agreeable, in the house' and consisted of 'fine copies' of the 'great cardinal classics' of English, Spanish and Portuguese, displayed alongside 'rare manuscripts' in Spanish and Portuguese (*DQW*, XIX: 416–18). Wordsworth, according to De Quincey, accused Southey of being 'finical' with books, but Southey found Wordsworth to be 'negligent', and 'self-indulgent', so that 'to introduce [him] into one's library, is like letting a bear into a tulip-garden' (*DQW*, XIX: 407). Southey's library is a place of masculine contemplation; even though he puts his library 'at the service of the ladies', De Quincey tells us, 'they did not intrude upon him' (*DQW*, XIX: 418). De Quincey twice repeats Coleridge's slur that the library was Southey's 'wife', as though to underline the incipient perversity of his relationship to it.

Daniel Roberts has written about the vexed relationship between Southey and De Quincey, the points of identification between them especially in their respective writing careers, and the forms of repudiation that are evident especially in De Quincey's later writing about Southey (Roberts 2006). It is interesting therefore to consider De Quincey's double-edged admiration of Southey's ostentatious library in light of this. De Quincey's book collection, like Southey's, was extensive and contained rare items; and like Heber, he was generous in lending books to others in order to consolidate friendships, especially with Coleridge (*DQW*, XIX: 337–8). But his description of the physical form of his library, however, emphasises a cosy familiarity that resembles Wordsworth's modest bookshelves rather than the splendours of Southey's grand library. Thus in the 1821 *Confessions* he invites us to picture him at home in his library, a room crammed with five thousand volumes, sipping tea—and laudanum. 'Let there be a cottage, standing in a valley, 18 miles from any town . . .', he writes, and from the rose-clad exterior of the cottage, leads us to his inner sanctum: '[p]aint me, then, a room seventeen feet by twelve, and not more than seven and a half feet high . . . Paint me a tea table' with two cups, and a 'lovely woman, sitting at the table', and a 'little golden receptacle of the pernicious drug [opium]' (although he adds that he would rather have the original) (*DQW*, II: 58, 60). This is a vision of a library as a private space, a library made domestic at the heart of the home; but curiously it conjoins the ordinary pleasures of tea with the extraordinary pleasures of laudanum. Traces of the exotic perversity hinted at in his account of Southey's library persist in the opium: the drug turns into a memento of desire among the bric-a-brac of domesticity, as books are converted from objects of his transgressive compulsion to the respectable equivalent of wallpaper. The illicit pleasures of the library are now those of consumption. The book buying episode in *Suspiria* suggested that the desire for books was De Quincey's primary addiction; so it is fitting perhaps that the library, the place of his books' accumulation, is here also the location of his opium taking.

Although in the *Confessions*, De Quincey describes an unusually adventurous and unorthodox early life, (and even though his biography tells us of a more difficult and socially liminal life, beset with the problems of addiction and poverty), all the autobiographies, including *Confessions*, tend to be written from the imagined vantage of domestic stability as an older man. For De Quincey the domestic interior is the site in which psychic interiority is displayed. Indeed, the French phenomenologist, Gaston Bachelard, picks out the scene in De Quincey's library for discussion in his *Poetics of Space*, precisely because in it De Quincey presents the domestic interior as the proper location of the psyche, a theme that Bachelard develops throughout his study (Bachelard 1969: 38–41). Much of De Quincey's autobiographical writing bears out this preference for domestic, interior and private spaces rather than public and exterior ones; especially *Suspiria de Profundis*, where he focuses on traumatic events of his early childhood. These invariably take place in the nursery and the bedrooms of his childhood home. These domestic scenes and sites thus accrue great significance, not only because he holds a proto-Freudian idea that childhood trauma is the cause of adult psychic development, but also because he argues that childhood dreams are more vivid than adult dreams, and only to be matched by the extreme visions conjured by opium. Indeed his baroque opium dreams (which he calls his Oxford visions because he starts taking opium while an Oxford undergraduate in 1804) are interesting here because they take him back to early childhood, and repeat his childhood dreams. In the logic of *Suspiria*, therefore, he returns obsessively to the events and sites of childhood from the vantage of maturity, skating over the period of early adulthood and his student days.[13] From one set of domestic chambers to another, from the nursery to his domestic library, what is skipped over here is his passage through other kinds of spaces—spaces which are neither entirely public nor private, and in which typically take place the exchange and purchase of books.

This structure recalls the episode with which this chapter began—the scene in the bookshop recounted in *Suspiria*. We might now see this as a staging of his own psyche, and the three characters as representing De Quincey at different phases of his life: the young boy, the young man, and the older man, the mature De Quincey who here is the narrator of the episode. The scene presents an uncomfortable confrontation with his young man's self—handsome, flirtatious, libidinous, the self that finds no other representation in *Suspiria*. Moreover, we might also consider that, in the context of this homoerotically charged scene, the difference in ages between the men is significant, for in Greek love (the dominant model of homosexual practice), the older man's attraction is for the young man (as in the case of Heber and Hartshorne) (Dover 1978). In another autobiographical essay, published in August 1834 in *Tait's*, he contemplates the threshold between boy and manhood when he asks: 'When, by what test, by what indication, does manhood commence?' The answer to the question that he finally settles on as the only criterion 'lies in the reverential feeling, sometimes suddenly developed, towards woman, and the idea of woman.... When the ideal of womanhood, in its total pomp of loveliness and purity, dawns like some vast aurora upon the mind, boyhood has ended; childish thoughts and inclinations have passed away for ever; and the gravity of manhood, with the self-respecting views of manhood have commenced' (*DQW*, X: 88 and 90).[14] The claim is a strange one for De Quincey in light of the reverence he continually records for women and girls even in childhood. But it draws attention to an anxiety surrounding this point of transition, this stage of life that is more uncertain, disordered, and sexually heterodox than he would like. And a stage which he repeatedly associates with book buying and borrowing.

That much of his time as an adolescent was spent in bookshops and libraries is clear from the diary that he wrote when he was seventeen, during a three month period spent at Everton, then just outside Liverpool, in 1803. Literary critics have been most interested in this diary because it records his youthful admiration of Wordsworth, his several drafts of the famous letter that he sent to him (Clej 1995: 117–31); but it is also a very interesting record of the cultural milieu in which he moved (Roberts 2000: 71–111). At this time, Liverpool was a thriving commercial and cultural centre; it had been the location of the first circulating library in England, the Liverpool Library, established in 1758, which became the focal point for a range of literary and scientific activities in the town (Longmore forthcoming). In the diary, De Quincey does not mention the Liverpool Library, but he does record visiting a surprising array of libraries and bookshops. The diary is a record of his day to day activities, which are dominated by reading. He reads an astonishing amount: poetry, novels (mostly gothic fiction), newspapers, periodicals. A typical entry reads thus: on Thursday May 12, he 'read "Edinburgh Review" No. 3 to Mrs. W. viz. Reviewal of Mdme. de Stael's *Delphine*;—part of d⁰· of Fiévée's *Lettres sur L'Angleterre*. N.B. I had just read the *whole* reviewal of this last. Look too at a {↑that day's} paper;—go on with Castles (Sunday eveng.) of A. & D. [Radcliffe's *Athlin and Dumbayne*];—dine alone with C.;—get parcel and letter from my mother;—talk of Edinburgh Review;' and so on (*DQW*, I: 27). Although his later self-representations describe him as a quiet home dweller, in this journal young De Quincey is peripatetic, walking energetically between Everton (where he lodges) and all the libraries and bookshops in Liverpool (among the libraries he mentions are Mrs Brown's Library, Miss J Bolton's Library,

Miss Turner's, O'Reilly's French Library), and extremely social. Reading is far from a solitary experience for him, but provides the hub of his social life: his friends the Wrights, with whom he spends a great deal of time, are bookshop owners, and their home appears to be above the shop; indeed the two social spaces merge into one, and the business of bookselling mingles with the day to day of domestic activity, of dressing, dining, and so on. De Quincey frequently meets people there, reads to 'the ladies', goes out from there to take walks along the shore, or in the new botanical gardens, to the theatre, or to tea parties with other friends, and to the libraries; but sometimes he finds no one at home, and sits down and reads on his own, until someone arrives, indicating that it is a place for public occupation too. Alongside his reading, the diary records his sexual activities—and the two often intermingle: his morning masturbations (always recorded in Greek) often merge with his reading (Rzepka 1995: 143–9): (on night of June 1, for instance 'goes to bed thinking of Coleridge . . . the greatest man that has ever appeared . . .', and directly afterwards in the entry for the following morning, records 'εφ σπ' (orgasm); then goes to library to return the third volume of the gothic novel that he's reading [DQW, I: 44–5]); and he also records his intercourse with prostitutes: May 22, for example, he writes: 'read the 19th book of Cowper's *Iliad*;—go home;—drink coffee and read a little more of *"The Foresters"*';—walk out;—{↑<enjoy a girl in the fields for 1{↑ s}. 6{↑ d}.>}. finish *"The Foresters"* and {↑ begin} <go on with> *"The Bachelor"*' (DQW, I: 35). A few days later, he records: 'go home with a whore' (DQW, I: 37) and so on. These sexual references have been reconstructed from erasures that have been made by a former 'careless but censorious reader' of the manuscript (DQW, I: 7);[15] but other passages have been physically excised, cut out with a knife, and these are even more intriguing. For instance, Friday, June 3: 'walk to and in <new> gardens—see Mr Thomas {↑ and a lady}—say 'How do you do Sir?' am locked in—am let out;—see Mr T. again;—say, in deep voice, 'Good night, Sir'; but do not touch hat as before because he did not return my bow before;—we {half a line cut away}—return at 10 o'clock' (DQW, I: 46). Most likely excised is a trip to a brothel, but striking is the fact that he goes with Mr Thomas, that even this is an exercise in sociability.

The diary ends in June. Six months later De Quincey had persuaded his mother to allow him go to Worcester College, Oxford. Given the kind of sociability that he records during his period in Liverpool, his insistence that he led a reclusive life as a student seems rather unconvincing. He was, by all accounts, a prodigious scholar; but he also records some extracurricular entertainments: going to the assizes, for instance, (in particular he writes of hearing the trial of two brothers who had allegedly abducted and raped Rachel Lee; the interest of the case was that the woman was the 'Female Infidel' who had visited his mother a number of years before) (DQW, XIX: 78–87; Roberts 2002) and, predictably, buying books and opium (Lindop 1981: 115–6; Japp 1891: I, 103–118).[16]

BUYING BOOKS IN OXFORD

To suggest the kind of sociability that De Quincey may have encountered in Oxford, I turn to an infamous case of book buying which occurred (tantalisingly) in the months directly after De Quincey's sudden departure in the middle of his finals, in June 1808. The case involved a fellow of All Souls College named Charles Shipley, and a nineteen-year-old book delivery boy, Charles Slatter, who worked for John Parker, bookseller of Broad Street, Oxford. In October 1808, Slatter accused Shipley of having kissed and 'frigged' him, when he made a delivery to Shipley's college rooms. By his own account Shipley had asked him 'how old he was, I asked him if he ever went after the girls, and chucked him under the chin' (Letter from Shipley to Montagu sent in Michaelmas, 1808, D.Coll. M.l no. 11, cited in McManners 2000: 8),[17] but he adamantly denied doing more than this. Slatter took out criminal proceedings against Shipley (paid for by Shipley's family—a clerical family of high standing—fairly secure in the belief that their son would be acquitted), and Shipley was found not guilty. The Governing Body of the College, however, thought differently, held its own trial, found him guilty, and withdrew his fellowship. The case is a fascinating one, and is examined at length by John McManners in *All Souls and the Shipley Case 1808–1810*.[18] While the case reveals much about Oxford, the internal organisation of colleges, and their complex relationship to the town in this period, a number of points that emerge from the records and from McManners' study bear specifically on the themes of this chapter. First, as in the case of Hartshorne and Heber, it is impossible to know exactly what happened in Shipley's college room. The fact that All Souls felt it expedient to expel him, however, despite the fact that he had been found innocent by a court of law, suggests that at the very least they found Shipley's style of conduct disturbing and potentially dangerous. Shipley was reputed to be flamboyant and open handed: his friends referred to him as 'a man whose extravagant habits were known to every scout in Oxford' (Heber 1808: 2 r.2), and indeed part of the evidence against him related to the fact that he had given Slatter a very generous tip. McManners also notes that he suffered from 'weak health' and 'irritable nerves', for which he had spent a long period in the previous year on a long cruise to Madeira as the guest of his brother who was a naval officer (McManners 2002: 3). Second, the likelihood is that Slatter had intended to blackmail Shipley, and the involvement of a second employee, William George, allows us to speculate that there may have been a more systematic participation of the bookshop in such dealings (McManners 2002:73). After the trial both Slatter and William George went to work at Mr Lunn's bookshop in Soho Square, although two years later Slatter was tried for stealing books and selling them to another book dealer—for which he served two years hard labour.[19] Third: Shipley was the best friend of Reginald Heber, younger half brother to Richard, who, as we have seen, would be in a similar predicament in 1825. Reginald Heber and Shipley had been at Brasenose together, and also at All Souls, and Reginald had recently married Shipley's sister. Heber was thus concerned to clear his wife's family name, and took it upon himself to find out about Slatter's background. He discovered that Slatter had a homosexual past: he had been a choirboy at New College (where he had a reputation for dishonesty), and at age sixteen had gone to London and lived with a man, whose bed he shared, and from whom he received gifts. Moreover, he had two brothers, one of whom (also while a choir boy) had made a charge against a gentleman; and the other of whom also lived with a man whom he had met while he was a chorister at Magdalen College. The Slatter boys seemed to be a bad lot, all of them involved in sexual activities with men that associated them with a criminal underworld. But in his private correspondence, Heber also writes of a purer kind of love between men which is also expressed physically. The remarks are all the more surprising as they come in a very frank private letter to the Warden of All Souls, in which he protested Shipley's innocence. Speculating on an attraction that Shipley may have had for Slatter, and Slatter's role in it, he says 'What that liking must have been which prompted such enormities, few boys of nineteen could have been ignorant, and fewer still who were not wholly depraved, would have acknowledged that they had without compulsion kissed and embraced one of their own sex, and anxiously sought an opportunity of again receiving similar caresses' (Heber, 1808: 1 v.2)—the implication being that if contact had happened it was more than likely consensual. Perhaps this was the kind of activity that was 'not secret but private' that Cobbett finds so disturbing twenty years later. While Heber suggests that it is a more common experience than might be expected, but it is one not to be acknowledged. Heber's letter is all the more surprising I think when we remember that this was a period of severe homosexual repression; as historians of sexuality have noted, there was an increase in prosecutions for sodomy, a capital offence, at the beginning of the nineteenth century (Harvey, 1978; Cocks, 2003: 22–30). When people write in the correspondence regarding the Shipley case that this is an 'accusation worse than death'—and they do frequently—there is a particular truth to this.[20]

There is no positive evidence that De Quincey knew any of the characters involved in the Shipley case, or that he had frequented the bookshop on Broad Street. By the time of the trial, he had already left Worcester College, so it is not likely that he was in the courtroom. But there is a more abstruse line of circumstantial details that brings them closer together. In an episode in his essay 'Sketches of Life and Manners' first published in *Tait's* in March 1838 (and revised as 'My Brother' in *Autobiographic Sketches*), he gives an account of his younger brother, Richard, also known as 'Pink', who was cursed by his extreme good looks. Pink's delicate beauty had been the cause of bullying at school, and to avoid this, he ran away to sea, not returning for a number of years. During the period that De Quincey was in Oxford (that is, sometime between 1804 and 1808), 'Pink' had returned to England, and unbeknown to his brother, had arrived in Oxford. He finds himself outside

138   *Thomas De Quincey*

All Souls (Shipley's College). There he met 'a gentleman gownsman, who (at the very moment of turning into the college gate) looked at Pink earnestly, and then gave him a guinea; saying at the time—I know what it is to be in your situation. You are a school boy, and you have runaway from school. Well I was once in your situation, and I pity you'(*DQW*, X: 230; XIX: 203). It is impossible not to remember Shipley here—his open handed generosity, his large tips for which he was famed all over Oxford, and his interest in pretty young men. Whether or not it was Shipley is unclear: on the face of it, it seems unlikely as De Quincey tells us that the man concerned was a 'gentleman commoner', recognisable by his velvet cap and silk gown, and not a fellow of the College like Shipley.[21] But the Shipley scandal entitles us at least to imagine that this sudden act of largesse between a young man and a beautiful boy may have meant more than it seemed.

I return one last time to the episode in the bookshop in *Suspiria*. The book that the boy De Quincey orders is a compendium of voyages around the world. It is likely that encrypted here is a reference to his father, who had recently returned from a long tropical voyage which he had undertaken to cure his illness. The voyage had been in vain, and the father had returned to die. But perhaps instead we might also see in the compendium of voyages a reference to 'Pink', who is certainly an intrepid traveller, a fugitive from homosexual desire.

This is a close rather than an ending and a speculative one at that. De Quincey's fantasies about books suggest that he at least is aware of the kinds of intimate sociability that seems to have existed around books and book collecting. To realise this tells us more about De Quincey's anxious masculinity; but it also opens up possibilities for writing a chapter in an as yet unwritten history of the sexual life of books.

ACKNOWLEDGMENTS

I would like to acknowledge gratefully the assistance of the following in preparing this chapter: George Rousseau, Simon Bailey, Archivist to the University of Oxford, Dr Norma Aubertin-Potter, of the Codrington Library, All Souls, Oxford, Stephen Knight, Joseph Bristow, Stefano Evangelista, Colin Jones, Ina Ferris, the organisers of and participants in the Oxford Romantic Realignments seminar, and especially the editors of this volume, who have pointed me to new material and suggested ways of extending my argument. I am grateful to The Warden and Fellows of All Souls College, Oxford for permission to cite material from the Shipley archive.

NOTES

1. The episode is recounted in *Suspiria*, *DQW*, XV: 163–8. John Barrell points out that the episode was included in the 1845 magazine publication of

Suspiria, but omitted from the first collected edition. See Barrell 1991: 22. For interpretations of the episode, see Barrell 1991: 53–54 and McDonagh 1994: ch. 3.
2. See Japp 1877: I, 38 and Eaton 1936: 28. Japp points out that De Quincey spent £700–£800 on books between 1806 and 1815. Japp, 1891: 113, cited in Rzepka 1995: 175. Cf. Rzepka on De Quincey's 'addiction' to books. Rzepka: 175–183. I follow Rzepka in noting the parallels between books and opium in De Quincey's writing, but depart from him in (1) setting the fascination for books in the context of a more widely expressed condition of 'bibliomania'; and (2) regarding books as De Quincey's first addiction, prior to opium.
3. Voyages around the world were favourite topics of children's illustrated books in the early nineteenth century. See, for example, Captain Samuel Prior (John Galt), *All the Voyages Round the World, from the first by Magellan in 1520, to that of Freycinet in 1820* (n.d.).
4. On De Quincey's reading of the *Arabian Nights*, see Barrell 1991: 54–57 and Plotz 2001: 145–59.
5. On his fascination with large appetites, see McDonagh 1994: 69 n. And with regulating his own, Plotz 2001: 184–190, Youngquist 2003: 109–126.
6. Ferriar was an enthusiast for Lawrence Sterne, and among his publications was *Illustrations of Sterne, with other Essays and Verses* (1798). See the entry on Ferriar in the *DNB*. On Dibdin, see Connell 2000: 30–33, Ferris 2004, Lynch 2004 and *DNB* entry for Dibdin.
7. See, e.g., Darwin 1801: I, 54. See McDonagh 2003: 77.
8. In a fragment of a manuscript De Quincey refers to 'the <9> volumes which are the jewels of my library—books of inestimable value from their rarity—and bought by me at the D. of Roxburghe's thrice famous sale in 1812' ('[Ransoming the Books]', *DQW*, X: 377). The piece refers to an incident in De Quincey's life in which a Penrith farmer, to whom he had entrusted his library, attempted to sell off volumes for personal gain. He refers to this in a letter to Adam Black, dated 14 July 1838. Cited by Clej in headnote, *DQW*, X: 377.
9. Cf. Barker 1964: 2, who notes that the books to be printed were chosen for their public benefit, rather than private gratification. The club's emphasis on eating and drinking, rather than 'reading or writing', was emphasised by an account of the club published by the *Athenaeum* newspaper in 1833. See Bigham 1928: 7.
10. A further parody of Dibdin's bibliomaniacal outpourings is Beckford 1817.
11. The fullest account of the scandal is given by Hunt 1993. See also new *DNB* entries for Hartshorne and Heber.
12. Hunt also demonstrates the way in which Heber and Hartshorne's network of friends organised around the Athenaeum Club came to the defence in this episode (Hunt 1993: 192).
13. On the temporal effects of *Suspiria*, see McDonagh 2005. Cf. Judith Plotz's account of De Quincey's love of children, and of his childish self. She presents compelling evidence to suggest that he unconsciously colludes in his body's denial of the adult state (Plotz 2001: 180–90). My point here is different, and that is that in the compulsive return to childhood, De Quincey is driven by an active repression of the period of being a young man, at Everton and as an Oxford undergraduate. This is the period covered in the *Confessions*, and so this 'repression' may amount to no more than a quest for novel material. But whatever the motivation, the effect remains the same.
14. This passage is in a section entitled 'Premature Manhood and Consequent Struggles' in *Tait's*, which, unusually, De Quincey does not reuse in the later *Autobiographic Sketches*. However, the intermediary status of a student, poised between boy and manhood, is discussed elsewhere in the *Tait's* essays,

and repeated in the *Autobiographic Sketches*. See *DQW*, X: 133–4; and XIX: 351.

15. The sexual content of the diary has been made explicit recently by the careful scholarship of Rzepka and especially Barry Symonds, the editor of the Pickering and Chatto edition, although Horace Eaton, the editor of the first published edition of the diary, also noted some references to De Quincey's visits to prostitutes.
16. As is well known, De Quincey travelled frequently between Oxford and London during his student years, and (as if to solder the places together, in the imagination at least) it was on Oxford Street, in London where he purchased his first opium. Correspondence with family members during this period reveals that they commissioned him to buy books for them and other relatives, including his uncle Penson, then residing in India.
17. Papers relating to the Shipley case are held in the archive of All Souls, and are, as yet, uncatalogued. John McManners, whose monograph on the case is based on this archive, produced his own reference system, and I have adopted this.
18. For the broader context of sexual scandals in Oxford colleges, see Rousseau forthcoming; on homosexuality and the law, see Cocks 2003.
19. There are also references in the correspondence to another case ten years before, involving a 'Mr Beaumont of BN Coll' [Brasenose College], who had faced a similar charge, and who had been acquitted at the assizes (Heber, letter to D'Oyley).
20. I also speculate that this context helps to explain the conceit behind De Quincey's essays 'On Murder Considered as One of the Fine Arts'; that is to say, the 'murderous' associations of gentlemen connoisseurs may indeed be the kind of pleasures allegedly enjoyed by Heber.
21. Gentlemen Commoners were independent members of the college, usually 'young men of family and fortune' who at some colleges would have been 'considered as Honorary Members of the High or Senior Fellows' Table'. As a Fellow of All Souls, on the other hand, Shipley was a dependent member of the college, and a member of the Governing Body of the College (Uwins 1815: 1–5). All Souls did not admit undergraduate students, but according to the *History of the University of Oxford*, did admit Gentlemen Commoners (Green 1986: 342). Of course De Quincey may have been mistaken, or misremembered the details of the scene.

WORKS CITED

Axon, William E. A. (1907) 'De Quincey and T. F. Dibdin', *The Library*, n.s. 8: 267–274.

Bachelard, Gaston. (1958) *La poetique de l'espace*, trans. Maria Jolas (1969) *The Poetics of Space*, Boston: Beacon Press.

Barker, Nicholas. (1964) *The Publications of the Roxburghe Club, 1814–1962*, Cambridge: privately printed.

Barrell, John. (1991) *The Infection of Thomas De Quincey: A Psychopathology of Imperialism*, New Haven, CT: Yale University Press.

Beckford, William. (1817) *A Dialogue in the Shades: Rare Doings at Roxburghe Hall*.

Bigham, Clive. (1928) *The Roxburghe Club, its History and its Members*, Oxford: Oxford University Press.

Black, Joel. (1991) *The Aesthetics of Murder: A Study in Romantic Literature and Contemporary Culture*, Baltimore: Johns Hopkins University Press.

De Quincey and the Secret Life of Books 141

Brewer, John. (1997) *Pleasures of the Imagination: English Culture in the Eighteenth Century*, London: Harper Collins.
Clej, Alina. (1995) *A Genealogy of the Modern Self: Thomas De Quincey and the Intoxication of Writing*, Stanford, CA.: Stanford University Press.
Cobbett, William. (1827) 'Heber and Hartshorne', *Weekly Register*, 64, no. 5 (Sat 27 October): 256–91.
Cocks, H. G. (2003) *Nameless Offences: Homosexual Desire in the Nineteenth Century*, London: I B Tauris.
Connell, Philip. (2000) 'Bibliomania: Book collecting, cultural politics, and the rise of literary heritage in romantic Britain', *Representations*, 71: 24–47.
Crompton, Louis. (1985) *Byron and Greek love: Homophobia in Nineteenth Century England*, London: Faber and Faber.
Darwin, Erasmus. (1801) *Zoonomia; or the Laws of Organic life* (4 vols.), London: Joseph Johnson.
Dibdin, Thomas Frognall. (1809) *The Bibliomania; or Book Madness, containing some account of the history, symptoms and cure of the fatal disease in an epistle addressed to Richard Heber*, London: Longman, Hurst, Rees, Orme and Brown.
———. (1811) *Bibliomania; or Book Madness: A Bibliographical Romance in Six Parts*, London.
D'Israeli, Isaac. (1807) *Curiosities of Literature* (5th edition, 3 vols.), London: Murray.
Dover, Kenneth. (1978) *Greek Homosexuality*, London: Duckworth.
Eaton, Horace Ainsworth. (1936). *Thomas De Quincey: A Biography*. New York: Oxford University Press.
Ferriar, John. (1809) *The Bibliomania, an Epistle to Richard Heber, Esq*. Warrington and London: J. Haddock and T. Cadell and W. Davies.
Ferris, Ina. (2004) 'Bibliographic Romance: Bibliophilia and the Book-Object', *Romantic Circles*. Retrieved 23 October 2006, from http://www.re.umd.edu/praxis/libraries/ferris/ferris.html
Green, V. H. H. (1986), 'The Social Life of the University', in *The History of the University of Oxford: The Eighteenth Century*, (eds.) L. S. Sutherland and L. G. Mitchell, 309–58. Oxford: Clarendon Press.
Hartshorne, Charles. (1825) *A geyfte ffor the neue yere: or, A playne, plesaunte, and profytable pathe=waie to the BLACK LETTRE Paradyse*. Cambridge.
Harvey, A. D. (1978) 'Prosecutions for Sodomy in England at the Beginning of the Nineteenth Century'. *Historical Journal*, 21 no. 4: 939–949.
[Haslewood, John] (1837) *Roxburghe revels, and other relative papers; including answers [by T.F. Dibdin] to the attack on the memory of the late Joseph Haslewood, with specimens of his literary productions*. Edinburgh.
Heber, Reginald. (1808) unpublished letter to Warden of All Souls, dated, Nov. 22 1808, MS in *Vaughan Papers*, All Souls College Archives.
Hunt, Arnold. (1993) 'A study in Bibliomania: Charles Henry Hartshorne and Richard Heber'. *The Book Collector* 42: 25–43, 185–212.
Jacobus, Mary. (1989) *Romanticism, Writing and Sexual Difference*. Oxford: Clarendon Press.
Japp, A. H. (1877) *Thomas De Quincey: His Life and Writings, with Unpublished Correspondence* (2 vols.) London: James Hogg.
———. (1891) *De Quincey Memorials. Being Letters and Other Records, Here first published* (2 vols.). London: Heinemann.
Keen, Paul. (1999). *The Crisis of Literature in the 1790s*. Cambridge: Cambridge University Press.
Lindop, Grevel. (1981) *The Opium Eater: A Life of Thomas De Quincey*. London: Dent.

Longmore, Jane. (forthcoming) 'The Urban Renaissance in Liverpool 1760–1800', in Elizabeth E. Barker and Alex Kidson (eds.), *Wright of Derby in Liverpool*. New Haven, CT: Yale University Press.

Lynch, Dierdre. (2004) '"Wedded to Books": Bibliomania and the Romantic Essayists', *Romantic Circles*. Retrieved 23 October 2006, from http://www.re.umd.edu/praxis/libraries/lynch/lynch.html

McDonagh, Josephine. (1994) *De Quincey's Disciplines* Oxford: Clarendon Press.

———. (2003) *Child Murder and British Culture 1720–1900*. Cambridge: Cambridge University Press.

———. (2005) 'De Quincey, Malthus and the Anachronism-Effect'. *Studies in Romanticism* 44 no.1, 63–80.

McManners, John. (2002) *All Souls and The Shipley Case: 1808–1810*. Oxford: All Souls College.

Oxford Dictionary of National Biography. (2004) Oxford: Oxford University Press.

Plotz, Judith. (2001) *Romanticism and the Vocation of Childhood*. New York: Palgrave.

Raven, James. (1996) 'From Promotion to Proscription: Arrangements for Reading and Eighteenth-Century Libraries', in James Raven, Helen Small, and Naomi Tadmore (eds.), *The Practice and Representation of Reading in England*, 175–201. Cambridge: Cambridge University Press.

Roberts, Daniel Sanjiv. (2000) *Revisionary Gleam: De Quincey, Coleridge, and the High Romantic Argument*. Liverpool: Liverpool University Press.

———. (2002) 'Wordsworth's Reading of Rachel Lee: De Quincey's Evidence'. *Notes and Queries* n.s. 49, no. 4: 465–67.

———. (2006) 'Beneath High Romanticism: "Southeian" Orientations in De Quincey'. In Lynda Pratt (ed.), *Robert Southey and the Contexts of English Romanticism*. Aldershot: Ashgate, 37–48.

Rousseau, George. (forthcoming) '"You have made me tear the veil from those most secret feelings": Arcadian Adolescents and Same-Sex Scandals in Mid-Victorian Oxford' in George Rousseau (ed.), *Children and Sexuality: The Greeks to the Great War*. Basingstoke: Palgrave.

Russett, Margaret. (1997) *De Quincey's Romanticism: Canonical Minority and the Forms of Transmission*, Cambridge: Cambridge University Press.

Rzepka, Charles. (1995) *Sacramental commodities: Gift, Text, and the Sublime in De Quincey*, Amherst: University of Massachusetts Press.

St Clair, William. (2004) *The Reading Nation in the Romantic Period*, Cambridge: Cambridge University Press.

Uwins, Thomas. (1815) *The Costume of the University of Oxford, Illustrated by a Series of Engravings from Original Drawings*. London: R. Ackermann

Youngquist, Paul. (2003) *Monstrosities: Bodies and British Romanticism*. Minneapolis: University of Minnesota Press.

8 National Bad Habits
Thomas De Quincey's Geography of Addiction

Joel Black

OPIUM PROPHET OR ADDICTION THEORIST

Thomas De Quincey's *Confessions of an English Opium-Eater* is often cited as a key factor behind the reversal in opium's reputation over the course of the nineteenth century from a popular household remedy to a potentially dangerous substance in need of medical supervision and governmental control. Although opium's addictive properties had been known for centuries before De Quincey's account of his experiences with the drug, they had been 'calmly accepted' for the most part, and 'quite rarely discussed' (Berridge 1999: xxiv). Put another way, the drug's addictive nature had been known, but not *widely* or *compellingly* known—at least not enough to prompt the medical community and society at large to limit its availability and use. In the absence of any consensus among medical authors about opium's benefits and dangers, and whether it should be classified as a sedative or a stimulant, it continued right up to the mid-nineteenth century to be widely available in a variety of forms as a popular pain killer and remedy for numerous ailments. It was tainted with none of the criminal penalties and little of the moral stigma with which it has since been associated.

All this was to change over the course of the century as the *Confessions* went through its numerous reprints following its original 1821 publication. De Quincey has been both credited and criticized for publicizing opium's effect as a stimulant, especially on imaginative, literary sensibilities like himself and Coleridge. While his book inspired some readers to experiment with the drug—prompting Alethea Hayter to call him 'the prophet of opium' who 'first aroused [nineteenth-century] addicts' curiosity' about the drug (1988: 104–05)—it also spurred the medical profession to study it more closely, and to catch up with him as an authority on its effects (Milligan, 2005: 541–46).

Yet beyond the attention that De Quincey brought to opium and that led to medical and legal controls on its availability, were his insights into addiction itself as a social, and ultimately global, issue. These insights are evident when we look beyond autobiographical works like the *Confessions* to his journalistic and political essays where addiction is considered in a more discursive (if hardly objective) manner,[1] and with respect to stimulants other than opium. Indeed, since the substance that was beginning to be recognized in the early nineteenth century as a general social problem in England, Europe, and North America was not opium but alcohol, it's illuminating to consider De Quincey's various observations on intemperance and 'inebriety' (as alcoholism was then known), and how this type of dependence might be overcome. So having suggested De Quincey's importance as a pioneering theorist in aesthetics (described by Kant as a state of disinterested desire) based on his writings on the unlikely subject of murder (Black 1991: 46–82), I now want to consider him as an early theorist of addiction (a form of 'interested' or compulsive desire if ever there was one) by reading his writings on opium in conjunction with his writings on alcohol. (Unavoidably, I'll also be referring to that other less potent but 'most important British addictive consumable' that was 'directly connected' to the opium trade—tea [Bello 2005: 18, 33]). Because his interest in addiction was not limited to his personal experiences with opium, but touched on some of the most significant social and political issues of the day, the subject offered him a way to explore the mysterious relation between individual subjectivity and national identity—their inseparable connection as well as their irresolvable contradiction.

OPIUM AND ALCOHOL

> He doses himself with Opium & drinks like a f[ish] . . .
>
> —Sara Hutchinson, describing De Quincey in 1815

From the early sixteenth century, the word 'addict' was marked by a curious ambiguity. On the one hand it carried a coercive, legal sense of obligation and constraint (*addictus*: assigned by decree, made over, bound)—of being delivered over to judgment and sentenced. On the other hand it conveyed a sense of willing or willful inclination, and was applied to those 'devoted' behaviours or acquired 'tastes' associated with products like strong drink and tobacco to which one was said, through habitual use, to be 'addicted' or to have 'addicted oneself'. Such antithetical meanings easily applied to a wide variety of activities and substances, but as a primal word, 'addiction' carried a double sense that was especially applicable to a drug or *pharmakon* like opium which was both pleasurable and painful, delightful and dangerous, seductive and addictive. Users might at first have a taste or inclination for the substance that later became an obligation, a necessity. By the mid-nineteenth century, the key issue was increasingly whether habitual *use* should be judged as *abuse*—whether a condition of dependence was more a medical disease or a sign of moral weakness, a failure of the user's will.

Although the medical view of addiction as a disease has since gained wide acceptance, the issue has by no means been settled.[2]

In the early nineteenth century, however, opium was not widely thought of as an addictive substance, nor was addiction itself generally recognized as a disease. 'Opium eating' was regarded as a relatively harmless indulgence, one of those 'devoted' behaviours or acquired 'tastes' like drinking or smoking. Even when De Quincey first 'confessed' his opium habit in 1821, it was, as Hayter notes, 'not considered an exotic and secret vice, but the excess of a normal indulgence', which she specifically compares to 'drunkenness' (1988: 34). Far from making De Quincey a social outcast or criminal, the *Confessions* turned him into a celebrity.

Yet despite, and in part because of, the social acceptability, legal immunity, and literary acclaim that he enjoyed as an opium addict, De Quincey was susceptible like other early nineteenth-century users to an intensely personal feeling of guilt—'not towards society and the law . . . but guilt towards God and their families and their own wasted talents' (Hayter 1988: 37–38). And while there may not yet have been any legal deterrent about obtaining the drug or much social stigma about its use, there were also no medical or social programs in place to assist users in overcoming their dependence as would later be the case. Opium addicts were largely on their own when it came to freeing themselves from a drug that De Quincey presents as a constant temptation—less a pain-reliever than a guilty pleasure which, once enjoyed, can be renounced only with the greatest difficulty, through a heroic act of will and self-discipline that was beyond most people's abilities.

While opium's addictive dangers were not immediately registered in Britain, intemperance was more quickly recognized. No doubt this was because of alcohol's far more obvious intoxicating effects which, for a time, opium in one form or another was actually used to treat.[3] Eight years before De Quincey's *Confessions of an English Opium-Eater*, the difficulties of giving up drink were vividly described in Charles Lamb's 'Confessions of a Drunkard'.[4] Repudiating the advice of 'sturdy moralist[s]' and 'water-drinking critics' that drinkers simply 'abstain', Lamb's alcoholic persona describes the drinker's condition in exaggerated terms that anticipate De Quincey's depiction of the horrors of opium addiction—namely as 'a state of death, almost as real as that from which Lazarus rose', where rehabilitation would require nothing less than a miracle. To the common-sense advice that the drunkard 'Begin a reformation and custom will make it easy', Lamb's persona replies

> But what if the beginning be dreadful, the first steps not like climbing a mountain but going though fire? what if the whole system must undergo a change violent as that which we conceive of the mutation of form in some insects? what if a process comparable to flaying alive be to be gone through? is the weakness that sinks under such struggles to be confounded with the pertinacity which clings to other vices, which have

induced no constitutional necessity, no engagement of the whole victim, body and soul? (Lamb 1903: I, 133–34)

Especially notable is Lamb's distinction between two temperaments or constitutional types which are affected altogether differently by alcohol. On the one hand are those with 'robust heads and iron insides, whom scarce any excesses can hurt'; on the other hand are 'weak' and 'nervous' addictive personalities like the author,

> who feel the want of some artificial aid to raise their spirits in society to what is no more than the ordinary pitch of all around them without it. This is the secret of our drinking. Such must fly the convivial board in the first instance, if they do not mean to sell themselves for term of life. (134)

Lamb's drunkard persona then records his attempt to escape his addiction by taking on another indulgence—namely tobacco—only to find that it intensified his desire to drink. And as in De Quincey's accounts of opium addiction, the drunkard's initial feeling of pleasure in his new habit soon gives way to overwhelming pain and misery.

> How a pipe was ever in my midnight path before me, till the vision forced me to realize it,—how then its ascending vapours curled, its fragrance lulled, and the thousand delicious ministerings conversant about it, employing every faculty, extracted the sense of pain. How from illuminating it came to darken, from a quick solace it turned to a negative relief, thence to a restlessness and dissatisfaction, thence to a positive misery. (136)

Lamb's persona presents himself as an example to others, as a warning of the effects of liquor on susceptible constitutions like his own. He insists that this is a matter of extremes, that there is 'no middle way betwixt total abstinence and the excess which kills you' (137). Alcohol is shown to usurp the mind as well as the body ('*reason shall only visit him through intoxication*' [138]), and ultimately one's moral sense: 'I dare not promise that a friend's honour, or his cause, would be safe in my keeping, if I were put to the expense of any manly resolution in defending it. So much the springs of moral action are deadened within me' (139).

Although known to have occasionally drunk to excess himself, De Quincey seems not to have developed a dependence on alcohol. 'I myself, . . . have never been a great wine-drinker', he writes in the *Confessions*, somewhat contradicting his previous admission that, whenever the opportunity presented itself in his pre-opium days, he 'never failed to drink wine—which I worshipped then as I have since worshipped opium' (*DQW*, II: 45, 34). In the spring of 1804 he boasted to Wordsworth that he wasn't tempted by the 'intemperance' he encountered while studying at Oxford.⁵ That fall, however, he experienced his fateful initiation into opium during a visit to London. And while Lamb's warning of the demoralizing effects of liquor in 1813 would be echoed in De Quincey's writings on opium, the tone of 'Confessions of a Drunkard' could not be more different from the latter's wry observations on alcohol fifteen years later in a review of the Scottish physician Robert Macnish's book *The Anatomy of Drunkenness*. Rather than generalize about intemperance, De Quincey notes its different manifestations in societies at different stages of development: 'It prevails most in a rude state of society; and as refinement increases, it gradually disappears'. He also draws on the key concept of 'national character' that had been the subject of a work by Kant he had freely translated four years earlier. Whereas the German philosopher had sketched a cultural geography of the world that compared nations on the basis of their 'sense of the sublime and beautiful', De Quincey's review parodied this idea by comparing nations based on their susceptibility to alcohol. Drunkenness was shown to be affected by national 'temperament', which itself was determined by geography and climate: 'The northern nations, too, where the temperament is more phlegmatic, and the air denser and colder, are more addicted to strong potations than the lively, volatile, inhabitants of the sunny south' (*DQW*, V: 283). It's not surprising, then, that De Quincey, who portrays himself as being less susceptible to alcohol than many of his countrymen, tended from earliest childhood to identify with the inhabitants of southern climes rather than with his northern, English heritage.⁶ This identification with the south—a region plagued by its own, far more powerful form of addiction—was a key factor in his emerging cultural geography.

As in his writings on murderers and opium-eaters, De Quincey is inclined to suspend moral judgment on persons who drink to excess. Drunkenness is less a matter of will and self-discipline than of temperature and temperament—of geography and genealogy. Whereas Lamb's drunkard presents his condition as having such a corrosive effect on his moral sense that even 'a friend's honour, or his cause, would [not] be safe in my keeping', De Quincey appears to find nothing morally wrong with intoxication in and of itself. In his 1845 essay on 'Coleridge and Opium Eating', he acknowledges that the act of 'violat[ing] a trust could never become right under any change of circumstances', but he makes a point of distinguishing such heinous deeds from socially unacceptable behaviours like the 'habit of intoxication'

> which are known to be wrong only by observing the consequences. If drunkenness did not terminate, after some years, in producing bodily weakness, irritability in the temper, and so forth, it would *not* be a vicious act. And accordingly, if a transcendent motive should arise in favour of drunkenness, as that it would enable you to face a degree of cold, or contagion, else menacing to life, a duty would arise, *pro hâc vice*, of getting drunk. (*DQW*, XV: 113)

De Quincey cites the example of an acquaintance who managed to overcome his inborn cowardice through drink: 'Therefore, in an emergency, where he knew himself suddenly loaded with the responsibility of defending a family, we approved highly of his getting drunk' (*DQW*, XV: 113). But the 'drunkard' in this case is not a habitual user of liquor, and is certainly not an addict. The claim that there is nothing intrinsically immoral about intoxication doesn't necessarily hold, at least in this instance, for addiction.

The subject of addiction *is* raised at the end of 'Coleridge and Opium Eating', but only (as the essay's title suggests) with respect to opium. After blaming the drug for having 'killed Coleridge as a poet' while stimulating 'his metaphysical instincts into more spasmodic life', he defends 'our friend the author of the *Opium Confessions*' against Coleridge's imputation that he and the 'Confessor' began taking the drug for entirely different reasons—that he sought 'to relieve pain, whereas the Confessor was surreptitiously seeking for pleasure' (*DQW*, XV: 122–24). De Quincey maintains that he and Coleridge both first took the drug as a pain remedy for rheumatism, but continued to use the drug because of the pleasurable effect it produced in them as a source of secret knowledge and imaginative power. However, he quickly adds that not everyone reacts to the drug this way; most people simply find it useful as a pain reliever and have little trouble giving it up when their pain subsides. But for those with philosophical sensibilities like Coleridge and the Confessor who were responsive to the drug's 'divine power to chase away the genius of ennui', it was all but impossible to avoid 'abusing this power. To taste but once from the tree of knowledge, is fatal to the subsequent power of abstinence' (*DQW*, XV: 124).[7] On the basis of this distinction between those who are immune to opium's capacity for intellectual stimulation and those 'whose nervous sensibilities vibrate to their profoundest depths under the first touch of the angelic poison', De Quincey proceeds to generalize about

> two classes of temperaments as to this terrific drug—those which are and those which are not, preconformed to its power; those which genially expand to its temptations, and those which frostily exclude them. Not in the energies of the will, but in the qualities of the nervous organization, lies the dread arbitration of—Fall or stand: doomed thou art to yield; or, strengthened constitutionally, to resist. (*DQW*, XV: 124)

De Quincey's distinction between 'two classes of temperaments' which respond altogether differently to the stimulant properties of opium and to its addictive potential echoes Lamb's distinction thirty-two years earlier in the 'Confessions of a Drunkard' between two constitutional types with respect to liquor—those with 'robust heads and iron insides, whom scarce any excesses can hurt', and those like his drunkard-persona with 'weak' and 'nervous', addictive personalities. For Lamb with respect to liquor as for De Quincey with respect to opium, addiction was less a matter of the user's will—of the power to resist temptation—than of the user's biological constitution and inborn nervous sensibility. But De Quincey went a step further, suggesting that temperament itself was influenced by the geographical region in which addicts (or their ancestors) happened to live. He came to envision addicts and alcoholics in a global context as individuals who had succumbed to national, rather than personal, bad habits. People became addicts and alcoholics less through any intention of their own or through a failure of their will, but through chance or fate—the constitution they happened to inherit, and the geographical region in which they happened to have been born. This was a view, we shall see, with profound geopolitical implications.

'A SUBSTITUTE FOR WILLPOWER'

Wine robs a man of his self-possession: opium greatly invigorates it.

—De Quincey, *Confessions* (*DQW*, II: 44)

Many drink, but few abuse; many smoke opium, but all abuse.

—Testimony presented to the Royal Commission on Opium, 1894

Nine months after his piece on 'Coleridge and Opium-eating' appeared, De Quincey returned to the subject of alcohol dependence in an article he wrote for *Tait's Magazine*. 'On the Temperance Movement in Modern Times'—an often overlooked essay that David Masson calls a 'waif from 1845' (1890: XIV, 7)—anticipates the medical profession's recognition of a connection between liquor and opium as addictive substances, and of the common difficulty that alcoholics and opium-eaters face in freeing themselves from their respective conditions.[8] Whereas De Quincey had formerly stressed the differences between opium and alcohol in their qualitative effects on consumers (*DQW*, II: 44), he now points up their similarities as addictive substances. And although his own experience of withdrawal the previous year had to do with opium rather than with alcohol—a substance on which he apparently never developed a 'dependence', apart from the fact that the form in which he commonly took opium was laudanum, a wine-based tincture[9]—he presents himself as an authority on the subject of intemperance and how it may be overcome.

> From opium I derive my right of offering hints at all upon the subjects of abstinence in other forms. But the modes of suffering from the evil, and the separate modes of suffering from the effort of self-conquest, together with the errors of judgment incident to such states

of transitional torment, are all nearly allied, practically analogous as regards the remedies, even if characteristically distinguished to the inner consciousness. I make no scruple, therefore, of speaking as from a station of high experience and of most watchful attention, which never remitted even under sufferings that were at times absolutely frantic. (*DQW*, XV: 245)

De Quincey here appears to lay the groundwork for a general theory of addiction that would complement the autobiographical record of his opium experiences in the *Confessions* upon which his literary reputation principally rests. Yet despite the gravity of the subject he has embarked on—the sufferings of those seeking to free themselves from the 'evil' of their addiction—the essay characteristically veers off into a breezy series of 'hints' for alleviating the torment of withdrawal. These suggestions, which make up the bulk of the article and include a lengthy digression on digestion, seem rather at odds with the serious tone of the essay's opening. Thus the relapses experienced by innumerable 'victims of alcohol', despite all their 'vast efforts' at 'emancipat[ion]', are blamed on their desperate attempts to use 'strong liquors' to relieve 'the horrors of indigestion' caused by 'the nervous irritations of demoniac cookery' (*DQW*, XV: 246). De Quincey—who claimed in the *Confessions* to have found 'no remedies but opium' for his own stomach ailment which he traced back to the 'extremities of hunger' suffered in his youth, but which in later years is likely to have resulted from his opium habit itself, however much he downplayed this possibility (*DQW*, II: 13, 84)—attributes the singular lack of success of British alcoholics and addicts in overcoming their dependence to the 'barbarous' state of 'English cookery' which he ranks only above that of the Chinese.[10]

The digressiveness and tonal disparity of the essay's midsection are typical of De Quincey's peculiar brand of romantic irony. Only in the article's opening and closing paragraphs does the author present a more 'sober' analysis of addiction—first, as a general phenomenon that applies (albeit in different ways) to opium and alcohol, and secondly, as a global phenomenon that applies (again, in different ways) to northern and southern nations.

The essay begins with a celebration of nineteenth-century temperance organizations as the 'most remarkable instance of a combined movement in society, which history, perhaps, will be summoned to notice' (*DQW*, XV: 244). De Quincey finds the American movement particularly impressive. Citing De Tocqueville's report that one organization had 270,000 members, and that Pennsylvania had reduced its consumption of intoxicating spirits by half a million gallons, he credits such movements, even at 'their earliest stage', with having 'obtained, both at home and abroad, a *national* range of grandeur'. He avoids any mention of the fact that the movement—especially in America where it would eventually lead to Prohibition—was for the most part a moral mission or crusade to rid society of liquor as a social scourge.

Instead he focuses on its supposed social and psychological value for alcoholics seeking to overcome their dependence. The movement's effectiveness is attributed not to morality or religion, but to the kind of group support, especially from fellow sufferers, that would become the working principle behind modern recovery organizations like Alcoholics Anonymous.[11] Rather than calling upon individuals to directly confront and renounce their 'original impulse of temptation' on their own, temperance advocates used group psychology to develop what De Quincey calls 'the secondary energies of resistance' (*DQW*, XV: 245).

> Having obtained from every confederate a pledge, in some shape or other, that he will give them his support, thenceforwards they bring the passions of shame and self-esteem to bear upon each member's personal perseverance. . . . Even to strengthen a feeble resolution by the aid of other infirmities, such as shame or the very servility and cowardice of deference to public opinion, becomes prudent and laudable in the service of so great a cause. (*DQW*, XV: 244)

This is not a very flattering view of human nature, to be sure, and yet it illuminates De Quincey's view of addiction in general, and of his own addiction in particular. Besides being a physical disease that was often inherited, it was, more specifically, a disease of the will over which the individual had limited control.[12] On their own, individuals weren't up to 'the effort of self-conquest' because the virtues of intellect, reason, and will were often powerless to resist temptation or vice. It took the more publicly oriented sense of conscience to shame individuals into changing their behaviour. It was simply too much to expect most people addicted to drugs or liquor to heal themselves, De Quincey argued, as much as they might dream of doing so: 'Yet still, so far as it is possible, every man sighs for a still higher victory over himself; a victory not tainted by bribes, and won from no impulses but those inspired by his own higher nature, and his own mysterious force of will; powers that in no man were ever fully developed' (*DQW*, XV: 245).

This sense of the inadequacy of the individual's will, and of the need for 'secondary energies of resistance' in the form of a social shaming mechanism, amounted to a personal credo for De Quincey. As Grevel Lindop notes, he 'was a great believer in making the disapproval of others a substitute for willpower' (1981: 259)—whether this applied to giving up opium, paying off debts, or finishing a work for publication. Thus it's not surprising that De Quincey believed the temperance movement to be so effective in helping alcoholics. Whether such a remedy might work in the case of opium remained to be seen. Opium was a far more powerful substance than alcohol, and the absence of a mass movement to help addicts cope with their problem made their attempts at withdrawal much more difficult.[13] (It also didn't help that opium, at the time, was one of the most 'widespread popular means of controlling and counteracting excessive drinking'! [Berridge, 1999: 33]).

There is some justification for the undercurrent of regret and even envy in the 'Temperance Movement' essay stemming from De Quincey's sense that a vast social movement was underway for the benefit of alcoholics but not opium addicts. The 1845 essay was written during an interim period when opium use continued to be tolerated and widely used by the general public while intoxicating liquors were being increasingly condemned on moral and medical grounds. Temperance organizations calling for restrictions or even a ban on liquor had been in full force in Britain since the 1830s,[14] but opium only came to be widely regarded as an addictive substance in the 1860s when addiction itself began to be recognized as a disease, and it wouldn't be until 1926 that legal drug maintenance treatment programmes first became available in Britain (Brodie and Redfield 2002: 6). Without any medical guidance or morally-driven mass movement to help them, opium-eaters like De Quincey were left to deal with their dependence on their own, and to confront their limitations and inadequacies, their individual failures of will, with virtually no social support.

While it is true that restrictions only began to be placed on opium's availability with the 1868 Pharmacy Act, and that a significant anti-opium movement corresponding (and often directly related) to the temperance movement did not emerge until the 1870s—more than a decade after De Quincey's death—fledgling anti-opium organizations had already begun to form in the 1840s, however 'short-lived' and lacking in 'public impact' they may have been (Berridge 1999: 175). Yet these groups were unlikely to have held much attraction for De Quincey since they were less concerned with the medical and social issue of opium use in England than with the moral and political issue of Britain's role in India's opium trade with China. And on this issue De Quincey was a staunch advocate of the commercial right of British and Indian merchants to ship opium to China despite that nation's ban on such imports—a dispute that led to the 1839–42 opium war. Although waged far from Britain, these 'mid-century wars' had a significant 'domestic impact', as Virginia Berridge notes, in that 'they initiated, at least in embryo, the connection between hostile reactions to opium use in the East and changed perceptions of opium in England'. Eventually opium would itself come to be linked with alcohol 'in the supposedly scientific concept of "inebriety"' as 'the drug, as much as alcohol, was viewed very much in the context of the temperance views which informed the work of medical men in this field' (Berridge 1999: 173, 154). So De Quincey's yearning for a temperance movement in England that would help addicts as well as alcoholics would be fulfilled, but in a way he is unlikely to have approved. For it was a movement driven, at least at first, more by moral than medical interests, and more by what seemed a concern for opium addicts in China than at home.

NATIONAL TEMPERANCE MOVEMENTS AND NATIONAL TEMPERAMENT

> The national mind is . . . best expounded by the direction of its moral feelings . . .
>
> —De Quincey, 'Kant on National Character in Relation to the Sense of the Sublime and the Beautiful' (*DQW*, IV: 151)

At the very end of the 'Temperance Movement' essay De Quincey finally returns to the topic announced in his title, a topic he had dropped for most of the piece in order to pursue his digression on digestion and his other 'Hints in Aid of the Self-Cure of Inebriates', as Masson describes them (1890: XIV, 7). His comments in this final section serve to explicate his opening remark that, even at their early stages, 'temperance movements had obtained, both at home and abroad, a *national* range of grandeur'. Now it is suggested that this modern movement has emerged at a critical time—indeed, *just* in time—during 'the greatest era by far of human expansion', when 'the greatest of our modern nations' are actively colonizing less developed but much older civilizations. Despite De Quincey's nationalist fervour, colonialism isn't shown here in a positive light. Returning to his earlier observation in the 'Anatomy of Drunkenness' that the tendency toward intoxication is 'modified by temperament', and that the northern nations, 'where the temperament is more phlegmatic, and the air denser and colder, are more addicted to strong potations than the lively, volatile, inhabitants of the sunny south', De Quincey now writes that in the process of 'colonizing warm climates' in the south, those great, northern nations 'propagate the contagion to their brothers' of their 'taste . . . for powerful liquors'. (He might have noted that 'the establishment, maintenance, and spread of European empires' in the first place was motivated by the 'demand for "tropical" (i.e., non-European) commodities' like tea [Bello 2005: 22].) De Quincey presents what amounts to a racial view of history in which two 'great races of men, our own in a two-headed form—British and American, and secondly, the Russians', have been 'tainted carnally' by climate and blood, and 'infect[ed]' by a 'contagion of habits', with an 'appetite for brandy, for slings, for juleps'. In contrast, 'all the great races', and 'consequently all the great empires' at the dawn of history arose amid 'the genial climates of the south' where 'man is naturally temperate'. As a result,

> the whole *ancient* system of civilization, all the miracles of Greece and Rome, Persia and Egypt, moved by the machinery of races that were *not* tainted with any such popular *marasmus*. The taste was slightly sowed, as an *artificial* taste, amongst luxurious individuals, but never ran through the labouring classes, through armies, through cities. The blood and the climate forbade it. (*DQW*, XV: 258)

As earlier in the essay he had credited the effectiveness of modern temperance movements to group psychology rather than to religious and moral zealotry, De Quincey here attributes the avoidance of alcohol he finds in the case of 'the Moor, or the Arab' to 'blood' and 'climate', ignoring the obvious religious reasons for their abstinence.

Playing on the temperance/temperate pun, De Quincey depicts a situation in which the northern, Anglo-American and Russian 'races' have combined 'like rising deluges' in 'their mission to overflow the earth'—a mission that threatens to instill a dependence on alcohol in those 'genial climates of the south' where 'man is naturally temperate' (*DQW*, XV: 257–58). At this critical historical moment—'the greatest era by far of human expansion' which will change 'the face of the world' in the 'next hundred years'—there was good reason to fear that the global spread of alcohol abuse would undermine 'the amelioration of the human race' undertaken by the enlightened nations of northern Europe. These nations which had offered the world the promise of salvation now stood to plunge it into perdition. Fortunately, a mass movement 'of resistance to intemperate habits' arose in those very northern nations just when it was most needed, offering salvation from the curse of alcoholism. (Elsewhere De Quincey acknowledges that crucial help also arrived from the temperate zones themselves in the form of tea.[15]) The essay optimistically concludes that

> as the case stands, the new principle of resistance nationally to bad habits has arisen almost concurrently with the new powers of national intercourse; and henceforward by a change equally sudden and unlooked for, that new machinery, which would else most surely have multiplied the ruins of intoxication, has become the strongest agency for hastening its extirpation. (*DQW*, XV: 259)

In this neo-Hegelian reading of nineteenth-century history, temperance is presented as a 'third movement' that promises to reconcile and humanize the 'two vast movements' of politics and technology ('the great revolutionary movement from political causes' and 'the great physical movement in locomotion and social intercourse'). De Quincey celebrates the modern temperance movement as a means of resisting 'bad habits' on the national level—a far more effective way of dealing with the problem than through the efforts of individuals themselves.[16] He is confident that the emergence of this movement in Britain, America, and Russia will make it possible for these modern, northern nations to avoid contaminating the ancient cultures of the south, and provoking the sort of deadly clash of modern and ancient civilizations that we hear so much about today.

Two points about the ending of the 'Temperance Movement' essay are worth noting. The first is De Quincey's repeated use of the word 'infection' to describe the unnatural craving and dependency for alcohol that northern, developed nations supposedly implant in the southern, temperate regions they colonize. This is precisely the opposite usage of the term that commentators like John Barrell have detected throughout this author's work—namely, one in which it is Western values and institutions that are constantly threatened with infection from exotic Eastern influences.[17] A second, more curious feature is De Quincey's avoidance of any mention in his essay of a far more obvious instance of the corruption of ancient, southern societies by modern, northern nations—Britain's opium trade with China.

This omission is especially noteworthy since De Quincey had addressed the subject at length shortly before the 'Temperance Movement' essay. In 'The Opium and the China Question', published in June 1840 at the start of the first opium war, he decried China's ban on British shipments of the drug smuggled into the country from India. Against claims by China's supporters that its government sought to protect its people from 'the national abuse of opium', he argued that opium consumption was a well-established national habit there which the Qing government, having 'long connived at the opium trade' itself, now wanted to exploit without foreign competition (*DQW*, XI: 534–35).[18] Ignoring the threat that the drug posed to China's public health and productivity, De Quincey summarily 'dismiss[ed] this opium part of the general [China] question' (*DQW*, XI: 544). Not only did this nation have no legitimate grounds for prohibiting British opium shipments, but in its uncivilized state it only stood to benefit from any contact it might have with the West. Far from Britain's being at fault in the opium trade, China itself had been 'the original tempter, inviter, hirer, clamorous suborner, of that intercourse which now she denounces' (*DQW*, XI: 565–66).

One might have expected the Sino-British opium trade, which De Quincey referred to in such detail in 1840, to have provided an obvious, contemporary parallel with the global situation outlined in the 1845 'Temperance Movement' essay in which modern, northern nations are shown to have 'infected' ancient, southern countries with their own bad habit of inebriety as an unfortunate (presumably unintended) side-effect of their inexorable 'colonizing' mission.[19] Yet no reference to the opium trade appears in this essay. Such a glaring omission, combined with the essay's peculiar use of the term 'infection', has only one explanation: De Quincey considered Britain's opium trade with China to be a relatively minor eddy flowing in the opposite direction of an overall opium flood moving from east to west. After all, opium originated in the 'East'—specifically, in the southern/eastern regions of Egypt and Arabia. Arab traders had spread the habit to Persia, India, and China, and had introduced opium to the Crusaders who had brought it back to Europe.[20] Thus, when De Quincey imagines the global flow of alcohol—its direction of infection—from north to south in the 'Temperance Movement' essay, he is actually mapping a westerly countercurrent to the easterly flow of opium.[21] In his view, any alcoholic contagion that northern nations are spreading to the south, and any opium habit that Britain might be fostering in China, are more than made up for by the influx in the West of southeastern nations' own indigenous habit-forming products like opium or, he might have added, tea. It was Britain's insatiable tea habit, after all, that drove it to export Indian opium into China in the first place as a way of balancing its trade deficit with that nation (Bello 2005: 33; Schmitt 2002: 77–78).[22]

Both the East and the West were, in effect, exchanging their own bad habits, or 'national sins'.[23] Of the two types of addiction, opium was a particularly 'vicious habit'—especially in the form of morphine injections as the British medical profession came to recognize later in the century (Berridge, 1999: 145). What made this disease so insidious was its 'connection to a larger social picture', as Barry Milligan has noted: 'it originated in the individual and his or her heredity, but it was taken as an indication of a general decline in the physical and moral health of Britons as a whole' (1995: 25). All the more reason for a national movement to provide the surrogate-will needed by individual addicts to overcome their addiction, as De Quincey had argued with respect to intemperance. But while northern nations had recognized their own alcohol problem and taken steps to rectify it before they contaminated the rest of the world, Eastern opium-producing nations like China lacked 'any principle of self-restoration', as he wrote in a later essay (*DQW*, XVIII: 134), and were either unwilling or unable to organize their own mass movement to counteract the ravages of opium, at home or abroad.

Of course, it might be pointed out that the Chinese government's ban on opium imports (as well as on domestic production) was itself just such an endeavour. Following De Quincey's logic in the opening section of the 'Temperance Movement' essay, however, such radical acts of *resistance* or attempts at *abstinence* have virtually no chance of success, either in the case of individuals or entire nations. In contrast, the moderating procedures employed by the more progressive *temperance* programmes supposedly had a proven record of success.[24] But since such programmes could only be effective when they play on the abuser's conscience and sense of shame, what chance could they have on a barbaric nation of such 'ineradicable perfidy and cruelty' as De Quincey believed China to be, a nation that was absolutely incapable of such moral feelings (*DQW*, XIII: 77)?

MANY NATIONS, UNDER THE INFLUENCE

> ... drugs become social problems only when they were moved out of their 'original' contexts to populations or nations which had not been habituated to their use ...
>
> —Carl A. Trocki (1999: xi)

> America is addicted to oil.
>
> —President George W. Bush, 2006 State of the Union address

National Bad Habits 157

We see how De Quincey, who so often 'confesses' to being a victim of opium, could be so insensitive towards the multitudes of fellow sufferers in China with whom he shared an addiction and towards whom we might have expected him to be sympathetic.[25] And we see how he can praise temperance movements in Britain and America to ameliorate the problem of alcoholism 'at home'—and even lament the lack of similar organizations to aid addicts like himself—while opposing the fledgling anti-opium movement in Britain. Whatever ambivalence De Quincey felt about opium, he was put off by its condemnation as an 'unmitigated evil' by moral reformers who sought to prohibit all non-medical uses of the drug in Britain and all efforts to market the drug in China (Blake 1996: 242). He was, after all, an *English* opium-eater, and was at pains to distinguish himself from the opium addicts—and especially from the stereotype of opium *smokers*—in the far East (Milligan, 1995: 115). In relation to Britain and, to a lesser degree, colonized territories like India, 'Oriental powers like China' were *uncolonizable*, as he writes in 'The Opium and the China Question'—not only 'incapable of a true civilisation, semi-refined in manners and mechanic arts, but incurably savage in the moral sense' (*DQW*, XI: 554). In Britain's dealing with such an 'accursed state', moral qualms about its trade policy would seem to be utterly irrelevant.

Nowhere is this point more vividly made than in a passage in 'The China Question' essay recounting what he calls that country's 'national crime of 1785': its execution of an aged Portuguese gunner aboard the *Lady Hughes*, a British vessel in the port of Whampoa, in retribution for the accidental death of a Chinese bystander killed by a shot from one of the ship's guns during a celebratory salute. 'Never in the history of human affairs,' writes De Quincey,

> was there a more absolute accident as respected the man who fired the gun. The man who loaded it was never discovered. But this wicked nation, who are so thoroughly demoralized as to perceive no moral difference between the purest case of misfortune terminating in a man's death and the vilest murder of premeditating malice, demanded (according to their practice) all the men to be given up who had in any way been parties to the loading, the priming, or the firing of the gun.

De Quincey proceeds to describe how, 'to the everlasting shame of poor dishonoured England, the innocent man, who had acted in obedience to absolute orders from his captain, was given up to the Canton devils, in order that they, under colour of avenging an imaginary murder, might perpetrate as real and foul a murder as human annals record' (*DQW*, XI: 550–51).

What strikes De Quincey as vile beyond measure is the inability or unwillingness of the Chinese in this instance to distinguish an accidental death *from* a murder, then to compound the tragedy of this accidental death by treating it *as* an intentional homicide, and finally, to take the life of an arbitrary victim, an entirely innocent individual, as compensation for the imagined murder that never took place. For De Quincey, this 'infamous doctrine that the intention, the motive, signifies nothing'—as he writes seventeen years later when he rehearses this event once again during the *second* opium war of 1856–60 (*DQW*, XVIII: 116)—is the epitome of depravity, and precisely the sort of disordered thinking or delirium that one might expect from someone—or some nation—under the influence of opium. But he immediately commits his own act of scapegoating, charging present-day China with imaginary crimes *it* has not (yet) perpetrated. He warns that, with the increase of British shipping in Asian waters, it is only a matter of time before this primal murder 'will revolve upon us' as China finds new 'opportunities for retaliation' whenever it believes its 'monstrous laws may happen to be infringed.... This people, who are bestial enough to think the will and the intention no necessary element in the moral quality of an act, are also savage enough to punish vicariously' (*DQW*, XI: 553–54). On the basis of this imaginary threat and a mere surmise that China will continue to repeat an act that took place more than a half-century earlier, De Quincey urges Britain to pursue an aggressive policy of military pre-emption.[26]

On one level, such lashing out at the savagery and immorality of the Chinese merely reflects the Celestial Empire's longstanding view of westerners as 'foreign devils' who had appropriated its cultural achievements and offered only its corrupting influence in return (Standage 2005: 184–85). But De Quincey's vehemence against China also seems a classic instance of projection—or what Andrew Blake calls a 'transposition of imperial guilt' (1996: 253)—screening De Quincey's own masochistic abuse.[27] Despite his profession to be an *English* opium-eater—possibly in an effort, as Cannon Schmitt suggests, to 'render the threat of Orientalization harmless by proclaiming from the start the Englishness of this particular consumer of opium' (2002: 70)[28]—he often seems tortured by the possibility that he is essentially no different from his description of the Chinese: opium-eaters and addicts who, while under the influence of the drug, are utterly incapable of seeing differences or setting priorities, and only too capable of committing unspeakable crimes. As an addict who has sunk to the depths of despondency, and who was only kept from sinking to the depths of depravity by the saving grace of his English identity,[29] De Quincey was all too familiar with opium's debilitating effect on the will. His own writings on the 'China Question' reveal that he himself was prone to what he calls 'this horrible Chinese degeneration of moral distinctions', this Eastern failure of the will that had begun to infect the Western world. Soon this moral relativism would manifest itself in guilt-ridden Europeans like Kafka's Joseph K., living in a world in which, to use De Quincey's words, 'the will and the intention' no longer determine 'the moral quality of an act'—a world where 'inevitable misfortune and malice aforethought[,] are equally criminal, punishable equally by the death of a dog' (*DQW*, XI: 551–52).[30]

De Quincey's imagined (albeit repressed) sense of his affinity with the moral savagery of China—'our vilest oriental enemy' (*DQW*, XVIII: 98)— and with what he describes as an Asiatic temperament typical of temperate nations susceptible to opium abuse, most often finds expression in the impassioned prose of his autobiographical works. In discursive, political writings like the 'China' essays, however, his guard is up: he has no trouble making moral distinctions and passing moral judgments, and dissociates himself entirely from Oriental savagery and immorality. Without a trace of irony or self-reflection, he presents opium addiction among the Chinese as a sign of *their* decadence. The British campaign to supply China with the drug is then easy to rationalize: Britain was merely providing the Chinese with what they wanted and deserved. Far from infecting China with a foreign addiction, Britain was merely catering to that nation's own bad habit. From De Quincey's perspective, the real victims of the global opium exchange were not Asians who had used the drug for millennia in their daily lives and who were accustomed to its effects, but Europeans like himself who were unprepared to deal with the dangers of this exotic substance. It was by presenting himself as one of opium's most wretched victims that De Quincey established his literary reputation, and in his more paranoid moments he could imagine himself as a kind of Manchurian candidate, the victim of an Eastern conspiracy to implant an insatiable craving for opium in the West, specifically in individuals with a certain predisposition or temperament like himself. This was not his private fantasy. His belief that Britain was becoming enslaved to opium would be echoed later in the century by the growing anti-opium movement which would argue that the empire's military and commercial venture in India and China was returning to haunt it as 'The Great Anglo-Asiatic Opium Curse' (Berridge 1999: 198–99). Yet De Quincey would have been appalled to learn that a primary exhibit in the movement's anti-opium campaign was his own *Confessions* which was cited in the first edition of its premiere journal, *Friend of China* (Blake 1996: 250–51).[31]

One may certainly deplore De Quincey's extravagant anti-Chinese animus and question his unswerving support of Britain's absolute right to promote its opium trade overseas. Yet there is something to be said for his 'pro-opium' position, especially in light of the sort of morally-motivated, anti-opium and anti-alcohol policies that have since been adopted by the new American empire that has largely assumed Britain's former global role. Having led the international movement in the early twentieth century to end the opium trade, and then embarked on the disastrous experiment of Prohibition, the U.S. endeavour to eradicate drugs at their source has proven to be counter-productive, most recently enabling an economy based on opium to flourish as never before in 'post-Taliban' Afghanistan. (As American efforts to shut down the international drug trade only seem to expand it, the interruption of Britain's drug trade with China during the opium wars coincided with an 'apparent increase in opium being brought into England' [Berridge

1999: 174].³²) Finally, De Quincey's insights into a geography of addiction are worth pursuing in view of the fact that, for nineteenth-century Britain as for twenty-first-century America, opium turns out ultimately to be of only secondary importance—merely a means to an end—in a global exchange involving these northwestern nations' far greater 'addictions', respectively, to the south- and mid-eastern commodities of tea and oil.³³

NOTES

1. Josephine McDonagh finds a related shift in the autobiographical works themselves as De Quincey 'demote[s] opium from its role as "the true hero of the tale" in *Confessions* in 1821' to a merely supportive role in the 1845 *Suspiria* where the subject is no longer 'the agent of addiction, but the addiction itself'. She notes a corresponding shift in 'his own literary reputation . . . from that of the popularizer of opium to that of a significant contributor to the broader fields of philosophy, literature, and political economy' (1994: 153, 180).
2. For a recent dissenting view, see Theodore Dalrymple's claim that 'addiction is a moral weakness par excellence', and his contention that the erroneous idea that it is a disease stems 'from the self-serving, self-dramatizing, and evasive and dishonest accounts of De Quincey and Coleridge' (2006: 109, 114).
3. Virginia Berridge reports that opium 'was popularly used to counteract the effect of too much drink' (specifically, delirium tremens), as an 'informal means of sobering up', and 'as a cheaper alternative to drink' (1999: 33–34, 106). She notes that the connection between opium and alcohol 're-emerges at many stages in nineteenth-century society—in the working-class opium-eating "scare", for instance, or in the concept of "inebriety" and the formulation of disease theories of addiction' (71).
4. First appearing as an unsigned letter in the quarterly magazine *The Philanthropist*, a revised version appeared in the *London Magazine* of August 1822.
5. Cited in Lindop, 1981: 119.
6. As children, Thomas and his older brother William imagined themselves as kings of fictitious countries—Tigrosylvania ruled by William in the far north, and Gombroon ruled by Thomas in the tropics. William's 'discovery that the people of Gombroon . . . had tails', and thus were 'degraded below the level of human existence' (Lindop, 1981: 18–19), anticipates De Quincey's later view of China as a barbaric nation to which he sensed himself to be profoundly linked.
7. As Hayter points out, however, De Quincey's gloomiest reflections about 'opium's worst powers' are to be found not 'in anything he wrote for publication', but 'in his private meditations, and letters to friends', especially during his own difficult attempt at withdrawal from laudanum in 1844 (1988: 116).
8. While noting that a late nineteenth-century doctor like Norman Kerr's 'interest in narcotic addiction was an offshoot of his prime concern for alcoholic inebriety', Berridge also observes that 'the linking of opium with alcohol in the supposedly scientific concept of "inebriety" meant that the drug, as much as alcohol, was viewed very much in the context of the temperance views which informed the work of medical men in this field' (Berridge 1999: 151, 154).
9. Regarding 'laudanum-drinkers', Hayter notes that 'some of [their] visions may be due to the alcohol in the laudanum rather than to the opium' (1988: 55). And citing the 'varying parts of alcohol and opium' in De Quincey's laudanum concoctions, McDonagh cautions against putting too much stock in his 'claims to know the distinct qualities of each substance' (1994: 160).

10. Cf. De Quincey's earlier 'Observations on Diet' from 1827 (*DQW*, V: 1–5). Whereas De Quincey suggests that alcohol was commonly used to alleviate indigestion, opium 'was used for hangovers and alcoholism' (Hayter 1988: 30).
11. Indeed, Robyn R. Warhol describes how the founders of AA revived the idea that 'alcoholism is a disease' in reaction to the nineteenth century 'ideology of temperance, which understood excessive drinking as a moral failing' (2002: 100).
12. Without referring specifically to this essay, Dalrymple rejects the idea that 'Addicts cannot possibly escape their chains without professional assistance', and calls for 'the closure of all clinics claiming to treat drug addicts' as 'the modern bureaucratic institutionalization of Romantic ideas' (2006: 36, 114). Dalrymple's fixation on De Quincey as a false prophet of opium keeps him from recognizing the latter's insights into addiction as a geographical and geopolitical phenomenon.
13. Contrast Dalrymple's claim that 'withdrawal from alcohol is much more serious' than withdrawal from opiates (ibid., 20).
14. The British and Foreign Temperance Society was founded in 1831; the British Association for the Promotion of Temperance in 1835.
15. As 'the most refined, elegant, and intellectual mode of stimulation that human research has succeeded in discovering', tea is credited with providing Britons with a 'substitute for the gross stimulation of ale and wine' (*DQW*, XVIII: 156).
16. Interestingly, religious leaders in the American Confederacy like the Presbyterian minister Benjamin Morgan Palmer considered intemperance an *individual* sin, along with swearing and Sabbath breaking, in contrast to *national* sins like the founders' failure 'to make "*a clear national recognition of God at the outset of the nation's career*"' (Foster 2002: 19–20). Predictably, Palmer overlooks what would seem to be America's greatest national sin—slavery.
17. Barrell makes only a passing reference to the 'Temperance Movement' essay (1991: 197 n11).
18. There is some merit to this claim. David A. Bello notes that despite the Qing government's prohibition policy (motivated by a concern to protect government revenues rather than by moral or medical concerns), opium production flourished in the interior regions of western China where 'Euro-American traffickers were completely absent'. However, he adds that Euro-Americans 'were unquestionably the deliberate instigators of the mass consumption of the drug in China proper' (2005: 6). And Tom Standage insists that 'Although China illegally produced as much opium, at the time, as was imported, that is no justification for state-sanctioned drug running on a massive scale, which created thousands of addicts and blighted countless lives merely to maintain Britain's supply of tea' (2005: 210).
19. One geographical group that De Quincey doesn't mention, but that confirms his observations, is Native Americans. As Gaines Foster notes, 'Few if any people suffered more from the ravages of alcohol than Native Americans, who learned to drink to excess from the Europeans' (2000: 13). While the Europeans' introduction of liquor into Native American society mirrors the British imposition of opium on the Chinese, the prohibitionist legislation eventually passed by Congress in the early nineteenth century, which restricted alcohol use by Native Americans who were deemed culturally inferior, was the opposite of Britain's policy at this time which amounted to forcing opium on the Chinese. The American writer James Fenimore Cooper showed a good deal more ambivalence in his works about the stereotype of the 'drunken Indian', which 'gave white imperialism the perfect formula for conquest without guilt'

(Warner 2002: 111), than De Quincey did about Chinese opium-smokers whom Britain could exploit with impunity.
20. Despite Britain's role in the opium trade between India and China, the bulk of the opium that made its way into England in the nineteenth century came from Turkey (Berridge 1999: 4).
21. Since the distillation of wine was a medieval Arab discovery and the word 'alcohol' itself is Arabic in origin, this substance travelled the same northwest route to Europe as opium. But given Muslims' widespread observance of the ban on alcoholic beverages, the Arabs used distilled wine primarily for medical and alchemical purposes. It wasn't until the technology spread to 'the cooler climes of northern Europe, where wine was scarce and expensive', that distilled 'drinks proved particularly popular' as De Quincey suggests (Standage 2005: 100).
22. De Quincey was clearly aware of Britain's dependence on China for tea, without which 'our daily life would, generally speaking, be as effectually ruined as bees without a Flora' (*DQW*, XVIII: 155). And he was well aware of China's economic dependence on Britain, suggesting that the surest way that 'opium-eating will prosper' in China is not by that nation's opening its markets to Britain, but by its closing them down, thereby depriving itself of the revenue it received from the 'English demand annually for forty millions of pounds' of tea (*DQW*, XI: 546). (Seventeen years later, he revised this figure to '100,000,000 pounds weight annually' [*DQW*, XVIII: 159].) After India became Britain's chief source of tea later in the century, the need for opium financing was eliminated and the Chinese economy devastated, much as De Quincey had predicted. One also shouldn't overlook the obvious parallel between China's confiscation and destruction of British merchants' supplies of opium which triggered the opium war, and the dumping of 'British' tea into Boston Harbor by American colonists some seventy years earlier which provoked the Revolutionary War.
23. See note 16.
24. Although De Quincey uses the terms 'abstinence' and 'temperance' interchangeably, and although many temperance organizations called for a total ban on sales of alcoholic beverages, the essay's opening argument boils down to a distinction between abstinence and moderation as alternative strategies for overcoming addiction. Of the two strategies, the latter is far more likely to be successful: while abstinence is essentially a zero-tolerance program, 'temperance' sets a more modest goal of moderating the abuse. As has recently been noted, 'Abstinence was long thought to be the only cure for addiction. But new treatments suggest that, for some, moderation may work better' (Carey 2006: 1).
25. It should be recalled that it was not until 1844—between the publication of 'The Opium and the China Question' and the 'Temperance Movement' essays—that De Quincey seems to have realized the full extent of his own addiction and that he was living 'under a curse' (Lindop 1981: 351).
26. Actually, Britain was provoked to declare war in the aftermath of a much more recent incident that stands in sharp contrast to the one De Quincey cites: the murder of a Chinese man by two British soldiers who were *not* surrendered by their superiors. In response, the British were expelled from Canton, which precipitated the opium war (Standage 2005: 211).
27. Cf. Milligan's suggestion of 'a form of masochistic repetition compulsion as an explanation of De Quincey's opium use' in contrast to addiction models based on 'stable definitions of pleasure and pain' (1995: 67–68). De Quincey's indulgence in 'the masochistic pleasures of addiction' and in 'the pleasurable loss of power incurred in addiction' is shown by McDonagh to extend to his aesthetic technique in the 'elaborately tortured text' of the *Suspiria*, and to his

insights in the 'China' essays regarding the 'economic corollary of addiction, the crisis in colonial trade' (1994: 180, 182).
28. Schmitt describes De Quincey's 'construction of English national identity' as a projection of his 'construction of autobiographical subjectivity'—namely, as a state of 'frailty', 'dependence', 'victimization', and 'openness to attack', that ultimately underwrites Britain's official policy of aggression after the Indian Rebellion of 1857 (2002: 68, 64–65, 84, 208 n60).
29. I am grateful to Robert Morrison and Daniel Roberts for pointing out this distinction.
30. Patrick Bridgwater has detailed several ways in which De Quincey is 'a precursor of Kafka', including both authors' Gothic sense of guilt:

> If De Quincey was obsessed by 'the fear of an imposed and unjust guilt', Kafka carried such a (partly self-imposed) burden throughout his life; Josef K. in *Der Proceß* embodies it. The idea of De Quincey incurring, in the form of his addiction to opium, what he, in his 'Preliminary Confessions', calls 'a captivity so servile' ... is not only Gothic, but Gothic in a late Romantic, Kafkaesque way, for the 'yoke of misery' is self-imposed. (2004: 157, 163)

31. It's worth noting that the decline of the Sino-British opium trade towards the end of the century had less to do with the anti-opium movement's moral-medical crusade than with the success of tea cultivation in India which then displaced China as Britain's principal source of tea. In 1857, two years before his death, De Quincey anxiously awaited news of the 'results in an experiment so vitally national' as the Assamese venture which held the possibility of 'making ourselves independent of a nation which at all times we had so much reason to distrust as the Chinese' (*DQW*, XVIII: 156). The ultimate irony is that, thanks to global warming, England itself is becoming a temperate zone where wine and even tea are now being cultivated.
32. Bello notes the analogous situation within China in the 1830s where the government's prohibition policies, based on 'their conviction that all opium users were serious, even dangerous addicts', actually 'resulted in a concept of opium consumers as serious addicts' that only aggravated the 'burgeoning in aggregate demand from Chinese consumers, whatever their degrees of addiction' (2005: 32).
33. In fact, opium functioned as a 'substitute for silver' in the Sino-British drug trade (Blake, 1996: 235; McDonagh, 1994: 175), since the silver that was traded for Chinese tea by the East India Company had itself been surreptitiously acquired from China in exchange for opium, which Standage describes as a kind of inexhaustible currency that Britain could 'grow as much [of] ... as it needed' (2005: 208). But as an 'addictive consumable' with immense 'revenue-generating power', opium was also an ideal commodity that soon 'supplant[ed] tea as the primary article of commerce' in the early nineteenth century 'because of its superior capacity for generating private and public wealth' by 'engender[ing] dependency or addiction in a critical number of users' (Bello 2005: 22, 32–33).

WORKS CITED

Barrell, John. (1991) *The Infection of Thomas De Quincey: A Psychopathology of Imperialism*, New Haven, CT: Yale University Press.

Bello, David A. (2005) *Opium and the Limits of Empire: Drug Prohibition in the Chinese Interior, 1729–1850*, Cambridge, MA: Harvard University Asia Center.

Berridge, Virginia. (1981; rev. ed. 1999) *Opium and the People: Opiate Use and Drug Control Policy in Nineteenth and Early Twentieth Century England*, London: Free Association Books.

Black, Joel. (1991) *The Aesthetics of Murder: A Study in Romantic Literature and Contemporary Culture*, Baltimore: The Johns Hopkins University Press.

Blake, Andrew. (1996) 'Foreign Devils and Moral Panics: Britain, Asia and the Opium Trade', in Bill Schwarz (ed.), *The Expansion of England: Race, Ethnicity and Cultural History*, London: Routledge, 232–59.

Bridgwater, Patrick. (2004) *De Quincey's Gothic Masquerade*, Amsterdam: Rodopi.

Brodie, Janet Farrell and Marc Redfield (eds.). (2002) *High Anxieties: Cultural Studies in Addiction*, Berkeley: University of California Press.

Carey, Benedict. (2006) 'Between Addiction and Abstinence', *New York Times*, 7 May, Sec. 4: 1, 14.

Dalrymple, Theodore. (2006) *Romancing Opiates: Pharmacological Lies and the Addiction Bureaucracy*, New York: Encounter Books.

Foster, Gaines M. (2002) *Moral Reconstruction: Christian Lobbyists and the Federal Legislation of Morality, 1865–1920*, Chapel Hill: University of North Carolina Press.

Hayter, Althea. (1968; rev. ed. 1988) *Opium and the Romantic Imagination: Addiction and Creativity in De Quincey, Coleridge, Baudelaire, and Others*, Wellingborough: Crucible.

Lamb, Charles. (1903) *The Works of Charles and Mary Lamb*, 5 vols., ed. E. V. Lucas, New York: Putnam's.

Lindop, Grevel. (1981) *The Opium-Eater: A Life of Thomas De Quincey*, New York: Taplinger.

Masson, David (ed.). (1890) *The Collected Writings of Thomas De Quincey*, 14 vols., Edinburgh: Adam and Charles Black.

McDonagh, Josephine. (1994) *De Quincey's Disciplines*, Oxford: Clarendon Press.

Milligan, Barry. (1995) *Pleasures and Pains: Opium and the Orient in Nineteenth-Century British Culture*, Charlottesville: University Press of Virginia.

———. (2005) 'Morphine-Addicted Doctors, the English Opium-Eater, and Embattled Medical Authority', *Victorian Literature and Culture* 33: 541–53.

Schmitt, Cannon. (2002) 'Narrating National Addictions: De Quincey, Opium, and Tea', in *High Anxieties: Cultural Studies in Addiction*, Janet Farrell Brodie and Marc Redfield (eds.), Berkeley: University of California Press, 63–84.

Standage, Tom. (2005) *A History of the World in 6 Glasses*, New York: Walker.

Trocki, Carl A. (1999) *Opium, Empire and the Global Political Economy: A Study of the Asian Opium Trade, 1760–1950*, London: Routledge.

Warhol, Robyn R. (2002) 'The Rhetoric of Addiction', in *High Anxieties: Cultural Studies in Addiction*, Janet Farrell Brodie and Marc Redfield (eds.), Berkeley: University of California Press, 97–108.

Warner, Nicholas O. (2002) 'Firewater Legacy: Alcohol and Native American Identity in the Fiction of James Fenimore Cooper', in *High Anxieties: Cultural Studies in Addiction*, Janet Farrell Brodie and Marc Redfield (eds.), Berkeley: University of California Press, 109–16.

9 On the Language of the Sublime and the Sublime Nation in De Quincey
Toward a Reading of 'The English Mail-Coach'

Ian Balfour

> No language is stationary...
>
> —Thomas De Quincey (*DQW*, XVII: 56)

Few writers or thinkers were ever so well poised to drink in the heady air of the sublime as was Thomas De Quincey. A voracious reader with a prodigious memory, his consciousness was usually swimming with passages from the ancients to the most contemporary of moderns. Raised in a modest hamlet in the orbit of Manchester, then an inhabitant alternately of one of the great metropolises of the world, a small town such as Oxford or a picturesque village such as Grasmere, he was exposed to a great diversity of social experience for someone confined to Britain. He came a little late in the period that would be consolidated as the Romantic era, meeting and getting to know, sometimes intimately, a number of the great writers of the half-generation before him. And he was well versed or at least immersed in German Idealist philosophy, especially that of Kant, author of by far the most consequential and influential account of the sublime, as well as other writings that caused a Copernican revolution of sorts and a few variously shattering 'Kant crises,' such as the one that debilitated Heinrich von Kleist. A highly educated person with the aura of elite provenance, De Quincey nonetheless led an unusually bohemian existence, complicated and sometimes enriched by the pains and pleasures of his opium-taking, whose consequences included instilling a sense of spatial and temporal sublimity.[1] It is no wonder, then, that for De Quincey, the sublime came to be something like second nature.

Where does one most readily locate the sublime in De Quincey's sprawling *oeuvre*? A short and only somewhat arbitrary list of sites might read: the universe, *Paradise Lost*, Wordsworth (the man and his best poetry), De Quincey's own mind and his dreams, London, England, and the English mail-coach. This is not just any list: a good deal of it is linked, as we shall see, via the force of metonymy or metaphor. Of course, the things that are plausibly sublime in De Quincey or even named by him explicitly as such are far greater in number. Even if the sublime is postulated as what is 'absolutely great' (Kant), we know that, in practice, there exists something of a sliding scale of sublimity, with some things pronounced 'more sublime' than others. This multiplication of sublimities is helped—or exacerbated—by De Quincey's penchant for upping the rhetorical ante whenever possible. As Virginia Woolf comments in her brief essay 'The English Mail Coach,' 'De Quincey's chief fault at least is one that under other circumstances becomes his chief virtue. He suffers from the gift of seeing everything a size too large, and of reproducing his vision in words which are also a size too large, unless indeed, they are applied, as, happily, is so often the case, to emotions which cannot be magnified' (Woolf 1996: 367). In what follows, the *topoi* or passages of sublimity I shall focus on will be ones where the rhetoric seems, at least momentarily, to be of the order of the *ne plus ultra*.

I shall ultimately be concerned in this essay with the under-examined overlap between the discourse of the sublime and the discourse of the nation especially as crystallized in De Quincey's work but first I want to establish some sense of what counts as sublime in De Quincey through some weighty (or is it lofty?) examples, many of which will turn out to have a covert or overt relation to the nation. The general terrain of the sublime might well have been mapped out for De Quincey by Kant, the thinker he spent a good deal of his life reading and/or avoiding. The possible bookends, as it were, of the sublime are set out by Kant in a famous passage at the end of a text often overlooked in the literature on the sublime, since it comes not from the *Critique of Judgment*, site of Kant's most extended analysis of the matter, but from the *Critique of Practical Reason*:

> Two things fill the mind with ever new and increasing admiration and awe (*Ehrfurcht*), the more often and more steadily one reflects on them: *the starry heavens above me and the moral law within me*. I do not need to search for them and merely conjecture them as though they were veiled in obscurity or in the transcendent region beyond my horizon: I see them before me and connect them immediately with the consciousness of my existence. The first begins from the place I occupy in the external world of sense and extends the connection in which I stand into an unbounded magnitude with worlds beyond worlds and systems of systems, and moreover into the unbounded times of their periodic motion, their beginning and their duration. The second begins from my invisible self, my personality, and presents me in a world which has true infinity but which can be discovered only by the understanding, and I recognize that my connection with that world (and thereby with all those visible worlds as well) is not merely contingent, as in the first case, but universal and necessary. The first view of a countless multitude of worlds annihilates, as it were, my importance as an *animal creature*, which must give back to the planet (a mere speck in the universe) the

matter from which it came, the matter which is for a little time provided with vital force (one knows not how). The second, on the contrary, infinitely raises my worth as an *intelligence* by my personality, in which the moral law reveals to me a life independent of all animality and even of the whole sensible world, at least so far as this may be inferred from the purposive determination of my existence by this law, a determination not restricted to the conditions and boundaries of this life but reaching into the infinite. (Kant, 1996, 270–71; translation modified slightly.)

All of De Quincey's touchstones of the sublime would fall somewhere on the spectrum from the all-encompassing but not-to-be-surveyed universe to the labyrinthine interiors of the self, opium-riddled or not. Descartes was the first Western thinker to expound what might be called infinite subjectivity, the subject as a locus of infinity, something that would be reiterated and recast by Kant and then all the more so by Hegel. De Quincey also certainly shares something of the shudder of the philosophers—and not just them—when contemplating the vastness of the universe. Even the rhetoric of the far more sober Kant features something of a De Quinceyean heightening when he invokes 'worlds beyond worlds,' or 'systems of systems,' as thought spirals outward far beyond what is available to the senses or to a 'meta'-level where only imagination and speculation can reign. When turning inward, De Quincey also shares the relatively newer awe in the face of the subject—Kant even thought that 'personality' as such was a locus of the sublime—though only sometimes is the inner self for De Quincey pre-eminently the site of 'moral law'.[2] (Kant, for a moment, is almost as hallucinatory as De Quincey sometimes is, when he somehow claims to 'see' [*sehe*] the moral law within him!) Yet in general for De Quincey, the self was opened up, by his reading of Kant as well as by his very experience, as a kind of epistemological abyss that comes with affective consequences. Kant's passage also shows, in miniature, a trajectory of the self that he elaborates at length in the third *Critique*, whereby the self is temporarily or momentarily annihilated, subject to death or something like it (if there is something *like* death), only to recognize its superiority, at the level of spirit or intelligence, to the world that defeated it on the terrain of the senses. De Quincey too will have recourse to such narratives, more or less improbably snatching victory from the jaws of defeat and all the more exhilarated or even ennobled for having done so.[3]

Unlike a good many of his contemporaries, De Quincey left no single extended or continuous reflection on the sublime or the beautiful, the two dominant categories that organized thinking on the aesthetic. But he came very close to formulating an aesthetics of the sublime in his landmark distinction between the literature of knowledge and the literature of power.[4] (We are accustomed nowadays, after Foucault, not to distinguish sharply between power and knowledge. Indeed Foucault usually couples them by hyphenation: power-knowledge. In De Quincey the distinction appears categorical. I recall the outlines of his claims from his celebrated review of Pope's works:

> There is first the literature of *knowledge*, and secondly, the literature of *power*. The function of the first is—to *teach*; the function of the second is—to *move* . . . The first speaks to the *mere* discursive understanding; the second speaks ultimately it may happen to the higher understanding or reason, but always *through* affections of pleasure and sympathy (*DQW*, XVI: 336).

In the much earlier 'Letters to a Young Man whose Education Has Been Neglected' of 1823 De Quincey already had starkly opposed knowledge to power, invoking *Paradise Lost* as a work to which one in no way should turn for knowledge but rather as a source or site of power. But would all of the literature of power, all literature that *moves*, be of the order of the sublime? No, as the invocation of the distinction at the outset of a general essay on Pope might suggest: hardly anyone would be tempted to call all or most of Pope sublime. Yet not just any examples of this literature of power are invoked by De Quincey. Some seem far more exemplary of power than others:

> When in King Lear, the height, and depth, and breadth of human passion is revealed to us—and for the purposes of a sublime antagonism is revealed in the weakness of an old man's nature, and in one night two worlds of storm are brought face to face—the human world, and the world of physical nature. . . . when I am thus suddenly startled into a feeling of the infinity of the world within me, is this power? or what may I call it? Space, again—what is it in most men's minds? The lifeless form of the world without us—a postulate of the geometrician, with no more vitality or real existence to their feelings, than the square root of two. But, if Milton has been able to *inform* this empty theatre—peopling it with Titanic shadows . . . so that, from being a thing to inscribe with diagrams, it has become under his hands a vital agent on the human mind; I presume that I may justly express the tendency of the Paradise Lost by saying that it communicates power . . . (*DQW*, III: 71)

The literature of power as De Quincey *defines* it is broad enough to encompass a wide swath, perhaps even all of what we too now tend to call literature, Literature with a capital L.[5] But the examples singled out tend to be, as here, textbook versions of the sublime, works that stretch (to) the limits of the human and stage the encounter of the human with the non-human to the extent of radically imperiling the self or subject, if only temporarily. The gloss on *King Lear* and the account of its effect on De Quincey marks it as participating in the frequent appropriation or transfer of power from the object to the subject in the sublime encounter (a dynamic superbly analyzed in Neil Hertz's work).⁶ It would be easy for any number of readers *not* to identify with *King Lear* or King Lear. Moreover, is there any necessary link between the infinity of the world outside and that within? Yet De Quincey, making the leap between Shakespeare's character and fictional world to himself, testifies to feeling—this is pure Kant—the infinity of the world within him, an inner infinity of which the vertiginous interiors of his opium-induced dreams, Piranesis of the self, would be only the most graphic expression.⁷

Milton is often invoked throughout De Quincey's writings as the most exemplary (not quite a contradiction in terms) instance of the literature of power: he is 'not an author amongst authors, not a poet amongst poets, but a power amongst powers; and the *Paradise Lost* is not a book amongst books, not a poem amongst poems, but a central force amongst forces' (*DQW*, XI: 436). The sublime might be considered, to mimic De Quincey's rhetoric, the power amongst powers. In the same essay, called simply 'Milton', he remarks: 'Let it be remembered, that, of all powers which act upon man through his intellectual nature, the very rarest is that which we moderns call the *sublime*' (*DQW*, XI: 437). De Quincey goes on to chart different modes of the sublime, the moral and the ethico-physical (entailing a synthesis of man and nature, of which *Prometheus Unbound* is the prime example), culminating in this pronouncement:

> Laying this one insulated case apart, and considering that the Hebrew poetry of Isaiah and Ezekiel, as having the benefit of inspiration, does not lie within the just limits of competition, we may affirm that there is no human composition which can be challenged as constitutionally sublime—sublime equally by its conception and by its execution, or as uniformly sublime from first to last, excepting the *Paradise Lost*. In Milton only, first and last, is the power of the sublime revealed. In Milton only does this great agency blaze and glow as a furnace kept up to a white heat—without intermission and without collapse. (*DQW*, XI: 437-38)

How can anyone who has a concept of the sublime maintain that one and only one poet achieved it, aside from those who 'officially' or according to scripture were beneficiaries of divine inspiration? Granted De Quincey retreats a bit in the lines prior and subsequent to the most extravagant claim, stressing that the particular distinction of Milton's sublime is its *continuous* character. Some passages of the same essay do acknowledge mere mortals, such as the author of *Prometheus Unbound*, to have achieved the sublime, but in this passage De Quincey pulls out all the stops or, at least, the absolute stop: 'in Milton *only*' (my emphasis). Elsewhere De Quincey will concede Homer a minimal sublimity in the same breath as he posits that Milton is 'many a thousand times more sublime' than the author of the *Iliad* and the *Odyssey* (*DQW*, XI: 9). Technically, this judgment has a place on the sliding scale of sublimity but in effect it moves 'off the scale' by virtue of the hyperbolic multiplication: 'many a thousand times more sublime'.

What to most arbiters of literary taste would stand as an outrageous comparison—Milton absolutely sublime, Homer hardly or not at all so—comes in the course of De Quincey's 'A Brief Appraisal of Greek Literature', which takes up the debate that the Romantics inherited in the wake of the seventeenth century's 'Quarrel of the Ancients and the Moderns'. Milton is crucial to De Quincey's case for weighing in on the side of the Moderns to the extent that it was an either/or decision, though De Quincey is not often constrained by the narrow constraints of the debate. De Quincey does allow for the greatness of Greek tragedy and its difference from English achievements in the same genre, without quite needing to decide on the superiority of one over the other. And, as De Quincey is the first to point out, at least he is well acquainted with Greek and Latin literature, as a good many partisans of the Moderns were not (especially the Greek).

Milton will rear his head again on our trajectory toward the national sublime in De Quincey but we might turn now to Wordsworth, arguably the most modern of the moderns in terms of the sublime. Wordsworth, not coincidentally for De Quincey, slots himself into the Miltonic line of the sublime by internalizing it, especially in *The Prelude*, where he claimed, in Book III that the recounting of 'what passed within' him was, in truth, 'heroic argument', (1805 Bk. III, 171-85) the Miltonic tag for the epic project now transferred to the Wordsworthian individual.[8] If one had to choose the most charged moment of De Quincey's life, I think one of the contenders would be the moment that he met William Wordsworth. The first of a series of long reflections on Wordsworth, entitled simply 'William Wordsworth,' opens with the *seeing* of the poet: 'In 1807 it was, at the beginning of winter, that I first saw William Wordsworth' (*DQW*, XI: 43). De Quincey's essay 'William Wordsworth and Robert Southey' opens, *in medias res*, with the very same moment—the first glimpse of the poet—but with a more elaborate description of its effect.

> That night—the first of my personal intercourse with Wordsworth—the first in which I saw him face to face—was (it is little, indeed, to say) memorable: it was marked by a change even in the physical condition of my nervous system. Long disappointment—hope for ever baffled, (and why should it be less painful because *self*-baffled?)—vexation and self-blame, almost self-contempt, at my own want of courage to face the man whom of all since the Flood I most yearned to behold... (*DQW*, XI: 110)

When one returns to the former reflection, one finds that the discussion focuses to a remarkable extent on the *face* of Wordsworth. Even given the long anticipation of meeting Wordsworth, in a 'face-to-face' encounter, it seems odd that there is so much attention to the literal face. But first, having sounded the theme of *seeing* Wordsworth, De Quincey backtracks to the pre-history of his encounter. It is a moment he approached with the utmost desire and trepidation, looking forward to it with immense anticipation and putting it off more than once, even when coming within a few miles of his express destination.⁹

The very setting was already, in his mind, awash with epic sublimity. Remarking how the yet unvisited sites of the Lake District cast 'local spells' upon him, 'equally poetic and elevating with the Miltonic names of Valdarno and Vallombrosa', he notes:

> ... they had a separate fascination, under the anticipation that very probably I might here form personal ties which would for ever connect me with their sweet solitudes by powers deep as life and awful as death. Oh! sense of mysterious pre-existence, by which, through years in which as yet a stranger to these valleys of Westmoreland, I viewed myself as a phantom-self ... (*DQW*, XI: 44)

But far more sublime than the arch-sublime setting of the fabled Lake District was the projected sight of one man who lived there: 'the very image of Wordsworth, as I prefigured it to my own planet-struck eye, crushed my faculties as before Elijah or St Paul' (*DQW*, XI: 45). Not only do the reputation and the idea and the texts precede Wordsworth, the man in the flesh, but the very *image* does so as well. A 'crushing of faculties' is stronger language than one tends to find even in Kant. This sublime effect is partly linked—or even explained—by Wordsworth by the (sublime) cause that precedes the sight of the poet:

> ... the real cause of my delay was the too great profundity, and the increasing profundity, of my interest in this regeneration of our national poetry; and the increasing awe, in due proportion to the decaying thoughtlessness of boyhood, which possessed me for the character of its author. (*DQW*, XI: 45)

The profundity and awe associated with the 'regeneration of our national poetry' somehow seem not quite dissociable from the image of Wordsworth. The specificity of Wordsworth's face is framed with a broader perspective on matters in which Wordsworth's face lives and moves and has its being:

> The movable part of a population is chiefly the higher part; and it is the lower classes that, in every nation, compose the *fundus*, in which lies latent the national face as well as the national character. Each exists here in racy purity and integrity, not disturbed in the one by alien intermarriages, nor in the other by novelties of opinion or other casual effects derived from education and reading. Now, look into this *fundus*, and you will find, in many districts, no such prevalence of the

round orbicular face as some people erroneously suppose: and in Westmoreland especially, the ancient long face of the Elizabethan period, powerfully resembling in all its lineaments the ancient Roman face . . . Wordsworth's face was, if not absolutely the indigenous face of the Lake district, at any rate a variety of that face, a modification of that original type. (*DQW*, XI: 57)

One way one faces the nation, then, lies in confronting it as a face, embodied in an exemplary way in Wordsworth. Wordsworth's face is at once regional, national, and poetic, aligned with the lower classes (as were the *Lyrical Ballads*) and yet having at the same time a kind of noble pedigree ('ancient Roman face'). De Quincey dilates on various aspects of the face, not failing to interpret them in the mode of popular phrenology (the pseudo-science is twice explicitly invoked) of which I excerpt just a section:

The nose, a little arched, and large, which, by the way, (according to a natural phrenology, existing centuries ago amongst some of the lowest amongst the human species,) has always been accounted an unequivocal expression of animal appetites organically strong. And that was in fact the basis of Wordsworth's intellectual power: his intellectual passions were fervent and strong; because they rested upon a basis of animal sensibility superior to that of most men, diffused through *all* the animal passions (or appetites); and something of that will be found to hold of all poets who have been great by original force and power, not (as Virgil) by means of fine management and exquisite artifice of composition applied to their conceptions. The mouth, and the region of the mouth, the whole circumjacencies of the mouth, were about the strongest feature in Wordsworth's face . . . (*DQW*, XI: 58)

We go back and forth in this passage, from literal nose and face to a far more general observation about the physiognomy and psychology of poets, and back again to the face itself. This passage accomplishes, in principle, one crucial thing subtended by both phrenology and physiognomy: it coordinates the internal (intellect, passions) with the external (face, body), such that everything is on one page, so to speak, with no possible discrepancy between inside and out. It should perhaps come as no surprise by now that a focus on the face of a poet would zoom in on the mouth, the best candidate of any facial part for the source of poetry. And as it happens, the mouth and area around it call to mind an astonishing incident. De Quincey recalls how he was once anxious, given his immense enthusiasm for Milton, to procure a copy of Jonathan Richardson's edition of Milton because it was thought to contain an 'unusually fine specimen' of the engraved portrait of the poet, one supposedly acknowledged by Milton's last surviving daughter to be a 'strong likeness' (*DQW*, XI: 59). Judge of our astonishment as we read what happens when De Quincey actually sees the portrait:

Judge of my astonishment when, in this portrait of Milton, I saw a likeness nearly perfect of Wordsworth, better by much than any which I have since seen, of those expressly painted for himself ... (*DQW*, XI: 59)

It seems a little too good to be true—but in De Quincey's logic it almost had to be true—that the regional, national, poetic face of Wordsworth would coincide with that of Milton, sometimes thought to be the only exemplar of the sublime, certainly of the continuous sublime, and certainly of the modern, English, poetic sublime. Such a face is not only 'exemplary to a nation,' to invoke a phrase of Milton's own, but also exemplary *of* it: this is the national poetic character literally *par excellence* (Milton 1957: 669).

No doubt the charged character of the meeting with—the *sight of*—Wordsworth had mainly to do with the profound effect the poetry had already had on him. The following formulation ranks among the most extravagant in all of De Quincey, even if its context, as a private letter to the praised poet in question, might qualify its status somewhat. He writes to Wordsworth in praise of his poetry:

> But I may say in general, without the smallest exaggeration, that the whole aggregate of pleasure I have received from some eight or nine other poets that I have been able to find since the world began—falls infinitely short of what those two enchanting volumes have singly afforded me. (Jordan 1963: 30)

Does this not in effect say that Wordsworth is, for De Quincey, the best poet ever? And it was not least the *sublimity* of Wordsworth's poetry that would come later to so enthrall De Quincey, a fact perhaps heightened by the latter's having access to that poetry in advance of almost everyone. Able to read (or hear) what would become *The Prelude* in the process of its long, discontinuous composition, De Quincey's experience of that epoch-making poetry was about as auratic as possible. With a fine eye and ear for what would become the canonical passages of his admired poet, De Quincey singles out the so-called 'dream of the Arab' for singled out its absolute singularity and sublimity:

> Wordsworth was a profound admirer of the sublimer mathematics; at least of the higher geometry. The secret of this admiration for geometry lay in the antagonism between this world of bodiless abstraction and the world of passion. And here I may mention appropriately, and I hope without any breach of confidence, that, in a great philosophic poem of Wordsworth's, which is still in M.S., and will remain in M.S. until after his death, there is, at the opening of one of the books, a dream, which reaches the very *ne plus ultra* of sublimity in my opinion, expressly framed to illustrate the eternity and the independence of all social modes

or fashions of existence, conceded to these two hemispheres, as it were, that compose the total world of human power—mathematics on the one hand, poetry on the other.

> The one that held acquaintance with the stars
> —undisturbed by space or time;
> The other that was a god—yea, many gods—
> Had voices more than all the winds, and was
> A joy, a consolation, and a hope. (*DQW*, XI: 80-81)

The '*ne plus ultra*' of sublimity is a quasi-tautology, since one way to define the sublime is precisely as the *ne plus ultra*: so the Dream of the Arab passage would be the sublime of the sublime, the *ne plus ultra* of the *ne plus ultra*. This sequence, commented at length with more quotations that can be rehearsed here, is perhaps sublime in just about anyone's estimation but it might have had a peculiar resonance for De Quincey, coming as it does in the form of a *dream* in the course of an autobiographical reflection, a kind of poetic version of what De Quincey would recount in his own *Confessions* and other writings about his own life. What begins as a sheer personal event (I had a dream . . .) is transformed into an event of apocalyptic tonality, a dynamic almost common in Romanticism but perhaps most pronounced in Blake, Wordsworth, and De Quincey.

Perhaps even more telling for De Quincey's establishment of Wordsworth as the sublime poet and regenerator of the national poetry is his response to a far more muted passage from the 'Boy of Winander' lyric, (also an episode in *The Prelude*) which elicits this response from De Quincey. Recounting Wordsworth's observations of how a sudden relaxation from an attentive state could allow one to penetrate one's 'capacity of apprehension with a pathos and sense of the infinite', De Quincey rehearses Wordsworth's framing of a key passage from the 'Boy Of Winander' that needs to be quoted at some length:

> '. . . Just now, my ear was placed upon the stretch, in order to catch any sound of wheels that might come down . . . at the very instant when I raised my head from the ground, in final abandonment of hope for this night, at the very instant when the organs of attention were all at once relaxing from their tension, the bright star hanging in the air above those outlines of massy blackness fell suddenly upon my eye, and penetrated my capacity of apprehension with a pathos and a sense of the infinite, that would not have arrested me under other circumstances'. (*DQW*, XI: 74)

This scenario parallels that of the Boy of Winander scene (when the young boy whose back-and-forth hooting with owls is suddenly greeted by silence), with the effect that:

> ... then, in that instant, the scene actually before him, the visible scene, would enter unawares—
>
> 'With all its solemn imagery'—
>
> This complex scenery was—What?
>
> 'Was carried *far* into his heart,
> With all its pomp, and that uncertain heav'n received
> Into the bosom of the steady lake'. (*DQW*, XI: 75)

De Quincey continues his commentary: 'This very expression, "far," by which space and its infinities are attributed to the human heart, and to its capacities of re-echoing the sublimities of nature, has always struck me as with a flash of sublime revelation' (*DQW*, XI: 75). It is one thing to sense the sublime in the blockbuster passages of *The Prelude* and quite another to register it in the simple word 'far' in this relatively unprepossessing lyric passage.

It should go without saying that the poetry that comes out of the mouths of De Quincey's most sublime poets is spoken (or written) in English. He conceives of the English language in general as 'noble' (*DQW*, XII: 12) and sees it as inexorably bound up as the vehicle of a national and trans-national destiny.[10] Yet (English) poetic language has a special role to play, a peculiar destiny. In forecasting Wordsworth being remembered in the future and indeed enshrined in the hearts of men, De Quincey argues for the special place eminent poets would hold in contrast to great philosophers, mathematicians, or reformers:

> How different, how peculiar, is the interest which attends the great poets who have made themselves necessary to the human heart; who have first brought into consciousness, and next have clothed in words, those grand catholic feelings that belong to the grand catholic situations of life, through all its stages; who have clothed them in such words that human wit despairs of bettering them! ... Mighty were the powers, solemn and serene is the memory, of Archimedes; and Apollonius shines like 'the starry Galileo,' in the firmament of human genius; yet how frosty is the feeling associated with these names by comparison with that which, upon every sunny brae, by the side of every ancient forest, even in the farthest depths of Canada, many a young innocent girl, perhaps, at this very moment—looking now with fear to the dark recesses of the infinite forest, and now with love to the pages of the infinite poet, until the fear is absorbed and forgotten in the love—cherishes in her heart for the name and person of Shakespeare (*DQW*, XI: 61).

If you can make it in Canada, De Quincey seems to suggest, you can make it anywhere. Whereas De Quincey tends not to go on and on about Shakespeare as he does about Milton, it still is breathtaking that the former is described as 'the infinite poet' (can one get more sublime than that?), with the artistic infinity all the more foregrounded by being contrasted with the natural sublimity of the 'dark recesses of the infinite forest'.[11] The unspoken logic of the passage seems to say: the infinite poet will be disseminated infinitely in space and, for all we know, time.

De Quincey then forecasts a similar destiny for Wordsworth because his fate is tied to the destiny of the English language in general:

> Such a place in the affections of the young and the ingenuous, no less than of the old and philosophic, who happen to have any depth of feeling, will Wordsworth occupy in every clime and in every land; for the language in which he writes, thanks be to Providence, which has beneficently opened the widest channels for the purest and most elevating literature, is now ineradicably planted in all quarters of the earth; the echoes under every latitude of every longitude now reverberate English words; and all things seem tending to this result—that the English and the Spanish languages will finally share the earth between them (*DQW*, XI: 61-62)

In an alternate formulation regarding the 'futures market' of world languages, De Quincey goes even further in his claims for the coming hegemony of English:

> The English language is travelling fast towards the fulfilment of its destiny.... the English language (and, therefore, the English literature) is running forward towards its ultimate mission of eating up, like Aaron's rod, all other languages. Even the German and the Spanish will inevitably sink before it; perhaps within 100 or 150 years. In the recesses of California, in the vast solitudes of Australia, *The Churchyard amongst the Mountains*, from Wordsworth's 'Excursion,' and many a scene of his shorter poems, will be read, even as now Shakespeare is read amongst the forests of Canada. (*DQW*, XIX: 366)[12]

This is the linguistic and cultural 'face' of English imperialism, however benign the reading of Wordsworth and Shakespeare might be. De Quincey remarks in 'How to Write English: Introductory Paper', first published in 1853, on how since the time of Hume the 'area of expectation for an English writer was prodigiously expanding under the development of our national grandeur, by whatever names of "colonial" or "national" it might be varied or disguised' (*DQW*, XVIII: 51). That De Quincey can shuttle between 'colonial' and 'nation' is symptomatic of an English 'Poetry Without Borders,' a version of the self-transcending nation so prominent throughout Romantic discourse but here best embodied in the sublime, infinite poets of the infinite, who best write the noble language 'travelling fast towards

On the Language of the Sublime and the Sublime Nation 177

the fulfilment of its destiny,' which, as De Quincey makes clear, is a state of affairs presided over by Providence.

We have already been approaching what we still have to determine as the national sublime via great English poetry and great English poets, Milton and Wordsworth above all. De Quincey's use of the word 'nation' is sometimes provocative, departing from its most usual meanings, as in the section from the *Autobiographic Sketches* entitled 'The Nation of London':

> It was a most heavenly day in May of this year (1800), when I first beheld and first entered this mighty wilderness, the city—no! not the city, but the nation—of London. Often since then, at distances of two and three hundred miles or more from this colossal emporium of men, wealth, arts, and intellectual power, have I felt the sublime expression of her enormous magnitude in one simple form of ordinary occurrence, viz., in the vast droves of cattle, suppose upon the great north roads, all with their heads directed to London, and expounding the size of the attracting body, together with the force of its attractive power, by the never-ending succession of these droves, and the remoteness from the capital of the lines upon which they were moving. A suction so powerful, felt along radii so vast, and a consciousness, at the same time, that upon other radii still more vast, both by land and by sea, the same suction is operating, night and day, summer and winter, and hurrying for ever into one centre the infinite means needed for her infinite purposes, and the endless tributes to the skill or to the luxury of her endless population, crowds the imagination with a pomp to which there is nothing corresponding upon this planet, either amongst the things that have been, or the things that are. (*DQW*, XIX: 109)

The word 'nation' can be invoked rather casually these days: Prozac Nation, hiphop nation, you-name-it nation. But what could De Quincey mean by calling London a 'nation'? It is likely invoked first to suggest the immense size of London, which surely then, as now, had more people than some whole nations. Granted, one index of the sublime here is a little bathetic: the huge number of cows entering London. Otherwise, these lines are littered with classic predicates of the sublime: mighty, colossal, enormous, never-ending, powerful, vast, infinite. In the motif of 'crowding the imagination,' De Quincey echoes one of Burke's signal phrases for the effect of the sublime.[12] The dizzying magnification and proliferation is rendered especially in two extremely long sentences that challenge one's ability to keep all the clauses in play and in memory, rather in the manner of several of the lengthy verse paragraphs of Wordsworth's account of London in Book VII of *The Prelude*.[13] The passage features accumulation (a technical term of Latin rhetoric De Quincey learned at school) and enumeration, suggesting that the description, as the experience, could go on and on. 'Infinite city' is a resonant phrase that pops up in a manuscript of 'The English Mail-Coach'

(*DQW*, XVI: 461) and if this London is not infinite, it's at least 'quasi-infinite' in the paradoxical phrase proposed by the artist/theorist Robert Smithson (Smithson 1996: 34). Once again, the rubric for all of this talk of sublimity is, crucially, the *nation*, the term invoked here instead of city to ratchet up the sense of magnitude and dignity.

The primary text in the eighteenth century where one could encounter the conjunction of the sublime and the nation (in its accepted sense!) was Kant's *Observations on our Feeling of the Beautiful and the Sublime* and it so happens that De Quincey would come, a full sixty years later, to publish a translation of the section of that text devoted to the aesthetics of the nation.[14] In the former text, published in 1764 and written in an empiricist mode more characteristic of Edmund Burke than of the later, transcendental Kant of the critical philosophy, the sage of Königsberg devotes one chapter to 'National Characteristics so far as They Depend upon the Distinct Feeling of the Beautiful and the Sublime.' Kant is typical of the late eighteenth century in thinking of the sublime as the *opposite* of the beautiful, as was consolidated with Burke. In this polarizing scheme, virtually every nation of the world is determined as having a feeling for the beautiful *or* the sublime, as in the text's inaugural, flatfooted pronouncement: 'Among the nations of our quarter of the globe, the Italians and the French are in my opinion those who are most distinguished for the sense of the Beautiful—the Germans, the English, and the Spaniards, for the sense of the Sublime' (*DQW*, IV: 150).[15] Kant acknowledges these pronouncements as generalizations 'which ought not to offend any one,—the blame being of such a nature that every man may toss off the ball to his neighbour' (*DQW*, IV: 150) but still the propositions sound as if they are categorical. Kant passes easily from 'the nation' to its exemplary inhabitants, from 'England' to 'the English' and back again: he sees no conceptual, much less rhetorical problem in doing so. One principle informing Kant's discussion of national aesthetics is the system of humours: melancholic, phlegmatic, sanguine, and choleric. So, for example, the Englishman (as he/she used to be called) turns out to be phlegmatic—and not melancholic as so widely assumed! This means that, here too, the nation is partly conceived as an individual, however generic, such that it can be slotted into one of four temperaments.

The nation, via its citizens or inhabitants who constitute a national character, perhaps even with a national face, behaves like an individual. We might well want to think that a nation does or should resist this sort of representation, the reduction of a complex, heterogeneous and always somewhat arbitrary collection of people, to a single type. But even some of the most serious intellectuals of the late eighteenth and early nineteenth centuries (Kant, Hume, Wollstonecraft, Jefferson, de Staël, etc.,) had little or no problem with the discourse of 'national character': indeed, they willingly indulged in it. In surveying the texts about national character from this period, an asymmetrical pattern emerges: the nation of the other turns out to be much easier to describe than one's own. A reductive, violent homogeneity is usually entailed in capturing (or is it producing?) this other, driving often by racism and ethnocentrism whose contours are familiar and whose nefarious tendencies inform even some of the most 'enlightened' and theoretically cosmopolitan thinkers, Kant included. The reduction of the other nation to a homogenous national character tends not to have a parallel when it comes to one's own nation. Thus in Hume we read 'the ENGLISH, of any people in the universe, have the least of a national character, unless this very singularity pass for such' (Hume 1987: 207), rather as today the American discourse of individualism allows for infinite difference within a putative identity (*e pluribus unum*). If the identity of one's own nation is postulated it tends to be a *complex* identity, as when Kant claims that the German is somehow a synthesis, in his relation to the sublime and the beautiful, of the Frenchman and the Englishman (*DQW*, IV: 153).

When De Quincey publishes the translation of Kant's chapter on 'National Characteristics' he certainly takes some distance from the source. On the text in general he remarks:

> He went so far even as to write an illustrative essay on the Sublime and the Beautiful, which he did his best to make popular, by making it determinately shallow and trivial; though, in the same spirit, he seasoned all his works with elegant citations from classical poets—always apposite, however trite. (*DQW*, 7: 51)

De Quincey adds a number of pointedly critical notes, as when he chastises Kant for his repeating Hume's outright dismissal of the cultural significance of any Africans—or even of such a possibility. The presence of these critiques might suggest that De Quincey was exposing Kant's chapter as not so 'sage' after all. Yet De Quincey by no means provides a global critique of the text: the project of dividing nations into groups and constructing them as embodied in aesthetic sensibilities on the model of a human subject is not really troubled by any of De Quincey's local barbs against this or that pronouncement. And his predecessor, Kant tends to move rather effortlessly between the nation and a national subject or character.

If Kant is the most insistent and extreme in his aesthetic paradigm of the sublime and beautiful nations and national characters, one finds other crucial determinations of the sublime nation in many of the prominent thinkers of the late eighteenth and early nineteenth centuries, as, say, in Burke's positioning of the English nation and its social contract that hearkens back before even the ancient constitution to an utterly immemorial time, on the one hand, and forward to the 'unborn' signatories of the future. Or in Fichte's extravagant appeal, in his notorious *Addresses to the German Nation*, backward to an origin of the pure 'German' and forward to a future that spirals out infinitely: he even bafflingly invokes a future nation exhibiting the 'more than infinite.' Together they combine to form a paradigm of the narrated nation moving backwards to a primeval past and forwards to a projected, if unrepresentable future.¹⁶ When the *story* of the self-manifestation of nation is grounded in a national personality or character and anchored in the more or less transcendental conceptual framework of Romanticism and/or German Idealism, the paradigm that emerges is that of the nation structured as an infinitely self-transcending subject.¹⁷

With this framework in mind, we approach, in closing, arguably the most spectacular expression of De Quincey's national sublime in his distinctive narrative/essay called 'The English Mail-Coach.' First designed as part of his autobiographical reflections in the *Suspiria de Profundis* but published separately, the text seems to have bewildered many of its early readers. Critics were hard-pressed to find the unity in a piece that moved from a history of the English mail-coach to the Chinese emperor, the character of crocodiles, the Napoleonic Wars, Christian versus Roman views on sudden death, and more. De Quincey subsequently publishes an explanatory 'postscript' to preface his essay on the movement of the post. He insists that the whole 'radiates as a natural expansion' from 'an appalling scene which threatened instant death' when a state mail-coach risks decimating a small non-governmental coach, so to speak. The scene forms the core of 'The Vision of Sudden Death,' and De Quincey relates that scene to the 'whole' in this way:

> What I had beheld from my seat upon the mail; the scenical strife of action and passion, of anguish and fear, as I had there witnessed them moving in ghostly silence; this duel between life and death narrowing itself to a point of such exquisite evanescence as the collision neared; all these elements of the scene blended, under the law of association, with the previous and permanent features of distinction investing the mail itself: which features at that time lay—1st, in velocity unprecedented; 2dly, in the power and beauty of the horses; 3dly, in the official connection with the government of a great nation; and, 4thly, in the function, almost a consecrated function, of publishing and diffusing through the land the great political events, and especially the great battles, during a conflict of unparalleled grandeur. (*DQW*, XX: 34)

Does this entirely clarify the enigmatic texture of 'The English Mail-Coach'? The passage does not do much more that restate numerous points already sounded at the outset of the first, un-prefaced version of the text. De Quincey seems to acknowledge further room for doubt and appeals to the logic of dream: '. . . if there be anything amiss—let the Dream be responsible. The Dream is a law to itself . . .' (*DQW*, XX: 35). De Quincey claims that the whole text radiates 'as a natural expansion' from the scene of sudden death and yet the title—which should in some way signify the 'whole'—is 'The English Mail-Coach'. So the question is: what is the relation of the mail-coach to sudden death? The most obvious answer is that the scene of sudden (near-)death is caused by and witnessed from the mail-coach. At one level, a simple case of metonymy or 'association', as De Quincey terms it. But 'the mail-coach' and 'the mail' seem, at least figuratively, more resonant than that.

De Quincey often abbreviates 'the mail-coach' as simply 'the mail,' a common enough practice, but here nonetheless a striking instance of metonymy, identifying the medium with the message, as it were. The mail-coach carries the mail but it also *is* the mail. The mail carries itself, delivers itself: it is, in part, its own message. Certainly, for De Quincey the mode of the diffusion is seen to partake of the same things as the letters and news the mail-coach carries, most notably: the fate of the nation and matters of life and death. Both the mail-coach and the mail, like the English language, are 'traveling fast' toward their destination or destiny. The 'unprecedented velocity,' cause of the sense of vitality as well as the permanent possibility of danger or even death, lends itself to the sublime already in the material or phenomenal forms but that sublimity is heightened by its political association:

> No dignity is perfect which does not at some point ally itself with the indeterminate and mysterious. The connexion of the mail with the state and the executive government—a connexion obvious, but yet not strictly defined—gave to the whole mail establishment a grandeur and an official authority which did us service on the roads, and invested us with seasonable terrors. (*DQW*, XVI: 414)

In this vision of what can only be called 'mail chauvinism', the word 'terrors' might be invoked casually here. Yet it is conspicuously the hallmark of the Burkean sublime, and it is bolstered by both the (again Burkean) categories of authority and grandeur. At the outset De Quincey had already noted that riding on the English mail-coach entailed an 'under-sense, not unpleasurable of a possible though indefinite danger' (*DQW*, XVI: 409). The sense of 'not unpleasurable danger,' already arch-sublime, is rendered all the more so, once again, by its articulation with the 'awful [read: awe-inspiring, awesome] political mission' of the mail-coach and its articulation, as the 'national organ,' of the most urgent and consequential news.

The news and the letters carried on the mail-coach are, typically, matters of life and death, as is the very delivery of that news. Sometimes life and death are closely, even inextricably connected as when De Quincey is on a coach bearing news of a great victory (life of the soldiers, life of the nation), only to find that a certain mother must learn that her son now lies among the fallen (*DQW*, XVI: 427-28). In the same vein, the word 'equipage' is invoked by De Quincey in contexts that range along the extremes from life to death. He appeals, in Miltonic and Burkean fashion to 'Death, the crownèd phantom, with all the equipage of his terrors, and the tiger roar of his voice' (*DQW,* XVI: 442) at the same time as he conceives elsewhere of all humanity as an 'equipage' (*DQW*, XIX: 112). An 'equipage' is, beyond its literal designation, a privileged figure for an entity moving (more or less fast) to a destination.

The 'Vision of Sudden Death' opens with the question 'What is to be thought of sudden death'? and then proceeds to rehearse various notions, Christian and pagan, about the topic. But we might ask, in our turn, what sort of thing is sudden death to write about? It is not so easy to convey suddenness in a text. A skillful writer can take one by surprise, in mid-sentence or mid-paragraph, or at the very opening or close of a segment, by the introduction of something brief and unexpected: a word, a phrase, an idea. De Quincey's discussion of sudden death is anything but sudden. He opts, Walter Shandy-like, to dilate and to digress, to draw out the action and inaction with painstaking and perhaps pain-causing procrastination, not least with talk of procrastination (*DQW*, XVI: 435). One passage at least is haunted by the great Shakespearean, 'English' procrastinator, Hamlet, with its appeal to doubt, guilt, action, distraction, and thought (*DQW*, XVI: 438)[18]—all brought to bear on the scene in which De Quincey wants to be able to warn the young couple in the fast-approaching gig of the impending danger. Facing the difficulties involved in representing a sheer moment, De Quincey nonetheless displays how much might be at stake leading up to and following from a 'moment' that has, in effect, no presence. He reconstructs the experience in slow motion, as it were. He narrates a single—but distended—moment and much of the tension of the text lies in the disjunction between the suddenness of the moment of death (or near-death) and the time it takes De Quincey to stage this moment, complete with the digressions and dilations characteristic of someone being paid by the word.[19]

More than once De Quincey stresses how the whole protracted experience felt somehow instantaneous. His general tendency to see temporally distinct things all at once applies with particular force to the 'appalling scene' of the coach's accident:

> .... this accursed gift I have, as regards *thought*, that in the first step towards the possibility of a misfortune, I see its total evolution: in the radix, I see too certainly and too instantly its entire expansion; in the first syllable of the dreadful sentence, I read already the last. (*DQW*, XVI: 438)

The marked discrepancy between the instantaneity of the moment of (near) sudden death and the actual elaboration of the text about it suggests the character of allegory. Paul de Man maintains that

> Allegory is sequential and narrative, yet the topic of its narration is not necessarily temporal at all, thus raising the question of the referential status of a text whose semantic function, though strongly in evidence, is not primarily determined by mimetic moments; more than ordinary modes of fiction, allegory is at the furthest possible remove from historiography. (de Man 1996: 51)

Thus in Spenser's *The Faerie Queene* we can read the *story* of something (a virtue such as holiness or chastity) that is not temporal: the text says something other than it means, says it in a mode (temporal) disjunctive from its referent (not temporal). In 'The English Mail-Coach' the disjunction between the suddenness of death or even near-death and the distended character of the narrative and reflection could hardly be more pronounced. Elsewhere de Man proposes that 'the paradigm for all texts consists of a figure (or a system of figures) and its deconstruction' (de Man 1979: 205). He pushes this further still to claim that 'allegories are always allegories of metaphor and as such always allegories of the impossibility of reading'. Whatever its merits as an absolute or general thesis, this seems particularly apt for 'The English Mail-Coach', given that the 'vehicle,' as we know from Aristotle's *Poetics*, is the oldest of metaphors for metaphor, transporting, as it does, sense from one place to another.[20] Metaphor transports us.

But if the text is an allegory of metaphor and the entire work is about the moment of sudden death, what then is the relation between that metaphor and the single, overarching topic or 'subject matter' of the text, between the mail-coach and (sudden) death? I would suggest that the metaphor in question is the letter, though the letter, consistent with Christian tradition, can be both dead and alive. The letter kills, St. Paul so famously says, but it cannot be killed. Indeed, it has a kind of life, a kind of undead life, especially when animated by the act of reading. As Milton says in *Areopagitica*: 'books are not absolutely dead things' (Milton 1957: 720). The letter, and its vehicle, the mail-coach, can be both dead and alive, and render other people or things dead and alive: that is one locus of sublime power.

In the final sequence of the text, the 'Dream-Fugue' on the theme of sudden death, De Quincey and company are travelling, in a dream, 'at a flying gallop' in an 'equipage' within an immense cathedral. We read:

> Forty leagues we might have run in the cathedral, and as yet no strength of morning light had reached us, when we saw before us the aërial galleries of the organ and the choir. Every pinnacle of the fret-work, every station of advantage amongst the traceries, was crested by white-robed choristers, that sang deliverance; that wept no more tears, as once their fathers had wept; but at intervals that sang together to the generations, saying—
> 'Chaunt the deliverer's praise in every tongue,'
> and receiving answers from afar,
> —'such as once in heaven and earth were sung.'
> And of their chaunting was no end; of our headlong pace was neither pause nor remission. (*DQW*, XVI: 446)

In this ending without any particular end, the tone of De Quincey's narrative essay becomes, through its motifs and its pervasively Biblical phrasing, thoroughly apocalyptic. We see the former coach transformed to an equipage at a higher level and if the literal post has been left behind we are now in the virtual presence of the 'deliverer' and deliverance, as if to answer the prayer uttered earlier in the text: 'From lightning and tempest; from plague, pestilence, and famine; from battle and murder, and from sudden death,—*Good Lord, deliver us*' (*DQW*, XVI: 430).

The metaphor of birth is inscribed in the very word for nation. That system of figuration seems to suggest that death would also be built into the nation, something entirely in keeping with the discourse of the sublime. But perhaps the singularity of the birth of the nation is that it is not accompanied by a corresponding death. At the very least, the nation resists imagining its own voluntary death. Certainly thinkers of the late eighteenth and early nineteenth centuries—Rousseau, Coleridge, Burke, Fichte, and others—seem incapable of imagining the death of nation: it is, rather, projected forward infinitely. The ending of 'The English Mail-Coach' stresses not death but transfiguration. Its closing vision of 'deliverance' entails, among other things, the apocalyptic character of the highly improbably event of a letter—or a coach or a nation or a language—arriving at its destination.

NOTES

1. See the *Confessions* (*DQW*, II: 66-7) for evidence of this. Here I want to express my gratitude to Robert Morrison and Daniel Sanjiv Roberts for their comments and suggestions for improvement on the drafts of this essay.
2. See, however, Proctor's discussion in 1943, Chapter III, section I C for some analysis of De Quincey's sublime in relation to the realm of the moral.
3. For an excellent series of readings attentive to this dynamic, see Hertz 1985.
4. The best, extended discussion of the sublime in De Quincey is Rzepka 1995, with a focus resolutely on the *Confessions*. Beer 1985 provides a wide-ranging conspectus on the topic. Proctor 1943 offers a short overview of the sublime in De Quincey. See also Devlin 1983, Chapter 4.
5. On De Quincey's place in the invention of a post-eighteenth century notion of 'literature,' see Bate. On the 'literature of power', see Roberts 2002.
6. Hertz shows how the Longinian sublime tends to consist in the collapse of entities and identities usually thought to be distinct: author and character, character and reader (or audience), author and reader (or audience).
7. Some characterizations of De Quincey's general psychic state assume the texture of the sublime. See the 1803 *Diary* where De Quincey asks himself: 'What shall be my character? . . . wild—impetuous—*splendidly* sublime? dignified—melancholy—*gloomily* sublime? or shrouded in mystery—supernatural—like the "ancient mariner"—*awfully* sublime?' (*DQW*, I: 26). Cf. also *DQW*, X: 142).
8. This sort of dynamic is expertly analyzed in Wilner 2000.
9. For De Quincey's account of the connotations of the word 'trepidation', see *DQW*, XIX: 111.
10. For helpful discussions of language in De Quincey, see McDonagh, 1994, especially Chapter Four, 'Style Slaves: De Quincey's Labour of Language'; Roberts 2000, especially Chapter Four, 'The Pains of Growth: Language and Cultural Politics'; Burwick 1985.

11. Elsewhere De Quincey speaks of 'the immeasurable and sea-like arena upon which Shakespeare careers—co-infinite with life itself—yes, and with something more than life' (*DQW*, X: 150).
12. In glossing one of the most sublime passages from Milton's *Paradise Lost* (I. 589-99), Burke comments: 'The mind is hurried out of itself, by a croud of great and confused images; which affect because they are crouded and confused' (Burke 1990: 57).
13. De Quincey repeatedly complained of Kant's very long sentences, sometimes comparing them to coaches that were overstuffed.
14. Daniel Sanjiv Roberts (2000) is the only critic I know of who has drawn attention to the pertinence of this Kantian scheme for the understanding of De Quincey's thinking about the nation. See his chapter on 'English Nationalism and the Mediation of Kant,' especially 127.
15. The exception is Holland, which (despite having produced some of the greatest painting of all time) is said to be 'a country in which neither feeling is very observable' (*DQW*, IV: 150).
16. On various practical and theoretical aspects of narrating nations, see Bhabha.
17. The passage begins 'I pretend to no presence of mind. On the contrary my fear is—that I am miserably and shamefully deficient in that quality as regards action'. See also one manuscript version of the passage, perhaps even more Hamlet-infused in its economy of motifs: *DQW*, XVI: 475.
18. For a study of this problematic see Miller 1965, for the excellent chapter on De Quincey.
19. On the vehicular character of metaphor and its very definition, see Derrida 1982: 231ff.

WORKS CITED

Bate, Jonathan. (1993) 'The Literature of Power: Coleridge and De Quincey' in eds. Tim Fulford and Morton D. Paley, *Coleridge's Visionary Language*, Cambridge: D. S. Brewer, 137-50.
Beer, John. (1985) 'De Quincey and the Dark Sublime: The Wordsworth-Coleridge Ethos,' in R.L. Synder (ed.) *Thomas De Quincey: Bicentenary Studies*, Norman: Oklahoma University Press, 164-198.
Bhabha, Homi K. ed. (1990) *Nation and Narration*. New York: Routledge.
Burke, Edmund. (1990) *A Philosophical Enquiry into the Origin of our Idea of the Sublime and the Beautiful*, Adam Phillips (ed.), Oxford and New York: Oxford University Press.
Burke, Edmund. (1970) *Reflections on the Revolution in France*. Connor Cruise O'Brien (ed.), Harmondsworth: Penguin.
Burwick, Frederick. (1985) 'De Quincey's Theory of Language,' in *Thomas De Quincey: Bicentenary Studies*, R.L. Synder (ed.), Norman: Oklahoma University Press, 279-307.
de Man, Paul. (1996) 'Pascal's Allegory of Persuasion', in Andrzej Warminski (ed.) *Aesthetic Ideology*, Minneapolis: University of Minnesota Press, 51–69.
———. (1979) *Allegories of Reading: Figural Language in Rousseau, Nietzsche, Rilke, and Proust*. New Haven and London: Yale University Press.
Derrida, Jacques (1982) 'White Mythology,' in *Margins of Philosophy*, Chicago: University of Chicago Press, 207–72.
Devlin, D. D. (1983) *De Quincey, Wordsworth and the Art of Prose*. London: Macmillan.
Fichte, Johann Gottlieb. (1968) *Addresses to the German Nation*, George A Kelly (ed.) New York: Harper & Row.

Frye, Northrop. (1968) *A Study of English Romanticism*. New York: Random House.
Hertz, Neil. (1985) *The End of the Line: Essays on Psychoanalysis and the Sublime*, New York: Columbia University Press.
Hume, David. (1987) *Essays Moral, and Political, and Literary*, Eugene F. Miller (ed.) Indianapolis: Liberty Classics.
Jordan, J. E. (1963) *From De Quincey to Wordsworth*, Berkeley: University of California Press.
Kant, Immanuel. (1996) *Practical Philosophy*, Mary Gregor (ed. and trans.), Cambridge: Cambridge University Press.
McDonagh, Josephine. (1994) *De Quincey's Disciplines*, Oxford: Clarendon Press.
Miller, J. Hillis. (1965) *The Disappearance of God*, New York: Shocken.
Milton, John. (1957) ed. Merritt Hughes. *Complete Poems and Major Prose*. Indianapolis: Odyssey.
Proctor, Sigmund K. (1943) *Thomas De Quincey's Theory of Literature*, Ann Arbor: University of Michigan Press.
Reed, Arden. (1985) '"Booked for Utter Perplexity" on De Quincey's *English Mail-Coach*'. in R.L. Synder (ed.) *Thomas De Quincey: Bicentenary Studies*, Norman: Oklahoma University Press, 279-307.
Roberts. Daniel Sanjiv. (2000) *Revisionary Gleam: De Quincey, Coleridge and the High Romantic Argument*. Liverpool: Liverpool University Press.
_____. (February 2002) 'Not "Forsworn with Pink Ribbons": Hannah More, Thomas De Quincey, and the Literature of Power'. *Romanticism On the Net* 25: 17 pars. http://www.erudit.org/revue/ron/2002/v/n25/006012ar.html
Rzepka, Charles J. (1995) *Sacramental Commodities: Gift, Text, and the Sublime*, Amherst: University of Massachusetts Press.
Smithson, Robert. (1996) ed. Jack Flam, *The Collected Writings*, Berkeley and Los Angeles: University of California Press.
Wilner, Joshua. (2000) *Feeding on Infinity: Readings in the Romantic Rhetoric of Internalization*, Baltimore: Johns Hopkins University Press.
Woolf, Virginia. (1986) 'The English Mail Coach' in *The Essays of Virginia Woolf*, Vol. 1. London: Hogarth, 365-68.
Wordsworth, William (1979). *The Prelude: 1799, 1805, 1850*. (ed.) Jonathan Wordsworth et al., New York: Norton.

10 Chambers of Horror
De Quincey's 'Postscript' to 'On Murder Considered as One of the Fine Arts'

Gregory Dart

Nobody knows precisely when De Quincey's 'Postscript' to 'On Murder Considered as One of the Fine Arts' was composed, but the internal evidence suggests that it was sometime in 1854, especially for inclusion in the fourteen-volume *Selections Grave and Gay*, which was the first authorised collection of the Opium-Eater's writings.[1] Intended as a belated sequel to his two original *Blackwood's* articles 'On Murder', which first appeared in 1827 and 1839 respectively, the 'Postscript' is a good deal longer and more ambitious than its name might suggest. But in other respects this unusual label is an apt one, for the essay does indeed present itself as a kind of afterword: the work of a man looking back on a lifetime's fascination with murder, and, just as importantly, on a thirty-year career in piece-meal, hand-to-mouth journalism, which the prospect of a collected edition was bringing to an unexpectedly triumphant end.[2]

The 'Postscript' returns to the Romantic period in order to relate a couple of true histories from what De Quincey considered to be the golden age of murder, cases sufficiently distant that they could be viewed aesthetically, unencumbered by contemporary concerns. The essay ends with a postscript to the postscript, consisting of a short, vivid description of the Manchester murderers the McKeons. But the main focus is on the notorious Ratcliffe Highway murders which took place in Wapping in 1811.[3] On Saturday 7 December of that year, shortly after midnight, a shopkeeper called Timothy Marr, his wife, his child and their young apprentice were all massacred, one after another, by an unknown intruder. This man, or men, broke into the shop at No. 29, Ratcliffe Highway, smashed each of them over the head with a ship's mallet, and then cut their throats. Only when Margaret Jewell, the Marr's servant-maid, came back to the shop from a late-night errand were suspicions aroused. A number of locals then broke into the warehouse but were too late to prevent the killers' escape. Twelve days later there was another household wreck in a pub on New Gravel Lane, a couple of minutes' walk from the main highway, when an old landlord by the name of Williamson, his wife and female servant were all despatched in a similar manner. This time the alarm was called by a young journeyman called John Turner, who happened to be lodging with the Williamsons at the time, and who saw an assassin at work in the front room of the tavern from a hidden vantage-point on the stairs. Creeping back up to his bedroom in terror, Turner chose not to disturb Williamson's little grandchild, who was sleeping peacefully in the room next door, but started tearing and tying up his own bedsheets in order to lower himself out of the back window. Once outside Turner raised the alarm, the murderer fled, and the little child in the upstairs room was saved.

The public reaction to these crimes, as De Quincey makes clear, was extraordinary. 'For twelve succeeding days,' he says, 'under some groundless notion that the unknown murderer had quitted London, the panic which had convulsed the mighty metropolis diffused itself all over the island'. During the inquest after the second murder, the coroner declared them 'a disgrace to this country', lamenting that from this day forward 'our houses are no longer our castles, and we are unsafe in our beds'.[4] Making as much as they could of their meagre resources, the Thames river police and Shadwell magistrates embarked upon an exhaustive search for the culprits, and on the 24 December they apprehended an Irish sailor by the name of John Williams. The case against him was strong if circumstantial, but in the event it never came to trial, for he hanged himself in his cell in Coldbath Fields Prison a few days later. Convinced that another man had been involved, the magistrates then spent some weeks hunting for Williams's accomplice—but no one else was ever charged. In keeping with the law respecting murderers and suicides, Williams was buried at the nearest crossroads to Ratcliffe Highway, which stood at the junction of Cannon Street Road and Cable Street, with a stake thrust through his heart.

Written well over forty years after the actual events, De Quincey's narrative is very close, in many respects, to the original reports in the Regency newspapers, to the *Times* articles for December 1811, and to the more extended accounts published soon after by Fairburn and the *Annual Register*.[5] Nevertheless, in certain key details we can see the Opium-Eater's desire intruding upon the story.[6] In most contemporary accounts of the murders Williams was described as a fierce, uncouth young man, who probably had an accessory.[7] But in De Quincey's the killer is a tiger-dandy, ferocious but fastidious, who stalks his victims in the costume of an old master and prides himself on acting alone.

By placing special emphasis upon Williams as a *solo virtuoso* De Quincey is able to develop an analogy, which had been implicit in his earlier papers on murder, between the solitary assassin and the Romantic artist, those twin types of transgressive genius.[8]

> Meantime, this solitary artist, that rested in the centre of London, self-supported by his own conscious grandeur, a domestic Attila, or 'scourge of God'; this man, that walked in darkness, and relied upon murder (as afterwards transpired) for bread, for clothes, for promotion in life, was silently preparing an effectual answer to the public journals; and on the

twelfth day after his inaugural murder, he advertised his presence in London, and published to all men the absurdity of ascribing to *him* any ruralising propensities, by striking a second blow, and accomplishing a second family extermination. (*DQW*, XX: 40)

When exploring the metaphor of murderer-as-artist in the 'Postscript', it is easy to assume that the word 'artist' is simply a synonym for 'writer'. But in fact Williams is compared to a number of different types of creator in the text. Like a great actor, Williams makes his 'début' on a dark Saturday night in December (only a couple of years before Edmund Kean was to burst upon the London stage as Shylock during the 'Great Frost' of 1813–4). And like De Quincey's own contemporary Benjamin Robert Haydon, who was completing a large canvas of *Macbeth* in the December of 1811, he has high hopes of immortality for any work 'turned out from his own *studio*' and flatly disdains a provincial reputation. The Opium-Eater reinforces this analogy between Williams and a great master by declaring that like another Titian, Rubens or Vandyke, he never practices his art but in 'full dress', i.e. a long blue surcoat of the very finest cloth, richly lined with silk.

Comparable to an actor, a painter, even a sculptor, Williams is also, in his covert dialogue with the public journals, akin to an anonymous periodical essayist, and in this respect has a good deal in common with the young Thomas De Quincey. Like Williams, De Quincey's assault upon the capital had been sudden and sensational. In the summer of 1821 his financial situation had been so appalling that he was forced to abandon his wife and children in the Lake District and move down to London in search of magazine work (Lindop 1985: 156–83). He then proceeded to make the most dramatic of double killings that same autumn, publishing the two parts of the *Confessions of an English Opium-Eater* in successive issues of the *London Magazine*. Throughout the composition of the *Confessions* De Quincey was on the run from duns and bailiffs, moving from lodging to lodging like a criminal in hiding; and this experience of having to leave his family for a fraught, fugitive existence in the city was to be repeated many times in future years. Hence his perverse identification with Williams at the beginning of the 'Postscript', and the paradoxical conjunction, in that text, between furtive private anonymity and public literary success; hence also perhaps his guilty sympathy for the escaping journeyman John Turner, a man forced to leave what remains of his family unprotected in order to save them.[9]

There were strong links between periodical journalism and assassination in the autumn of 1821. Exactly one year previous to this De Quincey had been egging his friend the *Blackwood's* stalwart John Wilson into battle against John Scott, his counterpart at the *London Magazine*, further fanning the flames of the 'Cockney School' controversy. A couple of months later Scott was dead, killed in a duel at Chalk Farm by the *Blackwood's* representative Jonathan Christie. By the summer of 1821 De Quincey had fallen out with the Blackwoodsmen and was down in London composing the

Confessions for the *London*. He was now fraternising freely with the Cockneys, including Lamb and Hazlitt, and living in John Scott's former lodgings at 4, York Street, Covent Garden. Robert Morrison highlights the piquancy of the situation in his introduction to Richard Woodhouse's *Causebook* for the *Harvard Library Bulletin*:

> De Quincey, who was fascinated by murder, often worried that he might be responsible for someone's death, such as the Malay's in the *Confessions*, or the young woman in the frail gig at the conclusion of 'The English Mail-Coach'. He undoubtedly recognised the grim ironies of writing his *Confessions* in the rooms of a man who had died because of animosity he had helped to incite, and of actively supporting the *London* when only a few months earlier he had been publishing in *Blackwood's* and speaking of the *London* with contemptuous abuse. (Morrison 1998: xix–xx)

De Quincey's situation was made even more complicated when John Wilson came down to London in the latter part of 1821, which resulted in the Opium-Eater embarking upon a dangerous double game, gossiping about the Blackwoodsmen to his new London acquaintances one moment while secretly seeking a rapprochement with their foremost representative the next. One night he confided to John Taylor that he had a sort of feeling or ominous anticipation 'that possibly there was some being in the world who was fated to do him at some time a great & inexpiable injury' and that 'many circumstances seemed to make it not improbable that Wilson might be that man' (Morrison 1998: 18).

Though opium certainly exacerbated these murderous fantasies—these fantasies of murdering and of being murdered—they were by no means peculiar to De Quincey. In the battle of the literary magazines the metaphor of periodical writer-as-serial assassin was often employed. Only a few short months after John Scott's death William Maginn was referring to Lockhart as 'wet with the blood of the Cockneys' and Wilson as one who had 'slain' many with his 'trenchant and truculent falchion' (quoted from *Blackwood's Magazine* for April 1821 in Morrison 1998: xviii). Economics, perhaps even more than politics, lay at the heart of it, for as David Higgins has suggested in his recent book on Romantic genius:

> Periodical writing on genius was not only partisan, but also often marked by anxiety and tension. Authors like John Wilson, Thomas De Quincey and Thomas Carlyle began writing for magazines because they could not subsist by producing more prestigious forms of literature; this sometimes lent a certain bitterness to their accounts of more fortunate and famous creative artists. And for many writers in the 1820s and 1830s the rise of newspapers and magazines was the reason for the apparent dearth of poets, dramatists and novelists of the first rank.

Original genius, it was claimed, was being swallowed up or stifled by the anonymous teeming mass of periodical writing. Like the urban crowd, the periodical press was imagined as being both dangerously various and fragmented, and disturbingly amorphous and uniform. (Higgins 2005: 8)

Periodical reviewers attacked the poets and dramatists of the day; they also attacked each other. And in the case of *Blackwood's* the very excessiveness of these attacks became a positive selling-point. In the fervid atmosphere of the early 1820s, fraught as it was with political and personal animosity, the ebullient Blackwoodsmen developed a particularly robust, sarcastic style that turned literary assassination into a sport. And 'The Opium-Eater' was always considered to be a natural player in this game, as can be seen from his rapid incorporation into *Blackwood's* fictional symposium, the 'Noctes Ambrosianae', as a gentleman-scholar brimming with murderous facetiousness.[10]

The first of De Quincey's two great *Blackwood's* articles 'On Murder Considered as One of the Fine Arts', which appeared in 1827, has always been credited with great originality. There was something very novel and challenging about its playful mixture of murder and Kantian metaphysics, and its ironic presentation of homicide as an artistic or sporting genre capable of being followed through history by a group of gentleman-amateurs. But the seeds of this dangerously flash attitude were already present in the Tory populism of the 1820s, in Pierce Egan's boxing journalism, and in *Blackwood's* own literary satires. Writing in the age of improvement, with the star of their sworn enemies the liberal utilitarians increasingly in the ascendant, both Egan and the Blackwoodsmen had a strong desire to use periodical journalism to preserve a realm of pleasure, an autonomous, hermetically sealed realm, at one remove from the claims of everyday politics and the 'new school of reform'. In Egan this realm is called sport, in *Blackwood's*, literature, but both fulfill similar functions as spaces where some of the more traditional—and violent—aspects of the British national culture could continue to be celebrated, as it were freely and irresponsibly. And it is this aspiration that De Quincey both advances and ironises in his first essay 'On Murder'.

'Everything in this world has two handles' De Quincey tell us, at the beginning:

> Murder, for instance, may be laid hold of by its moral handle, (as it generally is in the pulpit, and at the Old Bailey;), and *that*, I confess, is its weak side; or it may be treated *aesthetically*, as the Germans call it, that is, in relation to good taste. (*DQW*, VI: 114)

The influence of Pierce Egan can be felt in De Quincey's story of the Mannheim baker who goes twenty-six rounds with his assailant to avoid being murdered, for the whole episode is written in a mock-epic style reminiscent of the *Sporting Anecdotes*. Elsewhere one can feel the influence of *Blackwood's* and of the periodical warfare of the 1820s. In the delightful section devoted to famous philosophers who were nearly or actually murdered there is a comic rebellion of body against mind, practice against theory, as some of the grandest figures from intellectual history—Hobbes, Descartes, Malebranche, Kant—get cut down to size:

> Hobbes, but why, or on what principle, I never could understand, was not murdered. This was a capital oversight of the professional men of the seventeenth century; because in every light he was a fine subject for murder, [. . .] he had no right to make the least resistance; for, according to himself, irresistible power creates the very highest species of right, so that it is rebellion of the blackest dye to refuse to be murdered, when a competent force appears to murder you. (*DQW*, VI: 121)

Gathering momentum through a series of wicked puns and mutinous metaphors, we can see the revenge of the anonymous periodical journalist upon the independent man of letters, with the murder weapon of choice being a brilliant, fugitive irony. *Blackwood's* early caricature of the 'Opium-Eater' as a dandy assassin was deeply prophetic in this respect—for the late 1820s and early 30s see De Quincey engage in a number of biographical studies of famous writers—many of them his former friends—in which he slips casually into their private lives and then, with a peculiar mixture of generous insight and buried spite, both celebrates and exposes them. His sketches of Wordsworth and Coleridge are of this nature; so much so, indeed, that the Lakers' families soon came to regard him as something of a 'domestic Attila' in his treatment of them.[11]

What doesn't and can't get referred to in De Quincey's reviews is the economic necessity behind his gentle assassinations, the hidden needs driving his supercilious style. His criticism was built upon the fiction that he was a high-minded professional essayist, a subtle combination of new journalist and old-style gentleman of letters, but he discovered early on that there was money to be made by writing about his famous friends—and the temptation proved too great to resist. The notion of murder as a fine art represented a kind of allegory of De Quincey's position in this respect—since both depended on violence manifesting itself as a sly insinuation from a disinterested, even abstract realm, apparently devoid of any material or political motive.

This aspiration is expressed most forcibly in his second essay on murder, which was published some twelve years later, in 1839. In that piece, the character of Toad-in-the-Hole paints a vivid picture of all the various types of homicide that a dilettante must exclude:

> 'Gentlemen, I'll tell you the plain truth. Every day of the year we take up a paper, we read the opening of a murder. We say, this is good—this

is charming—this is excellent! But, behold you! scarcely have we read a little farther before the word Tipperary or Ballina-something betrays the Irish manufacture. Instantly we loathe it: we call to the waiter; we say, "Waiter, take away this paper; send it out of the house; it is absolutely offensive to all just taste." [. . .] Tithes, politics, or something wrong in principle, vitiate every Irish murder. Gentlemen, this must be reformed, or Ireland will not be a land to live in; at least, if we do live there, we must import all our murders, that's clear.' Toad-in-the-hole sat down, growling with suppressed wrath, and the universal 'Hear, hear!' sufficiently showed that he spoke the general feeling.

The next toast was—'The sublime epoch of Burkism and Harism!' (*DQW*, XI: 406)

Political murders, mass-produced murders, murders borne out of poverty or necessity—all these must be excluded from the true pantheon of crime as too impure and too modern for the taste of the true connoisseur. Instead the Edinburgh body-snatchers Burke and Hare are offered up as models of pure malignity—despite the fact that, as De Quincey himself probably knew only too well, they were both originally from Ulster.

Moving forward to the 'Postscript' of 1854, however, we can see that, despite being billed as the absolute *beau idéal* of the artist-assassin, Williams's relationship to the murders he commits is more complicated than De Quincey's second essay 'On Murder' might have led us to expect. He is, as we have already seen, a 'solitary artist', but he is also one who relies upon murder 'for bread, for clothes, for promotion in life'; like De Quincey himself therefore he hovers uneasily between the status of amateur and professional. With exquisite implausibility, Williams is described as having bright orange hair, a tiger character, a frozen corpse-like face and, at the very same time, a refined and suave manner. On the night of the Marrs' murders he appears first as a dispassionate aesthete most keen to 'execute a design which he had already sketched' who 'seems to have laid it down as a maxim—that the best person to murder was a friend'. But only a few lines later it is casually suggested that his motives may in fact have been far more concrete and mundane than that: jealousy of Marr's wife, greed, and the desire to revenge oneself for a past slight.

As the story of the night unfolds, the 'Postscript' is at first preoccupied with the practical difficulties of the murderer's task, sympathetically following his tight schedule, and offering the final outcome as a feat of great efficiency and daring. And yet, the suspicion remains that for De Quincey, above and beyond all Williams's good time-keeping, his real artistry is ultimately based on a talent for superfluity, not necessity. Financially, De Quincey insists, the Marr plot was a failure: Williams may have only got away with a 'few guineas' in the end. It is in the excessiveness, the sheer gratuitousness, of his actions that he revealed his sense of style. He smashed his victims' heads with a mallet and then used a chisel to cut their throats, brandishing the instruments of a sculptor to kill them—in effect—twice. There was nothing elegant—or stylish—in the *manner* in which he murdered the upstairs baby in the cradle; it was the utter needlessness of the action that marked it out: 'No one incident, indeed, in the whole tissue of atrocities', De Quincey writes, 'so much envenomed the popular fury against this unknown ruffian, as this useless butchery of the infant'. In the aftermath of the second spate of murders the London crowd wants to catch the killer in 'the carnival of his bloody revels', another indication that he is seen as an artist who conjures up around him a different kind of temporality. Left alone for a few moments in Coldbath Fields Prison, Williams also finds the time to commit suicide, an action at once pre-emptive and excessive, and one which instantly withdraws him from the disciplinary control of the state.

Somewhat surprisingly, perhaps, De Quincey does not attempt to disguise the fact that his Williams is (in actual fact) something of a workaday murderer: fast-moving, with a violent personality, clear motives, and a concretely material end. His aesthetic credentials are seen to lie in a capacity, every now and then, to go beyond the bounds of strict practical necessity, to open up, like a Romantic pianist making liberal use of *rubato*, vast new tracts of stolen time. Snatching a moment from the relentless time-discipline of the nineteenth century Williams is able to transform that moment into an eternal tableau of terror. And it is this ability to freeze nature in time that renders him a true artist, a sculptor of the real, and which explains the effect he has on the living as well as the dead. No sooner has he slaughtered the Marr family than Mary the maid-servant comes back from her midnight errand and knocks on the door of the shop. 'Yet how is this?' De Quincey writes:

> To her astonishment, but with the astonishment came creeping over her an icy horror, no stir nor rumour was heard ascending from the kitchen ... To pause, therefore, to impose stern silence upon herself, so as to leave room for the possible answer to this final appeal, became a duty of spasmodic effort. Listen, therefore, poor trembling heart; listen, and for twenty seconds be still as death. Still as death she was: and during that dreadful stillness, when she hushed her breath that she might listen, occurred an incident of killing fear, that to her dying day would never cease to renew its echoes in her ear. She, Mary, the poor trembling girl, checking and overruling herself by a final effort, that she might leave full opening for her young mistress's answer to her own last frantic appeal, heard at last and most distinctly a sound within the house. (*DQW*, XX: 49)

This sudden reverse shot enacts the same revolution of feeling De Quincey had noted many years before in his 1823 essay 'On the Knocking at the Gate in Macbeth'. The difference is, however, that in the earlier essay De Quincey's concept of the sublime murder was based entirely on a temporary identification with the murderer, an identification that was dramatically cancelled by the knocking at the gate (at which point the values of the outside world are suddenly re-presented to the audience, marking a return from the aesthetic to the moral). In the 'Postscript', however, the knocking ushers in an even more dramatic reversal—from the perspective of the murderer to that of the potential victim:

> Then the dreadful steps were heard advancing along the little narrow passage to the door. The steps—oh heavens! *whose* steps?—have paused at the door. The very breathing can be heard of that dreadful being, who has silenced all breathing except his own in the house. There is but a door between him and Mary. (*DQW*, XX: 49–50)

In the 'Knocking at the Gate' essay De Quincey had considered that the point of view of the would-be victim in a murder story could only be productive of 'coarse and vulgar horror'; the murderer was the only true point of interest (*DQW*, III: 151). But by the time he came to write the 'Postscript' thirty years later he had clearly changed his mind. How do we explain this shift? Why the 'Postscript's' relative lack of interest in Williams's psychology, his internal moral reasoning, and why the peculiar concentration on the figure of the prospective victim?

This shift has less to do with any fundamental change in De Quincey's psychological make-up—for as the 1821 *Confessions* and Woodhouse's *Cause Book* make clear, his tendency was always to identify equally with both assassins and their victims, with power and passive suffering, and late texts such as the 'Postscript' and 'The English Mail-Coach' (also revised in 1854) continue to bear this out. It is more closely related, I would suggest, to the changes that had taken place in English crime literature between the 1820s and 1854, changes which De Quincey can be seen to be responding to, in his indirect way. One of the most striking new genres to emerge in this period was the so-called 'Newgate Novel', an accumulation of loosely liberal and reformist fictions, which tended to offer sympathetic portraits of criminals maltreated by pre-modern society.[12] Sizeable, respectably-produced novels such as Bulwer-Lytton's *Paul Clifford* (1830) and Ainsworth's *Jack Sheppard* (which appeared in serial instalments in *Bentley's Miscellany* from 1839 to 1840), were extremely successful in giving a new and broader appeal to previously plebeian matter, and spawned a bewildering number of theatrical and pirate versions. Crowds burst into spontaneous applause when they saw Mrs. Keeley playing Sheppard at the Surrey Theatre, deftly slipping out of her prison chains, and the same scene was even more riotously received in the notorious 'bloodbath' theatres in the poorer parts of the capital (Taylor 1996: xvii). The fear among the ruling élite was that Newgate's anti-social, pro-libertarian heroes were exerting a positively radical, even revolutionary influence upon the lower-class reading public, and this led to vehement criticism of Bulwer, Ainsworth and even the Dickens of *Oliver Twist* in the contemporary press. The medium-term result of this was that by the late 1840s and early 1850s respectable novelists were steering clear of subjective portrayals of murderers: the position of criminal-as-hero was becoming increasingly difficult to defend.

Newgate was closely followed by the rapid burgeoning of cheap serial fictions in the 1840s, many of them revelling in gothic material. Of these, the most popular, and bloodthirsty, was probably G.W.M. Reynolds's long-running radical melodrama *The Mysteries of London* (first series 1844–46), which sold 40,000 copies a week (James 1963: 46), closely challenged by extraordinary 'penny dreadfuls' such as Thomas Peckett Prest's hugely successful *String of Pearls* (1846–47), which was rapidly adapted into a theatrical melodrama showpiecing the extraordinary serial-killer at its centre, Sweeney Todd. In the Prologue to *The Mysteries of London* Reynolds advertised his radical intentions from the outset. Crime, in his urban schema, was nothing but a mystery to be decoded, a sign that needed subsuming into the larger and more important categories of 'WEALTH' and 'POVERTY'. The gothic villain at the heart of *The Mysteries of London's* first series was a murderer, thief and body-snatcher called Anthony Tidkins, the Resurrection Man. There was a painful tension in Reynolds's representation of Tidkins. His role within the larger plot was relatively simple, that of a cool, calculating monster; but in the account of his early history the author offered a Newgate-influenced portrait of a young man slowly corrupted by social injustice after making repeated attempts to live within the law. Not only that, Reynolds gave such detailed descriptions of Tidkins's grave-robbing technique that one could not but acknowledge its business-like efficiency, and similarities were thereby established between the practical, systematic nature of low-life criminal practice and those larger, supposedly more legitimate systems of bodily exploitation, described in great detail elsewhere in the novel, perpetrated by the rich over the poor. Murder-as-business was also a feature of Peckett Prest's *The String of Pearls*, which was running at the same time as Reynolds's *Mysteries*. In Prest's narrative, the traffic of bodies down the underground tunnel connecting Todd's barbers' shop and Lovett's pie shop exploited contemporary anxieties about the mysterious relationship between capitalist production and consumption in the modern city, as well as preying upon more concrete fears about the adulteration of food. In the demon barber's story murder became one of the industrial arts—ruthless, efficient, and cleverly hidden from the public eye.

> Sweeney Todd walked into the back parlour and closed the door. There was a strange sound suddenly, composed of a rushing noise and then a heavy blow, immediately after which Sweeney Todd emerged from his parlour, and folding his arms, he looked upon the vacant chair where his customer had been seated, but the customer was gone, leaving not the slightest trace of his presence behind except his hat, and *that* Sweeney

Todd immediately seized and thrust into a cupboard that was at one corner of the shop. (Prest 1846: 3)

In both Reynolds and Prest there was a heady, if rather undigested mix of political allegory and sensational melodrama, a mix so heady, in fact, that the former was often completely swamped by the latter. This might explain why, quite contrary to all expectations, it was the polite Newgate Novel, as practised by Bulwer and Ainsworth that came in for the greatest criticism from the literary reviews, because it was in these works that the criminal was depicted with the greatest insight and understanding.

In 1847 Bulwer was forced to pen a little pamphlet entitled 'A Word to the Public' explaining and defending his recently published novel *Lucretia, or The Children of Night*, a three-volume work loosely based on the career of T. G. Wainewright the celebrated writer-turned-poisoner and former colleague of De Quincey's at the *London Magazine*. In his pamphlet Bulwer denied possessing, as his enemies claimed, 'a morbid and mischievous passion for treating crime and guilt', and would not accept that it was the prevailing character of his books 'to make heroes of criminals or felons'. Instead he proposed a version of the line that De Quincey had adopted in 'On the Knocking at the Gate', arguing that 'as guilt in Man, when accompanied with intellect or daring, contains a power infinitely exceeding the brute force of the mere animal, so crime is the customary material for tragic art, and furnishes the tremendous instrument for moving the human heart by the agency of terror'. It was this interest in the workings of the criminal mind that distinguished the old tragedy from the new, Bulwer claimed: 'With the Greek, Fate was the main instrument of woe and crime;—so with the Greek, there was little need of mental analysis—little need to show from what errors of his own man suffered and sinned . . . But with us, guilt or woe has its source in ourselves' (Bulwer-Lytton 1847: 54).

Crime was allowed on stage and in the popular press, Bulwer complained, but not in the novel, a strange state of affairs when one considered that fiction was best placed of all three to supply the requisite moral perspective:

> The essential characteristic of this age and land is *publicity*. There exists a press which bares at once to the universal eye every example of guilt that comes before a legal tribunal. In these very newspapers which would forbid a romance writer to depict crime with all that he can suggest to demonstrate its causes, portray its hideousness, insist on its inevitable doom, are everywhere to be found the minutest details of guilt,—the meanest secrets of the prison-house are explored, turnkeys interrogated, and pages filled with descriptions of the personal appearance of the felon, his dress at the bar, his courage at the gallows. To find the true literature of Newgate and Tyburn, you have only to open the newspaper on your table. (Bulwer-Lytton 1847: 28)

To return to the 'Postscript' in the light of this statement is to be reminded what a strange document De Quincey's essay really is—a piece of 'high literature' which nevertheless has far more in common with the popular newspapers and penny dreadfuls of its day than with the Whiggish productions of Bulwer. Where Bulwer had earnestly invested himself in characters such as Paul Clifford and Eugene Aram (employing a heated but still hopelessly patrician style that Thackeray satirized superbly in his *Punch* parody 'George de Barnwell'), there was something so facetiously excessive in De Quincey's early exaltation of Williams that the ground was always being prepared for the writer's future betrayal of him. Far from investing himself in Williams's psychology, 'the rational analysis of motivation and the moral interest of revenge' as Nigel Leask has noticed, 'is replaced by De Quincey by a fascination with revenge and a desire to sacrifice the criminal to a fate as ghastly as the crime he has perpetrated'. At around the same time as *Jack Sheppard* was taking the reading public—and London theatre world—by storm, De Quincey was, like Bulwer in his 'Word to the Public', contrasting Greek Tragedy with that of the English theatrical tradition. Following on from Lessing, Schlegel and Coleridge before him, De Quincey was fascinated by the primitive roots of Attic drama, its origins in the ritual murder of a heroic scapegoat. And in this light, as Leask points out, 'he seems to have understood catharsis in an almost sacramental sense' (Leask 1995: 196).

'In the ancient drama, to represent it justly,' De Quincey wrote, in 'A Brief Appraisal of Greek Literature' in 1838–39, 'the unlearned reader must imagine grand situations, impressive groups; in the modern tumultuous movement, a grand stream of action'.

> In the Greek drama, he must conceive the presiding power to be *Death*; in the English, *Life*. What Death?—What Life? That sort of death, or of life locked up and frozen into everlasting slumber, which we see in sculpture; that sort of life, of tumult, of agitation, of tendency to something beyond, which we see in painting. The picturesque, in short, domineers over English tragedy; the sculpturesque, or the statuesque, over the Grecian. (*DQW*, XI: 21–22)

De Quincey later expanded upon this theme in an article on the 'Theory of Greek Tragedy' that was published the following year in the more conservative *Blackwood's*. Great fixed situations were what Greek tragedy presented, not passions in states of growth, movement or conflict, and these situations were then 'held', De Quincey pointed out, 'like a statuesque attitude' for one or more acts. Hence 'the story of the tragedy was pretty nearly involved and told by implication in the *tableaux vivans*' (*DQW*, XI: 494).

> Hence, too, that habit amongst the tragic poets of travelling back to regions of forgotten fable and dark legendary mythus. Antiquity availed powerfully for their purposes, because of necessity it abstracted all petty

details of individuality and local notoriety; all that would have composed a *character*. It acted as twilight acts (which removes day's 'mutable distinctions',) and reduced the historic person to that sublime state of monotonous gloom which suited the views of a poet who wanted only the *situation*, but would have repelled a poet who sought also for the complex features of a character. (*DQW*, XI: 495–96)

In the context of a literary market-place swimming in representations of murder, it's tempting to read De Quincey's idealisation of the Greek tragic aesthetic during the 1840s as a Tory flight from liberal psychologising, and also from a broader tendency, in the popular crime literature of the period, to turn murder into economic or political allegory. Indeed one way of reading the 1854 'Postscript' is in terms of a long-standing desire on De Quincey's part to move away from the picturesqueness of English drama (and, one might add, English fiction), with its 'tendency to something beyond' and return to the deeply embodied yet abstract heart of Greek drama.

Some of the more excessive, almost deliberately extraneous elements in De Quincey's portrayal of the Ratcliffe Highway murders become explicable in this light. Larger than life with his orange hair, big robes and masklike face, Williams is a perfect candidate for Greek tragedy, and his status as holy scapegoat is only reinforced by the rather formal, ritualistic manner of his burial. More to the point, Williams is strongly associated with Oriental savagery in the essay (he has spent time in India, and developed a 'tiger quality'), but his Irishness, which was regularly referred to in the newspaper sources, is firmly suppressed.[13] This enables De Quincey to represent the killer as a figure of pure, rather than politically motivated, evil. At one point he is obliquely connected with the serial excesses of the Terror, his second outing being compared to 'the earthquake' which 'is not satisfied at once' in the revolutionary books of Wordsworth's recently published *Prelude*. But in a way this covert reference only goes to show how keen De Quincey is to de-politicise violence in the 'Postscript', and see it as part of a primitive natural cycle.

Williams is business-like in his preparations for murder, but he does not, like the Resurrection Man or Sweeney Todd, turn murder into a business: he is too much of an *amateur*, in both senses of the word. Most tellingly of all, Williams's 'twilight acts' are indeed sunk in 'monotonous gloom': like the protagonists of Greek Tragedy he has no character separate from his deeds. Where other literary criminals, the Resurrection Man included, are all possessed of an individual internal life that is prior to and in some sense separate from their crimes, Williams's individuality and his criminality, like that of Poe's 'Man of the Crowd' are indistinguishable from one another. And this is crucial to the aesthetic of ritual sacrifice and collective purification that De Quincey wants to create. Murder, in the second part of the 'Postscript' is no longer an allegory for anything—least of all the fine arts—but strives to be symbolic rather—its meaning inherent in itself. In the description of the second murder, there is a moment analogous to Mary's knocking at the door, when the young lodger comes down the stairs from his bedroom to see 'Marr's murderer now at work':

> Three separate death-struggles were by this time over; and the poor petrified journeyman, quite unconscious of what he was doing, in blind, passive, self-surrender to panic, absolutely descended both flights of stairs. Infinite terror inspired him with the same impulse as might have been inspired by headlong courage. In his shirt, and upon old decaying stairs, that at times creaked under his feet, he continued to descend, until he had reached the lowest step but four. The situation was tremendous beyond any that is on record. A sneeze, a cough, almost a breathing, and the young man would be a corpse, without a chance or a struggle for his life. The murderer was at that time in the little parlour—the door of which parlour faced you in descending the stairs; and this door stood ajar; [...] consequently two out of three corpses were exposed to the young man's gaze. Where was the third? And the murderer—where was he? [...] Very soon, however, he came into view; but, fortunately for the young man, at this critical moment, the murderer's purpose too entirely absorbed him to allow of his throwing a glance to the staircase, on which else the white figure of the journeyman, standing in motionless horror, would have been detected in an instant, and seasoned for the grave in the second. (*DQW*, XX: 58)

In the sudden slowing down of the narrative in these two key set-pieces we can see literature aspiring to sculpture. De Quincey errs slightly in the passage above when he tells us that Turner descends the stairs 'absolutely', because in fact he arrests himself four steps from the bottom, but this slight over-emphasis on the 'absoluteness' of the descent only serves to reveal the Opium-Eater's ambition for this passage all the more clearly: that it should conjure up a situation at one and the same time literal and metaphysical, temporal and eternal, a symbolic scene, in the Coleridgean or high German sense, with its meaning entirely inherent in its *mise en scène*.[14] A fatal fascination takes absolute control of Turner—and walks him down the stairs. Fundamental oppositions are brought into terrifying proximity: extreme physicality and extreme passivity, with only a whisker of a difference between motionless life and motionless death. The passage, which is longer than can be quoted here, seems to thicken and slow down as it proceeds, becoming ever more powerfully suspended in horror-stricken contemplation and ever more progressively absorbed by the stillness which that entails.

Like members of the Greek Chorus, first Mary then the journeyman stand in sublime horror at the scenes before them—before initiating the collective dance—the public hue and cry—that will eventually eject the murderer from the community.[15] In his book *Thomas De Quincey: Knowledge and Power*

Frederick Burwick writes illuminatingly of the dialectic of those mighty antagonisms 'infinite activity' and 'infinite repose' in De Quincey's writing. He sees the latter's poetic prose in terms of Pygmalion moments, in which images, characters, objects are suddenly released into motion, and Medusa moments, in which they are frozen as if forever. De Quincey's peculiar sensitivity to this dynamic was undoubtedly exacerbated by his opium-addiction, and reflects a chronic subjection to bouts of exhilarating mental activity and extreme passivity, delicious torpor and extreme nervous excitement. But it was also, as he knew from translating Lessing's *Laocoon*, a central feature of art as well, whose 'main attraction' 'is in the very antagonism between the transitory reality and the non-transitory image of it reproduced by Painting or Sculpture. The shows of Nature, which we feel we know to be moving, unstable, and transitory, are by these arts arrested in a single moment of their passage, and frozen as it were into motionless immortality' (*DQW*, VI: 40–41).

Burwick is very good on the terrifying alternation between movement and stasis in De Quincey, his prime example being the climactic 'Dream-Fugue' at the end of 'The English Mail-Coach'. Having been gathered up into a triumphal procession sweeping through the gates of a great city in celebration of the victory at Waterloo, the dreamer is suddenly confronted by the image of a Dying Trumpeter, in bas-relief, on the stone battlements: 'Solemnly from the field of battle he rose to his feet; and, unslinging his stony trumpet, carried it, in his dying anguish, to his stony lips', and no sooner has the trumpeter's proclamation of death been heard than 'by horror we, that were so full of life, we men and our horses, with their fiery fore-legs rising in mid air to their everlasting gallop, were frozen to a bas-relief. Then a third time the trumpet sounded; the seals were taken off all pulses; life, and the frenzy of life, tore into their channels again; again the choir burst forth in sunny grandeur, as from the muffling of storms and darkness' (*DQW*, XVI: 447). Like Keats's 'Ode on a Grecian Urn' this description of the frozen cavalcade is clearly inspired by the Elgin marbles, and offers a powerful image of tragic catharsis—of ritual terror and release.

At the beginning of the 'Postscript' De Quincey puts the full weight of his racist xenophobia into his presentation of Ratcliffe Highway. It is described as 'a public thoroughfare in a most chaotic quarter of eastern or nautical London and at this time . . . a most dangerous quarter'.

> Every third man at the least might be set down as a foreigner. Lascars, Chinese, Moors, Negroes, were met at every step. And apart from the manifold ruffianism, shrouded impenetrably under the mixed hats and turbans of men whose past was untraceable to any European eyes, it is well known that the navy [. . .] is a sure receptacle of all the murderers and ruffians whose crimes have given them a motive for withdrawing themselves for a season from the public eye. (*DQW*, XX: 41)

By the end of the narrative, however, the people of Wapping are rising from their beds in order to pursue the killer, discovering a new and sublime unity in their 'deadly roar of vengeance'. Like Hortense, the murderer in Dickens's *Bleak House* (1851–52) Williams functions as a scapegoat for the wider community. Unlike the Frenchwoman, however, his expulsion has real ritual force. The community unites and purifies itself in the act of getting rid of him, and the 'ferocious tumults' of London described in the essay's opening have exhausted and exorcised themselves by the end. At the beginning of the 'Postscript', as in De Quincey's previous essays on murder, there is a stark opposition between the aesthetic and the moral, but by the end of the piece they have both been resolved, through tragic ritual, into the religious. In a sense Williams dies so that De Quincey can live and reconcile himself to the London crowd—a crowd that he can imagine as English now that it is has been ritually purged of its foreignness. But it is the abstract nature of this process, its deliberate removal from any recognisable political context, that really renders De Quincey's treatment distinctive. The 'Postscript' presents crime not as a problem to be solved but as a ritual to be enacted. It is a very Tory take on the problem of the modern metropolis.

De Quincey's mixture of the Cockney and the classical in the 'Postscript' is remarkably reminiscent of another Tory form of the period that was particularly successful in its representation of murder. This was the waxworks of Madame Tussaud. Since its early years as a travelling exhibition Tussaud's show had been based on the most spectacular of theatrical—and class—divisions. It boasted a Main Room, costing 1 shilling a head, which specialised in effigies of kings and princes, statesmen, all the great and good; and it had an 'Adjoining Room', costing an extra sixpence, which focussed on figures from the French Revolution and criminals. By the late 1830s the Baker Street Bazaar had become the permanent home to an extensive gallery of malefactors, with the body-snatchers Burke and Hare among the most popular. There was a certain irony in this given that Madame was in her own polite way something of a body-snatcher herself, following hard upon the heels of celebrities and criminals in her search for authentic artefacts. 'Madame Tussaud modelled Burke during the trial,' Pamela Pillbeam tells us, 'and her sons completed Hare. She also acquired a cast of Burke's head done three hours after the execution'.

> Tussaud's 'Adjoining Room' became so famous that some villains donated their own clothes for their models before their executions. Sometimes the Tussaud's bought the entire content of a room where a particularly memorable murder had occurred, and reconstructed it in what 'Punch' christened, in 1846, the 'Chamber of Horrors'. (Pillbeam 2003: 108)

Many commentators thought wax-works inartistic and vulgar; De Quincey himself, in his first essay on murder, facetiously remarked that poisoning cases, compared with the legitimate style, were 'no better than wax-work by the side of sculpture' (*DQW*, VI: 127). But many others echoed the sentiments of Mrs. Jarley, the travelling wax-work owner in Dickens's *Old Curiosity Shop* (1841):

> 'It isn't funny at all,' repeated Mrs. Jarley, 'It's calm and—what's that word again—critical?—no—classical, that's it—it's calm and classical. No low beatings and knockings about, no jokings and squeakings like your precious Punches, but always the same, with a constantly unchanging air of coldness and gentility; and so like life, that if wax-works only spoke and walked about, you'd hardly know the difference. (Dickens 2001: 208)

It may seem strange to think of a wax-works exhibition in classical terms—but if we think of the paying public moving and milling about such spaces as, in effect, a kind of chorus, we can see that there might be more substance in Mrs. Jarley's assertion than at first appears. Certainly Dickens was in favour of a spectacle that replaced the boisterous, baiting mob of the old public executions with a crowd ready to be purged by pity and terror. Suggestions that the exhibition glamorized crime were heartily denied by the Tussaud family—indeed they inserted a piece in their catalogue assuring the public 'that so far from the exhibition of the likenesses of criminals creating a desire to imitate them, Experience teaches them that it has a direct tendency to the contrary'.

Certainly, there is no shortage of contemporary comment attesting to the powerful nature of the theatrical effect. As the 'Eyewitness' wrote in the January 1860 issue of *All the Year Round*: 'to enter the Chamber of Horrors rather late in the afternoon, before the gas is lighted, requires courage. To penetrate through a dark passage under the guillotine scaffold, to the mouth of a dimly-lit cell, through whose bars a figure in a black serge dress is faintly visible, requires courage'.[16] Responses were, if anything, even more acute at the beginning of the 1850s. In Bartlett's *What I Saw in London* of 1852, for example, the chamber of horrors is described, briefly but sincerely, as 'too horrible to gaze at' (Bartlett 1852: 55).

In part waxwork galleries were like theatrical *tableaux vivants* of the kind De Quincey mentioned in his 'Theory of Greek Tragedy'. But they also had the advantage of being three-dimensional spaces that could be entered and explored, spaces that gave spectators a heightened sense of perspective and proximity, of being *in* the scene. One description, by James Greenwood, of a particular tableau at a Birmingham waxworks shows the overwhelming feeling of presence and gradual revelation that they could generate. Its subject was the Esher tragedy which took place in 1854, the same year as De Quincey's 'Postscript' was composed, when six children were murdered by their mother, Mrs. Brough, the nurse to the Prince of Wales.

> But the crowning horror was in the further room. As you approached the half-open door you could see a bedstead foot; that was in no way

startling. From the position of the chamber it would naturally be used for sleeping in. You put your head in at the door, and you saw a sight that was almost enough to make you scream out 'Police!' There was a bedstead by the wall just where a bedstead usually stands, and with a bed on it—a made bed with sheets and bolster and pillows, exposing six children, each one with its throat cut in a manner so horrible that the shocked feelings of the beholder were immediately comforted by the reflection that their death must have been instantaneous. Gore on the little waxen faces, gore on the sheets, and on the hands that had been thrown up to protect their tender lives; and there was the murderess—she had left the razor in the windpipe of her last victim—with her throat cut as well, standing upright in her sprinkled nightdress, to welcome you, with a label round her neck that provided the edifying information that 'this woman was nurse to his Royal Highness the Prince of Wales'. (Greenwood 1873: 325)

Like the Chamber of Horrors, De Quincey's 'Postscript' organises itself around a series of static, tragic tableaux to be seen from the perspective of innocent bystanders.[17] It aspires to a theatre of meaning both embodied and abstract, a symbolic plane upon which, as De Quincey himself points out, the tragic drama will 'read aloud its own history'; in which significance will emerge naturally from a set of intimate spatial relations.

'It is really wonderful and most interesting,' he writes, of the first spate of murders:

> to pursue the successive steps of this monster, and to notice the absolute certainty with which the hieroglyphics of the case betray to us the whole process and movements of the bloody drama, not less surely and fully than if we had been ourselves hidden in Marr's shop, or had looked down from the heavens of mercy upon this hell-kite, that knew not what mercy meant. (*DQW*, XX: 47)

And this waxwork aesthetic is further revealed in the author's description of the murderer, with his 'corpse-like face' that 'wore at all times a bloodless ghastly pallor', and 'his eyes seemed frozen and glazed, as if their light were all converged upon some victim lurking in the far background' (*DQW*, XX: 42).

In the door scene, Mary leans forward to see if she can detect Williams's 'breathing', 'the breathing of that dreadful being who has silenced all breathing except his own' and becomes suddenly conscious of her own breathing as the one thing dividing her from oblivion. 'Still as death she was . . . during that dreadful stillness, when she hushed her breath that she might listen'. There is a similar moment in De Quincey's description of the Manchester murders at the end of the 'Postscript' when he describes how a young boy is forced to drain his face of all expression, slow the beating of his heart and counterfeit sleep, all in order to avert the murderer's suspicions of him. This is like the experience of a visitor to Madame Tussaud's in the presence of an individual wax-work. Both fascinated and appalled by the possibility that the frozen figure before him might suddenly, and perhaps almost imperceptibly, exhibit signs of life, the viewer becomes at once still and silent in the sublime contemplation of it, is turned into a wax-work himself, and, in fact, drawn into an unconscious sympathy with death. It is an uncanny experience, but it is also, like the image of the Dying Trumpeter at the end of 'The English Mail-Coach', ultimately a cathartic one, and one that relies on a curious combination of realism and abstraction to achieve its effect. Its final effect upon crime—in the case of the Chamber of Horrors—is simultaneously to sacralise it and separate it from ordinary social experience—to place it within a special, insulated chamber, 'a dangerous quarter' like Ratcliffe Highway itself, around which one might attempt to draw a reassuring *cordon sanitaire*.

The gallery is a sublime metaphor for life in De Quincey, not surprisingly, perhaps, given opium's tendency to expand and dovetail space and time. Witness the Piranesi-influenced nightmares in the 1821 *Confessions* and the image of the Whispering Gallery in the 1856 revision. One further example is contained in an 1844 manuscript draft of a projected third essay on murder—a piece that bears no obvious resemblance to the eventual 'Postscript' of 1854 except in so far as it anticipates some of the same themes and questions. This fragment begins with a mock-celebration of anonymity as the source of all true power. 'Note the power of murderers as fine-art professors to make a new start' De Quincey writes, 'to turn the corner, to retreat upon the road they have come ... this they owe to fortunate obscurity, which attests anew the wonderful compensations of life'. He fantasises a 'foreigner' landing in Calcutta, leaving his past behind him: 'it may be that in leaving Paris or Naples, he was simply cutting the connection with creditors who showed signs of *attachment* not good for his health. But it may also be that he ran away by the blaze of a burning inn, which he had fired in order to hide three throats he had cut'. Then, in a nod to his own middle-aged celebrity, he goes on to lament the lack of anonymity available to a member of the middle-classes. 'The privilege of safe criminality,' he says, 'is limited to classes crowded together like leaves in Vallambrosa; for them to run away into some mighty city, is to commence life anew'. But no sooner has he done this than he goes on to cite some instances of two unnamed men

> who wrote so many books, and perpetrated *so* many pamphlets, that at fifty they had forgotten much of their own literary villainies, and at sixty they commenced with murderous ferocity a series of answers to arguments which it was proved upon them afterwards that they themselves had emitted at thirty—thus coming round with volleys of shot on their own heads, as the Whispering Gallery at St. Paul's begins to retaliate any secrets you may have committed to its keeping in echoing

thunders after a time, or as Sir John Mandeville under Arctic skies heard in May all those curses thawing, and exploding like minute guns, which had been frozen up in November. (*DQW*, XV: 458)

On the one hand there is the life of serial criminality—of moving freely and invisibly from one place to another, of never looking back. On the other there is the image of the Whispering Gallery, in which all one's secrets—all one's sayings—rebound with a vengeance.

When De Quincey was engaged upon the 'Postscript' to 'On Murder Considered as One of the Fine Arts', he was just beginning to face the reality of gathering his innumerable writings together for the first collected edition, a task that he initially told his editor Hogg was 'absolutely impossible'. In part this was due to the sheer volume of manuscript material lying around. Seeking to explain De Quincey's extravagant system of living in later life Edward Sackville West wrote that:

> One of his reasons ... was a desire to escape from the importunities of friends. Another, more important, was his dislike of throwing anything—books, papers, manuscripts—away, combined with an even more intense objection to having his belongings 'tidied'. In this he did not differ from most men of letters; but few even of them can have collected such literary snow-drifts as De Quincey managed to amass during the last years of his life. When tables, chairs, bed and floor were entirely encumbered, and even the narrow path between the door and the fireplace had become silted up, he would simply lock the door of the room and betake himself to another lodging, there to remain until once more driven on by a similar set of affairs. At his death, no less than six sets of lodgings were found in this condition. (Sackville West, 1936: 275)

De Quincey was a man creatively haunted by the past, by early hardships and family tragedies, and this may help explain why, in relation to both his past writings and his past lives, he was simultaneously both excited and appalled at the prospect of having them 'tidied'. The prospect of collecting his separate serial performances into a timeless gallery was potentially a very disturbing one for him, as might be inferred from the nightmare vision of life depicted in his 1845 autobiography, the *Suspiria de Profundis*.

> ... I say if life could throw open its long suites of chambers to our eyes from some station *beforehand*, if from some secret stand we could look *by anticipation* along its vast corridors, and aside into the recesses opening upon them from either hand, halls of tragedy or chambers of retribution, simply in that small wing and no more of the caravanserai which we ourselves shall haunt, simply in that narrow tract of time and no more where we ourselves shall range, and confining our gaze to those and no others for whom personally we shall be interested, what

a recoil we should suffer of horror in our estimate of life! (*DQW*, XV: 198–99)

The spatial terms in which this vision is couched are, it hardly needs pointing out, strongly reminiscent of Madame Tussaud's, right down to the relationship between the halls and side-chambers, recesses and corridors. For De Quincey the vision of life as a gallery was a highly charged one, because it suggested a structure at once vast and labyrinthine, serial and simultaneous, in which, as in the mind of an addict under the influence of opium, time becomes space and space time.

De Quincey's 1854 'Postscript' retraces the narrative sketched out in his then unpublished 1844 manuscript on murder: it describes the furtive mobility of the serial assassin (or periodical journalist), it also captures the slow build-up of rebellious 'breathings' that will culminate in a retributive echo by the end. But there is an aesthetic benefit in conceiving of this nightmare as taking place *in camera*, in the serially connected chambers of Marr, Williamson and the Manchester tavern assailed by the McKeons, and it lies in the fact that, as with Madame Tussaud's, the closed settings which serve to amplify the horror are also those which strive to contain it, subjecting guilt's eternal reverberations to a continual, ritual catharsis.

NOTES

1. De Quincey only makes reference to one previous paper on murder at the beginning of the 'Postscript', which has led the Pickering editors to speculate that it might have been composed much earlier, that is, between 1827 (the date of the first essay) and 1839 (the date of the second). This one stray reference aside, however, there is still a great deal of internal evidence in the 'Postscript' suggesting that the piece was substantially composed and/or revised in the early 1850s (*DQW*, XX: 36–37).
2. 'The "Postscript" was first published in *Selections Grave and Gay*, an anthology of past writings in which De Quincey found himself at last free of the constraining magazine context and able to experiment with a new and more ambitious mode of address' (Leask 1995: footnote 46).
3. The most recent historical treatment of the murders is P.D. James's much-reprinted *The Maul and the Pear Tree*, which first appeared in 1971.
4. An account of the coroner's report was printed in *The Times*, December 23, 1811. This particular phrase was then taken up by the Rev. G. Williams of Gate Street Chapel in his *Substance of a Sermon on the Horrid Murders in Ratcliffe Highway and Gravel Lane preached on Sunday December 29, 1811* (1812).
5. See especially *Edinburgh Annual Register* 1813: 206–11, 219–31; *Fairburn's Account of the Dreadful Murder of Mr Marr and Family* (1812), *Fairburn's Account of the Life, Death and Interment of John Williams* (1812), *A Particular Account of a Most Shocking Murder* (1811), *Another Shocking Massacre in New Gravel Lane* (1811).
6. For a more detailed account of the various ways in which De Quincey has deviated from his sources in the 'Postscript' see especially Robert Morrison 2006: vii–xxvii, 166-201 (the introduction and the textual notes). Thomas

Burke's *The Ecstasies of Thomas De Quincey* (1928), Albert Goldman's *The Mine and the Mint: Sources for the Writings of Thomas De Quincey* (1965), and Margo Ann Sullivan's *Murder and Art: Thomas De Quincey and the Ratcliffe Highway Murders* (1987) are also worth consulting.

7. See especially *The Times* 1811: Dec 23, 24, 28, 30, 31 and 1812: Jan 1, 4, 13.
8. A.S. Plumtree offers a classic psychological reading of De Quincey's work in these terms: 'I would propose that De Quincey's conception of the murderer as artist springs from an intuition of the artist as murderer [...] when Sade referred to "the moral crime that is committed by writing" what he meant was that the writer is free to commit crimes of the imagination for which, in actual life, he might feel nothing but revulsion' (Plumtree 1985: 161).
9. Some contemporary commentators considered John Turner's abandonment of the child cowardly, but for De Quincey his decision to escape from the house and raise the alarm was unquestionably the right one.
10. The Opium-Eater's first appearance in the 'Noctes' is, in fact, a *tour de force* of murderous criticism. Not only does he refuse to take any responsibility for a series of alleged drug-related suicides brought about by the *Confessions*, he also launches into an unprovoked attack on Coleridge as an inveterate plagiarist. 'I mean no disrespect to a man of surpassing talents' the Opium-Eater continues, 'if he plead to the indictment, he is a dead man—if he stand mute, I will press him to death, under three hundred and fifty pound weight of German metaphysics'. Later in the same dialogue the character tells the Blackwoodsmen never to mix politics and literature, and warns them against sliding into 'coarseness' in their attacks on others. 'As a mere affair of taste' he concludes, 'use the dissecting-knife rather than the cleaver and leave the downright butchering business of literature to those to whom the perquisite of the offal may be of consequence' (*Blackwood's Edinburgh Magazine* XIV, 1823: 500–1).
11. Even more parasitic, Albert Goldman has argued, are his more formal book reviews, which frequently draw secretly on the volume under review for all their information while publicly damning them as worthless.
12. The classic study is still Keith Hollingsworth's *The Newgate Novel 1830–47*.
13. Fairburn tells us that Williams was born at Bandon in Ireland and speculates on the political background to his murderousness: 'whether he was in his native country at the time of the unhappy troubles of 1798, can now only be a matter of conjecture; but it is certainly not unnatural to suppose that a monster capable of committing the late atrocities, must early in life have lost that innate horror of bloodshed, which forms so striking a feature in the moral constitution of man. In the dreadful paths of rebellion, probably it was that he was first tempted to imbue his hands in the blood of his fellow-creatures, and, amidst those terrible scenes of midnight murder, which that unhappy country then afforded, might his sinful conscience have been seared to every feeling of repentance and remorse' (*Fairburn's Account . . . of John Williams*, 1812: 3).
14. In *The Statesman's Manual* Coleridge followed his German philosophical mentors Schlegel and Schelling in deploring the modern tendency to confuse symbol and allegory, insisting upon the philosophical and artistic superiority of the former: 'Now an allegory is but a translation of abstract notions into a picture-language which is itself nothing but an abstraction from objects of the senses; the principal being more worthless than even its phantom proxy, both alike unsubstantial, and the former shapeless to boot. On the other hand a Symbol is characterized by a translucence of the Special in the Individual or of the General in the Especial or of the Universal in the General. Above all by the translucence of the Eternal through and in the Temporal. It always partakes of the Reality which it renders intelligible; and while it enunciates the whole,

abides itself as a living part in that Unity, of which it is the representative' (Coleridge 1972: 30).
15. Later in the 'Postscript' the journeyman preparing his escape and the murderer preparing further destruction are described as working against each other 'like chorus and semi-chorus, strophe and antistrophe' (*DQW*, XX: 62).
16. 'An Eyewitness in Great Company', *All the Year Round*, 7 January 1860: 252.
17. On the 'Postscript' as an essentially non-satirical victim-story see Frederick Burwick 2001: 67–70.

WORKS CITED

Newspapers, Annuals, Journals and Pamphlet Sources

A Particular Account of a Most Shocking Murder. (1811) Cheapside: T. Batchelor.
Another Shocking Massacre in New Gravel Lane. (1811) Cheapside: T. Batchelor.
Fairburn's Account of the Dreadful Murder of Mr Marr and Family. (1812) London: Fairburn.
Fairburn's Account of the Life, Death and Interment of John Williams. (1812) London: Fairburn.
Williams, Rev. G. (1812) *Substance of a Sermon on the Horrid Murders in Ratcliffe Highway and Gravel Lane preached on Sunday December 29, 1811*, London: Fairburn.
The Times. (1812) Dec 23rd, 24th, 28th, 30th, 31st 1811 and Jan 1st, 4th, 13th.
Edinburgh Annual Register, (1813).
Blackwood's Edinburgh Magazine, (1823).
All the Year Round, (1860) Jan 7th.

Literary and Critical Sources

Altick, Richard. (1978) *The Shows of London*, Cambridge, MA: Belknap, Harvard University Press.
Bartlett, David W. (1852) 'Places and Sights: Madame Tussaud's', *What I Saw in London: or men and things in the great metropolis*, Auburn: Derby and Miller.
Bloom, Michelle E. (2003) *Waxworks: A Cultural Obsession*, Minneapolis: University of Minnesota Press.
Bulwer-Lytton, Edward. (1847) 'A Word to the Public', republished in *Lucretia, or the Children of Night*, 2nd edition, London: Saunders and Otley.
Burke, Thomas. (1928) *The Ecstasies of Thomas De Quincey*, London: n.p.
Burwick, Frederick. (2001) *Thomas De Quincey: Knowledge and Power*, Houndmills: Palgrave.
Coleridge, Samuel Taylor. (1972) *The Statesman's Manual* in *Lay Sermons, The Collected Works of Samuel Taylor Coleridge, Volume 6*, (ed.) R. J. White, Princeton, NJ: Routledge and Kegan Paul.
Chapman, Pauline. (1984) *Madame Tussaud's Chamber of Horrors*, London: Constable.
Dickens, Charles. (2000) *The Old Curiosity Shop*, Norman Page (ed.), Harmondsworth: Penguin.
Dickens, Charles. (2003) *Bleak House*, Nicola Bradbury (ed.), Harmondsworth: Penguin.
Dumas, Alexandre. (1860) *Causeries*, Paris: Michel Levy Freres.
Goldman, Albert. (1965) *The Mine and the Mint: Sources for the Writings of Thomas De Quincey*, Carbondale: Southern Illinois University Press.

Greenwood, James. (1873) 'The Onion Fair', *In Strange Company*, London: King.
Higgins, David. (2005) *Romantic Genius and the Literary Magazine*, London: Routledge.
Hollingsworth, Keith. (1963) *The Newgate Novel 1830–47*, Detroit: Wayne State University Press.
James, Louis. (1963) *Fiction for the Working Man 1830–50*, Oxford: Oxford University Press.
James, P.D. (2000) *The Maul and the Pear Tree*, Faber: London.
Joyce, Simon. (2003) *Capital Offenses: Geographies of Class and Crime in Victorian London*, Charlottesville: University of Virginia Press.
Leask, Nigel. (1995) 'Towards a Universal Aesthetic: De Quincey on Murder as Carnival and Tragedy', in John Beer (ed.) *Questioning Romanticism*, Baltimore: Johns Hopkins University Press.
Lindop, Grevel. (1985; 1st edn. 1981) *The Opium-Eater: A Life of Thomas De Quincey*, London: Weidenfeld and Nicholson.
Maxwell, Richard. (1992) *The Mysteries of Paris and London*, Charlottesville: University Press of Virginia.
McDonagh, Josephine. (1989) 'Do or Die: Problems of Agency and Gender in the Aesthetics of Murder', *Genders*, 5: 120–133.
Morrison, Robert (ed.) (2006) *De Quincey on Murder*, Oxford: Oxford University Press.
Morrison, Robert (ed.) (1998) 'Richard Woodhouse's *Cause Book*: The Opium-Eater, the Magazine Wars, and the London Literary Scene in 1821', *Harvard Library Bulletin*, 9: 1.
Peckett Prest, Thomas. (1846) *The String of Pearls, or The Barber of Fleet Street, A Domestic Romance*, London: E. Lloyd.
Pillbeam, Pamela. (2003) *Madame Tussaud and the History of Waxworks*, London and New York: Hambledon.
Plumtree, A. S. (1985) 'The Artist as Murderer: De Quincey's essay "On Murder Considered as One of the Fine Arts"' in Robert Lance Snyder (ed.) *Thomas De Quincey: Bicentenary Studies*, Norman: University of Oklahoma Press, 140–63.
Reynolds, G. W. M. (1996) *The Mysteries of London*, Keele: Keele University Press.
Roberts, Daniel (2000) *Revisionary Gleam: De Quincey, Coleridge and the High Romantic Argument*, Liverpool: Liverpool University Press.
Sackville West, Edward. (1936) *A Flame in Sunlight: the Life and Work of Thomas De Quincey*, London: Cassell.
Shatto, Susan. (1988) *The Companion to Bleak House*, London: Unwin Hyman.
Sullivan, Margo Ann. (1987) *Murder and Art: Thomas De Quincey and the Ratcliffe Highway Murders*, New York: Garland.
Taylor, George (ed.) (1996) *Trilby And Other Plays: Four Plays for Victorian Star Actors: Jack Sheppard, The Corsican Brothers, Our American Cousin, Trilby*, Oxford and London: Oxford University Press.

11 'A Deafening Menace in Tempestuous Uproars'
De Quincey's 1856 *Confessions*, The Indian Mutiny, and the Response of Collins and Dickens

Charles J. Rzepka

The impact of De Quincey's writings on the history of crime and detective fiction is widely recognized. 'On Murder Considered as One of the Fine Arts' (1827, 1839, 1854) occupies a prominent place in Joel Black's reflections on fictional and cinematic violence (Black 1991), and Robert Morrison has demonstrated the substantive relationship between the English Opium-Eater's writings and Edgar Allan Poe's prototypical stories of criminal pursuit and investigation (Morrison 2001). The protagonist of Peter Ackroyd's *Dan Leno and the Limehouse Golem*, a serial killer, uses De Quincey's essay as an instruction manual, while P. D. James and T. A. Critchley, investigating the Ratcliffe Highway murders that inspired De Quincey's droll reflections, have defended the innocence of their notorious 'genius', John Williams, in *The Maul and the Pear Tree*. The *Confessions of an English Opium-Eater* has also left its mark on the genres of crime and detection. Its particular influence on Wilkie Collins's *The Moonstone* (1868) and Charles Dickens's unfinished *The Mystery of Edwin Drood* (1870) has been the subject of essays by Christopher Herbert (Herbert 1974), Lawrence Frank (Frank 1976), and Joachim Stanley (Stanley 2004), as well as my own recent work (Rzepka 2005: 101–110).

How could a text first published in 1821 and, after a brief five years of brisk sales, republished only twice more in Britain before 1856, have achieved enough popular momentum at mid-century to influence the work not only of Collins and Dickens, but also of foreign writers like Charles Baudelaire, whose citations and translations of the *Confessions* appeared in *Les Paradis Arificiels* in 1860? Clearly, it was the greatly expanded 1856 *Confessions*, making up the fifth volume of *Selections Grave and Gay* (1853–1860) under the editorship of James Hogg, Jr., that re-awakened widespread public interest in the truancy and vagrancy, the opium 'debauches' in London and Grasmere, and the splendid reveries and insufferable nightmares of the Opium-Eater. This longer version of the *Confessions* was to go through numerous printings well into the twentieth-century, becoming the standard scholarly text upon its inclusion in David Masson's *Collected Writings of*

Thomas De Quincey (1889–1890) and remaining so until at least 1971, with the publication of Alethea Hayter's Penguin edition of the early version, followed not long afterwards by Grevel Lindop's 1985 edition for Oxford University Press.[1]

The renewal of interest in the 1821 *Confessions* that provoked De Quincey to revise it in 1856 arose from several sources. These included the publication of such major imaginative works as *Suspiria de Profundis* and 'The English Mail-Coach' during the previous decade, the republication of the original *Confessions* in the collected American edition of De Quincey's writings soon afterwards,[2] and growing public awareness of, and alarm over, the addictive properties of opium, whether imbibed as laudanum or smoked in pipes. As early as 1840, notes Barry Milligan (Milligan 1995: 21), future Prime Minister Gladstone had denounced the pernicious effects of the drug in the midst of England's First Opium War with China (1839–1842). The very year that the revised *Confessions* appeared marked the beginning of the Second Opium War, which ended in 1860 with China's forced legalization of opium and granting of trade concessions to the British. In 1857, the House of Lords' Select Committee on the Sale of Poisons heard testimony from pharmaceutical chemists and other professionals regarding abuse of the drug (Stanley 2004: 23n3). Eleven years later, Parliament decided that what was good for the Chinese goose would not do for the British gander, and passed the Pharmacy Act of 1868 preventing the sale of opium by anyone other than a licensed pharmacist (Milligan 1995: 22). Opium, in short, was in the air and, as Milligan notes, it was intimately related to the cultural dynamics of imperialism, particularly in the East.[3]

For all of these reasons, De Quincey's newly revised *Confessions* was sure to make an impact on contemporary letters. Its specific impact on *The Moonstone* and *The Mystery of Edwin Drood*, however, was enhanced by still another fortuitous conjunction of events. Britain's worsening drug problem and its second outbreak of hostilities with the Celestial Empire in 1856, the year De Quincey published his revised memoirs, were soon eclipsed in the public imagination by the Indian Mutiny of 1857, also known as the Sepoy Mutiny from the Hindi term for 'soldier', which was applied to the hundreds of thousands of enlisted men[4] drawn from the Indian population to fill the ranks of the Bengal, Madras, and Bombay Native Infantries serving on the subcontinent. Under the ultimate authority of the British East India Company and the Governor General of India, and commanded in the field by British commissioned officers, the sepoys, both Muslim and Hindu, had helped to consolidate colonial control over most of northern India during the previous half-century.

The causes of the mutiny were many: grievances over low pay, unsanitary housing, and lack of promotion were compounded by lax discipline, suspicions that British officers were attempting to Christianise the ranks, and smoldering resentment over the Company's ever more aggressive deposing of hereditary rulers in the northern provinces. Tensions reached the breaking point when stories began to circulate that the new Enfield rifles about to be issued to the enlisted men used cartridges greased with pig fat (anathema to Muslims) and cow fat (shunned by Hindus). To make matters worse, before loading the cartridges the soldiers were supposed to tear off the paper ends with their teeth.[5] On the evening of 10 May 1857, after a series of escalating rumours and minor acts of insubordination, the 20th Native Infantry mutinied at Meerut, northeast of Delhi. Local citizens from the bazaar rapidly swelled the ranks. Scores of Europeans were killed or wounded before the mutineers departed that night for Delhi, where the massacres were resumed (David 2002: 77–91). The women and children among the slain at Meerut were to become the first of many 'martyred innocents' in the newspaper accounts that began reaching home a month later, filling the British imagination with epical scenes of murder, mutilation, rape, and other atrocities to which 'Orientals' were, it went without saying, naturally prone. By the time hostilities ended in June 1858, the Indian Mutiny had devastated most of northern India, inciting horrific acts of inhumanity among combatants on both sides and making 'Cawnpore' and 'Lucknow' by-words among British readers for sepoy treachery, cruelty, and cunning.

The literary impact of the Mutiny has been concisely summarized by Patrick Brantlinger (Brantlinger 1988) and more extensively surveyed and analysed by Gautam Chakravarty (Chakravarty 2005). De Quincey's *Confessions*, however, does not figure in these accounts and nor, for that matter, does *The Moonstone* or *The Mystery of Edwin Drood*. Ronald Thomas has observed the mutiny's heightening of racist hysteria preparatory to the fictional appearance of the sinister Brahmins roaming the bucolic English countryside at the opening of Collins's novel (Thomas 1990: 208–09). The impact of these events would have been, perhaps, even more unsettling upon the first readers of *Drood*, who witnessed the ominous 'Orientalising', through opium addiction, of an otherwise respectable English choirmaster. John Jasper's implied methods of murdering and disposing of the body of his nephew, Edwin Drood, also bear a close and chilling resemblance, according to Howard Duffield and Edmund Wilson, to those used by the Thugs, the ritual 'Stranglers' of India, who began infiltrating British fiction soon after the publication of W. H. Sleeman's documentary *The Thugs or Phansigars of India* (1836) and Philip Meadows Taylor's fictional *Confessions of a Thug* (1839).[6] They remained very much in the forefront of public consciousness during the Mutiny itself, as indicated by the central position assumed by a representative 'Thug' in a rogues gallery of 'Hindoo' criminal types published by the *Illustrated London News* in November 1857. (See Figure 11.1).

The Moonstone, serialized in Dickens's *All the Year Round* beginning in January 1868, and *The Mystery of Edwin Drood*, appearing in six installments beginning in April 1870 and left unfinished at Dickens's death months later, mark a turning point in the history of crime and detective fiction. Hailed by T. S. Eliot as 'the first and greatest of modern English detective novels'

Figure 11.1. 'Hindoo Thugs and Poisoners'. The Thug is pictured just right of center, holding a 'roomal' or strangling kerchief diagonally in front of him. From *The Illustrated London News*, 14 November 1857, vol. 30, p. 433. Used by permission of Widener Library, Harvard College Library.

'A Deafening Menace in Tempestuous Uproars' 215

(Eliot 1932: 377), *The Moonstone* offered the first book-length, integrated detective plot in the history of the genre, while Dickens's incomplete mystery introduced English readers of Sensation Novels and subsequent crime fiction to the opium dens of London's East End and the morbidly split personalities that were later to figure prominently in Robert Louis Stevenson's *Dr. Jekyll and Mr. Hyde* and Oscar Wilde's *The Picture of Dorian Grey*. The influence of both books is apparent in Arthur Conan Doyle's earliest Sherlock Holmes stories of the late 1880s and early 1890s, epitomes of the genre. The plundered Moonstone inspired Doyle's choice of the Agra treasure as incentive to crime in the Holmes novella, *The Sign of Four* (Doyle 1890), where the three Brahmins that Collins set in pursuit of the gem reappear as three Muslim and Sikh conspirators who seize the treasure during the height of the Mutiny. *Drood*'s reach extends to Dr. Watson's discovery of Holmes working undercover in an East London opium den in 'The Man with the Twisted Lip' (Doyle 1891), seeking clues to the disappearance of City broker Neville St. Clair. Doyle's theme of respectable professionals—Isa Whitney, Holmes, St. Clair—leading secret lives in the smoke-filled basements of Limehouse is clearly indebted to the example of the respectable John Jasper of Cloisterham and his nocturnal forays to Princess Puffer's London establishment. And of course, Holmes's explanation for his own invidious drug habit, a release from 'the dull routine of existence' (Doyle 1890: 108) and the 'commonplace' events of this 'dreary, dismal, unprofitable world' (Doyle 1890: 113) whenever no worthier 'game is afoot' (Doyle 1892: 881),[7] reaches our ears like an eerie *fin de siecle* echo rebounding from the rafters of Jasper's gloomy apartment in the Gate House of Cathedral Close: 'I have been taking opium for a pain,' he tells his nephew, 'an agony that sometimes come over me', arising from 'the cramped monotony of my existence' (Dickens 1870: 47–48).

Critical examinations of the influence of the *Confessions* on Collins's and Dickens's novels have been, in general, either too piecemeal or too broadly thematic, and in any case incomplete. Lately I have come to believe that among the many forces, historical and literary, influencing the composition of *The Moonstone* and *The Mystery of Edwin Drood*, De Quincey's autobiographical memoir rates as the single most powerful and the most thoroughly integrated.[8] Not only is the *Confessions* pointedly referred to in the pages of the former, providing a template for the personality of the character who eventually solves the mystery of the gem's disappearance, but it also contains the germ of nearly every important feature of the living situation and opium dreams of the primary suspect in the latter. Moreover, the 1856 edition of the *Confessions* left its unique 'fingerprints', so to speak, on the scene of crime writing in both cases.

The central figure by which this influence was conveyed was the Malay who mysteriously appeared out of nowhere at the kitchen door of Dove Cottage in 1816, as described in the 'Introduction to the Pains of Opium' section of both the 1821 and 1856 editions. After 'bolt[ing]' at once the lips, and with eyes which ostentatiously looked anywhere rather than look in his face. The poor wretch was evidently no favourite in the house' (Collins 1868: 409). The fair and pretty face of the housemaid in juxtaposition to Jennings's 'gipsy-complexion' and generally 'unfavourable' demeanour recalls the young servant girl 'born and bred amongst the mountains, who had never seen an Asiatic dress of any sort', opening the door to admit the Malay in the *Confessions*. The tableau that strikes the Opium-Eater, who like Blake has just descended the stairs, places the girl, with 'her native spirit of mountain intrepidity', in the same frame as the 'tiger-cat before her', creating a 'striking picture' contrasting 'the beautiful face of the girl, and its exquisite fairness' with 'the sallow and bilious skin of the Malay, enameled or veneered with mahogany' (*DQW*, II: 56–7; 234–35).

In 1868, when *The Moonstone* began its serialization, readers would have imagined scenes like these in the light of widely disseminated newspaper accounts and memoirs describing sepoys murdering innocent English women and children in their homes, sometimes after treacherous professions of loyalty. One survivor of the massacres in Delhi provided the following account of a neighbouring family's ordeal:

> At length I nerved myself and stepped into the next room which was the hall. Oh! I had indeed need to nerve myself. Just before me pinned to the wall was poor Clark's little son with his head hanging down, and a dark stream of blood trickling down the wall into a large black pool which lay near his feet. And this cruel death they must have inflicted before the mother's eyes. I closed my eyes and shuddered, but I opened them upon, even as yet, a more dreadful sight. Clark and his wife lay side by side. But I will not, describe the scene . . . she was far advanced in pregnancy. (quoted in Robinson 1996: 43–44)

George Bruce Malleson's contemporary account of the 'charnel house' that met the eyes of the relief troops at Cawnpore became an iconic emblem of sepoy blood-lust toward women and children:

> The floor of the inner room was found two inches deep in blood,—it came over the men's shoes as they stepped. Ladies' hair, back combs, parts of religious books, children's shoes, hats, bonnets, lay scattered about the room; there were marks of sword-cuts on the walls low down, as if the women had been struck at as they crouched. From the well at the back of the house the naked bodies, limb separated from limb, protruded out. It was a sight sickening, heart-rending, maddening. (Malleson 1858: 2. 159).

Given the outcome of the Moonstone case, namely, that the thief turns out to be neither Hindu nor Anglo-Indian but the English Evangelical hypocrite, Godfrey Ablewhite, and that Ezra Jennings plays the crucial role in

(Eliot 1932: 377), *The Moonstone* offered the first book-length, integrated detective plot in the history of the genre, while Dickens's incomplete mystery introduced English readers of Sensation Novels and subsequent crime fiction to the opium dens of London's East End and the morbidly split personalities that were later to figure prominently in Robert Louis Stevenson's *Dr. Jekyll and Mr. Hyde* and Oscar Wilde's *The Picture of Dorian Grey*. The influence of both books is apparent in Arthur Conan Doyle's earliest Sherlock Holmes stories of the late 1880s and early 1890s, epitomes of the genre. The plundered Moonstone inspired Doyle's choice of the Agra treasure as incentive to crime in the Holmes novella, *The Sign of Four* (Doyle 1890), where the three Brahmins that Collins set in pursuit of the gem reappear as three Muslim and Sikh conspirators who seize the treasure during the height of the Mutiny. *Drood*'s reach extends to Dr. Watson's discovery of Holmes working undercover in an East London opium den in 'The Man with the Twisted Lip' (Doyle 1891), seeking clues to the disappearance of City broker Neville St. Clair. Doyle's theme of respectable professionals—Isa Whitney, Holmes, St. Clair—leading secret lives in the smoke-filled basements of Limehouse is clearly indebted to the example of the respectable John Jasper of Cloisterham and his nocturnal forays to Princess Puffer's London establishment. And of course, Holmes's explanation for his own invidious drug habit, a release from 'the dull routine of existence' (Doyle 1890: 108) and the 'commonplace' events of this 'dreary, dismal, unprofitable world' (Doyle 1890: 113) whenever no worthier 'game is afoot' (Doyle 1892: 881),[7] reaches our ears like an eerie *fin de siecle* echo rebounding from the rafters of Jasper's gloomy apartment in the Gate House of Cathedral Close: 'I have been taking opium for a pain,' he tells his nephew, 'an agony that sometimes come over me', arising from 'the cramped monotony of my existence' (Dickens 1870: 47–48).

Critical examinations of the influence of the *Confessions* on Collins's and Dickens's novels have been, in general, either too piecemeal or too broadly thematic, and in any case incomplete. Lately I have come to believe that among the many forces, historical and literary, influencing the composition of *The Moonstone* and *The Mystery of Edwin Drood*, De Quincey's autobiographical memoir rates as the single most powerful and the most thoroughly integrated.[8] Not only is the *Confessions* pointedly referred to in the pages of the former, providing a template for the personality of the character who eventually solves the mystery of the gem's disappearance, but it also contains the germ of nearly every important feature of the living situation and opium dreams of the primary suspect in the latter. Moreover, the 1856 edition of the *Confessions* left its unique 'fingerprints', so to speak, on the scene of crime writing in both cases.

The central figure by which this influence was conveyed was the Malay who mysteriously appeared out of nowhere at the kitchen door of Dove Cottage in 1816, as described in the 'Introduction to the Pains of Opium' section of both the 1821 and 1856 editions. After 'bolt[ing]' at once the enormous dose of opium given him by his gracious English host—'enough to kill three dragoons and their horses'—and disappearing into the hills, the Malay vengefully 'fastened afterwards upon' the Opium-Eater's dreams, bringing 'other Malays with him worse than himself, that ran "a-muck"' at him and led him 'into a world of troubles' (*DQW*, II: 57–58; see also 235–6).[9] No other source for Collins or Dickens aside from the *Confessions* offers such a highly charged 'involute,' as De Quincey himself might call it, for the amalgamation of Orientalist themes, the lure and threat of opium addiction, and the haunting sense of criminal guilt and dread that pervades both novels. To invoke the analogy with St. Paul's Whispering Gallery by which, in the 1856 edition, De Quincey sought to convey some sense of the portentousness of his decision to run away from Manchester Grammar School at the age of seventeen, the Indian Mutiny of 1857 took the softly murmured but 'solemn truth' of the Malay incident recorded in the 1821 *Confessions* and magnified its impact on the future of literary detection into 'a deafening menace in tempestuous uproars' (*DQW*, II: 155).

According to Christopher Herbert, Dickens had remarked to a visitor in 1869, while working on *Drood*, that of the books he most admired De Quincey's works were among his 'especial favorites' (Herbert 1974: 247). It is too much to claim, of course, that Collins and Dickens were familiar only with the 1856 *Confessions*, since much of the evidence of De Quincey's influence can be traced to material appearing, largely unchanged, in both editions. In any case, perhaps the most obvious impact of the *Confessions* on either novel is registered in Collins's characterization of Ezra Jennings, Dr. Candy's medical assistant and unofficial investigator into the mysterious disappearance of the Moonstone. Apparently wishing to dispel the 'Orientalist' stereotypes perpetuated by the recently republished *Confessions* and reinforced by the Mutiny hysteria, Collins uses Jennings to re-conceive the one Asian character in De Quincey's work that not only epitomized the Opium-Eater's racist fears and tyrannized over his dreams, but also most closely conformed to British stereotypes of the blood-thirsty sepoys.

To begin with, Jennings specifically recommends De Quincey's *Confessions* to the hapless suspect in the theft of the gem (and unwitting victim of opium intoxication), Franklin Blake (Collins 1868: 434–35), and his own life closely resembles both that of the English Opium-Eater and that of the Malay, with whom De Quincey thought he had achieved a secret understanding on the subject of the drug: 'On his departure', writes De Quincey, 'I presented him with a piece of opium. To him, as an Orientalist, I concluded that opium must be familiar: and the expression of his face convinced me that it was' (*DQW*, II: 57). In *Sacramental Commodities*, I provided a detailed analysis of the Malay's role as a De Quinceyan *Doppelgänger* (Rzepka 1995: 231–58) and Collins seems to have discerned the same specular consanguinity. Thus, far from causing Jennings to 'run a-muck' like the Egyptian and Asian figures in De Quincey's Malay-inspired opium dreams (*DQW*, II: 70–72, 261–62), opium becomes, as it does for

De Quincey himself, the settled study of his life. By means of that study Jennings alone is able to unlock the mystery of Franklin Blake's unconscious role in the Moonstone's disappearance.

In other ways as well, Jennings represents a racially hybridized version of the Malay and his English host. His 'gypsy darkness' and nose conforming to 'the fine shape and modeling so often found among the ancient people of the East' (Collins 1868: 358) visibly announce that Jennings was born and raised 'in one of our colonies', as he tells Blake, presumably India, by an English father and an Indian mother (Collins 1868: 411). Like the Malay roaming the rural villages of Cumberland, moreover, Jennings is a pariah wherever he goes. Despite the good he does as a physician's assistant, the locals shun him.[10]

However, Jennings also closely resembles the English Opium-Eater he professes to admire. First, like De Quincey, he is a relative new-comer to the village where he resides (Collins 1868: 359–60); second, he became addicted only after using the drug to relieve intense physical pain (Collins 1868: 421); third, he is tormented by memories of a lost beloved (Collins 1868: 420–21); fourth, he keeps a *Diary* of his experiences with the drug (Collins 1868: 511); and last, he is working on a major scientific work that he will never finish (Collins 1868: 414, 511–12). These last two documents accompany him, literally, to the grave.

Ezra Jennings's formal entrance into Collins's book is as portentous as that of the Malay into De Quincey's *Confessions*. As Franklin Blake and Gabriel Betteredge—spurned lover and head butler, respectively, of the young Rachel Verinder—pause in their reading of Roseanna Spearman's posthumous letter incriminating Blake as thief of Rachel's Moonstone, Blake announces that he is 'at the end of [his] resources': 'I don't know of a living creature who can be of the slightest use to me.' Just then a knock is heard. Enter Ezra Jennings, whose appearance at the back door of the Verinders' servants' quarters counterbalances the sinister appearance of the three Indian 'jugglers'—actually, three high-caste Brahmins in search of the Moonstone—at the Verinder mansion's front entrance early in the story (Collins 1868: 77–79). Jennings's entrance would also have recalled to knowledgeable readers the sudden intrusion of the Malay at the door of the Dove Cottage kitchen in the *Confessions*. Whether familiar or not with the *Confessions*, however, Collins's audience would have been put in mind of the tales of household invasion, murder, and mayhem appearing in news accounts of the Indian Mutiny little more than a decade previously. Collins heightens the similarities both to the Malay and the mutiny tales by later re-staging Blake's encounter with Jennings at the home of Dr. Candy, where Jennings resides. After descending the stairs on his way out, Blake is accosted by Jennings in the presence of a 'pretty housemaid' holding the street door open for him. 'The pretty servant girl,' says Blake, 'who was all smiles and amiability, when I wished her good morning on my way out—received a modest little message from Ezra Jennings [. . .] with pursed-up lips, and with eyes which ostentatiously looked anywhere rather than look in his face. The poor wretch was evidently no favourite in the house' (Collins 1868: 409). The fair and pretty face of the housemaid in juxtaposition to Jennings's 'gipsy-complexion' and generally 'unfavourable' demeanour recalls the young servant girl 'born and bred amongst the mountains, who had never seen an Asiatic dress of any sort', opening the door to admit the Malay in the *Confessions*. The tableau that strikes the Opium-Eater, who like Blake has just descended the stairs, places the girl, with 'her native spirit of mountain intrepidity', in the same frame as the 'tiger-cat before her', creating a 'striking picture' contrasting 'the beautiful face of the girl, and its exquisite fairness' with 'the sallow and bilious skin of the Malay, enameled or veneered with mahogany' (*DQW*, II: 56–7; 234–35).

In 1868, when *The Moonstone* began its serialization, readers would have imagined scenes like these in the light of widely disseminated newspaper accounts and memoirs describing sepoys murdering innocent English women and children in their homes, sometimes after treacherous professions of loyalty. One survivor of the massacres in Delhi provided the following account of a neighbouring family's ordeal:

> At length I nerved myself and stepped into the next room which was the hall. Oh! I had indeed need to nerve myself. Just before me pinned to the wall was poor Clark's little son with his head hanging down, and a dark stream of blood trickling down the wall into a large black pool which lay near his feet. And this cruel death they must have inflicted before the mother's eyes. I closed my eyes and shuddered, but I opened them upon, even as yet, a more dreadful sight. Clark and his wife lay side by side. But I will not, describe the scene . . . she was far advanced in pregnancy. (quoted in Robinson 1996: 43–44)

George Bruce Malleson's contemporary account of the 'charnel house' that met the eyes of the relief troops at Cawnpore became an iconic emblem of sepoy blood-lust toward women and children:

> The floor of the inner room was found two inches deep in blood,—it came over the men's shoes as they stepped. Ladies' hair, back combs, parts of religious books, children's shoes, hats, bonnets, lay scattered about the room; there were marks of sword-cuts on the walls low down, as if the women had been struck at as they crouched. From the well at the back of the house the naked bodies, limb separated from limb, protruded out. It was a sight sickening, heart-rending, maddening. (Malleson 1858: 2. 159).

Given the outcome of the Moonstone case, namely, that the thief turns out to be neither Hindu nor Anglo-Indian but the English Evangelical hypocrite, Godfrey Ablewhite, and that Ezra Jennings plays the crucial role in clearing the name of young Franklin Blake, we can only conclude that Collins, always critical of English middle-class prejudices, deliberately set out to evoke such historical resonances in order to dispel them.[11] In any case, they would not have been difficult to set reverberating. If, as De Quincey observes, '[T]here is no such thing as *forgetting* possible to the mind' (*DQW*, II: 67), and if, as Jennings insists, '[E]*very* sensory impression [. . .] is registered, so to speak, in the brain, and may be reproduced at some subsequent time' (Collins 1868: 432–3), then there can be little doubt that the vivid images of the Mutiny that found their way from the pages of its earliest accounts, such as Malleson's *The Mutiny of the Bengal Army* (1858), Charles Ball's *The History of the Indian Mutiny* (1858), and the *Illustrated London News*, into the brains of English readers in 1857 and 1858 would have been highly susceptible to imaginative 'reproduction' by even the faintest of allusions to them a decade later. (See Figure 11.2 and Figure 11.3).

I've been speaking so far of the impact of the *Confessions* regardless of edition, but there is evidence in *The Moonstone* of the specific impact of the 1856 version in Jennings's reference to the 'cloud of a horrible accusation' that 'has rested on me for years':

> I cannot bring myself to acknowledge what the accusation is. And I am incapable, perfectly incapable, of proving my innocence. [. . .] At the outset of my career in this country, the vile slander to which I have referred struck me down at once and for ever. (Collins 1868: 420)

This unspecified 'slander' against Jennings could refer, symbolically, to the prejudice against his race incited by the anti-sepoy hysteria of 1857–1858, a slander Collins is working actively to refute. More specifically, however, it recalls a prominent feature of De Quincey's Malay dreams in both editions of the *Confessions*: his intense but unfocussed sense of guilt. 'I fled from the wrath of Brama through all the forests of Asia: Vishnu hated me: Seeva laid wait for me. I came suddenly upon Isis and Osiris: I had done a deed, they said, which the ibis and the crocodile trembled at' (*DQW*, II: 71, 261–62). It is not difficult to find a cause for these feelings of recrimination in the autobiographical passages of the *Confessions*. For one thing, De Quincey had given the Malay what he suspected must have been a fatal overdose of opium when the man appeared at his door. For another, he had played truant and run off to London at seventeen to secure an advance on his patrimony without his mother's or his guardians' permission. Finally, he had not taken sufficient measures to keep track of the prostitute, Ann, whom he had befriended upon arriving in the capital and promised to help. But Jennings's agony clearly arises not from the performance of a shameful act, deliberate or not, but from being unable to escape the shameful 'slander' of having done so. He is not feeling guilty, but wronged.

The 1821 *Confessions* offers no situation or event experienced by De Quincey that is precisely analogous to the evil rumours that hound Jennings

Figure 11.2. 'The Massacre at Delhi'. A child flying through the air, upper left, is about to land on sepoy bayonets, while woman and children cower, lower right. Along the left margin, from top to bottom, three abductions are taking place, while on the porch, above center, a sepoy lunges to the right to behead a woman holding her infant. From Sir Colin Campbell, *Narrative of the Indian Revolt*, p. 1. Used by permission of Widener Library, Harvard College Library.

from village to village until pity moves Dr. Candy to hire him as his medical assistant and give him a home. In the 1856 edition, however, De Quincey spends an inordinate amount of time describing a complication that made his original truancy from Manchester Grammar School in 1802 a much more nerve-wracking affair than it appears to be in the 1821 version.

The day before his clandestine departure from the school, the young De Quincey received a letter in French, posted from Hamburg, addressed to a

'A Deafening Menace in Tempestuous Uproars' 221

Figure 11.3. 'The Campbells are Coming' (Awaiting Colin Campbell's Relief Forces at the Siege of Lucknow). From *The Illustrated London News*, 13 March 1858, vol. 31, p. 280. Used by permission of Widener Library, Harvard College Library.

'*Monsieur Monsieur De Quincy*' and mistakenly forwarded to him from the town of Chester, where his mother then resided. The letter, intended for a Quatremere de Quincy who was also a resident of Chester, contained a cheque for 40 guineas, a sum that the truant could readily have put to good use had he not felt conscience-bound to restore both letter and note to their rightful owner. However, he was unable to visit the post office immediately for the purpose. The delay preyed upon his mind. As he later put it, 'the suspense and progress of the case' might give rise to 'ugly rumours' that would 'cling to one's name among the many [people] that would hear only a fragmentary version of the affair' (*DQW*, II: 151). Journeying first to Chester upon leaving the school, De Quincey began to fear that the letter must have 'drawn the post-office into the ranks of [his] pursuers', along with the school authorities, 'forcing [him] into all sorts of indirect and cowardly movements at inns'. '[F]or beyond all things,' he adds, 'it seemed to me important that I should not be arrested, or even challenged, as the wrongful holder of an important letter, before I had testified, by my own spontaneous transfer of it, that I had not dallied with any idea of converting it to my own benefit' (*DQW*, II: 160–61). Eventually, anticipating his arrest if he should so much as enter the post office to return the letter, De Quincey entrusts it to a woman he meets walking along the River Dee, who after two hours returns to assure him that the postal authorities received it with relief and gratitude and that he no longer has anything to fear.

De Quincey treats the whole incident with levity from the long perspective of 1856, but the terror and anxiety it inspired at the time were apparently quite real. To judge from his family's reaction to an 'express' message from school stating that young Thomas had absconded with the misaddressed letter in his possession, these feelings were not unwarranted. Within an hour of receiving the news, and well in advance of De Quincey's arrival on their doorstep, '[a]larm spread through the Priory', his family home: 'The probability seemed that I must have violated the laws to some extent, either by forgery or by fraudulent appropriation' (*DQW*, II: 172). The boy's sister Mary and one of his guardians immediately departed in a carriage for the Lake District, home of Wordsworth, on the assumption that De Quincey had made good on his oft-expressed desire to visit his literary hero. In all they traveled some 600 miles and expended a total of 150 pounds on this wild goose chase. They had not returned when De Quincey left home several days later for a walking tour of Wales and, eventually, a miserable span of months in London.

The success of *The Moonstone* inspired Charles Dickens, who was Collins's close friend, traveling companion, fellow amateur thespian, and occasional collaborator, to begin writing *The Mystery of Edwin Drood* a year later. In both books the plot hinges on opium and its purported dissociative effects on personality; in both, persons and things Indian play a major role; and in both, the influence of De Quincey's *Confessions* is unmistakable. Dickens's response to the Indian Mutiny, however, was much more extreme than his friend's, verging on hysteria. In 'The Perils of Certain English Prisoners', which he wrote with the help of Collins and published in the 1857 Christmas number of *Household Words*, Dickens transplanted the revolt, siege, and murderous evacuation at Cawnpore to an island in the Caribbean off the coast of Honduras, replacing sepoy mutineers with treacherous 'Sambo' indigenes and pirates. As hostilities break out, Captain Carton, echoing almost verbatim sentiments expressed in Dickens's private correspondence (Brantlinger 1988: 206–7), announces that he feels commissioned by God 'to exterminate these people from the face of the earth' (Dickens 1857: 150).

To his credit, given the fact that his son John Paul Frederick had just returned from a tour of duty in India and his daughter Florence Baird Smith was living there with her husband when hostilities erupted in May, De Quincey responded in a less genocidal, if no less hyperbolic, manner in the three essays he published for *The Titan* in 1857 and 1858 on the causes of the Mutiny. The 'indignities past utterance inflicted upon our dear massacred sisters, and upon their unoffending infants,' writes De Quincey in 'Hurried Notices of Indian Affairs' (*DQW*, XVIII: 161–69), demand not the extermination of the race, but the abolition of the caste system, or in De Quincey's words, an 'everlasting retribution, inflicted upon the Moloch idolatries of India'. For '[u]pon the pride of *caste*', he continues, 'rests for its ultimate root all this towering tragedy' (*DQW*, XVIII: 163). Christianising imperialist to the core, De Quincey counsels England not to abandon its white man's burden in the face of sepoy treachery and ingratitude, but rather to accept the massacres as a 'ransom paid down on behalf of every creature groaning under the foul idol of caste' (*DQW*, XVIII: 163). The uprising, De Quincey adds in 'Suggestions Upon the Secret of the Mutiny', was fomented entirely by high-caste Brahminical and 'Mahometan misleading' (*DQW*, XVIII: 180). The rumours of the greased cartridges were only a pretext for rebellion, and the sepoy merely a 'poor simpleton [. . .] decoyed into this monstrous field of strife' by 'Indian princes and rajahs' as a test of his sincerity, and in order to lure him into the desperate position of having to abandon all hope of amnesty (*DQW*, XVIII: 185–86).

As in his essays on the Chinese Opium-Wars, where Britain's ambassadors to the Celestial Empire are applauded for refusing to 'kow-tow' to the Emperor, De Quincey makes much ado about ceremonial insult, spending two pages out of seven in his first *Titan* essay scolding British officers for not requiring the sepoys to rise from their seats as a sign of respect. Thus, 'under our British government', he continues, 'the lowest of our servants, a mass of carrion from a brotherhood of Thugs, shall have had free license to insult the leaders of the army which finds bread for him and his kindred' (*DQW*, XVIII: 168). This is the only reference in De Quincey's Mutiny essays to the Thugs, whose worship of the Hindu goddess of destruction, Kali (also known as Devi or Bhawanee), took the form of 'sacrificing' her victims—typically unwary travelers—by strangulation, followed by the personal appropriation of their belongings. (Interestingly, the Thugs, like the Native Infantry, included Muslims as well as Hindus.)

It was not long after the publication of Sleeman's and Taylor's books on the clandestine practice of 'Thuggee' in the late 1830s that the brotherhood began popping up in De Quincey's essays, beginning with his 'Second Paper on Murder Considered as One of the Fine Arts' in 1839 (*DQW*, XI: 403). 'The far-reaching power of this mysterious brotherhood', James Hogg later wrote of De Quincey's fascination with Thuggee, 'the swiftness and certainty of its operations, the strange gradations of official rank, and the curious disguises adopted—all these exercised an influence on his mind which seemed never to wane' (Hogg 1895: 174). A late reference to the Thugs occurs in the 1856 *Confessions* itself, where De Quincey explains his willingness to sleep out of doors in order to save money while vagabonding in Wales.

> There are, as perhaps the reader knows by experience, no jaguars in Wales—nor pumas—nor anacondas—nor (generally speaking) any Thugs. [. . .] Against Thugs I had Juvenal's license to be careless in the emptiness of my pockets (*cantabit vacuus coram latrone viator* [*The empty-handed traveler will whistle in the robber's face*]). But I fear that Juvenal's license will not always hold water. There are people bent upon cudgelling one who will persist in excusing one's having nothing but a bad shilling in one's purse, without reading in that Juvenalian *vacuitas* any privilege or license of exemption from the general fate of travellers that intrude upon the solitude of robbers. (*DQW*, II: 181)

It is highly unlikely that this passage alone could have inspired the many details of Thuggee with which, according to Duffield and Wilson, Dickens invested the appearance, personality, behaviour, and implied *modus operandi* of John Jasper, the prime murder suspect in *The Mystery of Edwin Drood*. However, Neville Landless's reasons for departing from Cloisterham on a walking tour the morning after Edwin Drood's disappearance recall the young De Quincey's motives for truancy among the Cambrian hills, and the manner of Landless's apprehension soon afterwards borrows something from the standard operating procedure of 'the profession' (Taylor 1839: 18).

Landless, a mixed-race Anglo-Indian recently arrived in Cloisterham from Ceylon with his sister, Helena, has been placed under the care and tutelage of the benevolent Minor Canon of the local cathedral, Septimus Crisparkle. Like Ezra Jennings, however, he has been ostracized by the townsfolk because of his race and, exacerbating this source of animosity, his infatuation with the fair young Rosa Bud, who is Edwin Drood's intended. Feeling himself to be 'unsettled and unhappy', and 'conscious of unsettling and interfering with other people', Neville persuades Crisparkle to let him abandon his studies for a fortnight's 'walking expedition' to clear his head and calm his nerves (Dickens 1870: 173–74)

However, Neville does not get far the next morning before he notices 'some other pedestrians behind him':

> As they were coming up at a faster pace than his, he stood aside, against one of the high banks, to let them pass. But their manner was very curious. Only four of them passed. Other four slackened speed, and loitered as intending to follow him when he should go on. [. . .] He looked at the four behind him and he looked at the four before him. They all returned his look. He resumed his way. The four in advance went on, constantly looking back; the four in the rear came closing up. [. . .] [L]et him diverge as he would to either side, there was no longer room to doubt that he was beset by these fellows. He stopped, as a last test; and they all stopped.
> 'Why do you attend upon me in this way?' he asked the whole body. 'Are you a pack of thieves?' (Dickens 1870: 185)

The manner in which this Cloisterham *posse* falls in with Neville before seizing him resembles the common practice of Thugs, who would often travel in small groups along a main highway, before and behind their intended victim, in order to allay suspicion, and then gradually begin to close ranks as they approached a prearranged site of attack (see, e.g., Taylor 1839: 163–64). Neville is released for lack of evidence after his arrest, but must labour, like Jennings and like the innocent recipient of the 1856 *Monsieur Monsieur* letter, under the cloud of a scandal that he is helpless to dispel. Eventually, again like De Quincey, Neville is forced to live a fugitive life in London.

The most obvious connections between *Drood* and the *Confessions* are to be found in the character of Jasper, beginning with the opening chapter—indeed, the opening paragraph—of Dickens's unfinished mystery.[12] Here we behold directly, for the first and last time, the mental panorama of Jasper's drug-induced, Orientalist fantasies as they unfold in the gray light of dawn penetrating the dingy windows of a London opium den:

> An ancient English Cathedral town? How can the ancient English Cathedral town be here! The well-known massive grey square tower of its old Cathedral? How can that be here! There is no spike of rusty iron in the air, between the eye and it, from any point of the real prospect. What IS the spike that intervenes, and who has set it up? Maybe, it is set up by the Sultan's orders for the impaling of a horde of Turkish robbers, one by one. It is so, for cymbals clash, and the Sultan goes by to his palace in long procession. Ten thousand scimitars flash in the sunlight, and thrice ten thousand dancing-girls strew flowers. Then, follow white elephants caparisoned in countless gorgeous colours, and infinite in number and attendants. Still, the Cathedral tower rises in the background, where it cannot be, and still no writhing figure is on the grim spike. (Dickens 1870: 37)

As has often been noted (see, e.g., Frank 1976: 163), the lamination of Cloisterham Cathedral and the Sultan's processions in Jasper's opium dreams represents the two layers of Jasper's split personality, his upright, conscious life as choirmaster of the cathedral and his clandestine, dissociated life as murderer of Drood and sexual predator of Drood's fiancee, Rosa Bud. The exotic Eastern imagery introducing the 'Oriental atmosphere' (Duffield 1930: 582) of the book as a whole reinforces Duffield's and Wilson's reading of Jasper's secret life as that of a Thug. Dickens provides, after all, definite indications that Jasper intends to kill his nephew and hide the body in the ritual manner of Thuggee, and Duffield even goes so far as to suggest he is an initiate of the cult (Duffield 1930: 583–86). The 'grim spike', however, does not correspond to the preferred method of Thuggee sacrificial ritual—strangling with a 'roomal', a large kerchief or sash (see Figure 11.1)—and this, as well as several details besides, connect this passage more closely to the opium dreams of the *Confessions* and De Quincey's comments on them.

The 'grim spike', for example, waiting to impale those who would threaten to steal the Sultan's possessions—presumably, given Jasper's fixation on Rosa, one of the consorts represented by the 'thrice ten thousand dancing-girls' in the procession—finds its corresponding instruments of torture and death in the 'Piranesi' sequence of 'The Pains of Opium' section, which was inspired, says De Quincey, by Coleridge's description of the Italian architect's engravings, *Carcieri d'Invenzionei*, or 'Imaginary Prisons':

> Some of them (I describe only from memory of Mr. Coleridge's account) represented vast Gothic halls, on the floor of which stood all sorts of engines and machinery, wheels, cables, pulleys, levers, catapults, &c. &c. expressive of enormous power put forth, and resistance overcome. (*DQW*, II: 68, 258–59)

These rack-like engines of torture, analogous in function to the 'grim spike' in Jasper's dreams, appear at the foot of a soaring 'Gothic' structure, resembling the tower of Cloisterham Cathedral. 'Creeping along the sides of the walls', De Quincey continues, 'you perceived a stair-case; and upon it, groping his way upwards, was Piranesi himself: follow the stairs a little further, and you perceive it come to a sudden abrupt termination, without any balustrade, and allowing no step onwards to him who had reached the extremity, except into the depths below' (*DQW*, II: 68, 259). At this point, De Quincey perceives what he takes to be Piranesi mounting another staircase higher up the wall, and the sequence continues in this vertiginous manner, multiplying staircases, impending plunges, and ascending Piranesis *ad infinitum*, with a 'power of endless growth and self-reproduction' (*DQW*, II: 68, 259).

This theme of reiterated, dizzying ascent and pending fall to destruction takes a religiously inflected architectural form in De Quincey's Malay dreams: 'I ran into pagodas: and was fixed, for centuries, at the summit, or in secret rooms; I was the idol; I was the priest; I was worshipped; I was sacrificed' (*DQW*, II: 71, 261). The theme is adumbrated in turn, with similarly religious overtones, in Dickens's initial focus on the pagoda's Western counterpart in Jasper's dawn reverie, the Gothic Cathedral tower, and further developed at two important points in *Drood*. In Chapter 12, 'A Night with Durdles', Jasper takes a nocturnal tour of the Cathedral with the taciturn sexton, Durdles. In the course of his search (it is implied) for a place in which to hide Edwin's body, and, perhaps, a convenient spot in which to murder him as well, Jasper ascends the Cathedral tower, 'up the winding staircase [. . .] toilsomely, turning and turning', 'through strange places', including 'level, low-arched galleries' 'look[ing] down into the moonlit nave' (Dickens 1870: 156). This recapitulation of the tortuous ascent of the Piranesi dreams in reverse perspective is later reprised in Jasper's account to Princess Puffer, in her London opium den, of what seems to be the climactic moment of the 'journey' that he has repeated, 'over and over again', 'hundreds of thousands of times', in the homicidal fantasies he has induced by smoking opium. In the end, the actual murder of his nephew pales in comparison to these imaginary anticipations:

> 'It was a journey, a difficult and dangerous journey. That was the subject in my mind. A hazardous and perilous journey, over abysses where a slip would be destruction. Look down, look down! You see what lies at the bottom there?'
> He has darted forward to say it, and to point at the ground, as though at some imaginary object far beneath. [. . .]
> 'Well; I have told you. I did it, here, hundreds of thousands of times. What do I say? I did it millions and billions of times. I did it so often, and through such vast expanses of time, that when it was really done, it seemed not worth the doing, it was done so soon.' (Dickens 1870: 269)

It was only after he reached the murderous climax of his dreams, says Jasper, that the 'changes of colours and the great landscapes and glittering processions began. They couldn't begin till it was off my mind' (Dickens 1870: 270). At this point we suddenly realize the full, tantalizing significance of Dickens's opening paragraph: he has begun his book at the instant in Jasper's obsessive reveries immediately following the choirmaster's imagined murder of his nephew. The key to the 'mystery' of the book's title thus lies, alluring and irretrievable, in the instant before its narrative begins—on page 0, as it were.

'Changes of colours' are not a prominent feature of De Quincey's dream narratives, but 'visionary colours' (*DQW*, II: 66; 256) and 'great landscapes' are: magnificent cloud castles, 'translucent lakes [. . .] seas and oceans', 'all the forests of Asia', and towering mountains of 'more than Alpine height' (*DQW*, II: 69, 71–72; 259-61, 262). 'Glittering processions' like the one in Dickens's opening paragraph appeared regularly, says De Quincey (*DQW*,

II: 68, 258), and the dilation of time and space remarked by Jasper is both explicitly noted in the *Confessions* (*DQW*, II: 66–67; 256) and frequently observed in its later dream sequences. One especially noticeable psychological effect, says De Quincey, is 'that whatsoever I happened to call up and trace by a voluntary act upon the darkness was very apt to transfer itself to my dreams':

> [W]hatsoever things capable of being visually represented I did but think of in the darkness, immediately shaped themselves into phantoms of the eye; and, by a process apparently no less inevitable, when thus once traced in faint and visionary colours, like writings in sympathetic ink, they were drawn out by the fierce chemistry of my dreams, into insufferable splendour that fretted my heart. (*DQW*, II: 66, 256)

This effect is captured with brilliant compression in Dickens's representation, on *Drood*'s first page, of Jasper's inability to control his thoughts regarding the 'grim spike', thoughts which dart instantly from speculation to accomplishment: '*Maybe*, it is set up by the Sultan's orders for the impaling of a horde of Turkish robbers, one by one. *It is so*, for cymbals clash, and the Sultan goes by to his palace in long procession' (Dickens 1870: 37; emphasis added).

The rich stores of De Quincey's dream journals supplied Dickens with the imagery of bottomless depths as well as looming heights. Jasper's eliciting of information from Durdles on how to 'sound' the walls of the Cathedral and its crypt for hidden recesses and anonymous 'old 'uns', as Durdles calls the ancient, forgotten cadavers stashed away in the foundations, has raised suspicions in many readers' minds that he is looking for a suitable spot in which to hide Edwin's body after killing him. Dickens later picks up this theme in Edwin Drood's own conversation with Rosa Bud concerning his plans to bring modern engineering to backward Egypt. 'You are not going to be buried in the Pyramids, I hope?' rejoins Rosa, having just described the near-death of the pioneering Italian Egyptologist (and former circus strongman) Giovanni Belzoni, who upon entering the great pyramid of Cheops was 'dragged out by the legs, half choked with bats and dust' (Dickens 1870: 59). Not only does the reference to Belzoni foreshadow Drood's strangulation as a sacrificial victim of Thuggee (Duffield 1930: 586), but it recalls still another important 'Oriental' detail of De Quincey's Malay dreams: 'I was buried, for a thousand years, in stone coffins, with mummies and sphynxes, in narrow chambers at the heart of eternal pyramids' (*DQW*, II: 71).

Several other points of correspondence between De Quincey's *Confessions* and Dickens's *Drood* could be adduced here indicative of the broad impact the English Opium-Eater's memoir had on Dickens's work. At least one among these, in addition to the 'Thug' reference mentioned above in connection with Neville's departure from Cloisterham, seems to point to the specific influence of the 1856 edition.

In the material De Quincey added to his revisions he included a much more circumstantial account of his living quarters at Manchester Grammar School, a 'quiet study, lifted by two storeys above the vapours of earth, and liable to no unseasonable intrusion', unless it were 'the bells of the collegiate church' (*DQW*, II: 138–39):

> Naturally, however, this means of retirement tended to sequester me from my companions: for, whilst liking the society of some amongst them, I also had a deadly liking (perhaps a morbid liking) for solitude. To make my present solitude the more fascinating, my mother sent me five guineas *extra*, for the purchase of an admission to the Manchester Library; [. . .] These two luxuries were truly and indeed such: but a third, from which I had anticipated even greater pleasure, turned out a total failure; [. . .] This was a pianoforte. (*DQW*, II: 137)

Since De Quincey was too lazy to practice his lessons, this 'luxury' soon 'became useless', remaining in his room 'for months as a lumbering monument of labour misapplied, of bubbles that had burst, and of musical visions that, under psychological tests, had foundered for ever' (*DQW*, II: 138).

The apartment of Dickens's English opium-eater, also a second-story affair, is located above the Gate House of the Cathedral Close, making Jasper, like his De Quinceyan predecessor, a reclusive, diary-keeping (Dickens 1870: 132) inhabitant of a sequestered community, 'with its hoarse Cathedral-bell' (Dickens 1870: 51) punctuating the daily routine. De Quincey's room is 'airy and cheerful' (*DQW*, II: 137) while Jasper's is 'a little sombre' and 'mostly in shadow' (Dickens 1870: 43), but in both of them the only piece of furniture worthy of remark is the piano.

Talent-wise, of course, no two characters could be more dissimilar: De Quincey does not even attempt to practice, while Jasper is a professional choirmaster and piano instructor to Rosa Bud. But both English opium-eaters seem to understand the power of music as a wordless discourse of feeling, particularly when allied with the seductive properties of opium. De Quincey's description of his experiences at the Italian Opera on Saturday night 'debauches' of opium vividly conveys his sense of music's power: 'The choruses were divine to hear: and when [the Italian contralto Josephina] Grassini appeared in some interlude [. . .] I question whether any Turk, of all that ever entered the Paradise of opium-eaters, can have had half the pleasure I had' (*DQW*, II: 48; 225). Despite the erotic overtones sounded by the appearance of the gorgeous Grassini, a former mistress of Napoleon (*DQW*, II: 225n), De Quincey insists that this pleasure is purely 'intellectual'. In any case, it arises not from the communication of 'ideas', but from 'a language of representative feelings' (*DQW*, II: 48; 225).

De Quincey's reference to the Turks and their Paradise alludes to a contrast he has just made between the intellectually stimulating effect of opium on English constitutions and the purely sensual 'narcotic influence' the drug supposedly has on non-Western peoples like the Ottoman Turks, who are 'absurd enough to sit, like so many equestrian statues, on logs of wood as stupid as themselves' (*DQW*, II: 47; 224). These references to Turkish opium-eaters and the 'Paradise' they glimpse under the effects of the drug apparently helped to provide a hint for the extravagant fantasies of specifically Ottoman power, lust, and vengeance—'Sultan's orders', 'Turkish robbers'—that unfold in Dickens's opening paragraph describing Jasper's opium fantasies. In particular, the multitude of lovely, dark-eyed virgins or *houri* that, according to the Qur'an (55.56; 44.51–54), inhabit this Paradise, waiting to embrace the faithful Islamic worshipper after death, seem to have become incarnated in the log-like Jasper's visions of 'thrice ten thousand dancing-girls' (Dickens 1870: 37).

The themes and images thus constellated through De Quincey's domestic arrangements at Manchester Grammar School, particularly his useless but 'monumental' piano, and his erotically charged reflections on opium and music insinuate themselves into the most sinister facet of Jasper's submerged personality, namely, his musical power of seduction over Rosa Bud. This power is conveyed, like that of Italian Opera to the mind of the English Opium-Eater, not by distinct 'ideas' but by a 'language of representative feelings'. Rosa herself describes its irresistible effects to Helena Landless:

> He has forced me to understand him, without his saying a word; and he has forced me to keep silence, without his uttering a threat. When I play, he never moves his eyes from my hands. When I sing, he never moves his eyes from my lips. When he corrects me, and strikes a note, or a chord, or plays a passage, he himself is in the sounds, whispering that he pursues me like a lover, and commanding me to keep his secret. (Dickens 1870: 95)

Taken as yet another among a multitude of suggestive similarities to the *Confessions* evident in both *The Moonstone* and *The Mystery of Edwin Drood*, the sexual threat posed to Dickens's fair representative of English maidenhood by this most explicitly 'Orientalised' of his English villains points to the profound if indirect impact of the events of the Indian Mutiny of 1857 not only on British fiction of the latter half of the nineteenth century, but on that fiction's modes, and peculiar manner, of appropriating the works that preceded it.

NOTES

1. Both the 1821 and 1856 editions, as edited by Lindop, are now available in Volume 2 of *The Works of Thomas De Quincey* (2000–03). In his publication history of the 1821 *Confessions*, Lindop notes that the only two re-printings to appear in England after 1826, those of 1845 and 1853, were undertaken by John Taylor, publisher of the original 1821 *Confessions* in *The London Magazine*, 'to retain his control of the work' under the Copyright Act of 1842

(*DQW*, II: 8). That is to say, these two re-printings did not reflect continuing public demand, which seems to have fallen off somewhat after 1826 (no new editions appeared for nearly twenty years afterwards), but were precautionary moves to retain ownership in reaction to the appearance of *Suspiria de Profundis* in 1845, which was advertised as a 'Sequel' to the *Confessions*, and to the announcement by the James Hoggs, father and son, of a new British edition of De Quincey's works in 1853. In the United States, the 1821 edition underwent a sudden revival of popularity after three desultory decades with its republication in 1850 and 1851 by Ticknor, Reid, and Fields of Boston, who subsequently included it in their American edition of De Quincey's collected works in 1852 and in separate stereotyped editions in 1853 and 1854 (*DQW*, II: 90). An unscientific scanning of WorldCat reveals some ninety editions of the *Confessions*, both original and revised, appearing in the United States and Great Britain between 1856 and 1900, which suggests that the 1856 edition was a major factor in reviving public interest in its older, but shorter, sibling.

2. De Quincey felt that the *Confessions* would require fattening up in any case if the volume of the *Selections* in which it appeared was to approach the size of the other thirteen: 'How could 7s. 6d. be reasonably charged to the public for what obviously was but a third part in bulk of the other volumes? No. Mr H[ogg]., the publisher, who knows, of course, so much more than I do about such cases, assures me that nothing so much annoys the trade as any interruption of the price scale upon a series of volumes. Such being the case, no remedy remained but that I should *doctor* the book, and expand it into a portliness that might countenance its price' (quoted in Japp 1890: 387–88).

3. For the relationship between De Quincey's response to the Chinese Opium Wars and his theorizing of a 'literature of power,' see Rzepka (1991).

4. In 1857, Indian troops in the Native Infantry numbered close to a quarter of a million, compared to some 45,000 European enlistees, a ratio of approximately 5:1 (David 2002: 9).

5. According to Saul David (David 2002: 55), there is no evidence that any such cartridges were ever manufactured, let alone delivered to the troops, who, after voicing their objections, were allowed to prepare their own cartridge grease.

6. For an excellent brief survey of Thug-related fiction leading up to *Drood*, see Duffield (Duffield 1930: 587–88).

7. Cocaine, of course, 'a seven-percent solution,' but also, apparently, morphine, the distilled and highly addictive form of opium that became injectable by hypodermic syringe during the 1870s. 'Which is it today,' Dr. Watson asks Holmes at the beginning of *The Sign of Four*, 'morphine or cocaine?' (Doyle 1890: 105).

8. Christopher Herbert shares this opinion with respect to *Drood*, 'an opium tale in which the influence of the English Opium Eater is pervasive' (Herbert 1974: 247). However, he devotes most of his essay on the subject of De Quincey and Dickens to other, more popular novels in Dickens's *oeuvre*.

9. Here and in subsequent references to the *Confessions*, I shall provide pagination from both the 1821 and 1856 editions for any passages appearing in both.

10. Moving accounts of the discrimination suffered by mixed-race children of British fathers and Indian mothers, in Britain as well as on the sub-continent, are to be found in chapter two of Vyvyen Brendon's *Children of the Raj*, '"A Forlorn Race of Beings": Eurasian Offspring' (Brendon 2005: 41–67). Martha Graham, an Englishwoman residing in India early in the century, considered it 'a cruelty to send children of colour to Europe, where their complexion must subject them to perpetual mortification' (quoted in Brendon 2005: 55).

11. This would tend to reinforce John R. Reed's classic interpretation of the novel as an indictment of British imperialism and colonial depredation.
12. '[I]ndeed', writes Christopher Herbert, 'the novel's opening paragraph, with its phantasmagoric vision of exotic Oriental pageantry, amounts to something very like a dedication to De Quincey'. Herbert does not specify the details adding up to this 'dedication', however, since his aim, as he says, 'is not to enumerate the overt echoings which occur between De Quincey's works and Dickens' [. . .] but rather to define if I can a complex of subjects lying at the heart of each writer's work' (Herbert 1974: 247).

WORKS CITED

Ackroyd, P. (1994) *Dan Leno and the Limehouse Golem*, London: Sinclair-Stevenson.

Ball, C. (1858) *The History of the Indian Mutiny: giving a detailed account of the Sepoy insurrection in India*, London: London Printing and Publishing Company.

Black, J. (1991) *The Aesthetics of Murder: A Study in Romantic Literature and Contemporary Culture*, Baltimore, MD: Johns Hopkins University Press.

Brantlinger, P. (1988) *Rule of Darkness: British Literature and Imperialism, 1830–1914*, Ithaca, NY: Cornell University Press.

Brendon, V. (2005) *Children of the Raj*, London: Weidenfeld and Nicolson.

Campbell, C. (1858) *Narrative of the Indian Revolt from its Outbreak to the Capture of Lucknow*, London: G. Vickers.

Chakravarty, G. (2005) *The Indian Mutiny and the British Imagination*, Cambridge: Cambridge University Press.

Collins, W. (1868; reprinted 1982) *The Moonstone*, A. Trodd (ed.), Oxford: Oxford University Press.

David, S. (2002) *The Indian Mutiny, 1857*, London: Viking Press.

Dickens, C., and W. Collins (1857) 'The Perils of Certain English Prisoners', in *Posthumous Papers of the Pickwick Club—Volume II and Christmas Stories*, Philadelphia: John D. Morris and Company.

Dickens, C. (1870; reprinted 1974) *The Mystery of Edwin Drood*, A. J. Cox (ed.), London: Penguin Books.

Doyle, A. C. (1890; reprinted 1986) *The Sign of Four*, in Loren Estleman (ed.), *Sherlock Holmes: The Complete Novels and Stories*, Vol. 1, New York: Bantam Books.

———. (1891; reprinted 1986) 'The Man with the Twisted Lip', in Loren Estleman (ed.), *Sherlock Holmes: The Complete Novels and Stories*, Vol. 1, New York: Bantam Books.

———. (1892; reprinted 1986) 'The Adventure of the Abbey Grange,' in Loren Estleman (ed.), *Sherlock Holmes: The Complete Novels and Stories*, Vol. 1, New York: Bantam Books.

Duffield, H. (1930) 'John Jasper—Strangler', *The Bookman* 70: 581–88.

Eliot, T. S. (1932) 'Wilkie Collins and Dickens', in *Selected Essays: 1917–1932*, New York: Harcourt, Brace, and Co., 373–82.

Frank, L. (1976) 'The Intelligibility of Madness in *Our Mutual Friend* and *The Mystery of Edwin Drood*', *Dickens Studies Annual* 5: 150–95, 207–09.

Herbert, C. (1974) 'De Quincey and Dickens', *Victorian Studies* 17: 247–63.

Hogg, James. (1895) *De Quincey and His Friends*. London: S. Low, Marston and Co.

James, P. D., and T. A. Critchley (1971) *The Maul and the Pear Tree: The Ratcliffe Highway Murders 1811*, London: Constable.

Japp, A. (1890) *Thomas De Quincey: His Life and Writings*, London: J. Hogg & Co.
Malleson, G. B. (1858) *The Mutiny of the Bengal Army. An Historical Narrative*, London: Bosworth and Harrison.
Milligan, B. (1995) *Pleasures and Pains: Opium and the Orient in Nineteenth-Century British Culture*, Charlottesville: University Press of Virginia.
Morrison, R. (2001) 'Poe's De Quincey, Poe's Dupin', *Essays in Criticism* 51: 424–41.
Reed, J. R. (1973) 'English Imperialism and the Unacknowledged Crime of *The Moonstone*', *Clio* 2: 281–90.
Robinson, J. (1996) *Angels of Albion: Women of the Indian Mutiny*, London: Penguin.
Rzepka, C. J. (1991) 'The Literature of Power and the Imperial Will: De Quincey's Opium War Essays', *South Central Review* 8: 37–45.
———. (1995) *Sacramental Commodities: Gift, Text, and the Sublime in De Quincey*, Amherst: University of Massachusetts Press.
———. (2005) *Detective Fiction*, Cambridge: Polity Press.
Sleeman, W. H. (1836; reprinted 1839) *The Thugs or Phansigars of India*, Philadelphia: Carey and Hart.
Stanley, J. (2004) 'Opium and *Edwin Drood*: Fantasy, Reality, and What the Doctors Ordered', *Dickens Quarterly* 21: 12–27.
Taylor, P. M. (1839) *Confessions of a Thug*, London: R. Bentley.
Thomas, R. (1990) *Dreams of Authority: Freud and the Fictions of the Unconscious*, Ithaca, NY: Cornell University Press.
Wilson, E. (1929; reprinted 1997) *The Wound and the Bow*, Athens: Ohio University Press.

Contributors

Ian Balfour is a professor of English and in the Graduate Programme in Social and Political Thought at York University, Toronto. He is the author of *The Rhetoric of Romantic Prophecy* and a monograph on Northrop Frye. He has recently co-edited, with Atom Egoyan, *Subtitles: On the Foreignness of Film* and co-edited, with Eduardo Cadava, *And Justice for All? The Claims of Human Rights*. He is currently completing a book on the sublime.

Joel Black teaches Comparative Literature at the University of Georgia. His work on De Quincey includes his book *The Aesthetics of Murder: A Study of Romantic Literature and Contemporary Culture* (1991) and essays in *Comparative Literature* and *Thomas De Quincey: Bicentenary Studies*. He has also contributed a chapter on Romantic Science to the "Romanticism" volume of the *Cambridge History of Literary Criticism* (2000), and is the author of *The Reality Effect: Film Culture and the Graphic Imperative* (2002). He is presently completing a cultural history of the Prohibition period.

Gregory Dart was educated at Clare College Cambridge between 1986 and 1993, whereupon he taught for seven years in the English Department at the University of York, Heslington. In 2000, he moved to the Department of English at UCL. His main work to date is a full-length study of the influence of Rousseau and the French Revolution upon a series of English writers such as Wordsworth, Wollstonecraft, Godwin and Hazlitt entitled *Rousseau, Robespierre and English Romanticism* (CUP, 1999). He has also published articles on Hazlitt, Dickens, Pierce Egan and Ford Madox Brown, and a short book on stalking called *Unrequited Love*. His current research comprises a book on the early nineteenth century as represented in literature and the visual arts.

Josephine McDonagh is professor of Victorian Literature at the University of Oxford, and Fellow of Linacre College, Oxford. She is author of *De Quincey's Disciplines* (1994), *George Eliot* (1997), *Child Murder and British Culture 1720–1900* (2003), and is currently working on a study of place in nineteenth-century British literature in the context of migration.

Contributors

Barry Milligan is professor of English at Wright State University. His publications include *Pleasures and Pains: Opium and the Orient in Nineteenth-Century British Culture* (1995), the Penguin edition of De Quincey's *Confessions of an English Opium-Eater and Other Writings* (2003), and several articles on drugs, medicine, and Romantic and Victorian culture.

Robert Morrison is Queen's National Scholar in the English department at Queen's University, Kingston, Ontario. He has edited writings by Thomas De Quincey, Leigh Hunt, Jane Austen, Richard Woodhouse, and John Polidori. His work on De Quincey has appeared in the *Keats-Shelley Journal*, *The Wordsworth Circle*, *Romanticism*, *Essays in Criticism*, and *Victorian Periodicals Review*. He is currently writing a new biography of De Quincey.

Julian North is a lecturer in English at the University of Leicester. She is the author of *De Quincey Reviewed: Thomas De Quincey's Critical Reception, 1821–1994* (1997), editor of volume 11 and co-editor of volume 20 of *The Works of Thomas De Quincey* (Pickering and Chatto, 2003). She has also published on autobiography, biography and nineteenth-century drug literature.

Daniel Sanjiv Roberts is a reader in English at Queen's University Belfast. He has edited Thomas De Quincey's *Autobiographic Sketches* (2003) and Robert Southey's *The Curse of Kehama* (2004) for major collected editions of these writers; the latter was honoured as a Distinguished Scholarly Edition by the M.L.A. in 2005. His book *Revisionary Gleam: De Quincey, Coleridge and the High Romantic Argument* appeared from Liverpool University Press in 2000. His current research interests include interfaces between Romantic literature and India.

Charles J. Rzepka, professor of English at Boston University, has written extensively on the major Romantic writers, including several essays and a book, *Sacramental Commodities* (1995), on Thomas De Quincey. In recent years he has turned to the study of fictional crime and detection, publishing a cultural history of the genre, *Detective Fiction*, in 2005. An essay on race and genre in the Charlie Chan novels is forthcoming in the October 2007 issue of *PMLA*.

John Whale is professor of Romantic Literature in the School of English, University of Leeds. He is the author of *Thomas De Quincey's Reluctant Autobiography* (1984), *Imagination Under Pressure* (2000) and *John Keats* (2005) as well as co-editor of *Beyond Romanticism* (1992) and editor of *Burke's Reflections on the Revolution in France* (2000). He co-edited volume 13 and edited volume 14 of the *Works of Thomas De Quincey*, under the General Editorship of Grevel Lindop. He is currently working on two projects: pugilism in the Romantic period, and William Roscoe and Liverpool.

Index

Page references in **bold** refer to chapter(s) which deal mainly with that subject. Page references in *italics* refer to illustrations

Abernethy, John 56, 57
Abolition 63, 74; *see also* Slavery
Ackroyd, Peter 8, 211
Adams, Robert Martin 2
Addiction: to books 124, 130, 133, 139n. 2 (*see also* bibliomania); to substances 5, 6, 13, 14, 68, 133, **143–164**, 201, 213, 216 (*see also* Alcohol; Oil; Opium; Tea; Tobacco)
Ainsworth, William Harrison 197; *Jack Sheppard* 195, 198
Album, The 5
Alcohol and alcoholism 13, 48, 54, 63, 68, **143–164**
Alcoholics Anonymous 151, 161n. 11
Alden, H.M. 4
Alexander the Great 35
Alexandria 35
All Souls College, Oxford 12, 136, 137, 138, 140n. 21
All the Year Round 203, 213
Allegory 182–183, 192, 197, 199, 208n. 14
America, United States of 13, 55, 56, 115, 230n. 1; American Confederacy 161n. 16; California 176; Native Americans 161n. 19; temperance movement in 144, 150, 153, 154, 156, 157, 159–160, 161n. 18
Amis, John 2
Anglican Church 37
Ann (Oxford Street prostitute) 30–31, 41n. 20, 64–65, 66, 67, 81, 219

Annual Register 188
Antiquarianism 33, 125, 126, 127, 128, 130
'Anxiety of reception' 11, 99, 101
Apollonius 175
Arabia and its culture 47, 154, 155, 162n. 21; 'Dream of the Arab' 173–174; *Arabian Nights* 124, 125
Archimedes 175
Aristotle 183
Asiatic Researches 33, 40n. 9
Asiatic Society 13, 24, 27, 41n. 18
Atheism 23, 39n. 7, 41n. 14, 56, 70, *71*
Athenaeum Club 128, 139n. 12
Australia 176
Author-reader relationship: *see* readership and audience
Axon, William E.A. 129

Bachelard, Gaston 133
Baillie, Joanna 103, 112
Baird Smith, Florence (*née* De Quincey; DQ's daughter): *see* Smith, Florence Baird
Balfour, Ian 13
Ball, Charles 219
Balzac, Honoré de 8
Barker, Nicholas 128, 139n. 9,
Barrell, John 7, 10, 39n. 2, 41n. 20, 42n. 21, 48, 64, 82, 117n. 10, 138n. 1, 139n. 4, 155, 161n. 17
Bartlett, David 203
Bate, Jonathan 96n. 15, 100, 116n. 6, 184n. 5

Index

Bateson, F.W. 5
Baudelaire, Charles 8, 81, 95n. 1, 211
Baxter, Edmund 7, 63, 83
Beautiful (aesthetic category) 13, 83, 147, 153, 167, 178–179
Beckford, William 139n. 10
Beddoes, Thomas 46, 53, 54, 55, 59n. 4
Beer, John 3, 184n. 4
Bell, Charles 56
Bello, David A. 144, 153, 156, 161n. 18, 163nn. 32, 33
Belzoni, Giovanni 89, 228
Bengal 8, 27; Native Infantry 212; *Mutiny of the Bengal Army* (Malleson) 219
Bentham, Jeremy 72, 100
Berridge, Virginia 143, 152, 156, 159, 160nn. 3, 8, 162n. 20
Bhabha, Homi K. 185n. 16
Bible and biblical scholarship 10, 19–43, 49, 51, 57, 59n. 5, 183; *see also* Genesis; Jeremiah; New Testament; Noah; Old Testament; Revelation
Bible Society 32
Bibliomania 12–13, 125, 126–131, 132; *see also* Books and book collecting
Bichat, Marie François Xavier 56
Bigham, Clive 128, 139n. 9
Black, Joel 2, 4, 13, 144, 211
Blackwood, William 64, 118n. 24
Blackwood's Edinburgh Magazine 4, 12, 14, 45, 64–65, 69, 70, 72, 76, 88, 99, 100, 102, 118n. 18, 129, 187, 189–192, 198
Blair, Alexander 95n. 8
Blake, Andrew 157, 158, 159, 163n. 33
Blake, William 21, 49, 55, 67; *Songs of Experience* 67
Blessington, Lady 119n. 36
Boccaccio, Giovanni 128
Bodleian Library 124, 128
Bombay Native Infantry 212
Books and book collecting **123–142**; DQ's library 131–135, 139n. 8; *see also* Bibliomania
Boon, Marcus 6, 67
Booth, Martin 67
Borges, Jorge Luis 8
Boston Tea Party (1773) 162n. 22
Boswell, James 103
Bouterwek, Friedrich 117n. 9

Bowdler, Henrietta Maria 118n. 24
Brahmins 23, 39n. 6, 213, 215, 217
Braithwaite, Helen 60n. 10
Brantlinger, Patrick 213, 223
Brasenose College, Oxford 137, 140n. 19
Brendon, Vyvyen 231n. 10
Brewer, John 126
Bridgwater, Patrick 4, 163n. 30
British Library 125, 128
British Museum 125
British Quarterly Review 1
Brodie, Janet Farrell 152
Brougham, Henry 70
Broughton, Elizabeth 118n. 23
Brown, John 11, 46, 51–55, 57–58, 68; *Elementa Medicinae* 46, 51, 53, 55; *see also* Brunonianism
Brunonianism 11, 46, 51–61, 68; *see also* Brown, John
Bryant, Jacob 40n. 8
Budgen, Frank 8
Bulwer-Lytton, Edward 197; *Lucretia* 197; *Paul Clifford* 195; 'A Word the Public' 197–198
Burke and Hare (Edinburgh body-snatchers) 193, 202
Burke, Edmund 10, 41n. 17, 68, 74, 83, 177, 178, 179, 181, 184, 185n. 12; *Reflections on the Revolution in France* 68
Burke, Thomas 207n. 6
Burnett, James: *see* Monboddo, Lord
Burroughs, W. S. 8
Burwick, Frederick 7, 184n. 10, 201, 209n. 17
Bush, George W. 156; Bush-Blair alliance 36
Butler, Lady Eleanor: *see* Ladies of Llangollen
Butler, Marilyn 60n. 11, 63
Byron, George Gordon, Lord 69

Cafarelli, Annette Wheeler 5
Calcutta 41n. 18, 205
Campbell, Colin 220, 221
Cambridge 126, 130
Canada 116, 175, 176
Carey, Benedict 162n. 24
Carlyle, Thomas 3, 190
Caroline, Queen 68
Chakravarty, Gautam 213
'Chaldee Manuscript' (1817) 70

Chamber of Horrors 202, 203, 204, 205; see also Tussaud, Madame; Waxworks
Champollion, Jean François 33
Chatterjee, Bankim Chandra 8
Childhood 7, 99, 103, 160n. 6; books in 123–124, 133, 134, 139n. 13; role of religion in 20, 21–22, 29–30, 36, 42n. 21
China and Chinese culture 13, 19, 27, 31, 37; role in opium trade 152, 155–156, 157, 158, 159, 160n. 6, 161n. 18, 162nn. 21, 22, 163nn. 31, 33; see also Opium wars
Christ, Ronald 8
Christianity 10, 49, 95n. 2, 180, 182, 183, 212, 223; oriental scholarship and 20, 21, 22–24, 26, 28, 29, 31, 32–38, 39nn. 3, 7, 41n. 15; see also Evangelicalism; Protestantism
Christie, Jonathan 64, 189
Clarkson, Thomas 11, 74
Class: see social class
Clej, Alina 7, 48, 63, 134, 139n. 8
Clive, Robert (Clive of India) 32
Clowes, Alice 72
Cobbett, William 56, 130, 131, 137; *Weekly Political Register* 131
Cockneys 63, 64, 70, 190, 202; Cockney School 69, 189
Cocks, H.G. 137, 140n. 18
Coldbath Fields Prison 188, 194
Colebrook, Henry Thomas 39n. 5, 41n. 18
Coleridge, Hartley 5
Coleridge, Samuel Taylor 2, 3, 4, 5, 6, 9, 31, 41n. 13, 53, 56, 83, 84, 86, 89, 90, 92, 95n. 7, 103, 106, 113, 115, 132, 135, 184, 192, 198, 200, 208nn. 10, 14, 226; audience, attitude towards 107–108; opium and 143, 148, 160n. 2; see also under De Quincey, Works
 Works: *Biographia Literaria* (1817) 6, 92, 106, 116n. 6; *The Friend* 108, 115; see also Plagiarism
Coleridge, Sara (STC's daughter) 5
Coleridge, Sara (STC's wife) 108
Collins, Wilkie 4, 211; *The Moonstone* 14, 211, 212, 213, 215, 216–220, 222, 230

Colonialism 8, 10, 11, 14, 32, 115, 116, 153, 162n. 27, 176, 212, 232n. 12
Connell, Philip 125, 126, 127, 128, 131, 139n. 6
Conservative ideology 10, 11, 21, 22, 45, 56, 58, 58n. 2, 63, 72, 77, 104–105, 126; see also Toryism
Cooper, Astley 56
Cooper, James Fenimore 161n. 19
Copyright (literary) 56, 103, 115, 125
Corfu 130
Cowper, William 113, 135
Crime literature 195–197, 211, 213, 215; see also 'Newgate Novel'; Collins; Dickens
Critchley, T.A. 211
Crusaders 155
Cullen, Margaret 103, 107–108
Cullen, William 51, 54

Dalrymple, Theodore 6, 160n. 2, 161nn. 12, 13
Daniell, David 21
Darbishire, Helen 2
Darlington, Beth 119n. 30
Dart, Gregory 13–14
Darwin, Erasmus 139n. 7
David, Saul 213, 231nn. 4, 5
Davy, Humphry 55
Delhi 213, 218; 'The Massacre at Delhi' 220
De Luca, V.A. 2, 67, 75
De Man, Paul 182–183
Dendurent, H.O. 15n. 1
De Quincey, Elizabeth (DQ's mother and sister): see Quincey, Elizabeth
De Quincey, Florence (DQ's daughter): see Smith, Florence Baird
De Quincey, Margaret (DQ's wife) 107, 119n. 30
De Quincey, Paul Frederick (DQ's son) 223
De Quincey, Richard ('Pink') (DQ's brother) 12, 137–138
De Quincey, Thomas (1785–1859) 'literature of knowledge' 3, 34, 93, 125, 167–168; 'literature of power' 3, 93–94, 100, 101, 114, 117n. 9, 125, 167–169

De Quincey, Thomas (*continued*)
Works: *Autobiographic Sketches*
(1853–4) 10, 14 21, 29, 32,
33, 41n. 20, 81, 87, 132, 137,
139n. 14, 177
'The Avenger' (1838) 4
'A Brief Appraisal of Greek Literature' (1838–39) 170, 198
'Coleridge and Opium Eating'
(1845) 147–148, 149
Confessions of an English Opium-Eater (1821; rev. 1856) 5–6,
7, 8, 10–11, 14, 19, 20, 26,
31, 32, 45, 46, 51, 54, 56, 57,
60nn. 12, 13, **63–79** (Morrison), 81, 87, 89–90, 102,
132, 133, 139n. 13, 143, 145,
146–147, 148, 149, 150, 159,
174, 189, 190, 195, 205,
208n. 10, **211–233** (Rzepka);
'The Pleasures of Opium'
46–50, 53–54, 57, 58
Diary (1803) 14, 118n. 22, 119n.
35, 134–135, 184n. 7, 217
'The Dourraunee Empire' (1841)
40n. 9
'The English Mail-Coach' (1849)
2, 7–8, 13, 14, 36, 46, 58,
87, 177–178, 180–181, 183,
184, 190, 195, 201, 205; 'The
Dream-Fugue' 8, 183, 201;
'The Vision of Sudden Death'
7, 180, 182
'The Essenes' (1840) 34, 39n. 3, 41n.
15
'Greece under the Romans' (1844) 34
'How to Write English: Introductory
Paper' (1853) 176–177
Klosterheim (1832) 4
'Lake Reminiscences' (1839) 11,
100, 101, 102, 103, 105, 108,
114, 115, 116n. 2, 119n. 38,
170
'Letter to Mr Tait Concerning the
Poetry of Wordsworth' (1838)
113, 114–116
'Letters to a Young Man whose
Education has been Neglected'
(1823) 41n. 18, 92–93, 125,
168
'Life and Adventures of Oliver Goldsmith' (1848) 114
'Milton' (1839) 169

'Notes on Gilfillan's "Gallery of
Literary Portraits"' (1845)
41n. 14
'Novels' (1830) 119n. 35
'Observations on Diet' (1827) 161n.
10
'On Christianity as an Organ
of Political Movement'
(1846) 34
'On Murder Considered as One of
the Fine Arts' (1827 and 1839)
3, 4, 129, 140n. 20, 187,
191–193, 206, 211, 224
'On the Knocking at the Gate in
Macbeth' (1823) 3, 194–195,
197
'On the Present Stage of the English
Language' (1840) 37
'On the Supposed Scriptural
Expression for Eternity'
(1853) 34
'On the Temperance Movement in
Modern Times' (1845) 13,
149–151, 152, 153–155, 156,
162n. 25
'On Wordsworth's Poetry' (1845)
100, 113–114, 115, 116
'The Opium and the China Question' (1840) 118n. 23, 155,
157, 158, 162n. 25, 223
'The Pagan Oracles' (1842) 34
'Passing Notices of Indian Affairs'
(1857) 40n. 8
'Postscript' (to 'On Murder Considered as One of the Fine Arts',
1854) 4, 14, **187–210**
'Protestantism' (1847–48) 34, 40n.
12
'Schlosser's Literary History' (1847)
117n. 11
Selections Grave and Gay (1853–60)
1, 10, 187, 207n. 2, 211,
231n. 2
'Sketch of Professor Wilson' (1829)
89, 91
'Sketches of Life and Manners'
(1834–1841) 100, 101,
102–104, 107, 112, 114,
116n. 2, 137
'The Street Companion' (under
pseud. Rev. Tom Foggy
Dribble) 129
'Style' (1840) 101, 118n. 19

Suspiria de Profundis (1845) 7, 13, 14, 38, 48, 49, 123, 125, 126, 133–134, 138, 160n. 1, 162n. 27, 180, 206–207, 212, 230n. 1; 'The Apparition of the Brocken' 38–39
'Theory of Greek Tragedy' (1840) 198–199, 203
'William Wordsworth and Robert Southey' 132, 170–175, 176
'The Works of Alexander Pope' (1848) 93, 116n. 5, 168
De Quincey, William (DQ's brother): see Quincey, William
Derrida, Jacques 68, 185n. 19
Descartes, René 167, 192
Desmond, Adrian 56, 60n. 11
De Tocqueville, Alexis 150
Devlin, D.D. 6, 184n. 4
Dibdin, Thomas Frognall 127, 128–130, 139nn. 6, 10
Dickens, Charles 8, 66, 203; *Bleak House* 202; *The Mystery of Edwin Drood* 14, 211, 212, 213, 215, 222, 224–227, 228, 229, 230; *Old Curiosity Shop* 203; *Oliver Twist* 195–196; 'The Perils of Certain English Prisoners' 223
Disney, Walt 2
Disraeli, Benjamin 45, 58
D'Israeli, Isaac 126, 127
Dostoevsky, Fyodor 8
Dover, Kenneth 134
Doyle, Arthur Conan 4, 14, 'The Man with the Twisted Lip' 215; *The Sign of Four* 215
Dreams and nightmares 2, 4, 5, 6, 7, 10, 11, 49, 63, 67, 82, 133, 165, 169, 180, 205, 206–207, 211, 226, 227–228; childhood 99, 133; 'Dream of the Arab' 173–174; orientalist 19, 20, 27, 29–31, 32, 36, 38, 39, 41n. 20, 87; see also Malay episode
Duffield, Howard 213, 224, 226, 228, 231n. 6
Duffy, Cian 99, 100, 101

Easley, Alexis 101–102, 117nn. 12, 13, 15, 17
East India Company 10, 22, 24–25, 27, 32, 35, 41n. 17, 163n. 33, 212

Eaton, Horace 139n. 2, 140n. 15
Eclectic Review 1, 5
Edgeworth, Maria 117n. 16
Edinburgh 5, 64; Edinburgh University 51, 54, 55, 59n. 9, 70
Edinburgh Literary Gazette 89
Edinburgh Philosophical Society 51
Edinburgh Review 70, 107, 119n. 43, 134
Egan, Pierce 91, 191, 192
Egypt and Egyptian culture 153, 155, 216, 228; Biblical scholarship and 19, 22, 26, 27, 31, 33, 35
Eichhorn, Johann Gottfried 21, 28, 31
Eldon, John Scott, Lord 56
Elgin marbles 201
Elijah 105, 171
Eliot, T.S. 213, 214–215
Ellis, Sarah Stickney 117n. 16
Enlightenment, the 21, 31, 38, 39; Scottish Enlightenment 41n. 18
Erskine, Thomas 11, 68–69
Esher tragedy 203
Essenes, the 36, 41n. 15; see also under De Quincey, Works
Evangelicalism 95n. 2, 129; imperialism and 10, 20, 21–22, 23–24, 26–27, 31, 32–33, 34, 35, 37, 39, 41n. 18
Evans, Eric 63

Fairburn, John 188, 208n. 13
Femininity and the feminine 81–82, 90, 93, 94, 104, 105, 108, 109–110, 111, 112
Feminism 12, 101, 117n. 14
Ferriar, John 127–128, 139n. 6
Ferrier, Susan 103, 118n. 23
Ferris, Ina 126, 128, 139n. 6
Fichte, Johann Gottlieb 179, 184
Field, Barron 85
Fielding, Henry 108
Foote, Samuel 41n. 17
Foster, Gaines M. 161nn. 16, 19
Foucault, Michel 65, 167
Fox, Charles James 68
France and French culture 8, 55, 72, 178, 179, 202, 220, 222; see also French Revolution
Frank, Lawrence 211, 226
French Revolution 29, 51, 56, 76, 202
Friend of China (journal) 159
Frey, Anna 39n. 2

242 *Index*

Fulford, Tim 12, 83

Galileo (Galileo Galilei) 175
Garland, Cannon 39n. 7
Gautier, Théophile 8
Gender and gendering 9, 11, 12, 14;
    readership and 102, 103, 104,
    105, 118n. 18; writing and 81,
    82–83, 89, 92–94, 94; *see also*
    Femininity; Masculinity
Genesis 39n. 4, 49, 59n. 6
Gentlemen Commoners 140n. 21
George IV 125
George, William 136
Germany, German culture and influence
    4, 5, 38, 41n. 14, 76, 191, 200,
    208n. 10; Biblical critics 28,
    31, 59n. 5; Idealist philosophy
    3, 11, 103, 165, 176, 178,
    179–180; *see also* Kant; Schlegel; Schelling
Gibbon, Edward 39n. 7
Gilfillan, George 4, 37–38; *see also
    under* De Quincey, works
Gillray, James 59n. 7
Gladstone, William 212
Goethe, Johann Wolfgang von 8
Goldman, Albert 3, 208n. 11
Gore, Catherine 101, 117n. 16
Gothic, the 4, 134, 135, 163n. 30, 196,
    226
Grant, Charles 24
Grasmere 85, 165, 211
Grassini, Giovanna 229
Greece and Greek culture 103, 153,
    200; Biblical scholarship and
    19, 27, 33, 34–35, 36, 40n.
    12, 41n. 19; tragedy 170, 197,
    198–199; nationalism 130; sex
    and 134, 135
Green, J.A. 15n.1
Green, V.H.H. 140n. 21
Greenwood, James 203–204
Groves, David 64

Hall, Samuel 123
Hamilton, Elizabeth 103
Hare, Julius 5
Hartshorne, Charles 12, 130, 134, 136,
    139n. 12
Harvey, A.D. 137
Haslam, Fiona 59n. 7
Haslewood, John 130
Hastings, Warren 22, 32, 41n. 17

Haydon, Benjamin Robert 189
Hayter, Alethea 1, 6, 57, 143, 145,
    160nn. 7, 9, 161n. 10, 212
Hazlitt, William 11, 70–72, 74, 94–95,
    190; *Essay on the Principles
    of Human Action* 70; *Reply
    to the Essay on Population by
    . . . Malthus* 71; *Liber Amoris*
    71, 94
Heber, Reginald 136–137
Heber, Richard 12, 109, 127, 128,
    129, 130–132, 134, 136,
    137, 139nn. 11, 12, 140nn.
    19, 20
Hebrew and Hebraic culture 28, 31,
    33, 34–35, 40n. 12, 41n. 19,
    70, 169
Hegel, Friedrich 154, 167
Helfand, William H. 59n. 7
Hell-Fire Club 128, 129
Hemmings, F.J.W. 1
Henderson, Willie 73
Herbert, Christopher 211, 216, 231n. 8,
    232n. 12
Hertz, Neil 169, 184nn. 3, 6
Higgins, David 99, 190–191
Hinduism 22, 24, 26, 27, 33, 212, 213,
    218, 223–224; practice of
    sati 24, 25, 40n. 11; *see also*
    Brahmins
Hitler, Adolf 37
Hobbes, Thomas 192
Hogg, James 206, 211, 224, 230n. 1
Holland 185n. 15
Hollingsworth, Keith 208n. 12
Homer 169, 170; *Iliad* 169; *Odyssey*
    169
Homoeroticism 125, 134
Homosexuality 12, 131, 134, 136–138,
    140n. 18
Hope, Thomas 69
Houghton, W.E. 100, 116n. 3, 117nn.
    12, 13
House of Lords 212
Household Words 223
Howitt, Mary 101, 117n. 16
Hume, David 70, 71, 176, 178, 179
Hunt, Arnold 130, 131, 139nn. 11, 12
Hutchinson, Sara 144
Hyde, M. 116n. 4

Imperialism 7, 9, 10, 11, 63, 64, 161n.
    19, 176, 212, 232n. 11; influence of evangelicalism and

DQ's attitude to 20, 26, 27,
34, 35, 36, 37, 38, 39, 39n.
2, 41n. 20, 42n. 21; *see also*
Colonialism; Evangelicalism
Inchbald, Elizabeth 103
India and Indian culture 75, 109, 140n.
16; Biblical scholarship and
22–23, 24, 27, 31, 32, 33,
36, 37, 39n. 5, 40n. 8, 40n.
11; 'Indomania' 22, 24, 27,
31, 33; 'Indophobia' 22, 24,
27, 31; opium trade 152,
155, 156, 157, 159, 162nn.
20, 22, 163n. 31; violence
and 199, 212, 213, 217, 222,
223, 231n. 4, 10; *see also*
East India Company; Indian
Mutiny
Indian Mutiny (1857) 7, 14, 36,
212–213, *214*, 215, 216, 217,
219, 220, *221*, 222, 223, 230,
231n. 4
Intoxication and inebriation: opium
and 48–49, 53, 54, 216; alcohol and 144, 145–148, 152,
153, 154, 155, 160nn. 3, 8; *see
also* Alcohol; Opium
Ireland and Irish culture 117n. 14, 188,
193, 199, 208n. 13
Isis 27, 219
Islam and Islamic culture 29, 36, 40n.
9, 162n. 21, 212, 213, 215,
224, 230

Jacobinism 51, 55, 56
Jacobitism 55
Jacobus, Mary 82
Jacyna, L.S. 56
Jaggarnath carnival (India) 24, *25*
James, Louis 196
James, P.D. 207n. 3, 211
Jameson, Anna 117n. 14
Japp, A.H. 10, 135, 139n. 2, 231n. 2
Jefferson, Thomas 178
Jeffrey, Francis 70, 119n. 43
Jeremiah's *Lamentations* 41n. 20
Jerusalem 29, 30, 35, 41n. 20
Jewell, Margaret ('Mary' in DQ's
account) 187, 194, 195, 200,
204
'John Bull' 59n. 7, 63, 77
John Bull (Tory newspaper) 130–131
Johnson, Joseph 55, 60n. 10
Johnson, Samuel 67

Johnstone, Christian 12, 101–102,
103–104, 108, 109, 112–113,
117n. 12, 118n. 18, 119n.
36; see also *Tait's Edinburgh
Magazine*
Jones, John 59n. 8, 67
Jones, Sir William 22–23, 24, 27, 33,
39n. 7, 40nn. 8, 9, 41n. 18
Jordan, John E. 2, 3, 5, 15n. 1, 84,
95nn. 3, 5, 118n. 27, 173
Joyce, James 8
Judaism and Jewish culture 23, 31, 35,
40n. 9, 41nn. 15, 20

Kafka, Franz 158, 163n. 30
Kant, Immanuel 3, 53, 60n. 13, 72,
102, 103, 115, 144, 147, 153,
166, 167, 178, 191, 192;
Critique of Judgment 166;
Critique of Practical Reason
166–167; *Observations on . . .
the Beautiful and the Sublime*
13, 178; the sublime and 165,
166–167, 169, 171, 178–179
Kean, Edmund 189
Keats, John 11, 69–70, 74, 85; 'egotistical sublime' 86; *Endymion*
69; *Hyperion* 69–70; *Lamia,
Isabella, the Eve of St Agnes,
and Other Poems* 70; 'Ode on
a Grecian Urn' 201; 'Ode to a
Nightingale' 70, 74
Keen, Paul 125
Kerr, Norman 160n. 8
Keswick, Lake District 75
Kleist, Heinrich von 165
Knight, Charles 72
Kopf, David 26
Koran, the 29, 230

Ladies of Llangollen 103
Lady Hughes (ship) 157
Lake District 75, 107, 171–172, 189,
222
Lake poets 12, 29, 56, 103, 104, 192
Lamb, Charles 66, 190; 'Confessions
of a Drunkard' 145–147,
148–149
Lamb, Mary 103
Lancet 56
Llandaff, Bishop of 31, 108
Landor, Walter Savage 77
Latin 28, 51, 123, 170, 177; *see also*
Roman culture

Lawrence, Christopher 53, 54, 55
Lawrence, D. H. 8
Lawrence, William 56, 57, 60n. 11
Leask, Nigel 6, 39n. 2, 63, 64, 68, 75, 198, 207n. 2
Lee, Harriet 103, 108
Lee, Rachel 135
Lee, Sophia 103, 119n. 35
Legendre, Adrien Marie 70
Leighton, Angela 1, 12, 82, 110, 117n. 10
Le Sage, Alain René 108
Leslie, John 11, 70, 71
Lessing, Gotthold Ephraim 198; *Laocoon* 201
Libraries and bookshops 125, 126, 127, 129, 132, 134–135; national libraries 103, 125
Lindop, Grevel 3, 8, 9, 38, 57, 58n. 2, 59n. 9, 70, 87–88, 90, 95nn. 3, 7, 96nn. 10, 11, 118nn. 18, 27, 119n. 30, 135, 151, 160nn. 5, 6, 162n. 25, 189, 212, 230n. 1
Linton, Eliza Lynn 101
Liverpool 70, 74–75, 84, 134–135; Liverpool Library 134; Liverpool reverie 70, 74
Lockhart, John Gibson 72, 190
London 8, 11, 29, 30 (and illus.), 46, 47, 48, 126, 128, 137, 140n. 16, 147, 165, 177–178; in the *Confessions* (1821) 63, 64–65, 66, 75; murder and crime in 188–189, 190, 194, 198, 201, 202, 211, 215, 219, 222, 225, 227; East End 63, 215; Oxford Street 57, 64, 66, 81, 140n. 16; Soho Square 66; Wapping 14, 187, 202; *see also* Whispering Gallery
London Magazine 6, 14, 45, 64–65, 69, 75, 77, 92, 99, 100, 102, 129, 189–190, 197
Longmore, Jane 134
Lowth, Robert 21, 28–29, 33, 34, 41n. 19
Lynch, Deirdre 126, 129, 139n. 6
Lyon, Judson S. 8
Lyrical Ballads 65, 83, 85, 87, 103, 113, 114, 172

Macaulay, Thomas Babington 24
Macnish, Robert 147

Madeira 136
Madras Native Infantry 212
Magdalen College, Oxford 137
Maginn, William 70, 190
Malay episode (in *Confessions*) 10, 11, 63–64, 67, 190, 215–217, 218, 219, 226, 228
Malden, Henry 72
Malebranche, Nicolas 192
Malleson, George Bruce 218, 219
Manchester 65, 165, 187, 204, 207; Manchester Grammar School 30, 65, 76, 216, 220, 229, 230; Manchester Library 229
Maniquis, Robert 2, 8, 39n. 2
Marr family 187, 193, 194, 200, 204, 207; *see also* Ratcliffe Highway murders
Martineau, Harriet 5, 101, 117n. 16
Masculinity 12, **81–97**, 104, 105, 106, 111; bibliophily and 126, 127, 128, 131, 132, 138; *see also* gender
Masson, David 10, 14, 149, 153, 211–212
Mathias, T.J. 103
Maturin, Charles 69
Maurice, Thomas 39n. 6
McDonagh, Josephine 2, 8, 11, 12–13, 39n. 2, 45, 48, 63, 82, 96n. 15, 138n. 1, 139nn. 5, 7, 13, 160nn. 1, 9, 162n. 27, 163n. 33, 184n. 10
McFarland, Thomas 2, 8, 12, 81–82
McKeons (murderers) 187, 207
McManners, John 136, 140n. 17
McQueen, James 72
Medical community and discourse 6, 9, 10, 11, 12, 14, 46, 47, 51–58, 59nn. 4, 8, 68, 126, 127; and addiction 143, 144–145, 149, 152, 156, 157, 160n. 8, 161n. 18, 162n. 21, 163n. 31; *see also* Brunonianism
Medusa 201
Mellor, Anne K. 39n. 1
Metaphor 38, 49, 50, 51, 85, 88, 93, 165, 183, 184, 185n. 19, 189, 190, 192, 205
Metonymy 165, 180, 181
Michaelis, J.D. 21, 28, 29, 31
Mill, James 24, 39n. 5, 72
Millar, Mrs 103, 107–108

Miller, J. Hillis 7, 10, 185n. 18
Milligan, Barry 7, 10, 11, 68, 143, 156, 157, 162n. 27, 212
Milton, John 168, 169–170, 172–173, 175–176, 177; *Areopagitica* 183; Miltonic influence 7, 50, 170, 181; *Paradise Lost* 165, 168, 169, 185n. 12
Missionaries 20, 27
Mitford, Mary Russell 69, 101, 103, 112
Monboddo, Lord (James Burnett) 27
Montgomery, James 6
More, Hannah 23, 103, 118n. 24
Morgan, Sydney Owenson, Lady 117n. 14
Morrison, Robert 3, 4, 10–11, 15n. 1, 45, 60n. 12, 70, 74, 76, 88, 91–92, 95n. 9, 96nn. 13, 14, 99, 102, 118n. 26, 190, 207n. 6, 211
Mosaic ethnology 22, 23, 31, 33, 40nn. 8, 9
Müller, Max 39n. 5
Murder 1, 3–4, 14, 75, 87, 129, 144, 147, 157–158, 162n. 26, 184, **187–210**; influence of Indian Mutiny in depictions of 211, 213, 217, 218, 224, 226, 227; *see also* De Quincey, Works
Murray, Alexander 41n. 18

'Nabob' 41n. 17
Napier, MacVey 70
Naples 205
Napoleonic Wars 13, 46, 180
Nationalism and nationality 11, 12, 13, 63, 64, 67, 82, 91, 125, 126, 130, 131; national poetry and character 170–181; national sublime 177, 178–186; national temperament 143–144, 153–164, 191;
Nerval, Gérard de 8
New College, Oxford 137
'Newgate Novel' 14, 195, 197
New Historicism 9
Newlyn, Lucy 11, 99, 100, 119n. 40
New Monthly Magazine 75
New Testament 50, 58
Nietzsche, Friedrich 4
Nightmares: *see* Dreams
Noah and the flood 22–23, 39n. 6, 40n. 8, 49, 59n. 5

'Noctes Ambrosianae' 191, 208n. 10
North British Review 100
North, Christopher: *see* Wilson, John
North, Julian 11–12, 15n. 1, 106
Norton, Frederick 130

Oddie, Geoffrey 24
Oil 156, 160
Old Testament 28, 35, 50
Onwhyn, Thomas 117n. 17
Opie, Amelia 101
Opium 3, 4, 6, 10, 11, 13, 26–27, 32, 38, **45–61** (Milligan), 89, 95n. 9; **143–164** (Black), 165, 167, 169, 190, 201, 205, 207; addiction to books and 124, 132–133, 135, 139n. 2, 140n. 16; anti-opium movement 152, 157, 159, 163n. 31; *Confessions* (1821) and 63, 64, 65, 67–68, 69, 70, 74, 75; crime literature and 211, 212, 213, 215–216, 219, 222, 225, 226, 227, 229–230, 231n. 7; opium trade 13, 144, 152, 155, 159, 162n. 20, 163nn. 31, 33
Opium wars 159, 162nn. 22, 26, 223; First Opium War (1839–42) 152, 155, 212; Second Opium War (1856–60) 158, 212
O'Quinn, Daniel 42n. 22, 63
Orientalism 7, 10, 14, **19–43**, 46, 59n. 5, 67, 82, 87, 157, 158, 159, 199; crime literature, influence in 213, 216, 225, 226, 228, 230, 232n. 12
Osiris 27, 219
'Other', the 11, 19, 82, 110
Overmeier, Judith A. 55
Owen, W.J.B. 100, 116nn. 6, 7
Owenson, Sydney: *see* Morgan, Lady
Oxford 64, 75, 88, 126, 136–138, 139n. 13, 140n. 16, 165; Oxford University 102, 128, 130

Paganism 31, 36, 38–39, 39n. 3, 95n. 2, 182
Paine, Thomas 52, 60n. 10, 68
Palmer, Benjamin Morgan 161n. 16
Paris 205
Parker, John 136
Patriotism 8, 32, 33, 40n. 8, 126
Patterson, C.I. 117n. 9

Peckett Prest, Thomas 196–197; *String of Pearls* 196; *see also* Sweeney Todd
Peignot, Gabriel 127
Persia 153, 155
Pharmacy Act (1868) 152, 212
Pilkington, Mary Hopkins 119n. 35
Pillbeam, Pamela 202
'Piranesi' sequence (in *Confessions*) 205, 226, 227
Plagiarism: Coleridge and 5, 208n. 10; De Quincey and 3, 5, 71
Plato 8, 72, 91
Plotz, Judith 39n. 2, 90, 96n. 10, 139nn. 4, 5, 13
Plumtree, A.S. 4, 208n. 8
Poe, Edgar Allan 4, 8, 199, 211
Ponsonby, Sarah: *see* Ladies of Llangollen
Pope, Alexander 168; *see also under* De Quincey, Works
Porter, Roger J. 6
Porter, Roy 59n. 4
Portugal and Portuguese culture 132, 157
Praz, Mario 4
Priestley, Joseph 55
Proctor, Sigmund 3, 184nn. 2, 4
Prohibition 150, 159
Prometheus 50; *Prometheus Unbound* 169
Prostitutes and prostitution 11, 30, 40n. 11, 41n. 20, 64, 66–67, 77, 102, 135, 140n. 15, 219; *see also* Ann of Oxford Street
Protestantism 10, 20, 21, 22, 34, 38, 40n. 12; *see also* Christianity; Evangelicalism
Proust, Marcel 8
Ptolemy 35
Pygmalion 201

Quarterly Review 75, 106
Quincey, Elizabeth (DQ's sister) 7, 8, 29, 32, 41n. 16, 81
Quincey, Elizabeth (*née* Penson) (DQ's mother) 23–24, 32, 34, 35, 36, 37, 41n. 16, 134, 135, 229
Quincey, William (DQ's brother) 160n. 6

Race and racial issues 9, 11, 27, 48, 63, 65, 153, 219, 224, 231n. 10; racism 63, 179, 201, 213, 216
Radcliffe, Ann 103, 108
Radicalism 10, 11, 14, 29, 36, **45–61**, 99, 100, 102, 114, 118n. 18, 195, 196; in the *Confessions* (1821) 64, 72, 73, 75, 76, 77
Ratcliffe Highway murders 187–188, 199, 201, 205, 211; *see also* Williams, John
Readership and audience 6, 11–12, 28–29, 34, 40n. 12, 90, **99–121**, 125, 184n. 6, 195, 198, 217
Redfield, Marc 152
Reed, John R. 232n. 11
Reeves, Clara 119n. 35
Reform 70, 72, 73, 145, 175, 191, 195; medical 46, 53, 54, 56; moral 129, 157; Reform Bill (1832) 100; *Tait's* and 99, 100, 101, 102, 117nn. 13, 14
Rendell, Jane 41n. 18
Resurrection Man (Reynolds character) 196, 199
Revelation, Book of (NT) 50
Reynolds, G.W.M. 196, 197
Rheumatism 67, 148
Ricardo, David 11, 53, 58, 72–73, 73
Richardson, Jonathan 172
Richter, Harvena 8
Richter, Jean Paul 2
Roberts, Daniel Sanjiv 5, 10, 45, 59n. 5, 67, 95n. 2, 132, 134, 135, 184nn. 5, 10, 185n. 14
Roberts, Emma 109
Robin Hood 91
Robinson, Henry Crabb 4, 5, 69, 95n. 6
Robinson, J. 218
Robinson, Mary 119n. 35
Roman culture 2, 35, 36, 39nn. 3, 7, 41n. 20, 106, 153, 172, 177, 180; *see also* Latin
Roscoe, William 11, 74–75
Rose, Michael 2
Rousseau, George 140n. 18
Rousseau, Jean Jacques 7–8, 63, 71, 118n. 19, 184
Rowlandson, Thomas 59n. 7
Roxburghe Club 12, 128–129, 130
Royal College of Surgeons 56
Rubens, Peter Paul 189
Rushdie, Salman 8
Russell, Alexander 29
Russett, Margaret 8, 42n. 21, 118n. 26, 125
Russia 153, 154

Ruston, Sharon 56, 60n. 11
Rzepka, Charles 6, 13–14, 39n. 2, 66, 124, 135, 139n. 2, 140n. 15, 184n. 4, 211, 216, 231n. 3

Sackville West, Edward 2, 206
Sade, Marquis de 4, 67, 208n. 8
Said, Edward 19–20, 27, 36, 39n. 2
Sanskrit 27, 33
Satan 50
Schelling, Friedrich von 208n. 14
Schlegel, August von 117n. 9, 198, 208n. 14
Schmitt, Cannon 156, 158, 163n. 28
Scott, John 64, 69, 189–190
Scott, Sir Walter 4, 126
Sedgwick, Eve Kosofsky 4–5
Semele 105
Septuagint, the 34–35
Sex and sexuality 9, 11, 12, 14, 24, 30, 63, 66, 67, 82, 84, 94, 104–105, 110, 119n. 35, 226, 230; bibliophily and 125, 126, 129, 131–132, 134, 135, 137, 138, 140nn. 15, 17; *see also* Homosexuality; Homoeroticism
Shackell, Edward 131
Shaffer, Elinor 41n. 13
Shakespeare, William 84, 115–116, 169, 175–176, 182, 185n. 11; Hamlet (character) 182, 185n. 17; *King Lear* 168–169
Sharp, Ronald A. 95n. 4
Shelley, Percy Bysshe 11, 41n. 14, 50, 56, 60n. 12, 69, 75–77; *Revolt of Islam* 76
Shepherd, Revd. William 119n. 36
Sheridan, Richard Brinsley 68
Shipley, Charles 12, 136–138, 140n. 21
Shiva (Seeva) 27, 219
Shore, John 39n. 7
Silver 163n. 33
Simmons, Diane 39n. 2, 42n. 21
Sinophobia 29, 42n. 21
Slatter, Charles 136–137
Slavery and the slave trade 11, 74, 75, 77, 161n. 16; *see also* Abolition
Sleeman, W.H. 213, 224
Smith, Adam 72
Smith, Charlotte 119n. 35
Smith, Elizabeth 103, 118n. 24
Smith, Florence Baird (*née* De Quincey; DQ's daughter) 223
Smith, Stevie 8
Smithson, Robert 178
Smollett, Tobias 108
Snyder, Robert Lance 3, 4
Social class 11, 46, 48, 50, 51, 58, 63, 66, 102, 103, 115, 202, 205; middle class 46, 47, 99, 100, 102, 127, 205, 219; working classes 11, 63, 66, 101, 117n. 13, 153, 160n. 3, 171–172, 195
Society for the Suppression of Vice 129
Sotheby, H.W. 4
Southey, Robert 5, 41n. 14, 56, 106, 170, 132, 133, *The Curse of Kehama* 40n. 11
Spain and Spanish culture 132, 176
Spector, Stephen J. 7
Spenser, Edmund 104, 183; *The Faerie Queene* 183
Sporting Anecdotes 192
Spring, L.W. 4
Staël, Madame de 134, 178
Standage, Tom 158, 161n. 18, 162nn. 21, 26, 163n. 33
Standard (newspaper) 73
Stanley, Joachim 211, 212
St Clair, William 125
Stephen, Leslie 3
Sterne, Laurence 2, 139n. 6
Stevenson, Robert Louis 8; *Dr. Jekyll and Mr. Hyde* 215
Stevenson, William 72
Stickney, Sarah: *see* Ellis, Sarah Stickney
St. Paul 103, 171, 183
Sublime (aesthetic category) 3, 13, 83, 113, 115, 116, 119n. 42, 147, **165–186**, 194, 199, 200, 202, 205
Sudan, Rajani 39n. 2
Sullivan, Margo Ann 207n. 6
Swann, Elsie 95n. 8
Sweeney Todd (Peckett Prest character) 196, 199
Swift, Jonathan 2
Symonds, Barry 42n. 21, 64, 69, 70, 140n. 15

Tait, William 100, 101, 117n. 12, 118n. 23
Tait's Edinburgh Magazine 11–12, 14, **99–121**, 134, 137, 139n. 14, 149
Taussig, Gurion 95n. 4

Tave, Stuart 73
Taylor, George 195
Taylor, John (publisher) 230n. 1
Taylor, Philip Meadows 213, 224
Tea 132–133, 135; as addictive substance 144, 153, 154, 156, 160, 161n. 15, 161n. 18, 162n. 22, 163nn. 31, 33
Temperance movement 13, 151, 152, 153–156, 157, 161n. 14; *see also under* De Quincey, Works
Thackeray, William Makepeace 198
Thomas, Ronald 213
Thron, E. Michael 1
'Thug' 213, *214*, 223–224, 225, 226, 228; 'Thugee' 224, 226, 228
Ticknor, Reid, and Fields (Boston publishers) 230n. 1
Times, The 188
Titan, The (journal) 223
Titian (Tiziano Vecellio) 189
Tobacco 144, 145, 146
Tooke, John Horne 55
Toryism 14, 32, 45, 46, 58, 102, 130, 191, 199, 202; tensions between radicalism and 63, 64, 70, 71, 72, 73, 77
Trautmann, Thomas 22, 24
Trocki, Carl A. 156
Trollope, Frances 103, 110
Turkey and Turkish culture 67, 162n. 20, 225, 228, 229–230
Turner, J.M.W. 29, *30*
Turner, John 187–188, 189, 200, 208n. 9
Tussaud, Madame 202–203, 205, 207

Utilitarianism 20, 24, 27, 39n. 5, 41n. 18, 72, 191
Uwins, Thomas 140n. 21

Vandyke, Sir Anthony 189
Vatican Library 124
Vellore Mutiny (1806) 24
Vespasian (Roman emperor) 41n. 20
Vickers, Neil 11, 55
Victorian period and culture 9, 13–14, 36, 39
Vishnu 27, 219
Vitality/Vitalism Debate 56, 57, 58, 60n. 11
V.R. 2

Wainewright, T.G. 197

Wakley, Thomas 56
Wales 65, 222, 224
Walker, Sarah 71
Warhol, Robyn R. 161n. 11
Warner, Nicholas O. 161n. 19
Warton, Joseph 103
Waterloo 201
Waugh, Evelyn 8
Waxworks 202–204, 205; *see also* Tussaud, Madame
Weekly Political Register; *see under* Cobbett, William
Wellek, René 3
Wellesley, Richard 32
Wellington, Arthur Wellesley, Duke of 32
Westmorland Gazette, The 76
Whale, John 6, 11, 12, 96nn. 15, 16, 99
Whiggism 63, 68, 70, 72, 73, 74, 198
Whispering Gallery (St. Paul's Cathedral) 205–206, 216
Wilberforce, William 11, 37, 74
Wilde, Oscar 215
Wilford, Captain Francis 33
Wilkins, Charles 22
Williams, Rev. G. 207
Williams, John 4, 188–189, 193–194, 195, 198, 199, 202, 204, 208n. 13, 211
Williams, Jonathan 8
Williamson family 187–188, 207
Wilner, Joshua 184n. 8
Wilson, Edmund 213, 224, 226
Wilson, Horace Hayman 39n. 5
Wilson, John (Christopher North) 12, 69, 76, 81, 86, 87–92, 94, 95nn. 8, 9, 96n. 14, 105, 106, 189, 190; see also *Blackwood's Edinburgh Magazine*
Wolfson, Susan 39n. 1
Wollstonecraft, Mary 55, 103, 178
Women 12, 81–83, 94, 134; as readers and writers **99–121**
Woodhouse, Richard 64, 66, 76, 91, 190, 195
Woolf, Virginia 2, 8, 166
Worcester College, Oxford 66, 135, 137
Wordsworth, Dorothy 12, 103, 104, 107, 109, 110–113, 119n. 38
Wordsworth, Jonathan 4
Wordsworth, Mary 109–110, 119n. 30
Wordsworth, William 2, 5, 6, 7, 10, 29, 55, 56, 65, 75, 132, 134,

146, 192, 199, 222; audience, attitude towards 11, **99–121**; relationship with DQ 12, 81, 83–87, 88, 89, 90, 92, 95nn. 2, 6, 8; the sublime in 165, 170–175, 176, 177

Works: 'The Beggars' 110, 112; 'Composed upon Westminster Bridge' 29; *Convention of Cintra* 118n. 26; 'Essay Supplementary to the Preface' 100, 106; *The Excursion* 114, 119n. 43, 176; *The Prelude* 6, 170, 173, 174, 175, 177, 199; 'Ruth' 111–112; 'She was a Phantom of Delight' 109–110; 'The Thorn' 109; 'Tintern Abbey' 107

Wright, David 5
Wright family 135
Wu, Duncan 39n. 1, 119n. 34

Xenophobia 11, 63, 201

Young, Edward 113
Youngquist, Paul 60n. 13, 139n. 5

Zeus 105

Lightning Source UK Ltd.
Milton Keynes UK
11 May 2010

154053UK00001B/114/P